Texts in Computer Science

Series Editors

David Gries, Department of Computer Science, Cornell University, Ithaca, NY, USA

Orit Hazzan ⓘ , Faculty of Education in Technology and Science, Technion—Israel Institute of Technology, Haifa, Israel

Titles in this series now included in the Thomson Reuters Book Citation Index!

'Texts in Computer Science' (TCS) delivers high-quality instructional content for undergraduates and graduates in all areas of computing and information science, with a strong emphasis on core foundational and theoretical material but inclusive of some prominent applications-related content. TCS books should be reasonably self-contained and aim to provide students with modern and clear accounts of topics ranging across the computing curriculum. As a result, the books are ideal for semester courses or for individual self-study in cases where people need to expand their knowledge. All texts are authored by established experts in their fields, reviewed internally and by the series editors, and provide numerous examples, problems, and other pedagogical tools; many contain fully worked solutions.

The TCS series is comprised of high-quality, self-contained books that have broad and comprehensive coverage and are generally in hardback format and sometimes contain color. For undergraduate textbooks that are likely to be more brief and modular in their approach, require only black and white, and are under 275 pages, Springer offers the flexibly designed Undergraduate Topics in Computer Science series, to which we refer potential authors.

Marco T. Morazán

Animated
Program Design

Intermediate Program Design
Using Video Game Development

 Springer

Marco T. Morazán
Department of Computer Science
Seton Hall University
South Orange, NJ, USA

ISSN 1868-0941   ISSN 1868-095X   (electronic)
Texts in Computer Science
ISBN 978-3-031-04319-2   ISBN 978-3-031-04317-8   (eBook)
https://doi.org/10.1007/978-3-031-04317-8

This Springer imprint is published by the registered company Springer Nature Switzerland AG
The registered company address is: Gewerbestrasse 11, 6330 Cham, Switzerland

To my students for educating me on how to teach problem solving and program design.

Marco

Preface

Everybody engages in problem solving, and this book is about the science of problem solving. It aims to teach its readers a new way of thinking about designing solutions to problems that takes them beyond trial-and-error thinking. Trial and error is, indeed, a fundamental problem-solving technique but must be tightly coupled with design to be effectively used. Trials or experiments must be thought out and planned. What does this mean? It means that problem solvers must engage in careful and thorough consideration of the different options they have to solve a problem. Problem-solving techniques must be used appropriately, and different solutions to a problem must be evaluated to choose the best one. The evaluation of a solution is done both mathematically and empirically. That is, theory and practice play a pivotal role in problem solving. Rest assured that the problem-solving and programming techniques you learn may be used to solve problems using any programming language.

This textbook continues the journey started in *Animated Problem Solving* and completes a year-long (two semesters) curriculum for first-year students. Readers of this book are likely to be familiar with writing expressions, defining data, divide and conquer, iterative design, designing functions using structural recursion, abstraction and abstract functions, and even distributed programming. Indeed, you are likely to already be very powerful problem solvers and programmers. Now it is time to become even more powerful programmers. How is this achieved? This book aids this quest by exploring with you new types of recursion, by introducing you to the use of randomness, by taking the first steps into experimental Computer Science and algorithm analysis, by taking a peek into Artificial Intelligence, and by presenting a disciplined approach to the use of mutation—also known as assignment which is routinely abused and misused every day giving rise to the majority of programming bugs today.

At the heart of this exploration is the *design recipe*—the steps to go from a problem statement to a working and tested solution. The new design recipes studied in this textbook are less prescriptive than those used for solutions based on structural recursion. In this regard, they are akin to the design recipe for distributed programming found in *Animated Problem Solving*. One of the most attractive features of structural recursion is that it suggests how to divide and conquer a problem. For example, structural recursion suggests that solving a problem for a nonleaf binary tree is done by solving the same problem for the left and/or right subtrees. In contrast, heap sorting, an efficient sorting algorithm studied in this textbook, creates a new binary tree to solve the problem. In essence, there is no prescriptive design recipe for divide and conquer when structural recursion is not used. In such cases, a problem solver must rely on insights gained from problem analysis to perform divide and conquer. An interesting and powerful consequence is that a solution to a problem using structural recursion may be refined/improved based on insights gained to use other forms of recursion.

You may already have butterflies in your stomach anticipating a wealth of knowledge from the pages of this book. If that is the case, then you are on your way. Enthusiasm for knowledge and understanding is essential for a problem solver. Problem solving, however, can and ought to also be fun. To this end, this book promises to design and implement a video game using modern Artificial Intelligence techniques with you. To achieve this, however, there is a great deal about problem solving and programming you must learn. The game is developed using iterative refinement. That is, as your problem solving and programming knowledge grows, improved versions of the game are developed. Buckle up for fascinating and fun journey to expand your mind!

1 The Parts of the Book

The book is divided into four parts. Part I presents introductory material. It starts by reviewing the basic steps of a design recipe. It does so using a problem solved using structural recursion on a list. It then proceeds to review code refactoring—the restructuring of a function without changing its external behavior. Refactoring is a common technique used to refine programs when a better or more elegant way is found to solve a problem. For example, a problem involving a list may be solved using structural recursion and explicit use of `first` and `rest`. The solution may be refactored to eliminate low-level functions like `first` and `rest` by using a `match` expression. In turn, this solution may be refactored to eliminate recursive calls by using abstract functions like `map` and `filter`. Part I then moves to review abstract running time. In addition, this part introduces the N-Puzzle problem—the video game developed throughout the book—and introduces the use of randomness in problem solving.

Part II explores a new type of recursion called generative recursion. Instead of exploiting the structure of the data to make recursive calls, this type of recursion creates new instances of the data to make recursive calls. The study of generative recursion navigates the reader through examples involving fractal image generation, efficient sorting, and efficient searching techniques such as binary, depth-first, and breadth-first search. This part concludes presenting two refinements to the N-Puzzle game using generative recursion and the problems that they have including the loss of knowledge. Throughout, complexity analysis and empirical experimentation are used to evaluate solutions.

Part III explores a new type of recursion called accumulative (or accumulator) recursion. Accumulative recursion introduces one or more accumulators to a function designed using structural or generative recursion. Accumulators are used to solve the loss of knowledge problem or to make programs more efficient. Examples used include finding a path in a graph, improving insertion sorting, and list-folding operations. The study of list-folding operations leads to new abstract functions with an accumulator: `foldl` and `foldr`. The expertise developed using accumulative recursion is used to refine the N-Puzzle game to perform a heuristic search using the A* algorithm—an algorithm used in Artificial Intelligence. Part III ends with a chapter introducing an important and powerful program transformation called continuation-passing style. Continuation-passing style allows programmers and compilers to optimize programs. Throughout, complexity analysis and empirical experimentation are used to evaluate solutions.

Part IV explores mutation. Mutation (or changing the value of a state variable) allows different parts of a program that do not call each other to share values. Interestingly enough, most textbooks on programming that use mutation fail to mention this. Abstracting over state variables leads to interfaces and object-oriented programming. The use of mutation, however, comes at a heavy price: the loss of referential transparency. That is, (f x) is not always equal to (f x). This means programmers must be disciplined about the order in which mutations are done because knowing that a program works is suddenly much harder. To aid you in properly sequencing mutations, this part of the book teaches you about Hoare Logic and program correctness. In addition, it introduces vectors, vector processing, and in-place operations. Part IV ends by presenting a solution to the chicken or egg paradox in programming. Throughout, complexity analysis and empirical experimentation are used to evaluate solutions.

2 Acknowledgments

This book is the product of over 10 years of work at Seton Hall University building on the shoulders of giants in Computer Science and on the shoulders of Seton Hall undergraduate CS1 and CS2 students. A heartfelt thank you is offered to all the students that throughout the years helped me understand what works and does not work when teaching program design. Many of the giants in Computer Science that have informed my teaching efforts are members of the PLT research group, especially those responsible for developing the student programming languages used in this textbook and for penning *How to Design Programs*—an inspiration for *Animated Problem Solving* and for *Animated Programming*. It is impossible not to explicitly express my heart-felt appreciation for Matthias Felleisen from Northeastern University and Shriram Krishnamurthi from Brown University for having my back, for debating with me, and for encouraging the work done at Seton Hall University—all of which led to this textbook.

There are many other professional colleagues that deserve credit for inspiring the lessons found in this textbook. Chief among them is Doug Troeger, my Ph.D. advisor, from City College of New York (CCNY). Together, we taught CCNY undergraduates about program correctness. Some of the material in Part IV of this textbook is inspired by those efforts. A great deal of the material in this textbook is based on my Computer Science Education peer-reviewed publications. I was mostly blessed with thoughtful and conscientious reviewers that offered honest feedback on the good and the bad, but that always made an effort to provide thought-provoking comments and suggestions for future work. Collectively, they have also influenced the lessons in this book. I am deeply appreciative to the venues that have published my articles such as the Trends in Functional Programming in Education Workshop, the Journal of Functional Programming , and the Trends in Functional Programming Symposium.

Finally, there is a gifted group of individuals that have been or still are invaluable in making the courses taught using the material in this textbook successful: my undergraduate research/teaching assistants. They have been responsible for making sure I explain the material clearly and for helping answer student questions using their own perspective on the material. This group includes: Shamil Dzhatdoyev, Josie Des Rosiers, Nicholas Olson, Nicholas Nelson, Lindsey Reams, Craig Pelling, Barbara Mucha, Joshua Schappel, Sachin Mahashabde, Rositsa Abrasheva, Isabella Felix, Sena Karsavran, and Julia "Ohio" Wilkins. Their feedback and the feedback they collected from enrolled students have influenced every topic presented. In closing, my appreciation goes out to Seton Hall University and its Department of Computer Science for supporting the development of the work presented in this textbook.

South Orange, NJ, USA   Marco T. Morazán

Contents

Part IV Mutation

Part I
Basic Problem Solving and Program Design

Chapter 1
The Science of Problem Solving

This textbook continues the study of problem solving and program design that began in *Animated Problem Solving* that exposes its readers to typed-based programming, structural recursion, abstraction, and distributed programming. In this textbook we move beyond structural recursion to other forms of recursion that require insights into a problem beyond what may be suggested by the structure of the data. We shall start, however, with a review of the concepts needed to successfully navigate this textbook.

The basic concepts you need to be familiar with are:

- Variables
- Functions
- Design recipe
- Abstract functions (generic programming)
- Abstract running time

Variables are used to store values. A variable may be declared as a parameter to a function or locally using a `local`-expression. Functions are abstractions over similar expressions used to compute a value. Each difference among similar expressions is captured as a function parameter. The function body is created by choosing one of the similar expressions and substituting each difference with the parameter that represents it. Abstraction over the types processed by similar functions gives rise to abstract functions and generic programming. An abstract function, therefore, may process different types of input. For example, `map` and `filter` may be used to process a list of numbers, a list of aliens, or a list of criminal records. Finally, abstract running time is a measure of the number operations executed in relation to the size of the input. It allows us to compare the efficiency of programs regardless of the computer hardware used.

Let us review the basic concepts by developing a couple of programs. First, we review the fundamental design recipe steps for function development. We then illustrate the design process by developing functions to compute the area of a triangle and to double the elements in a list of numbers.

© The Author(s), under exclusive license to Springer Nature Switzerland AG 2022   3
M. T. Morazán, *Animated Program Design*, Texts in Computer Science,
https://doi.org/10.1007/978-3-031-04317-8_1

Fig. 1 The general design recipe for functions

1. Perform data analysis and outline a design idea.
2. Define constants for the value of sample expressions.
3. Identify and name the differences among the sample expressions.
4. Write the function's signature and purpose.
5. Write the function's header.
6. Write tests.
7. Write the function's body.
8. Run the tests and, if necessary, redesign.

3 The Design Recipe

To design and implement a function we follow the steps of the design recipe. A design recipe is a series of steps that take a problem solver from a problem statement to a working solution. Each step has a specific outcome that helps others understand how a problem is solved. Remember that one of the primary tasks of a programmer is to communicate how a problem is solved.

As you may know there are many design recipes that vary according to the type of data that needs to be processed. Figure 1 displays a general design recipe for functions (not specialized for any specific datatype). It contains eight steps that may be described as follows:

Step 1 Define the types of values processed and describe how the needed value is computed.

Step 2 Write sample expressions for computing a needed value.

Step 3 Identify the differences among the sample expressions and choose descriptive variable names for them.

Step 4 Write the function's signature and purpose statement.

Step 5 Write the function header using the variable names chosen in Step 3.

Step 6 Write tests illustrating the function's expected behavior.

Step 7 Write the function's body by substituting the differences in any sample expression with the names chosen in Step 3.

Step 8 Run the tests and debug your design if errors or failed tests arise.

4 Computing the Area of a Triangle

To begin consider the problem of finding the area of a triangle when the lengths of each side are known. Figure 2 displays two triangles with known lengths. How is the area of a triangle with known lengths computed? Heron's formula tells us that the area of a triangle is given by the square root of the product of the sum of the sides divided by 2, the difference of the sum of the sides divided by 2 and the first side, the difference of the sum of the sides

Fig. 2 Two triangles with known lengths

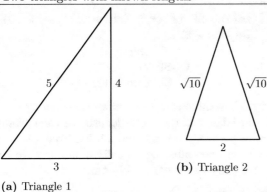

(a) Triangle 1

(b) Triangle 2

divided by 2 and the second side, and the difference of the sum of the sides divided by 2 and the third side.[1] Let's design and implement a function to compute the length of a triangle following the steps of the design recipe.

For Step 1 we can observe that three positive numbers are needed as input—one for the length of each side of a triangle. A positive number may be defined as follows:

```
;; A positive number, number>0, is a number greater than 0.
```

Our design idea is to compute a triangle's area using Heron's formula. To simplify the formulation we define the semi-perimeter, sp, of a triangle as the sum of its lengths (s1, s2, and s3) divide by 2:

$$sp = \frac{s1 + s2 + s3}{2}$$

Using sp we may formulate the area of a triangle as:

$$A(s1,s2,s3) = \sqrt{sp*(sp-s1)*(sp-s2)*(s-s3)}$$

To satisfy Step 2 we write sample expressions to compute the areas for the triangles displayed in Fig. 2. Following our design idea from Step 1, a local-expression is used to define a variable for the semi-perimeter of the triangle and, therefore, avoiding having to write the same expression repeatedly. The sample expressions are:

```
;; Sample expressions for the area of a triangle
(define AREA-T1 (local [(define SP (/ (+ 3 4 5) 2))]
                  (sqrt (* SP (- SP 3) (- SP 4) (- SP 5)))))
```

---

[1] Heron of Alexandria was a Greek mathematician and engineer that lived in Roman Egypt c. 10–70 AD.

```
(define AREA-T2 (local
                  [(define SP (/ (+ 2 (sqrt 10) (sqrt 10)) 2))]
                  (sqrt (* SP
                           (- SP (sqrt 10))
                           (- SP 2)
                           (- SP (sqrt 10))))))
```

For Step 3 we observe that there are three differences among the expressions for the areas of the triangles: the three lengths of each triangle. We name the three lengths, respectively, s1, s2, and s3. For Step 4 it is straightforward to conclude that the area must be a positive number. Now we may write the contract and purpose statement as follows:

```
;; number>0 number>0 number>0  → number>0
;; Purpose: Compute the area of the triangle from the
;;          given lengths
```

Completing Steps 3 and 4 naturally leads to the development of the function header to satisfy Step 5:

```
(define (triangle-area s1 s2 s3)
```

Observe that a descriptive function name that suggests the purpose of the function to any reader of the code is chosen.

For Step 6, we write two types of tests to illustrate that the function works. The first type uses the values of the sample expressions developed in Step 2. The second uses concrete sample values. The tests may be written as follows:

```
;; Tests using sample computations
(check-within (triangle-area 3 4 5) AREA-T1 0.01)
(check-within (triangle-area 2 (sqrt 10) (sqrt 10))
              AREA-T2
              0.01)


;; Tests using sample values
(check-within (triangle-area (sqrt 5) 2 (sqrt 5)) 2 0.01)
(check-within (triangle-area 1 2 (sqrt 5)) 1 0.01)
```

To satisfy Step 7 a sample expression is chosen and the identified differences in Step 3 are substituted with their corresponding variables. This leads to the following function body:

```
(local [(define SP (/ (+ s1 s2 s3) 2))]
  (sqrt (* SP (- SP s1) (- SP s2) (- SP s3))))
```

The resulting program is displayed in Fig. 3. Finally, for Step 8 run the tests. If no bugs are manifested and all tests pass, you may be cautiously optimistic that your program works. Otherwise, debug your program by checking the results for each step of the design recipe.

Fig. 3 Program to compute the area of a triangle with known lengths

```
;; Sample expressions for the area of a triangle
(define AREA-T1 (local [(define SP (/ (+ 3 4 5) 2))]
                  (sqrt (* SP (- SP 3) (- SP 4) (- SP 5)))))

(define AREA-T2 (local [(define SP (/ (+ 2 (sqrt 10) (sqrt 10)) 2))]
                  (sqrt (* SP
                           (- SP (sqrt 10))
                           (- SP 2)
                           (- SP (sqrt 10))))))

;; A positive number, number>0, is a number greater than 0.

;; number>0 number>0 number>0  → number>0
;; Purpose: Compute the area of the triangle from the given lengths
(define (triangle-area s1 s2 s3)
  (local [(define SP (/ (+ s1 s2 s3) 2))]
    (sqrt (* SP (- SP s1) (- SP s2) (- SP s3)))))

;; Tests using sample computations
(check-within (triangle-area 3 4 5) AREA-T1 0.01)
(check-within (triangle-area 2 (sqrt 10) (sqrt 10)) AREA-T2 0.01)

;; Tests using sample values
(check-within (triangle-area (sqrt 5) 2 (sqrt 5)) 2 0.01)
(check-within (triangle-area 1 2 (sqrt 5)) 1 0.01)
```

4.1 Exercises

1 Design and implement a function to compute the area of a rhombus.

2 Design and implement a function to extract the first element of a given string.

3 Design and implement a function to double the size of a given image.

5 Doubling a List of Numbers

Consider the problem of doubling every number in a list of numbers. This is an example where exploiting the shape or structure of the data can guide our problem-solving process. To do so we must carefully define a list of numbers.

5.1 Step 1: Data Analysis and Design Idea

The first thing to note is that a list of numbers is data of arbitrary size. To us, as problem solvers, this means that a recursive data definition is needed. Recall that a recursive data definition must have at least two variants: one nonrecursive and one recursive. It may, of course, have more than one of either. We define a list of numbers as follows:

```
;; A list of numbers, lon, is either:
;;  1. empty
;;  2. (cons number lon)
```

For every data definition define sample instances. These must include at least one instance for each variant. We may define sample lon instances as follows:

```
;; Sample lon
(define ELON '())
(define LON1 '(2 3 4 5))
(define LON2 '(8 -2 0))
```

We use a data definition to develop a template for functions that process a lon. The template captures how the structure of a lon is exploited to solve problems. Observe that there are two lon variants. This means that any function that processes a lon must distinguish between the variants using a conditional expression. Further observe that the second variant, the nonempty lon, contains a self-reference. This means that the rest of a nonempty lon ought to be processed recursively. These observations allow to develop the following template for functions on a lon:

```
#| Template for functions on a lon

        ;; lon ... → ...
        ;; Purpose:
        (define (f-on-lon a-lon ...)
          (if (empty? a-lon)
              ...
              ...(first a-lon)...(f-on-lon (rest a-lon))))

        ;; Sample expressions for f-on-lon
        (define ELON-VAL ...)
        (define LON1-VAL ...)
        (define LON2-VAL ...)
            :

        ;; Tests using sample computations for f-on-lon
        (check-expect (f-on-lon ELON ...) ...)
        (check-expect (f-on-lon LON1 ...) ...)
```

```
    (check-expect (f-on-lon LON2 ...) ...)
        ⋮

    ;; Tests using sample values for f-on-lon
    (check-expect (f-on-lon ... ...) ...)
        ⋮
|#
```

Every function on a `lon` must take as input at least a `lon` and have a purpose statement. The function header must have at least one parameter for the `lon` to process. The body of a function to process a `lon` has a conditional. In this case the conditional is an `if`-expression because there are only two varieties (a `cond`-expression works just as well). The sample expressions must illustrate how the different variants are processed (usually using the defined sample instances). Finally, the template outlines the tests required. There must be tests for every variant. Commonly, the tests use sample computations (derived from the sample expressions) and sample values (to illustrate that the function works for values beyond the sample instances).

The design idea for doubling a `lon` must include both variants. If the list is empty then there are no numbers to double and the answer is the empty list. If the `lon` is not empty then an answer is created by `cons`ing the doubling of the first element of the given `lon` and recursively doubling the rest of the given list.

The function template is the proverbial yellow brick road we follow to solve problems involving the processing of a `lon`. That is, when a `lon`-problem is solved this function template is specialized. This specialization is done following the rest of the steps of the design recipe.

5.2 Step 2: Sample Expressions

The sample expressions use concrete values to illustrate how the answer for the `lon` varieties is computed. Following our design idea we may define sample expressions as follows:

```
;; Sample expressions for lon-double
(define DOUBLE-ELON '())
(define DOUBLE-LON1 (cons (* 2 (first LON1))
                          (lon-double (rest LON1))))
(define DOUBLE-LON2 (cons (* 2 (first LON2))
                          (lon-double (rest LON2))))
```

Observe that we are faithful to the design idea. If the empty `lon` is doubled, the answer is the empty list. Otherwise, a new list is created using the value of doubling the first element and the value of doubling the rest of the list.

5.3 Step 3: Differences Among Sample Expressions

The differences among sample expressions are done by variant. For the empty
lon there are no differences because the answer is always the empty list. For
the nonempty we observe there is only one difference: the lon processed.

   This analysis informs us that our function only needs the lon to process
as input. Put differently, the function only needs one parameter of type lon.
A descriptive name for this variable is a-lon.

5.4 Steps 4–5: Signature, Purpose Statement, and Function Header

We have determined that the only parameter must be a lon. It is not difficult
to see that the returned value is also a lon. Given that a single input value
is needed the function header only requires a single parameter. Finally, it is
highly advisable to pick a descriptive function name. Do not forget that a
primary goal of programming is to communicate how a problem is solved. Descriptive function names help readers of our code to understand each function.
We shall use the descriptive function name lon-double for our function.

   The above analysis allows us to write the following signature, purpose
statement, and function header:

```
;; lon → lon
;; Purpose: Double the numbers in the given list of numbers
(define (lon-double a-lon)
```

5.5 Step 6: Tests

The tests must cover all variants of the data being processed. Whenever
possible start by writing tests using sample computations. These use lon
sample instances and the values of sample expressions. We write the following
tests using sample computations:

```
;; Tests using sample computations
(check-expect (lon-double ELON) DOUBLE-ELON)
(check-expect (lon-double LON1) DOUBLE-LON1)
(check-expect (lon-double LON2) DOUBLE-LON2)
```

The test using sample values, on the other hand, is not based on the sample
expressions. Instead, concrete values are used to illustrate that the function
works. We may write the following tests using sample values:

```
;; Tests using sample values
(check-expect (lon-double '(-8 -10)) '(-16 -20))
(check-expect (lon-double '(23 -850 209)) '(46 -1700 418))
```

Observe that these tests, for example, illustrate that the function works for lons with different characteristics. For instance, it works for lists that only contain negative numbers.

5.6 Step 7: Function Body

To develop the function body we modify, if necessary, a sample expression for each variety. These define the expressions needed for each branch of a conditional expression. For the empty lon we use the sample expression for DOUBLE-ELON. This sample expression contains no differences and, therefore, remains unchanged. For the nonempty lon we use the sample expression for DOUBLE-LON1.[2] In this expression we substitute LON1 with a-lon.

The above analysis yields the following conditional expression for the function's body:

```
(if (empty? a-lon)
    '()
    (cons (* 2 (first a-lon)) (lon-double (rest a-lon))))
```

Observe how we independently reason about and write each branch of the conditional expression. Remember to always reason about the variants one at a time.

5.7 Step 8: Run Tests

Figure 4 displays the solution developed to double a list of numbers. Running the tests reveals no errors nor failed tests. Therefore, we may be cautiously optimistic that our solution works.

A question you should always ask yourself is whether or not there is a better solution. This question has two dimensions. The first is whether or not there is a faster solution. The second is whether or not there is a more elegant or easier to understand solution.

---

[2] The sample expression for DOUBLE-LON2 works equally well.

Fig. 4 Program to double a list of numbers

```
;; A list of numbers, lon, is either:
;;  1. '()
;;  2. (cons number lon)

;; Sample lon
(define ELON '())
(define LON1 '(2 3 4 5))
(define LON2 '(8 -2 0))


#| Template for functions on a lon

    ;; lon ... → ...
    ;; Purpose:
    (define (f-on-lon a-lon ...)
      (if (empty? a-lon)
          ...
          ...(first a-lon)...(f-on-lon (rest a-lon))))

(check-expect (f-on-lon '() ...) ...)
(check-expect (f-on-lon ... ...) ...)
    ...
(check-expect (f-on-lon ... ...) ...)
|#


;; lon → lon
;; Purpose: Double the numbers in the given list of numbers
(define (lon-double a-lon)
  (if (empty? a-lon)
      '()
      (cons (* 2 (first a-lon)) (lon-double (rest a-lon)))))

;; Sample expressions for lon-double
(define DOUBLE-ELON '())
(define DOUBLE-LON1 (cons (* 2 (first LON1))
                         (lon-double (rest LON1))))
(define DOUBLE-LON2 (cons (* 2 (first LON2))
                         (lon-double (rest LON2))))

;; Tests using sample computations
(check-expect (lon-double ELON) DOUBLE-ELON)
(check-expect (lon-double LON1) DOUBLE-LON1)
(check-expect (lon-double LON2) DOUBLE-LON2)

;; Tests using sample values
(check-expect (lon-double '(-8 -10)) '(-16 -20))
(check-expect (lon-double '(23 -850 209)) '(46 -1700 418))
```

5.8 Exercises

4 Design and implement a function to count the number of 'm in a list of symbols.

5 Design and implement a function to return the `posn` furthest away from the origin in a given list of `posn`.

6 Design and implement a function to add all the whole numbers in the interval `[a..b]`, where a and b are whole numbers.

7 Design and implement a function to multiply two positive natural numbers, n and m, without using multiplication. HINT: 4 * 5 = 4 + 4 + 4 + 4 + 4.

6 Code Refactoring

Code refactoring restructures existing functions without changing their external behavior. There may be many reasons to refactor a function. These include finding a faster or more elegant way of solving a problem. The idea is to change the implementation of a function without changing its signature or its purpose. Among other things, this means that when a function is refactored the existing tests must still pass without editing them.

The design of `lon-double` in the previous section exploits structural recursion. From the start you may have thought that our design idea makes the solution unnecessarily long and you realized that there is a more elegant solution. This is precisely a scenario in which code refactoring may be used.

If you carefully reason about what the code does, you can observe that the given list is traversed one element at a time. Each element is doubled and a list of the doubled elements is created. In essence, this means that the same function is applied to each element of the list. Recall that there is an abstract function, `map`, that traverses a given list and applies a given function to every element to create a list of the function application results. We can, therefore, refactor `lon-double` to use `map` as follows:

```
;; lon → lon
;; Purpose: Double the numbers in the given list of numbers
(define (lon-double a-lon)
  (map (λ (a-num) (* 2 a-num)) a-lon))
```

The body of the function applies `map` to an anonymous function that doubles its input and to the given lists of numbers. Observe that the function's signature and purpose remain unchanged. You may run the tests and they will all pass. Most code readers familiar with abstract functions would argue that this solution is more elegant and easier to understand. This means that this solution is superior because it better communicates how the problem is solved.

Alternatively, `lon-double` may be refactored to eliminate the use of list selectors by introducing local variables for the components of a list. This may be achieved using a `match`-expression. Recall that a `match`-expression dispatches on the type of the data processed. To process a list of numbers two stanzas are needed: one for each `lon` variant. The stanza for the nonempty `lon` allows us to introduce local variables for its components. We can refactor `lon-double` as follows:

```
;; lon → lon
;; Purpose: Double the numbers in the given list of numbers
(define (lon-double a-lon)
  (match a-lon
    ['() '()]
    [(cons frst rst) (cons (* 2 frst) (lon-double rst))]))
```

Observe that low-level selectors like `first` and `rest` are not utilized. Instead two local variables, `frst` and `rst`, are declared for the first element and the rest of the elements of a nonempty list. Unlike the refactored version using `map`, in this version of the function the use of structural recursion is explicit.

A local variable for the elements of a list may also be introduced by refactoring `lon-double` to use a `for`-loop. The use of `for`-loops allows us to declare variables for sequences of values. The `for`-loop iterates through the sequences to compute a result. For `lon-double` there is only one sequence of values of interest: the elements of the given `lon`. As before, the elements of the sequence must be doubled to create the solution list. We can also refactor `lon-double` as follows:

```
;; lon → lon
;; Purpose: Double the numbers in the given list of numbers
(define (lon-double a-lon)
  (for/list ([a-num a-lon]) (* 2 a-num)))
```

The local variable `a-num` is used to capture each element of the sequence defined by the elements of `a-lon`. The loop, `for/list`, creates a list of the results obtained from evaluating the loop's body, `(* 2 a-num)`, as the sequence is traversed.

6.1 Exercises

8 Design and implement a recursive function to move the elements of a list of posns by 5 on the x-axis. Refactor your function to eliminate the explicit use of recursion.

9 Design and implement a recursive function to extract the strings with a length greater than 5 from a given list of strings. Refactor your function to eliminate the explicit use of recursion.

10 Design and implement a recursive function to return a list of the first n natural numbers. Refactor your function to eliminate the explicit use of recursion.

11 Design and implement a recursive function to determine if a given list of numbers contains a given number. Refactor your function to eliminate the explicit use of recursion.

12 Design and implement a recursive function to determine if all the posns in a given list of posns are in the first quadrant. Refactor your function to eliminate the explicit use of recursion.

7 Abstract Running Time

Abstract running time relates a function's input size with the number of *abstract steps* needed to solve the problem. We say abstract steps because we do not count the actual number of computer operations performed. Instead, we count the number of general steps taken like the number of function calls or the number of comparisons made. Naturally, you are probably wondering why we do not count the actual number of computer operations performed. This is perfectly good question and it is important to understand the answer. The short answer is that we need a way to compare a program's expected performance independent of the computer used to run the program.

Consider, for example, running lon-double from Fig. 4 on a computer made in 1997 and on a computer made in 2021. It is unlikely to surprise you that it runs faster on the computer from 2021. Did the program magically become faster? Clearly, that is not the case. The program runs faster because the hardware used to execute it is faster. The algorithm implemented by the program remains unchanged when using a different computer. How

List length	Number of function calls
0	1
1	2
2	3
3	4
4	5
⋮	⋮

Table 1: Number of function calls in relation to list length for `double-lon`

do we remove differences in hardware to fairly compare the expected performance of the program? The answer is to count something that remains unchanged regardless of the hardware used for execution. This hypothetical something is called the number abstract steps. Observe, for example, that the number of function calls (or the number of multiplications performed) is the same regardless of the hardware used. If the number of abstract steps is the same regardless of the hardware used, how do we explain that it runs faster on a computer from 2021? The answer to this question comes from how the abstract operations are implemented by different machines. For example, making a recursive call on the 2021 machine may be faster because it can be done using fewer computer operations.

The next question to answer is: how are abstract operations counted? Consider, for example, the number of function calls performed for `double-lon` (from Fig. 4) displayed in Table 1. If the function is called with the empty list, only one function call is made. We know this by observing that when the given list is empty, the function returns the empty list without making any function calls. The only function call is the one made by the user. When the length of the list is 1 we can observe that two function calls are made: one (recursive) call in the else branch of the `if`-expression and the number of calls needed to process the empty list (i.e., `(rest a-lon)`). For a list of length 2 the number of function calls is 3: one (recursive) call in the else branch of the `if`-expression and the number of function calls needed for a list of length 1 (which we know is 2). The number of function calls is computed the same way for all rows.

Counting the actual number of abstract steps (like the concrete number of function calls) is of little use because it deprives us the power to predict the function's behavior given an arbitrary valid input. Therefore, the number of abstract operations is counted in relation to the size of the input. Intuitively, this ought to make sense given that the larger the input is the more abstract operations need to be performed. From Table 1 it is clear that there is a relation between the size of the input (i.e., the length of the list) and the number of function calls made. The number of function calls is always one more than the length of the list. That is,

```
number-function-calls(L) = (length L) + 1.
```

List length	n	n^2
0	0	0
1	1	1
2	2	4
3	3	9
4	4	16
5	5	25
$\vdots$	$\vdots$	$\vdots$
1,000,000	1,000,000	1,000,000,000,000

Table 2: Growth of n and n^2

This means that the only thing that varies from one row to another in Table 1 is the length of the list. If we let the length of the list be denoted by n, then the number of function calls is n+1.

If the number of abstract operations is n+1, then the number of computer operations is k*(n+1) (or k*n + k), where k is the number of computer operations needed to perform an abstract operation. This means that the number of computer operations is proportional to the number of abstract operations. We say that k is the constant of proportionality. Any increase in the number of computer operations performed is solely due to a change in n. Therefore, we ignore the constants when describing the abstract running time of a program. A program's abstract running time or *complexity* is usually written using Big O notation. For example, the complexity of lon−double is O(n). Observe that the constant of proportionality is ignored.

If a program is O(n) we say that it is linear. That means that if the size of the input is doubled, then we expect the number of abstract operations performed to be doubled. If a program is $O(n^2)$ and the size of the input is double, we expect the number of abstract operations to be quadrupled. Why? It is worth noting that programs may have an exponential running time. For example, a program might be $O(2^n)$. If a program has exponential complexity, it is unlikely to be useful other than for very small inputs. Consider, for example, a list-processing function that is $O(2^n)$. For a relatively small list with only 30 elements, the expected number of computer operations is proportional to over a billion operations. If the size of the list is doubled to 60, the number of computer operations is proportional to over a quintillion operations. A computer that is capable of executing two billion (computer) operations per second would roughly take over 160 thousand hours (i.e., over 18 years) to process a list with 60 elements. You can easily see why programs that have an exponential abstract running time are not practical.

Finally, the function for the abstract running time may have more than one component that depends on the size of the input. For example, such a function might be f(n) = $3n^2$ + 4n + 10. What is the complexity of such a program? We might be tempted to say that it is O(n^2 + n) (remember that we ignore the constants). Observe, however, the values for n and n^2 displayed in Table 2. It is clear that n^2 grows faster than n. For small values of n we can say that there is not much difference between the values of n and n^2. As n grows, however, it is clear that the value of n^2 is much larger. This means that the number of operations is proportional to n^2 and not to n. Therefore, we say that the complexity is $O(n^2)$. In general, the complexity of the program is the fastest growing component of its abstract running time function.

7.1 Exercises

13 Design and implement a recursive function to reverse a list of numbers. What is the complexity of your program?

14 Without using any local variables design and implement a function to extract the largest number of a list of numbers. What is the complexity of your program?

15 Design and implement a function to determine if a given number is a member of a given binary tree of numbers. What is the complexity of your program?

16 Design and implement a function to determine if a given number is a member of a given binary search tree of numbers. What is the complexity of your program?

8 What Have We Learned in This Chapter?

The important lessons of this chapter are summarized as follows:

- Variables are used to store values.
- Functions are abstractions over similar expressions.
- Abstraction over the types processed by similar functions gives rise to abstract functions and generic programming.
- Abstract running time relates the number of operations executed to the size of the input.
- A design recipe is a series of steps that take a problem solver from a problem statement to a working solution.
- One of the primary tasks of a programmer is to communicate how a problem is solved.
- For data of arbitrary size a recursive data definition is needed.

- A data definition is used to develop a function template.
- When solving a problem that requires processing data of arbitrary size, reason about each variant independently.
- Code refactoring restructures existing functions without changing their external behavior to make them faster or easier to understand.
- A program's complexity is usually written using Big O notation.

Chapter 2
The N-Puzzle Problem

One of the goals as you progress through this textbook is to implement an N-puzzle video game. This game is interesting because it is a problem that allows us to explore Computer Science topics that are usually relegated to advanced courses such as heuristic searching. If you do not know what heuristic searching is, there is no need for you to be concerned. We shall discuss it later in this textbook.

The N-puzzle is a sliding puzzle that has N tile positions, where N+1 is a square (e.g., N = 8 or 15). The tiles are typically numbered 1–N and there is an unoccupied tile space (that we shall call the empty tile space or simply the empty space). The board is organized as a square with $\sqrt{N+1}$ rows and $\sqrt{N+1}$ columns. Figure 5 displays sample boards for the eight puzzle. The player's goal is make a series of moves to take an unsolved puzzle as the one displayed in Fig. 5a to the puzzle's solution displayed in Fig. 5b. The player advances the game by swapping the empty tile space with a tile that is directly above, below, to the right, or to the left. For example, a player may swap the empty tile space with either the 5, 8, 4, or 3 tiles in Fig. 5a.

The player may feel she needs help to solve the puzzle. Therefore, the game offers a mechanism for the player to ask for help. This help comes in the form of a single move every time the player requests it. Making a move for the player is what makes the N-puzzle very interesting from a problem-solving perspective. How does the program decide what move to make? If the player makes no moves and only requests help, the program ought to eventually solve the puzzle. How does the program solve the puzzle? Another interesting question is how do we make sure that providing help does not make the program slow? After all, is there anything worse than a slow video game? These are the questions that we shall try to answer as we improve the implementation of the game. As you may have already guessed we will follow the process of iterative refinement. Each refinement of the game shall bring us closer to successfully answering these questions. Buckle up and enjoy this adventure of the mind, problem solving, and programming!

© The Author(s), under exclusive license to Springer Nature Switzerland AG 2022   21
M. T. Morazán, *Animated Program Design*, Texts in Computer Science,
https://doi.org/10.1007/978-3-031-04317-8_2

Fig. 5 Sample eight puzzles

1	5	2
4		3
7	8	6

1	2	3
4	5	6
7	8	

(a) An Unsolved 8-Puzzle.   (b) A Solved 8-Puzzle.

We shall implement an eight-puzzle game following a top-down design methodology. That is, we shall start with a **run** function containing a **big-bang** expression. All the auxiliary functions needed shall be designed following the steps of the design recipe. The bulk of the code developed in this chapter shall remain unchanged throughout the book. In fact, the only function that shall be refined is the one that makes a move every time the player requests help.

9 The world and the run Function

The sole purpose of the **run** function is to start the game by evaluating a **big-bang** expression. We encapsulate the **big-bang** expression inside a function to provide an easy way for the player to run the game. In other words, the function's purpose is to run the game and does not solve a problem. Therefore, this function shall be the only one that is not tested.

We must decide how to represent the game's world. Think carefully about what changes as the game advances. Clearly, the board changes as the player or the program swaps the empty tile space with a neighboring tile. Is there anything else that changes? Let's see. This game only has a board of tiles. Therefore, there is nothing else that may change, meaning that the game's world is the value of the board.

How can the value of the board be represented? The board contains nine positions that we shall number 0–8. The top row from left to right contains board positions 0–2. The middle row from left to right contains board positions 3–5. The bottom row from left to right contains board positions 6–8.

This suggests the following board position data definition, sample values, and template for functions of a board position:

```
;; A board position, bpos, is an integer in [0..8]

;; Sample bpos
(define TRCRNR 0)   ;; top right corner
(define CENTER 4)   ;; center position
(define MLEFTC 5)   ;; middle left column

#|
;; bpos ... → ...
;; Purpose:
(define (f-on-bpos a-bpos ...)
  (cond [(= a-bpos 0) ...]
        [(= a-bpos 1) ...]
        [(= a-bpos 2) ...]
        [(= a-bpos 3) ...]
        [(= a-bpos 4) ...]
        [(= a-bpos 5) ...]
        [(= a-bpos 6) ...]
        [(= a-bpos 7) ...]
        [else ...]))

;; Sample expressions for f-on-bpos
(define TRCRNR-VAL ...)
(define CENTER-VAL ...)
(define MLEFTC-VAL ...)

;; Tests using sample computations for f-on-bpos
(check-expect (f-on-bpos TRCRNR ...) ...)
(check-expect (f-on-bpos CENTER ...) ...)
(check-expect (f-on-bpos MLEFTC ...) ...)

;; Tests using sample values for f-on-bpos
(check-expect (f-on-bpos ... ...) ...)
      ⋮
|#
```

Observe that the definition's template body contains a conditional expression to distinguish among the eight bpos variants.

Each board position may contain a tile or be empty. A tile may be represented by the number on the tile: 1–8. How can the empty tile space be represented? We are free to pick any representation that we like. Without loss of generality, we choose to represent the empty tile space as 0. This leads

us to the following data definition, sample values, and template for functions
on a tile value:

```
;; A tile value, tval, is an integer in [0..8]

;; Sample tval
(define BLNK 0)
(define FOUR 4)
(define FIVE 5)

#|
;; tval ... → ...
;; Purpose:
(define (f-on-tval a-tval ...)
  (cond [(= a-tval 0) ...]
        [(= a-tval 1) ...]
        [(= a-tval 2) ...]
        [(= a-tval 3) ...]
        [(= a-tval 4) ...]
        [(= a-tval 5) ...]
        [(= a-tval 6) ...]
        [(= a-tval 7) ...]
        [else ...]))

;; Sample expressions for f-on-tval
(define BLNK-VAL ...)
(define FOUR-VAL ...)
(define FIVE-VAL ...)

;; Tests using sample computations for f-on-tval
(check-expect (f-on-tval BLNK ...) ...)
(check-expect (f-on-tval FOUR ...) ...)
(check-expect (f-on-tval FIVE ...) ...)

;; Tests using sample values for f-on-tval
(check-expect (f-on-tval ... ...) ...)
        ⋮
|#
```

Do not erroneously conclude that bpos and tval are the same. A bpos refers
to a fixed position on the board. A tval refers to a tile value that may be
located at any bpos value. For example, a bpos equal to 0 always indicates
the top right corner board position, while a tval equal to 0 indicates the
empty tile space (that may be at any board position). In short, we use the
same representation for two different data types.

Based on the previous definitions, we can now define a world as nine board positions, each containing a tile value. This suggests the following world structure, sample worlds, and template for functions on a world:

```
;; A world is a structure:
;;    (make-world tval tval tval tval tval tval tval tval tval)

(define-struct world (t0 t1 t2 t3 t4 t5 t6 t7 t8))

;; Sample worlds
(define WIN     (make-world 1 2 3
                            4 5 6
                            7 8 0))

(define A-WRLD (make-world 1 5 2
                           4 0 3
                           7 8 6))

#|
;; world ... → ...
;; Purpose:
(define (f-on-world a-world ...)
  (... (f-on-tval (world-t0))
       (f-on-tval (world-t1))
       (f-on-tval (world-t2))
       (f-on-tval (world-t3))
       (f-on-tval (world-t4))
       (f-on-tval (world-t5))
       (f-on-tval (world-t6))
       (f-on-tval (world-t7))
       (f-on-tval (world-t8)) ...))

;; Sample expressions for f-on-world
(define WIN-VAL ...)
(define A-WORLD-VAL ...)

;; Tests using sample computations for f-on-world
(check-expect (f-on-world WIN ...)      WIN-VAL)
(check-expect (f-on-world A-WORLD ...) A-WORLD-VAL)

;; Tests using sample values for f-on-world
(check-expect (f-on-world ... ...) ...)
     ⋮
|#
```

The name of the fields may be interpreted as *tile value at board position n.* For example, t0 is the tile value at board position 0. Observe that the definition template contains expressions that suggest calling functions to process a tile value.

We can now turn our attention to designing the function to run the game. This function shall take as input a name, represented as a symbol or a string, to be placed on the game's window frame and returns a world (i.e., the value when the game ends). We need to decide what handlers are needed by the big-bang expression. Clearly, a handler is needed to draw the world and to detect when the game is over. In addition, we shall define a function to draw the final world when the puzzle is solved. The only decision left for us to make is how the player shall interact with the game. There are two choices. We may design the game to allow the player to use either the keyboard or the mouse to swap the empty tile space with one of its neighbors. We arbitrarily choose to have the player interact with the game using the keyboard. This means that we need a keystroke-processing function. This analysis leads to the following run function:

```
;; A name is either a symbol or a string

;; name → world
;; Purpose: Run the 8-puzzle game
(define (run a-name)
  (big-bang
    A-WRLD
    (on-draw draw-world)
    (on-key process-key)
    (stop-when game-over? draw-last-world)
    (name a-name)))
```

We need to design and implement four functions and any auxiliary functions these four main functions need. The big-bang expression is where we start the top-down design process. The following sections fully outline the design and implementation of each handler. Remember that run must be the last function in your file.

10 Useful Constants

Before proceeding with the design of the handlers, it is useful to outline useful constants. We know that a scene to draw the world in is needed. The scene must fit three tile images across and three tile images down for a total of nine tiles. Therefore, it makes sense to define the width and the height of the scene in terms of a tile's width and height.

A tile's image has a width and a length. In addition, a tile's image has a background color. The text on a tile has a font size and a color. We are free to choose these characteristics to our liking. If each tile image is made a square, then only a length is needed to define it. These observations lead to the following constants:

```
(define TILE-LEN 100)

(define TILE-COLOR 'green)

(define BORD-COLOR 'black)

(define TEXT-COLOR 'black)

(define TEXT-SIZE 36)

(define SCENE-LEN (* 3 TILE-LEN))

(define e-scene (empty-scene SCENE-LEN SCENE-LEN))
```

A tile image is defined as having a length of 100 pixels and its background color is green. A tile's text is black and has a font size of 36. The empty scene's length is defined as three times the tile length. The scene's length is used to create an empty scene that is a square that fits nine tiles.

The foundation image for a tile is two overlayed squares of the same size. The top is an outline square using BORD-COLOR to make tile borders visually pleasing. The bottom square is created using TILE-COLOR. Over this foundation image a text image containing the tile number is overlayed. We may define the empty tile, the one tile, and the two tiles as follows:

```
(define T0 (overlay (square TILE-LEN 'outline TEXT-COLOR)
                    (square TILE-LEN 'solid   TILE-COLOR)))

(define T1 (overlay (text (number->string 1)
                          TEXT-SIZE
                          TEXT-COLOR)
                    (square TILE-LEN 'outline TEXT-COLOR)
                    (square TILE-LEN 'solid   TILE-COLOR)))

(define T2 (overlay (text (number->string 2)
                          TEXT-SIZE
                          TEXT-COLOR)
                    (square TILE-LEN 'outline TEXT-COLOR)
                    (square TILE-LEN 'solid   TILE-COLOR)))
```

At this point you ought to realize that the remaining tile images are defined in the same manner as T1 and T2. This approach leads to a lot of repeated

Fig. 6 A tile image generating function

```
;; tval → image
;; Purpose: Return the tile image for the given tile number
(define (make-tile-img a-tval)
  (if (= a-tval 0)
      (overlay (square TILE-LEN 'outline BORD-COLOR)
               (square TILE-LEN 'solid TILE-COLOR))
      (overlay (text (number->string a-tval) TEXT-SIZE TEXT-COLOR)
               (square TILE-LEN 'outline BORD-COLOR)
               (square TILE-LEN 'solid TILE-COLOR))))

;; Sample expressions for make-tile-img
(define T0 (overlay (square TILE-LEN 'outline BORD-COLOR)
                    (square TILE-LEN 'solid TILE-COLOR)))

(define T1 (overlay (text (number->string 1) TEXT-SIZE TEXT-COLOR)
                    (square TILE-LEN 'outline BORD-COLOR)
                    (square TILE-LEN 'solid TILE-COLOR)))

(define T2 (overlay (text (number->string 2) TEXT-SIZE TEXT-COLOR)
                    (square TILE-LEN 'outline BORD-COLOR)
                    (square TILE-LEN 'solid TILE-COLOR)))

;; Tests using sample computations for make-tile-img
(check-expect (make-tile-img 0) T0)
(check-expect (make-tile-img 1) T1)
(check-expect (make-tile-img 2) T2)

;; Tests using sample values for make-tile-img

(check-expect (make-tile-img 8) ⬛ )

(check-expect (make-tile-img 5) ⬛ )
```

code. What does this suggest? It suggests abstracting over the expressions to define a function to create tile images. Observe, however, that the expression used for T0 is different from those used for T1 and T2. We would like to create a function to create all tile images, but currently we are unable to abstract over all the expressions. At this point if you are thinking about refactoring the expressions, you are on the right track.

We can use a conditional expression to distinguish when to create the empty tile space image and when to create a nonempty tile image. This design idea yields the following definitions for tile image constants:

```
(define T0 (if (= 0 0)
              (overlay (square TILE-LEN 'outline TEXT-COLOR)
                       (square TILE-LEN 'solid   TILE-COLOR))
              (overlay (text (number->string 0)
                             TEXT-SIZE
                             TEXT-COLOR)
                       (square TILE-LEN 'outline TEXT-COLOR)
                       (square TILE-LEN 'solid   TILE-COLOR))))

(define T1 (if (= 1 0)
              (overlay (square TILE-LEN 'outline TEXT-COLOR)
                       (square TILE-LEN 'solid   TILE-COLOR))
              (overlay (text (number->string 1)
                             TEXT-SIZE
                             TEXT-COLOR)
                       (square TILE-LEN 'outline TEXT-COLOR)
                       (square TILE-LEN 'solid   TILE-COLOR))))

(define T2 (if (= 2 0)
              (overlay (square TILE-LEN 'outline TEXT-COLOR)
                       (square TILE-LEN 'solid   TILE-COLOR))
              (overlay (text (number->string 2)
                             TEXT-SIZE
                             TEXT-COLOR)
                       (square TILE-LEN 'outline TEXT-COLOR)
                       (square TILE-LEN 'solid   TILE-COLOR))))
```

It may seem silly to test two values for equality when they are obviously equal or not equal, but remember that the goal is to abstract over these expressions to create a function. The expressions above are the sample expressions for the new function.

Observe that the only difference between the expressions is the tile's tval. We may name the single parameter needed a-tval. This leads to the signature, purpose statement, and function header for make-tile-img displayed in Fig. 6. The body of the function is obtained by substituting the only difference with the parameter name. The tests using sample computations use the concrete tval values employed in the sample expressions and the values the sample expressions evaluate to. Finally, the tests using sample values illustrate that tile images are correctly created for other concrete tvals.

We now define the rest of the tile images as follows:

```
(define T3 (make-tile-img 3))

(define T4 (make-tile-img 4))

(define T5 (make-tile-img 5))
```

```
(define T6 (make-tile-img 6))

(define T7 (make-tile-img 7))

(define T8 (make-tile-img 8))
```

Observe how elegant these definitions are. They are both concise and easy for any reader of the code to understand.

We proceed to the design and the implementation of the handlers. Be advised that we shall write encapsulated functions. That is, for each handler the auxiliary functions are locally defined. This has two implications for problem solving using a computer. The first is that it prevents us from writing tests for the local functions. Therefore, you ought to first write a proposed local function at the global level and test it thoroughly before making it local. The second is that it prevents us from writing sample expressions given that local functions are out of scope at the global level where tests must be written. The solution is the same as for tests. Design and implement non-locally first and then encapsulate. We discuss the design of all local functions, but sample expressions and tests for local functions do not appear in the finalized version of the code presented.

1 Customize tile images using colors, fonts, and shapes of your liking. You are strongly encouraged to be creative and personalize your game.

11 The draw-world Handler

The universe abstract procedure interface (API) informs us that the drawing handler must take as input a world and return an image. We can think of a board image as having three rows above each other. The top row has the tile images for the tiles in board positions 0–2. The middle row has the tile images for the tiles in board positions 3–5. Finally, the bottom row has the tile images for the tiles in board positions 6–8. To create the image the top row is placed above the middle row which is placed above the bottom row. Each row is created by placing the appropriate three tile images beside each other.

Based on the above design idea we can outline sample expressions as follows:

```
(above (beside (tile-img (world-t0 WIN))
               (tile-img (world-t1 WIN))
               (tile-img (world-t2 WIN)))
       (beside (tile-img (world-t3 WIN))
               (tile-img (world-t4 WIN))
               (tile-img (world-t5 WIN)))
```

```
                (beside (tile-img (world-t6 WIN))
                        (tile-img (world-t7 WIN))
                        (tile-img (world-t8 WIN)))))

   (above (beside (tile-img (world-t0 A-WRLD))
                  (tile-img (world-t1 A-WRLD))
                  (tile-img (world-t2 A-WRLD)))
          (beside (tile-img (world-t3 A-WRLD))
                  (tile-img (world-t4 A-WRLD))
                  (tile-img (world-t5 A-WRLD)))
          (beside (tile-img (world-t6 A-WRLD))
                  (tile-img (world-t7 A-WRLD))
                  (tile-img (world-t8 A-WRLD)))))
```

The (yet-to-be designed and local) auxiliary function `tile-img` returns the
tile image for the `tval` it is given as input. Observe that the only difference
between the sample expressions is the world drawn and we name the difference
`a-world`. Also note that constants for these expressions cannot be defined in
the finalized code because `tile-img` is locally defined in `draw-world`.

The function signature, purpose statement, and header are:

```
;; draw-world: world → image
;; Purpose: To draw the given world in the empty-scene
(define (draw-world a-world)
```

This allows us to write tests for the `draw-world` as follows:

```
;; Tests using sample values for draw-world
```

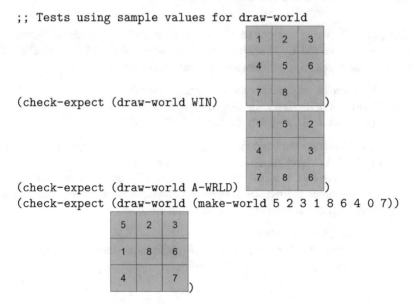

```
(check-expect (draw-world WIN)                              )

(check-expect (draw-world A-WRLD)                           )
(check-expect (draw-world (make-world 5 2 3 1 8 6 4 0 7))
                                                           )
```

Observe that only tests using sample values appear in the finalized code given
that we are unable to include sample expressions for `draw-world`.

The body of the function is obtained from abstracting over the proposed sample expressions. The concrete `world` value found in the proposed sample expressions is substituted with `a-world` to obtain:

```
(above (beside (tile-img (world-t0 a-world))
               (tile-img (world-t1 a-world))
               (tile-img (world-t2 a-world)))
       (beside (tile-img (world-t3 a-world))
               (tile-img (world-t4 a-world))
               (tile-img (world-t5 a-world)))
       (beside (tile-img (world-t6 a-world))
               (tile-img (world-t7 a-world))
               (tile-img (world-t8 a-world)))))
```

The design of `tile-img` specializes the template for function on a `tval`. Each branch of the conditional returns the appropriate image constant defined in Sect. 10. The complete code for the draw-world is displayed in Fig. 7. Run the tests and make sure you thoroughly understand the design.

2 Write sample expressions and tests for `tile-img` if it were not local in Fig. 7.

12 The `game-over?` Handler

The game is over if the `world` is the same as, `WIN`, the winning board. This may be determined by checking the given world and `WIN` for equality. This design idea leads to the following sample expressions:

```
;; Sample expressions for game-over?
(define WIN-OVER    (equal? WIN WIN))
(define A-WRLD-OVER (equal? A-WRLD WIN))
```

The only difference between the sample expressions is the world that is compared to `WIN`. We may name this difference `a-world`.

The universe `API` informs us the game over handler must take as input a world and must return a Boolean. This allows us to write the following signature, purpose statement, and function header:

```
;; world → Boolean
;; Purpose: Determine if the game has ended
(define (game-over? a-world)
```

Fig. 7 The draw-world handler

```
;; draw-world: world → image
;; Purpose: To draw the given world in the empty-scene
(define (draw-world a-world)
  (local [;; tval → image
          ;; Purpose: Return the image for the given tile value
          (define (tile-img a-tval)
            (cond [(= a-tval 0) T0]
                  [(= a-tval 1) T1]
                  [(= a-tval 2) T2]
                  [(= a-tval 3) T3]
                  [(= a-tval 4) T4]
                  [(= a-tval 5) T5]
                  [(= a-tval 6) T6]
                  [(= a-tval 7) T7]
                  [else T8]))]
    (above (beside (tile-img (world-t0 a-world))
                   (tile-img (world-t1 a-world))
                   (tile-img (world-t2 a-world)))
           (beside (tile-img (world-t3 a-world))
                   (tile-img (world-t4 a-world))
                   (tile-img (world-t5 a-world)))
           (beside (tile-img (world-t6 a-world))
                   (tile-img (world-t7 a-world))
                   (tile-img (world-t8 a-world))))))

;; Tests using sample values for draw-world
```

```
(check-expect (draw-world WIN)
```

```
(check-expect (draw-world A-WRLD)                    )
(check-expect (draw-world (make-world 5 2 3 1 8 6 4 0 7))
```

```
                                                     )
```

Fig. 8 The game-over? handler

```
;; world → Boolean
;; Purpose: Determine if the game has ended
(define (game-over? a-world) (equal? a-world WIN))

;; Sample expressions for game-over?
(define WIN-OVER (equal? WIN WIN))
(define A-WRLD-OVER (equal? A-WRLD WIN))

;; Tests using sample computations for game-over?
(check-expect (game-over? A-WRLD) A-WRLD-OVER)
(check-expect (game-over? WIN)    WIN-OVER)

;; Tests using sample values for game-over?
(check-expect (game-over? (make-world 5 2 3 1 8 6 4 0 7)) #false)
```

We can write tests for this function as follows:

```
;; Tests using sample computations for game-over?
(check-expect (game-over? A-WRLD) A-WRLD-OVER)
(check-expect (game-over? WIN)    WIN-OVER)

;; Tests using sample values for game-over?
(check-expect (game-over? (make-world 5 2 3 1 8 6 4 0 7))
              #false)
(check-expect (game-over? (make-world 4 3 1 0 7 2 8 5 6))
              #false)
```

The tests using sample computations illustrate that the function returns the same answer as the evaluated sample expressions. The tests using sample values illustrate that the function works for other world values.

The body of the function is obtained by abstracting over the sample expressions. The complete code for this handler is displayed in Fig. 8. Run the tests and make sure you understand the design.

To inform the user that the game is over, the function for the last scene returns the board's image with the message PUZZLE SOLVED!!! on it. The result of following the steps of the design recipe is displayed in Fig. 9. The puzzle solved message is placed at the bottom of the top row as illustrated by the sample expressions. There is only one difference among the sample expressions and, therefore, the function has only one parameter as required by the universe API. The set of tests, as before, illustrates that the function works for the concrete values used in the sample expressions and for concrete values not used in the sample expressions.

Fig. 9 The function to draw the last world

```
;; world → image
;; Purpose: Draw the final world
(define (draw-last-world a-world)
  (overlay/xy (text "PUZZLE SOLVED!!!" 28 'brown)
              -25
              -75
              (draw-world a-world)))

;; Sample expressions for draw-last-world
(define WIN-FIMG (overlay/xy (text "PUZZLE SOLVED!!!" 28 'brown)
                             -25
                             -75
                             (draw-world WIN)))

(define A-WRD-FIMG (overlay/xy (text "PUZZLE SOLVED!!!" 28 'brown)
                               -25
                               -75
                               (draw-world A-WRLD)))

;; Tests using sample computations for draw-last-world
(check-expect (draw-last-world WIN)     WIN-FIMG)
(check-expect (draw-last-world A-WRLD) A-WRLD-FIMG)

;; Tests using sample values for draw-last-world
(check-expect (draw-last-world (make-world 4 3 1 0 7 2 8 5 6))
```

```
)
(check-expect (draw-last-world (make-world 5 2 3 1 8 6 4 0 7))
```

```
)
```

---

3 The universe API guarantees that the function to draw the final world is only called when game-over? returns #true. Observe that this may only occur when the given world is WIN. Redesign draw-last-world to return an image defined as a constant. This is not a refactoring exercise because it requires revisiting all the steps of the design recipe.

13 The process-key Handler

This handler is responsible for managing interactions with the user. That is, it is the handler that moves the empty tile space and that makes a move when the player requests help. In this version of the game the request for help shall not be implemented. When the player requests help, nothing occurs and the game continues. In future refinements the game shall make a move for the player when help is requested.

   The player can hit any key, but the game only reacts to keys for moving the empty space and for requesting help. An intuitive set of keys that may be used to move the empty space is the set of arrows. Each of the four arrows allows the user to move the space in the corresponding direction as long as it is a valid move. We shall allow the player to use the space bar to request help. This data analysis suggests the following data definition for valid keys:

```
;; A valid key, vk, is either
;; 1. "up"
;; 2. "down"
;; 3. "left"
;; 4. "right"
;; 5. " "

;; Sample vk
(define UP     "up")
(define DOWN   "down")
(define LEFT   "left")
(define RIGHT  "right")
(define HKEY   " ")

;; Template for functions on a vk
#|
;; vk ... → ...
;; Purpose:
(define (f-on-vk a-vk ...)
  (cond [(key=? a-vk UP)    ...]
        [(key=? a-vk DOWN)  ...]
        [(key=? a-vk LEFT)  ...]
        [(key=? a-vk RIGHT) ...]
        [else ...]))

;; Sample expressions for f-on-vk
(define UP-VAL    ...)
(define DOWN-VAL  ...)
(define LEFT-VAL  ...)
(define RIGHT-VAL ...)
(define HKEY-VAL  ...)
```

```
;; Tests using sample computations for f-on-vk
(check-expect (f-on-vk UP     ...) UP-VAL)
(check-expect (f-on-vk DOWN   ...) DOWN-VAL)
(check-expect (f-on-vk LEFT   ...) LEFT-VAL)
(check-expect (f-on-vk RIGHT  ...) RIGHT-VAL)
(check-expect (f-on-vk HKEY   ...) HKEY-VAL)

;; Tests using sample values for f-on-vk
(check-expect (f-on-vk ...  ...) ...)
        ⋮
|#
```

The set of vk values is an enumerated type with five variants. This is why the body of the definition template has a cond-expression with five stanzas. It is also why the template suggests writing at least five sample expressions and at least five tests using sample computations. The template also suggests writing at least one test using sample values because a computation may depend on multiple inputs beyond a valid key.

The design idea is for the function to distinguish between vk and non-vk keystrokes. If the given key is a vk then it must be processed to advance the game by creating a new world. Otherwise, the given key is not processed and the given world is returned. This allows us to begin outlining the process-key handler as follows:

```
;; world key → world
;; Purpose: Return next world after the given key event
(define (process-key a-world a-key)
  (local [...
          (define (vk? a-key) ...)
          ...
          (define (process-vk a-world a-vk) ...)]
    (if (vk? a-key)
        (process-vk a-world a-key)
        a-world)))
```

The signature of the function is the one required by the universe API. The purpose statement clearly explains that the function returns the next world after a key event (i.e., a keystroke). An auxiliary function, vk?, is used to determine if the given key is a valid key. If so, an auxiliary function, process-vk, is called to process the given world and the given valid key. Otherwise, the given world is returned. The auxiliary functions vk? and process-vk are encapsulated to make sure the final version of the code is well-organized.

We can now illustrate the expected behavior of the function by writing tests. Think carefully about what needs to happen when a valid key is pressed for a given world. Let us examine a possible set of tests in the final program:

```
;; Tests for process-key
(check-expect (process-key A-WRLD "m") A-WRLD)
(check-expect (process-key A-WRLD "d") A-WRLD)
(check-expect (process-key WIN UP)
              (make-world 1 2 3
                          4 5 0
                          7 8 6))
(check-expect (process-key (make-world 0 1 2
                                       3 4 5
                                       6 7 8)
                           UP)
              (make-world 0 1 2
                          3 4 5
                          6 7 8))
(check-expect (process-key (make-world 0 1 2
                                       3 4 5
                                       6 7 8)
                           DOWN)
              (make-world 3 1 2
                          0 4 5
                          6 7 8))
(check-expect (process-key WIN DOWN) WIN)
check-expect (process-key A-WRLD LEFT)
              (make-world 1 5 2
                          0 4 3
                          7 8 6))
(check-expect (process-key (make-world 1 5 2
                                       0 4 3
                                       7 8 6)
                           LEFT)
              (make-world 1 5 2
                          0 4 3
                          7 8 6))
(check-expect (process-key A-WRLD RIGHT)
              (make-world 1 5 2
                          4 3 0
                          7 8 6))
(check-expect (process-key WIN RIGHT) WIN)
(check-expect (process-key A-WRLD HKEY) A-WRLD)
```

The goal of our tests is to illustrate that the function works as expected. The first two tests illustrate that the same (unchanged) input world is returned when a non-vk keystroke is given as input. The rest of the tests illustrate how the function works when a vk keystroke is given as input. The third and fourth tests illustrate the behavior when the up arrow is pressed by the player. In test three the 0 and the 6 are swapped given that the empty space may be moved up. In contrast, the fourth test illustrates that input world is returned when the empty space cannot be moved up (because 0 is in the top row). The fifth and sixth tests illustrate what happens when the down arrow is pressed. In the fifth test the space moves down (i.e., 0 is swapped with 3). In the sixth test, on the other hand, the empty space cannot be moved down in the winning board (because the empty space is in the bottom row). The seventh and eighth tests illustrate that the space moves left when possible, while the ninth and tenth tests illustrate that the space moves right when possible. Finally, the 11th test illustrates what happens when the player requests help. Recall that in this version of the game the program does not make a move for the player and, therefore, the input world to `process-key` is returned.

13.1 The Design of `vk?`

Determining whether an arbitrary key is a `vk` is relatively straightforward. The given key must be tested for equality with all the `vk` values. If it matches any of the `vk` variants, then this predicate returns `#true`. Otherwise, it returns `#false`.

This function is first defined and tested as a global function. Once you are satisfied that the function is correctly implemented, it is made local to `process-key`. The local function definition is:

```
;; key → Boolean
;; Purpose: Determine in given key is a vk
(define (vk? a-key)
  (or (key=? a-key UP)
      (key=? a-key DOWN)
      (key=? a-key LEFT)
      (key=? a-key RIGHT)
      (key=? a-key HKEY))))
```

Observe that an `or`-expression is used to determine if the given key matches any `vk` variant.

13.2 The Design of `process-vk`

We discuss the design of `process-vk`, but only display the code that is localized. When the player hits a valid key, one of two things may happen. Either an empty space moving key is processed or a help request is processed. This suggests that a conditional expression is needed to distinguish between these two possibilities. We may outline the function as follows:

```
;; world vk → world
;; Purpose: Return the next world after given vk
(define (process-vk a-world a-vk)
    (local [(define (blank-pos a-world) ...)
               (define (get-target-bpos a-world a-vk) ...)
               (define (swap-empty a-world target) ...)
               (define (make-move a-world) ...)]
      (if (or (key=? a-vk UP)   (key=? a-vk DOWN)
               (key=? a-vk LEFT) (key=? a-vk RIGHT))
          (swap-empty a-world (get-target-bpos a-world a-vk))
          (make-move a-world))))
```

Observe that the second input for this function is a vk and not an arbitrary
key. Make sure you understand why. If an empty space moving vk is given as
input, a (local) function to swap the empty space in the requested direction is
called. The target bpos for the empty space is computed by a local function
called get-target-bpos. If the given input is HKEY then a function to make
a move for the player is called. In addition, there is a function to return the
position of the empty space. This function is local to process-vk because it
is used by several functions under it.

13.2.1 Computing the Position of the Empty Space

The empty space's bpos is computed by examining a given world. To determine the position of the blank space, the tvals at each board position are ex-
amined. The board position that has a tval of 0 is the value of BLNK-POS. The
function is obtained by specializing the template for functions on a world:

```
;; world → bpos
;; Purpose: Return the bpos for the blank
(define (blank-pos a-world)
   (cond [(= (world-t0 a-world) 0) 0]
            [(= (world-t1 a-world) 0) 1]
            [(= (world-t2 a-world) 0) 2]
            [(= (world-t3 a-world) 0) 3]
            [(= (world-t4 a-world) 0) 4]
            [(= (world-t5 a-world) 0) 5]
            [(= (world-t6 a-world) 0) 6]
            [(= (world-t7 a-world) 0) 7]
            [(= (world-t8 a-world) 0) 8]))
```

13.2.2 The Design of get-target-bpos

We discuss the design of get-target-bpos, but only display the code that
is made local to process-vk. This function processes a vk other than HKEY.

Its goal is to compute a new board position for the empty space. We have three questions to answer:

1. **What is the target board position if the empty space cannot be moved?**
2. **How can we determine if the empty space may be moved in the given direction?**
3. **How is the target board position computed when the empty space can be moved?**

To answer the first question think about what happens to the blank's position if it cannot be moved. In such a case, the position of the blank in the new `world` constructed is the same as in the world given to `process-key`. This means we can make the target board position the board position of the empty space. Observe that swapping the empty space board position with itself is the same as not moving it.

To answer the second question we ought to reason about each of the four possible `vk` values and the position of the blank space. If the given `vk` is `UP` then the empty space may move only if it is not in the top row. That is, moving up can only occur if the blank's position is greater than or equal to 3. If the given `vk` is `DOWN` then the empty space may move only if it is not in the bottom row. That is, moving down can only occur if the blank's position is less than or equal to 5. If the given `vk` is `LEFT` then the empty space may move only if it is not in leftmost column. This means that it is not in board positions 0, 3, or 6. How can we detect this condition? We can test if the blank's position is any of those values. A more elegant solution uses modular arithmetic. Observe that 0, 3, and 6 are the only board positions divisible by 3 in the eight puzzle. This means that the empty space may be moved left if the blank's position is not divisible by 3. That is, the remainder when dividing by 3 is not 0. If the given `vk` is `RIGHT` then the empty space may move only if it is not in the rightmost column. This means that it is not in board positions 2, 5, or 8. Observe that these are the only board positions in the eight puzzle that have a remainder of 2 when divided by 3. Therefore, the empty space may be moved right when the remainder of dividing the blank's position and 3 is not 2.

To answer the third question we again reason about each of the four possible `vk` values. What happens to the blank's position if it is moved up? Observe that it is decremented by 3. Notice that moving down is the inverse of moving up. Consequently, the blank's position is incremented by 3 when it is moved down. What happens to the blank's position if it is moved left? Moving left decrements the blank's position by 1. Given that moving right and moving left are inverses of each other, it follows that the blank's position is incremented by 1 when moving right.

Based on this data analysis and design idea, the code for `get-target-bpos` is:

```
;; world vk → bpos
;; Purpose: Return the bpos to move the blank into
(define (get-target-bpos a-world a-vk)
  (local [(define BLNK-POS (blank-pos a-world))]
    (cond [(key=? a-vk UP)
           (if (< BLNK-POS 3)
               BLNK-POS
               (- BLNK-POS 3))]
          [(key=? a-vk DOWN)
           (if (> BLNK-POS 5)
               BLNK-POS
               (+ BLNK-POS 3))]
          [(key=? a-vk LEFT)
           (if (= (remainder BLNK-POS 3) 0)
               BLNK-POS
               (sub1 BLNK-POS))]
          [else
           (if (= (remainder BLNK-POS 3) 2)
               BLNK-POS
               (add1 BLNK-POS))])))
```

Observe that the position of the blank is locally defined. For each possible vk value, the function tests if the empty space position may be moved. If it cannot be moved the empty space board position is returned. Otherwise, the new board position for the empty space is returned.

13.2.3 The Design of `swap-empty`

To swap the empty space a new world must be created with each board position containing its new value (which may be the same as its current value). This function gets a `bpos` value as input but does not process it. Instead, it is only responsible for constructing a new `world`. To do so it has a new `t-val` computed for each board position. We outline `swap-empty` as follows:

```
;; world bpos → world
;; Purpose: Move the blank to the given bpos
(define (swap-empty a-world target)
  (local [...
          (define (new-tile-value a-world a-bpos) ...)]
    (make-world (new-tile-value a-world 0)
                (new-tile-value a-world 1)
                (new-tile-value a-world 2)
```

```
                    (new-tile-value a-world 3)
                    (new-tile-value a-world 4)
                    (new-tile-value a-world 5)
                    (new-tile-value a-world 6)
                    (new-tile-value a-world 7)
                    (new-tile-value a-world 8))))
```

The local function `new-tile-value` takes as input a `world` and a board position and computes new tile value for the given board position. Observe that the `tval` for a given board position only changes if it is equal to `target` or to the empty tile position. Otherwise it remains unchanged. If the given board position is equal to `target`, then the new `tval` is 0 (the value representing the empty space). If the given board position is equal to empty tile position, then the new `tval` is the tile value at `target`. Simply stated, the values at blank's position and at `target` are swapped. This analysis suggests the use of a conditional expression to distinguish among the three possible cases. The function's implementation may be outlined as follows:

```
;; world bpos → bval
;; Purpose: Return new value of given bpos
(define (new-tile-value a-world a-bpos)
  (local [...
          (define (get-tile-value a-world a-bpos) ...)]
        (cond [(= target a-bpos) 0]
              [(blank-pos a-world)
               (get-tile-value a-world target)]
              [else (get-tile-value a-world a-bpos)])))
```

The local function `get-tile-value` returns the `tval` at the given `bpos`. Observe that `target` is in scope and, therefore, may be accessed (it is a parameter of the enclosing `swap-empty` function).

The function `get-tile-value` processes the given `bpos`. It is implemented by specializing the template for functions on a `bpos`. It is implemented as follows:

```
;; world bpos → bval
;; Purpose: Return the given bpos' bval
(define (get-tile-value a-world a-bpos)
  (cond [(= a-bpos 0) (world-t0 a-world)]
        [(= a-bpos 1) (world-t1 a-world)]
        [(= a-bpos 2) (world-t2 a-world)]
        [(= a-bpos 3) (world-t3 a-world)]
        [(= a-bpos 4) (world-t4 a-world)]
        [(= a-bpos 5) (world-t5 a-world)]
        [(= a-bpos 6) (world-t6 a-world)]
        [(= a-bpos 7) (world-t7 a-world)]
        [else (world-t8 a-world)]))
```

13.2.4 The Design of `make-move`

In this version of the game this function is the easiest to design, but in future refinements of the game, this is the function that captures our interest. This is the function that will be redesigned to make the game better. More specifically, it is refined to make a helping move for the player.

In this version of the game, however, this function is supposed to do nothing. It does nothing because we still have not discussed how to make a move on behalf of the player. The input to this function is a `world` and it returns a `world`. It is implemented as follows:

```
;; world → world
;; Purpose: Make a move on behalf of the player
(define (make-move a-world) a-world)
```

Observe that this function truly does nothing for the player. In other words, it provides no help when the player requests it (by pressing HKEY). It is now very easy to see that this function needs to be refined. Before doing so, however, we need to learn more about problem solving and program design.

In programming a function like `make-move` above is called a `stub` (or `function stub`). A stub is a function written to temporarily fill in for some programming functionality that is not yet developed. You may think of it as a function placeholder. Stubs are useful during software development. They allow for a partially developed program to be executed and tested.

4 A brilliant CS student, Josh, complains that it is silly to define the `world` as a structure because it makes the implementation of `get-tile-value` unnecessarily complicated. He suggests that the world ought to be a (`listof tval`). Then `get-tile-value` may be implemented as follows:

```
;; a-world bpos → bval
;; Purpose: Return the given bpos' bval
(define (get-tile-value a-world a-bpos) (list ref a-world a-bpos))
```

What do you think? Is Josh onto something? Redesign the game's implementation using a list-based representation for the world. Be careful when defining the world. Remember that it is not data of arbitrary size. Why is this observation important?

14 What Have We Learned in This Chapter?

The important lessons of this chapter are summarized as follows:

- The same representation may be used for different data types.
- Abstracting over similar expressions to create functions results in more elegant and easier to understand code.
- Functions are designed at the global level and are encapsulated after thorough testing.
- Encapsulation yields better organized code.
- It is important to program to satisfy an API (like `universe`).
- Modular arithmetic may be used to design more concise and elegant solutions.
- A stub is a function written to temporarily fill in for some programming functionality.
- Using stubs allows for partially developed programs to be executed and tested.

Chapter 3
Randomness

Chapter 2 left us with the problem of how to make a move for the player in the eight-puzzle game. Given the choices available to make a move, how do we want the program to decide which move to make? At this point you have probably played and solved the eight puzzle several times. How did you decide what move to make next? This may be a difficult question for you to answer. Equally difficult to answer is how should the program decide which move to make.

Given our inability to express how a human solves the puzzle, what can we do? You have probably already thought that the program ought to randomly pick among the possible moves. This potential solution is attractive because of its simplicity. The idea is to determine the empty space's neighbors, randomly pick one, and use it to make a move for the player. This requires redesigning `process-key`'s local function `make-move`. Let us explore this design idea. One thing to note is that by randomly picking a move `make-move` becomes a *nondeterministic function*. That is, it becomes a function whose result cannot be predicted. As we shall see, this has profound implications for writing tests and guaranteeing that our programs terminate.

15 ISL+'s `random` Function

Before proceeding with the redesign of `make-move`, we need to know how randomness may be used in ISL+. In programming, randomness requires the generation of random numbers. That is, the computer needs to generate a sequence numbers that cannot be predicted. The level of unpredictability of the next number to be generated is called *entropy*. Ideally, a random number generator ought to maximize the level of entropy. For example, the generation of a random integer in `[0..n-1]` ought to make it equally likely that any integer in the given range is the next number generated. This means that the probability of generating any integer `i` in the given range is $\frac{1}{n}$. This

© The Author(s), under exclusive license to Springer Nature Switzerland AG 2022   47
M. T. Morazán, *Animated Program Design*, Texts in Computer Science,
https://doi.org/10.1007/978-3-031-04317-8_3

is important so that no one (and no program) can predict the outcome of generating the next number. Can you imagine the consequences of someone being able to predict the next number at a roulette table?

It turns out that generating random numbers is an incredibly difficult problem. Computers can produce long sequences of numbers that appear random. They do so by using a mathematical formula that requires an input value that is called a *seed*. You can now see that the numbers generated are not truly random. Anyone that knows the formula used and the seed value can predict the sequence of numbers generated. This is called a *pseudorandom number generator*. In practice a pseudorandom number generator suffices for most applications including security-critical ones.

In ISL+, the `random` function may be used to generate pseudorandom natural numbers. It takes as input a natural number, n, and returns a natural number in [0..n-1]. The following are sample uses:

```
> (random 10)
8
> (random 10)
9
> (random 10)
8
> (random 10)
3
```

As you can see (`random n`) may be used to generate a sequence of numbers in [0..n-1] that appears random. Be mindful of the fact that if you evaluate the same expression on your computer, you are likely to generate a different sequence of numbers in [0..n-1].

So the good news is that we can simulate randomness in ISL+. The bad news is that randomness breaks our mental model of what a function is. Throughout **Animating Programs** and this textbook so far we have assumed that the functions we write are *deterministic* as the ones you have studied in mathematics courses: applying a function to a given value always yields the same result. When this condition holds functions exhibit what is called *referential transparency*. Referential transparency is the property that an expression may always be substituted with its value. That is, (`f x`) is always equal to (`f x`).

Now run the following test:

```
(check-expect (random 10) (random 10))
```

The test fails (fairly frequently)! The same expression does not always evaluate to the same value. This means that when `random` is used, we lose referential transparency. That is, (`f x`) is not always equal to (`f x`). If this feels like a nightmare from a horror sci-fi movie, you are not alone. Nonetheless, randomness has its role in computing and you must learn to use it responsibly.

The use of randomness makes the job of a problem solver more difficult. It is more difficult because we are unable to predict the result of a function that uses randomness. If it is not possible to predict the output of a function, then how can the function be tested? There are two techniques that may be used. The first technique, introduced in `Animating Programs`, is property-based testing. Instead of testing for the specific value of an expression, we test properties that the value of the expression ought to have. For example, for (random 10) we may test that result is always in [0..9] as follows:

```
(check-expect (<= 0 (random 10) 9) #true)
(check-expect (<= 0 (random 10) 9) #true)
```

When these tests are executed both pass. ISL+ provides a more elegant way of testing properties using `check-satisfied`. This type of test checks if the value of a given expression satisfies a given one-input predicate. For example, we may test (random 10) as follows:

```
(check-satisfied (random 10) (λ (n) (<= 0 n 9)))
(check-satisfied (random 10) (λ (n) (<= 0 n 9)))
```

You may ask yourself why the same test is written more than once. Remember that they are not the same test because the value of (random 10) is not predictable.

The second technique involves making sure that the two expressions tested use the same seed for their corresponding uses of `random`. If the same seed is used then the pseudorandom number generator produces the same numbers for both tested expressions. This is achieved by using `check-random`, for example, as follows:

```
(check-random (random 10) (random 10))
(check-random (random 50) (random 50))
```

Both tests pass because for each test the use of `random` in the left expression uses the same seed as the use of `random` in the right expression. We can only test if both expressions in a test that use the same seed produce the same result. Keep in mind that this requires that both expressions request random numbers in the same order in the same interval. Therefore, the following tests fail:

```
(check-random (random 20) (random 60))
(check-random (+ (random 10) (random 20) (random 30))
              (+ (random 20) (random 10) (random 30)))
```

In the first test both expressions request a random number in the same order but use different intervals. In the second test the same intervals are used but the random numbers are requested in a different order.

Fig. 10 The function to make a random move for the player in the N-puzzle game

```
;; world arrow world
;; Purpose: Make a move for the player
(define (make-move a-world)
  (local [(define neighbors '((1 3)
                              (4 0 2)
                              (1 5)
                              (0 4 6)
                              (7 1 3 5)
                              (2 4 8)
                              (3 7)
                              (8 4 6)
                              (5 7)))

          (define BLNK-NEIGHS (list-ref neighbors (blank-pos a-world)))]
    (swap-empty (list-ref BLNK-NEIGHS (random (length BLNK-NEIGHS))))))
```

16 N-Puzzle Version 1

Instead of doing nothing, this version of the N-puzzle game makes a random move when the player requests help. The only function that requires redesign is make-move (which means the behavior of process-key is changed). To make a move the board positions neighboring the empty tile space need to be known. A neighboring board position is randomly chosen and swapped with the empty tile space.

The neighbors of every board position are fixed and may be defined as a constant. We may use a list of length 9 to represent the neighbors of each bpos[3] as follows:

```
(define neighbors '((1 3)
                    (4 0 2)
                    (1 5)
                    (0 4 6)
                    (7 1 3 5)
                    (2 4 8)
                    (3 7)
                    (8 4 6)
                    (5 7)))
```

The ith element of neighbors contains a (listof bpos) that are neighbors to the ith board position. The neighbors of the empty space position may be defined as follows:

---

[3] See Sect. 9 for the data definition.

```
(define BLNK-NEIGHS (list-ref neighbors
                              (blank-pos a-world)))
```

Given these constants the body for `make-move` must be:

```
(swap-empty (list-ref BLNK-NEIGHS
                      (random (length BLNK-NEIGHS))))
```

The complete function to make local inside of `process-key` is displayed in Fig. 10.

This means that we have changed the design of `process-key`. The processing `HKEY` now creates a new `world`. Therefore, the following test fails:

```
(check-expect (process-key A-WRLD HKEY) A-WRLD)
```

How do we write tests for the processing of `HKEY`? Using randomness means that `process-key` is nondeterministic and we cannot predict the `world` that is returned when processing `HKEY`. Therefore, we cannot write tests that look as follows:

```
(check-expect (process-key ... HKEY) (make-world ...))
```

The best we can do is to check properties of the value returned by `process-key`. What properties should the `world` returned by `process-key` have? We know that (`process-key ...HKEY`) and (`make-world ...`) ought to be different `world`s that are a single move away. How can this be tested? A single move away means that the two `world`s only have different tiles in two board positions. Furthermore, the tile value in the first world at the blank's board position in the second world must equal the tile value in the second world at the blank's board position in the first world.

The needed predicate is displayed in Fig. 11. The body of the function determines if the number of tile differences between the `world`s is 2 and if the empty space has been properly swapped. To achieve this the empty space's board position in each `world`, a function to determine the board position of the empty space, a function to get a board position's tile value, and a function to count the tile differences between two given `world`s are locally defined.

The `process-key` tests using `HKEY` are updated as follows:

```
(check-expect
  (one-move-away? A-WRLD (process-key A-WRLD HKEY))
  #true)
(check-expect (one-move-away? WIN (process-key WIN HKEY))
              #true)
```

We are unable to use `check-random` because we cannot call `process-vk` (it is local to `process-key`). We are also unable to use `check-satisfied` directly with `one-move-away?` because this predicate requires two inputs (not one as must be the case to use `check-satisfied`). You may, however, use a λ-expression to define a predicate that takes as input a world and calls `one-move-away?`. As an exercise rewrite the tests above using `check-satisfied`.

Fig. 11 Predicate to test HKEY processing

```
;; world world → Boolean
;; Purpose: Determine if the given worlds are one move away
(define (one-move-away? w1 w2)
  (local [;; world → bpos
          ;; Purpose: Return the blank's bpos in given world
          (define (get-empty-bpos a-world)
            (cond [(= (world-t0 a-world) 0) 0]
                  [(= (world-t1 a-world) 0) 1]
                  [(= (world-t2 a-world) 0) 2]
                  [(= (world-t3 a-world) 0) 3]
                  [(= (world-t4 a-world) 0) 4]
                  [(= (world-t5 a-world) 0) 5]
                  [(= (world-t6 a-world) 0) 6]
                  [(= (world-t7 a-world) 0) 7]
                  [(= (world-t8 a-world) 0) 8]))
          ;; world bpos → bval   Purpose: Return the given bpos' bval
          (define (get-tile-value a-world a-bpos)
            (cond [(= a-bpos 0) (world-t0 a-world)]
                  [(= a-bpos 1) (world-t1 a-world)]
                  [(= a-bpos 2) (world-t2 a-world)]
                  [(= a-bpos 3) (world-t3 a-world)]
                  [(= a-bpos 4) (world-t4 a-world)]
                  [(= a-bpos 5) (world-t5 a-world)]
                  [(= a-bpos 6) (world-t6 a-world)]
                  [(= a-bpos 7) (world-t7 a-world)]
                  [else (world-t8 a-world)]))
          (define BLNK-W1 (get-empty-bpos w1))
          (define BLNK-W2 (get-empty-bpos w2))
          ;; world world → Boolean  Purpose: Count number of differences
          (define (cnt-diffs w1 w2)
            (+ (if (= (world-t0 w1)(world-t0 w2)) 0 1)
               (if (= (world-t1 w1)(world-t1 w2)) 0 1)
               (if (= (world-t2 w1)(world-t2 w2)) 0 1)
               (if (= (world-t3 w1)(world-t3 w2)) 0 1)
               (if (= (world-t4 w1)(world-t4 w2)) 0 1)
               (if (= (world-t5 w1)(world-t5 w2)) 0 1)
               (if (= (world-t6 w1)(world-t6 w2)) 0 1)
               (if (= (world-t7 w1)(world-t7 w2)) 0 1)
               (if (= (world-t8 w1)(world-t8 w2)) 0 1)))]
    (and (= (cnt-diffs w1 w2) 2)
         (= (get-tile-value w1 BLNK-W2)
            (get-tile-value w2 BLNK-W1)))))
;; Tests using sample values for one-move-away?
(check-expect (one-move-away? WIN    (make-world 1 2 3 4 5 6 7 0 8))
              #true)
(check-expect (one-move-away? A-WRLD (make-world 1 5 2 4 8 3 7 0 6))
              #true)
(check-expect (one-move-away? A-WRLD (make-world 0 1 2 4 5 3 7 8 6))
              #false)
```

1 Carefully argue that the `make-move` implementation is correct.

2 An alternative design idea for `one-move-away?` in Fig. 11 is to compute the board positions that differ and then check that the board values are properly swapped. Redesign `one-move-away?` to use this idea. Is it necessary to still check that there are only two differences between the boards? Why or why not?

Run the game several times using (`make-world 1 2 3 4 5 6 7 0 8`) as the initial `world`. For each run only request help (i.e., only press the space bar). Observe that despite solving the puzzle is only one move away, the program does not always make the right move. Are you satisfied with this implementation to help the player? The answer ought to be an unequivocal no. Offering help ought to mean making a move that gets the player closer to solving the puzzle. That is clearly not the case when using randomness. We still need to find a solution to the problem of helping the player.

There is another more subtle problem with our program. Imagine a player that only wants to see the moves to solve a puzzle. Such a player repeatedly requests help until the puzzle is solved. Observe that the player may request help for hours (or millennia if she could live that long!). We cannot argue that the puzzle is solved in a reasonable amount of time. In fact, we cannot convincingly argue that the puzzle will be solved. We simply do not know if the pseudo number generator will ever produce the right sequence of moves. Potentially this may run forever and an algorithm that may run forever to find the solution to a problem is not a practical solution. This observation suggests that we need to learn techniques to approximate answers when finding a solution may take too long.

Using randomness to make a move was tempting due to its simplicity. It turned out to be a poor choice for making a move in the N-puzzle. The lesson to walk away with is that randomness must be used with care and as problem solvers you must recognize when using randomness is a good choice. As a general statement we can say that the use of randomness ought to be considered when it is important not to be able to predict a function's value. Using randomness is appropriate, for example, when simulating natural phenomena such as radioactive decay, implementing games of chance such as roulette and games that require card shuffling, and generating encryption keys or passwords for network security. We now proceed to implement two applications in which randomness is useful: password generation and a distributed fortune teller game.

17 Generating Random Passwords

Cybersecurity experts always remind us that we ought to use strong unique passwords that are not easy to predict for our online accounts. This is important to prevent bad actors from gaining access, for example, to our bank accounts and email accounts. A strong password is a string of at least ten characters that includes a combination of at least one uppercase letter, one lowercase letter, one number, and one special character. Special characters include, for example, $, &, and *.

A password character, pwdchar, may be represented as a string of length 1. The four sets of password characters needed to create a strong password may be represented using (listof pwdchar)s. We may define these four sets as follows:

```
(define UCASE (map symbol->string
                   '(A B C D E F G H I J K L M
                     N O P Q R S T U V W X Y Z)))
(define LCASE (map string-downcase UCASE))
(define NUMBS (map number->string '(0 1 2 3 4 5 6 7 8 9)))
(define SCHRS '("$" "&" "*" "+" "@" "#" "_" "!" "?"))
```

A password is defined as follows:

```
#|
A password, pw, is a string that has a minimum length of 10
and contains at least one of each: lower case letter, upper
case letter, number, and special character.
|#
```

Observe that a strong password ought to be difficult to predict. This suggests the use of randomness to generate passwords. The user may specify the length of a password using a natural number. The characters that may be used from each set are randomly chosen as long as there is at least one element of each set and the sum of the number of characters from each set is equal to the length provided by the user. The chosen elements may be randomly used to generate a password. This design idea allows us to outline a random password generating function as follows:

```
;; natnum → pw throws error
;; Purpose: To generate a random password of the given length
(define (generate-password passwd-len)
  (if (< passwd-len 10)
      (error "The password length must be at least 10.")
      (local [(define UC-NUM (add1 (random 7)))
              (define LC-NUM (add1 (random (- passwd-len
                                              UC-NUM
                                              2))))
```

```
                   (define NB-NUM (add1 (random (- passwd-len
                                                    UC-NUM
                                                    LC-NUM
                                                    1)))))
                   (define SC-NUM (- passwd-len
                                     UC-NUM
                                     LC-NUM
                                     NB-NUM))

                   ;; (listof X) natnum → (listof X)
                   ;; Purpose: Randomly pick the given number of
                   ;;          elements from the given list
                   (define (pick lst n)
                     (build-list
                        n
                        (λ (i) (list-ref lst (random (length lst))))))

                   ;; ...
                   ;; Purpose: ...
                   (define (generate ...) ...)
                   ]
             (generate (pick UCASE UC-NUM)
                       (pick LCASE LC-NUM)
                       (pick NUMBS NB-NUM)
                       (pick SCHRS SC-NUM)))))
```

If the given length is less than 10, an error with an informative message is
generated. If the given length is valid a password is generated by randomly
picking elements from each of the four sets. The number of elements to pick
from each set is randomly generated and locally defined. The number of
elements from the set of uppercase letters is randomly chosen to be between
1 and 7. Observe that the number of uppercase letters may not be more than
7 because there must be at least one element from each of the other sets.
The maximum number of lowercase letters used is the given password length
minus the number password elements already chosen (i.e., UC-NUM) and the
minimum number of elements (i.e., 2) that must be reserved for numbers
and special characters. The maximum number of numbers used is the given
password length minus the number password elements already chosen (i.e.,
UC-NUM + LC-NUM) and the minimum number of elements (i.e., 1) that must
be reserved for special characters. Finally, the number of special characters
used is the password length minus the number password elements already
chosen (i.e., UC-NUM + LC-NUM + NB-NUM). Finally, picking a given number
of elements, n, from a given list, lst, is done by randomly picking elements.
Observe that any element may be chosen more than once.

Fig. 12 A function to generate a random string from given lists of strings

```
;(listof string) (listof string) (listof string) (listof string) → string
;; Purpose: Generate a string using all the strings in the given lists
(define (generate L0 L1 L2 L3)
  (if (and (empty? L0) (empty? L1) (empty? L2) (empty? L3))
      " "
      (local [(define 1st-num (random 4))]
        (cond
          [(= 1st-num 0)
           (if (empty? L0)
               (generate L0 L1 L2 L3)
               (string-append (first L0) (generate (rest L0) L1 L2 L3)))]
          [(= 1st-num 1)
           (if (empty? L1)
               (generate L0 L1 L2 L3)
               (string-append (first L1) (generate L0 (rest L1) L2 L3)))]
          [(= 1st-num 2)
           (if (empty? L2)
               (generate L0 L1 L2 L3)
               (string-append (first L2) (generate L0 L1 (rest L2) L3)))]
          [(= 1st-num 3)
           (if (empty? L3)
               (generate L0 L1 L2 L3)
               (string-append (first L3)
                              (generate L0 L1 L2 (rest L3))))]))))
```

3 For `generate-password` carefully argue that the sum of the number of elements chosen from each set is equal to the given password length.

The next task is to design the function that generates a random string using the elements from each set. This function takes as input four (`listof string`) (i.e., the sets to use) and returns a `string`. If all four given lists are empty, then the empty string is returned given that there are no more elements to add. Otherwise, a list is randomly chosen. If the chosen list is empty, then a recursive call is made without changing any of the given lists. If the chosen list is not empty, then its first element is appended with the result of recursively processing the rest of the chosen list and the other lists. This design idea may be implemented as displayed in Fig. 12. Observe that a list is chosen by randomly picking a number in [0..3]. Also note that there is something different about this function. There are recursive calls with the given arguments. This suggests that there may be an *infinite recursion*. An infinite recursion occurs when a function fails to make progress towards termination. In this case, it means that it fails to move all four arguments towards becoming empty. Essentially, we hope that each given list is chosen enough times to become empty. Although extremely unlikely with a good pseudorandom number generator, it is possible for this program to run forever because one of the lists is never chosen. This possibility ought to make you very uncomfortable because it means this solution may be impractical.

As you well know it is necessary to write tests for `generate-password`. Illustrating that an error is generated is straightforward as shown by the following test:

```
(check-error (generate-password 6)
             "The password length must be at least 10.")
```

The question now is: how do we test the function when a password is actually generated? The use of randomness means that `generate-password` is nondeterministic and, therefore, we may employ property-based testing. The following are examples of the needed tests:

```
(check-satisfied (generate-password 10) valid-passwd?)
(check-satisfied (generate-password 12) valid-passwd?)
```

We need to design and write a predicate to determine if a given string is a valid password.

How do we determine if a given string is a valid password? The string must have a minimum length of 10. In addition, it must have at least one uppercase letter, one lowercase letter, one number, and one special character. Finally, the string must contain no other characters.

To write such a predicate a local variable may be used to store the value of converting the string into a list. This list is filtered four times to define a local variable for the elements of each of the four sets. Each of these filtered lists must have a length greater than 0 and summing their lengths must equal the length of the given string. The predicate is implemented as follows:

```
;; string natnum → Boolean
;; Purpose: Determine of the given string is a pw
(define (valid-passwd? str)
  (local [(define lststr (explode str))
          (define uc (filter (λ (s) (member s UCASE)) lststr))
          (define lc (filter (λ (s) (member s LCASE)) lststr))
          (define nc (filter (λ (s) (member s NUMBS)) lststr))
          (define sc (filter (λ (s) (member s SCHRS)) lststr))]
    (and (>= (string-length str) 10)
         (= (length lststr)
            (+ (length uc) (length lc)
               (length nc) (length sc)))
         (> (length uc) 0)
         (> (length lc) 0)
         (> (length nc) 0)
         (> (length sc) 0))))

;; Tests using sample values for valid-passwd?
(check-expect (valid-passwd? "?$Isdwer67G")   #true)
```

```
(check-expect (valid-passwd? "Z!jwqx8t2sY32") #true)
(check-expect (valid-passwd? "abcdefgh")      #false)
(check-expect (valid-passwd? "a2cZdEfghJ8")   #false)
```

4 Carefully argue that any string that satisfies `valid-passwd?` only contains uppercase letters, lowercase letters, numbers, and elements of the defined set of special characters.

18 Distributed Fortune Teller Game

The fortune teller game provides a random fortune every time a player requests it. We shall design and implement a distributed fortune teller game that allows multiple players to request fortunes. The design recipe for distributed computing is reviewed before proceeding with the program's design.

18.1 Design Recipe for Distributed Computing

The design recipe for distributed programming is:

1. Divide the problem into components.
2. Draft data definitions for the different components.
3. Design a communication protocol.
4. Design marshaling and unmarshaling functions.
5. Design and implement the components.
6. Test your program.

Step 1 is problem analysis. It asks you to outline how the components cooperate to solve a problem. This step clearly defines the task (or tasks) carried out by a component. Step 2 asks you to define the types required by each component. Remember that the types required for each component are not necessarily the same.

Step 3 asks you to develop a communication protocol. This protocol must capture all the communication chains that may occur. A communication chain is sparked by an event like a keystroke or a clock tick. As part of this step you must develop data definitions for `to-server messages` and `to-client messages`. These data definitions are used to design the message-processing function for the server and for the clients.

Step 4 asks you to design marshaling and unmarshaling functions used to make data transmissible. In order for a message to be transmissible it must be a symbolic expression defined as follows:

A symbolic expression, sexpr, is either a:
   1. string
   2. symbol
   3. number
   4. Boolean
   5. character
   6 (listof sexpr)

To transmit any data that is not a `sexpr` a marshaling function is needed to transform it into a `sexpr` and an unmarshaling function is needed to convert it back to its original form. These functions must be inverses of each other.

Step 5 asks you to develop the programs for each component. This means that you need to develop at least two programs: one for the server and one for each client. The client program may or may not be the same for all clients. Nonetheless, there must be a separate program (different or copy) for each client. Observe that this means that a distributed program is written in at least two different files.

Step 6 asks you to run and test your program. As always, if any tests fail you must redesign.

18.2 The Components

For this game there are an arbitrary number of players and a server. All the players are almost the same. That is, they all perform the same functions and, therefore, execute a copy of the same code. Each player, however, must have a unique name for the server to distinguish among players. Players are responsible for maintaining a world, drawing the world, processing keystrokes, detecting the end of the game, and processing messages from the server. Based on the responsibilities assigned to a player program, the player's **run** function is:

```
;; A name is a string or a symbol

;; name → world
(define (run a-name)
  (big-bang
    INIT-WORLD
    (on-draw draw-world)
    (on-key process-key)
    (stop-when finished? draw-final-world)
    (on-receive process-message)
    (register LOCALHOST)
    (name a-name))))
```

Six player handlers must be designed and implemented. The input to run is
the proposed player name. If the given name is not already in use by another
player, the server accepts to connect the player to the game. Otherwise the
server rejects connecting the player.

The server is responsible for adding new players, removing players, and
processing messages from the players. Based on this outline the function to
run the server is:

```
;; Any → universe
;; Purpose: Run the universe server
(define (run-server a-z)
  (universe
    INIT-UNIV
    (on-new add-new-iworld)
    (on-msg process-message)
    (on-disconnect rm-iworld)))
```

Three server handlers must be designed and implemented. The input is of
type Any. This means that the input may be any type of data. The type of
the input does not matter because a-z is a dummy parameter (i.e., it is never
used). The only reason this function has a parameter is because ISL+ does
not allow us to write functions with zero parameters.

18.3 Data Definitions

18.3.1 Player Data Definitions

To draw the world the player needs a scene. This scene needs to have a
length, a width, and a color. In addition, the text for the fortune as well as
the instructions must have a text color and a text font size. The values for
these constants are defined as follows:

```
(define ESCN-LEN    700)
(define ESCN-HEIGHT 200)
(define ESCN-COLOR  'darkblue)
(define TXT-SIZE    36)
(define TXT-COLOR   'gold)
(define TXT-SIZE2   16)
(define TXT-COLOR2  'pink)
```

The first text size and color are for fortunes and the second two are for
instructions. In addition, constants are defined for the instructions, for when
the player quits, and for when the server rejects connecting a player as follows:

```
(define INSTR-STR
        "Press q to quit or any other key to get a fortune")
```

```
(define DONE-STR   "Bye...")
(define DENIED-STR
       "Connection denied: name is already in use.")
```

The background of the empty scene is defined as a constant. Given that the instructions, the farewell message, and the rejected connection message do not change as the game progresses, we may define images for them as constants. These constants are defined as follows:

```
(define ESCN-BCKGRND (rectangle ESCN-LEN
                                ESCN-HEIGHT
                                'solid
                                ESCN-COLOR))
(define INSTR-IMG    (text INSTR-STR TXT-SIZE2 TXT-COLOR2))
(define BYE-IMG      (text DONE-STR TXT-SIZE TXT-COLOR))
(define RJCT-IMG     (text DENIED-STR TXT-SIZE TXT-COLOR))
```

These constants allow us to define three different empty scenes. The first is used when the game is running to draw fortunes. The second is used when the player quits the game. The third is used when a player's connection to the server is rejected. The empty scene constants are defined as follows:

```
(define E-SCN (place-image INSTR-IMG
                           (/ ESCN-LEN 2)
                           (* 0.8 ESCN-HEIGHT)
                           ESCN-BCKGRND))
(define E-SCN2 (place-image BYE-IMG
                           (/ ESCN-LEN 2)
                           (* 0.3 ESCN-HEIGHT)
                           ESCN-BCKGRND))
(define E-SCN3 (place-image RJCT-IMG
                           (/ ESCN-LEN 2)
                           (* 0.3 ESCN-HEIGHT)
                           ESCN-BCKGRND))
```

5 There are repeated expressions in the definition of the different empty scenes. Define and use constants to eliminate repeated expressions.

For a player the only data that changes as the game progresses is the fortune to display. A fortune, and therefore the world, may be represented as a string of a length that fits in the empty scene. The world and sample worlds are defined as follows:

```
;; A world is a string of length less than 45.

;; Sample worlds
(define W1 "You will live long and prosper.")
```

```
(define W2 "Logic is the beginning of wisdom, not the end.")
(define W3 "The trial never ends")
(define W4 DONE-STR)
(define W5 DENIED-STR)
(define INIT-WORLD "")
```

A length of less than 45 is an arbitrary choice and you are encouraged to customize the game to your liking. Observe that any function on a string may be applied to a world. The first three sample worlds are sample fortunes. The fourth world is the string used when the player quits. The fifth world is the string used when a player's connection to the server is denied. Finally, the initial world is defined as the empty string because the player is yet to request and receive a fortune from the server.

Finally, the player quits and requests fortunes using the keyboard. Two types of keys are defined:

```
;; A game key, gk, is either:
;;   1. "q"
;;   2. any other key

;; sample gk
(define QUIT-GK "q")
(define OTHR-GK "z")
```

The first subtype is used by the player to quit the game. The second subtype is used to request a fortune. The template for functions on a gk is:

```
#|
Template for functions on a gk

;; gk ... → ...
;; Purpose:
(define (f-on-gk a-gk ...)
  (if (key=? a-gk QUIT-GK)
      ...
      ...))

;; Sample expressions for f-on-gk
(define QGK-VAL ...)
(define OGK-VAL ...)

;; Tests using sample computations for f-on-gk
(check-expect (f-on-gk QUIT-GK ...) QGK-VAL)
(check-expect (f-on-gk OTHR-GK ...) OGK-VAL)
      ⋮

;; Tests using sample values for f-on-gk
```

```
(check-expect (f-on-gk ... ...) QGK-VAL)
       .
       .
       .
  |#
```

The choice of "q" as the key used to quit is arbitrary. Once again, you are encouraged to personalize the game.

18.3.2 Server Data Definitions

The server needs a database of fortunes to randomly pick one from when a player's request arrives. This is a sample database of fortunes represented using a (listof string):

```
(define FORTUNES
        '("Do not violate the prime directive"
          "0.67 seconds is an eternity for an android"
          "Don't be left with nothing but your bones"
          "Stay down, honor has been served"
          "Reach for the final frontier"
          "I canna' change the laws of physics"
          "No one can summon the future"
          "You can use logic to justify almost anything"
          "There is a way out of every box"
          "Make it so"
          "Don't grieve if it is logical"
          "Live long and prosper"
          "Resistance is futile"
          "Set your phasers to stun"
          "Without followers, evil cannot spread"
          "I fail to comprehend your indignation"
          "Things are only impossible until they're not"
          "A lie is a very poor way to say hello"
          "Time is the fire in which we burn"
          "Make now always the most precious time"
          "Perhaps man wasn't meant for paradise"
          "To survive is not enough"
          "To be human is to be complex"))
```

The server must track the players connected to it. The number of players is arbitrary and the universe API represents each as an iworld. This observation leads to the following data definition:

```
;; A universe is a (listof iworld)

(define INIT-UNIV '())
(define UNIV2 (list iworld1))
```

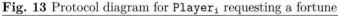

Fig. 13 Protocol diagram for `Player`$_i$ requesting a fortune

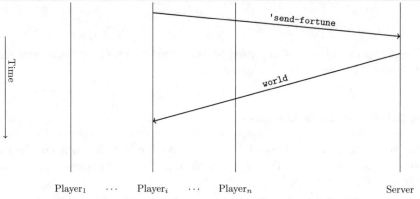

The initial universe is defined as empty because when the server starts running, no players have connected. The other sample universe uses a predefined `iworld` provided by the `API`. The template for a function on a universe is obtained by specializing the template for a function on a (`listof X`).

18.4 Communication Protocol

Ask yourself when messages must be exchanged between a player and the server. The answer reveals the communication chains that must be implemented. An event that starts a communication chain is `Player`$_i$ requesting a fortune. This chain is sparked when `Player`$_i$ hits any key other than `"q"`. When this occurs a message must be sent to the server indicating that a fortune is requested. In turn, the server must send a fortune to `Player`$_i$. Figure 13 displays the protocol diagram for this communication chain. The request from `Player`$_i$ is communicated by sending to the server the symbol `'send-fortune`. The server communicates back by sending a fortune. Observe that a sending a fortune is the same as sending a world.

A communication chain is also sparked when `Player`$_i$ quits the game. A message informing the server must be sent. There is no need (and it would make no sense) for the server to generate any messages. This communication chain is captured in the protocol diagram displayed in Fig. 14. When `Player`$_i$ hits `"q"` the server is informed by sending the symbol `'bye`.

Finally, a communication chain is started when `Player`$_i$'s request to join the game is rejected. This occurs when `Player`$_i$'s name is already in use by another player. Figure 15 displays the protocol diagram for this communication chain. When a player attempts to register, a message is sent by the `universe API` implementation to the server (indicated by a dashed line).

Fig. 14 Protocol diagram for Player_i leaving the game

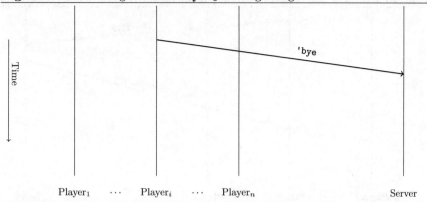

Player_i is informed that the request to join the game is denied by sending a message that contains the symbol 'connection-denied.

Based on this design a to-server message is an enumerated type defined as follows:

```
#|
A to-server message, tsm, is either:
  1. 'bye
  2. 'send-fortune
|#

;; Sample tsm
(define BYE 'bye)
(define SFT 'send-fortune)
```

The template for a function on a tsm is:

```
#|
;; tsm ... → ...
;; Purpose:
(define (f-on-tsm a-tsm ...)
  (if (eq? a-tsm 'bye)
      ...
      ...))

;; Sample expressions for f-on-tsm
(define BYE-VAL ...)
(define SFT-VAL ...)

;; Tests using sample computations for f-on-tsm
(check-expect (f-on-tsm BYE ...) BYE-VAL)
```

Fig. 15 Protocol diagram for Player$_i$ unsuccessfully joining the game

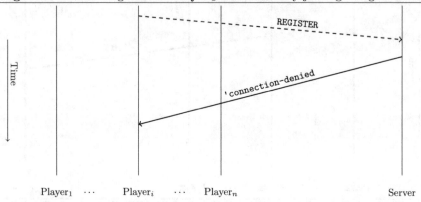

```
(check-expect (f-on-tsm SFT ...) SFT-VAL)

;; Tests using sample values for f-on-tsm
(check-expect (f-on-tsm ... ...) ...)
      ⋮
 |#
```

A to-player message is an enumerated type defined as follows:

```
#|
A to-player message, tpm, is either:
  1. 'connection-denied
  2. world
|#

;; Sample tpm
(define CDEN 'connection-denied)
(define WTPM W3)
```

The template for a function on a tpm is:

```
#|
;; tpm ... → ...
;; Purpose:
(define (f-on-tpm a-tpm ...)
  (if (eq? a-tpm 'connection-denied)
      ...
      ...))

;; Sample expressions for f-on-tpm
(define CDEN-VAL ...)
```

```
(define WTFP-VAL ...)

;; Tests using sample computations for f-on-tpm
(check-expect (f-on-tpm CDEN ...) CDEN-VAL)
(check-expect (f-on-tpm WTPM ...) WTPM-VAL)

;; Tests using sample values for f-on-tpm
(check-expect (f-on-tpm ... ...) ...)
    .
    .
    .
|#
```

18.5 Marshaling and Unmarshaling Functions

Observe that all tsms and tpms are sexprs. This means that all messages are transmittable. There is no need for marshaling and unmarshaling functions.

18.6 The Player Component

In this section the player handlers are designed and implemented. Their design is based on the previous steps of the design recipe. That is, we use the developed data definitions and communication protocol to write the player's handlers.

18.6.1 The draw-world Handler

The draw-world handler is displayed in Fig. 16. The sample expressions convert a sample world into a text image. This image is placed in the horizontal middle and one third of the way down on the vertical in the empty scene for fortunes. The tests using sample values illustrate the handler correctly computes the same value as the sample expressions. The tests using sample values illustrate that the handler works for arbitrary world values not previously defined. The body of the handler is obtained from abstracting over the sample expressions. The only difference is the world drawn and, therefore, the handler only has one parameter as expected by the universe API.

Fig. 16 The `draw-world` handler for distributed fortune teller game

```
;; world → image
;; Purpose: Draw the given world
(define (draw-world a-world)
  (place-image (text a-world TXT-SIZE TXT-COLOR)
               (/ ESCN-LEN 2)
               (* 0.3 ESCN-HEIGHT)
               E-SCN))

;; Sample expressions for draw-world
(define W1-IMG (place-image (text W1 TXT-SIZE TXT-COLOR)
                            (/ ESCN-LEN 2)
                            (* 0.3 ESCN-HEIGHT)
                            E-SCN))

(define W2-IMG (place-image (text W2 TXT-SIZE TXT-COLOR)
                            (/ ESCN-LEN 2)
                            (* 0.3 ESCN-HEIGHT)
                            E-SCN))

(define W3-IMG (place-image (text W3 TXT-SIZE TXT-COLOR)
                            (/ ESCN-LEN 2)
                            (* 0.3 ESCN-HEIGHT)
                            E-SCN))

;; Tests using sample expressions for draw-world
(check-expect (draw-world W1) W1-IMG)
(check-expect (draw-world W2) W2-IMG)
(check-expect (draw-world W3) W3-IMG)

;; Tests using sample values for draw-world
(check-expect (draw-world "Insufficient facts always invite danger.")
```

```
                                                                      )
(check-expect (draw-world "Boldly go where no one has gone before." )
```

```
                                                                      )
```

18.6.2 The `process-key` Handler

The process-key handler is displayed in Fig. 17. It is developed specializing the template for functions on a `gk`. The protocol diagram in Fig. 14 informs us that when the player quits a `'bye tsm` must be sent. In addition, the world must become a value that allows the program to detect the game has ended. For this purpose we choose DONE-STR. These actions are illustrated by the packages created by the first two sample expressions. Observe that DONE-STR

Fig. 17 The process-key handler for the distributed fortune teller game

```
;; world key → package
;; Purpose: Create the next world after the given key event
(define (process-key a-world a-key)
  (if (key=? a-key "q")
      (make-package DONE-STR 'bye)
      (make-package a-world  'send-fortune)))

;; Sample expressions for process-key
(define W1Q-PK (make-package DONE-STR 'bye))
(define W2Q-PK (make-package DONE-STR 'bye))
(define W2*-PK (make-package W2       'send-fortune))
(define W1a-PK (make-package W1       'send-fortune))

;; Tests using sample computations for process-key
(check-expect (process-key W1 "q") W1Q-PK)
(check-expect (process-key W2 "q") W1Q-PK)
(check-expect (process-key W2 "*") W2*-PK)
(check-expect (process-key W1 "a") W1a-PK)

;; Tests using sample values for process-key
(check-expect (process-key W3 "q") (make-package DONE-STR 'bye))
(check-expect (process-key W1 "z") (make-package W1 'send-fortune))
```

is a valid world value. The protocol diagram in Fig. 13 informs us that when the player requests a fortune a 'send-fortune tsm must be sent. The world remains unchanged in this case (recall that the world changes when the new fortune is received). These actions are illustrated by the packages created by the second two sample expressions. The first two tests using sample values illustrate that the function works when the player quits (i.e., hits "q") using, respectively, W1 and W2. The second two of these tests illustrates that the function works when the world is W2 and the player hits "*" and when the world is W1 and the player hits "a". The tests using sample values illustrate the behavior of the handler with other input values.

In the body of the function the then-branch of the if-expression is obtained by abstracting over the first two sample expressions. There are no differences and, therefore, the literal expression found in these sample expressions is used. The else-branch is obtained by abstracting over the second two sample expressions. The only difference is the world used. This corresponds to the world parameter expected by the universe APIand, therefore, a-world is used.

18.6.3 The process-message Handler

The process-message handler is designed specializing the template for functions on a tpm. The protocol diagram in Fig. 15 informs us that the server

Fig. 18 The `process-message` handler for the distributed fortune teller game

```
;; world tpm → world
;; Purpose: Create new world after receiving the given to player message
(define (process-message a-world a-tpm)
  (if (eq? a-tpm 'connection-denied)
      DENIED-STR
      a-tpm))

;; Sample expression for process-message
(define PM-DN DENIED-STR)
(define PM-W2 "Warp speed now")
(define PM-W3 "This far and no further")

;; Test using sample computation for process-message
(check-expect (process-message INIT-WORLD DENIED-STR) PM-DN)
(check-expect (process-message W2 "Warp speed now") PM-W2)
(check-expect (process-message W3 "This far and no further") PM-W3)

;; Test using sample value for process-message
(check-expect (process-message "Make it so" "Resistance is futile")
              "Resistance is futile")
(check-expect (process-message "It will all work out" "Time to let it go")
              "Time to let it go")
```

sends a message containing `'connection-denied` when the player's connection to the server is refused. In this case the new world value is `DENIED-STR` in order for the game to end and correctly draw the last scene. The protocol diagram in Fig. 13 informs us that the other type of message a player may receive is a `world` value. In this case the new world is the received message. This design idea is reflected in the sample expressions in Fig. 18. The first illustrates the result of receiving `DENIED-STR`. The other two show the result of receiving a `world` when the current worlds are, respectively, W2 and W3. The tests illustrate that the function computes the values of the sample expressions and works for other arbitrary worlds.

In the function's body the then-expression is the world defined to end the game that is used in the first sample expression. The else-expression is obtained by abstracting over the second and third sample expressions. The only difference is the value of the new `world` which is the received `tpm`.

18.6.4 The `finished?` Handler

The game needs to halt when the `world` is either `DONE-STR` or `DENIED-STR`. To detect these conditions the value of the given `world` may be checked for equality with both of these predefined `worlds`. In Fig. 19, the first sample expression tests if a non-ending world is `DONE-STR`. The second sample expres-

Fig. 19 The `finished?` handler for the distributed fortune teller game

```
;; world → Boolean
;; Purpose: Determine if the simulation has ended
(define (finished? a-world)
  (or (string=? a-world DONE-STR)
      (string=? a-world DENIED-STR)))


;; Sample expressions for finished?
(define NFNSHD (string=? W1 DONE-STR))
(define FNSHD  (string=? W4 DONE-STR))
(define DND    (string=? W5 DENIED-STR))
(define NDND   (string=? W3 DENIED-STR))


;; Tests using sample computations for finished?
(check-expect (finished? W1) NFNSHD)
(check-expect (finished? W4) FNSHD)
(check-expect (finished? W5) DND)
(check-expect (finished? W3) NDND)


;; Tests using sample values for finished?
(check-expect (finished? DONE-STR)    #true)
(check-expect (finished? "Stop being highly illogical") #false)
(check-expect (finished? DENIED-STR) #true)
```

sion tests if an ending world is DONE-STR. The third sample expression tests
if the given (non-ending) world is DENIED-STR. Finally, the fourth sample
expression tests if a (ending) world is DENIED-STR.

The tests using sample computations illustrate that the function computes
the same values as the evaluation of the sample expressions. The tests using
sample values illustrate that the handler works for other concrete values.

The body of the function is obtained by abstracting over the sample expressions for each condition and oring the result for each expression. Observe
that among the expressions for each condition, there is only one difference:
the world tested. Therefore, this function only requires one parameter as
expected by the universe API.

The function to draw the last world is designed assuming that it is always
called with an ending world. If the given world is DONE-STR then the scene
image, E-SCN2, for when the player quits is returned. Otherwise, the scene
image, E-SCN2, for when the player's request to connect to the game is rejected is returned. This design idea is reflected in the two sample expressions
below:

```
;; world → image
;; Purpose: To draw the last world
;; ASSUMPTION: Given world is either W4 or W5
(define (draw-final-world a-world)
  (if (string=? DONE-STR a-world)
      E-SCN2
      E-SCN3))
```

```
;; Sample expression for draw-final-world
(define DFW1 E-SCN2)
(define DFW2 E-SCN3)

;; Tests using sample computations for draw-final-world
(check-expect (draw-final-world W4) DFW1)
(check-expect (draw-final-world W5) DFW2)

;; Tests using sample values for draw-final-world
(check-expect (draw-final-world W4)
```

```
)
(check-expect (draw-final-world W5)
```

```
)
```

Both sets of tests use the same world input given that there are only two possible input values. The test using sample computations illustrates that sample expressions and the function application evaluate to the same value. The tests using sample values illustrate the concrete images that are returned by the handler.

18.7 The Server Component

In this section the server handlers are designed and implemented. As with the player's handlers, their design is based on the previous steps of the design recipe.

18.7.1 The add-new-iworld Handler

When a player registers with the server, it is either added to the game or its request to connect is rejected. To decide this handler checks if the new player's name is in use because the name is how it distinguishes between players. If it is and according to Fig. 15 a connection denied message is sent to the player and the player is not added to the universe. The third sample expression in Fig. 20 illustrates how this may be done using UNIV2. A bundle is created with the same universe, a list containing a single connection denied tpm for the given player, and an empty list of iworlds[4] to disconnect from the game.

---

[4] Recall that an iworld is an API structure used to represent a player at the server.

Fig. 20 The handler to process `Player`$_i$'s request to connect to the game

```
;; universe iworld → bundle
;; Purpose: Add the given world to the given universe
(define (add-new-iworld u iw)
  (if (member? (iworld-name iw) (map iworld-name u))
      (make-bundle u
                   (list (make-mail iw 'connection-denied))
                   '())
      (make-bundle (cons iw u) '() '())))

;; Sample expressions for add-new-world
(define ADD1 (make-bundle (cons iworld1 INIT-UNIV) '() '()))
(define ADD2 (make-bundle (cons iworld2 UNIV2) '() '()))
(define ADD3 (make-bundle UNIV2
                          (list (make-mail iworld1
                                           'connection-denied))
                          '()))

;; Tests using sample computation for add-new-world
(check-expect (add-new-iworld INIT-UNIV iworld1) ADD1)
(check-expect (add-new-iworld UNIV2     iworld2) ADD2)
(check-expect (add-new-iworld UNIV2     iworld1) ADD3)

;; Tests using sample values for add-new-world
(check-expect (add-new-iworld (list iworld2) iworld3)
              (make-bundle (list iworld3 iworld2) '() '()))
(check-expect (add-new-iworld (list iworld2 iworld3) iworld3)
              (make-bundle (list iworld2 iworld3)
                           (list (make-mail iworld3
                                            'connection-denied))
                           '()))
```

The first two sample expressions illustrate what needs to be done when the new player is allowed to join the game. Recall that there is no communication chain sparked when a player is allowed to join the game. A bundle is created with a new **universe** that contains the new player's **iworld**, an empty list of **tpm**, and an empty list of **iworlds** to disconnect.

The tests illustrate that the function computes the same value obtained from evaluating the sample expressions and that it works for a couple of arbitrary inputs. The body of the function uses an **if**-expression to determine if a player is added to the **universe**. The condition tests if the given **iworld**'s name is the name of any **iworld** in the **universe**. The then-expression is obtained by abstracting over the third sample expression and the expression used in the second test using sample values. The else-expression is obtained by abstracting over the first two sample expressions.

Fig. 21 The handler to remove `Player`$_i$ from the game

```
;; universe iworld → universe
;; Purpose: Remove the given iworld from the given universe
(define (rm-iworld u iw)
  (filter (λ (w) (not (equal? w iw)))  u))


;; Sample expressions for rm-iworld
(define RM1 (filter (λ (w) (not (equal? w iworld2))) UNIV2))
(define RM2 (filter (λ (w) (not (equal? w iworld1))) INIT-UNIV))


;; Tests using sample computations for rm-iworld
(check-expect (rm-iworld UNIV2 iworld2) RM1)
(check-expect (rm-iworld UNIV2 iworld1) RM2)


;; Tests using sample values for rm-iworld
(check-expect (rm-iworld (list iworld1 iworld2 iworld3)
                         iworld2)
              (list iworld1 iworld3))
```

18.7.2 The `rm-iworld` Handler

This handler is used when a player abruptly disconnects from the game (e.g., closing the game's window or losing their Internet connection). The player's `iworld` needs to be removed from the `universe` in order to allow that player or another player with the same name to connect to the game in the future.

The handler is displayed in Fig. 21. The sample expressions illustrate that a given `universe` is filtered to remove the given `iworld`. The tests illustrate that the function correctly computes the values of the sample expressions and that the function works for arbitrary sample values. The body of the function is obtained by abstracting over the sample expressions.

18.7.3 The `process-message` Handler

According to our design there are two subtypes of `tsm`: `'bye` and `'send-fortune`. When a player quits the game its `iworld` must be removed from the `universe`. As illustrated in the first sample expression in Fig. 22, this is done by creating a bundle whose `universe` is the result of removing the given `iworld` from the given `universe`, whose list of `tpm mails` is empty, and whose list of `iworlds` to remove only contains the given `world`. When a player requests a fortune, a `bundle` is created with the given `universe`, a list with a single `tpm mail` for the given world that contains a randomly selected fortune, and an empty list of `iworlds` to remove from the server. This is illustrated by the second sample expression in Fig. 22.

Observe that the result of processing a `'bye tsm` is predictable and may be tested using `check-expect` as done in the first test using sample compu-

Fig. 22 The process-message handler for tsms

```
;; universe iworld tsm → bundle
;; Purpose: To process the given to-server message
(define (process-message u iw m)
  (if (eq? m 'bye)
      (make-bundle (rm-iworld u iw)
                   '()
                   (list iw))
      (make-bundle u
                   (list (make-mail
                          iw (list-ref FORTUNES
                                       (random (length FORTUNES)))))
                   '())))
;; Sample expressions for process-message
(define PM1 (make-bundle (filter (λ (w)
                                   (not (equal? (iworld-name w)
                                                (iworld-name iworld1))))
                                 UNIV2)
                         '()
                         (list iworld1)))
(define PM2 (make-bundle UNIV2
                         (list (make-mail
                                iworld1
                                (list-ref FORTUNES
                                          (random (length FORTUNES)))))
                         '()))
;; Tests using sample computations for process-message
(check-expect (process-message UNIV2 iworld1 'bye) PM1)
(check-random (process-message UNIV2 iworld1 'send-fortune)
              (make-bundle UNIV2
                           (list (make-mail
                                  iworld1
                                  (list-ref FORTUNES
                                            (random (length FORTUNES)))))
                           '()))
;; Tests using sample values for process-message
(check-random
  (process-message (list iworld3 iworld2) iworld2 'send-fortune)
  (make-bundle (list iworld3 iworld2)
               (list (make-mail iworld2
                                (list-ref FORTUNES
                                          (random (length FORTUNES)))))
               '()))
(check-random
  (process-message (list iworld1 iworld2) iworld1 'send-fortune)
  (make-bundle (list iworld1 iworld2)
               (list (make-mail iworld1
                                (list-ref FORTUNES
                                          (random (length FORTUNES)))))
               '()))
```

tations. To test processing a `'send-fortune tsm` we would like to write a
test like:

```
(check-expect (process-message UNIV2 iworld1 'send-fortune)
              PM2)
```

This, however, cannot be done because `process-message` is nondeterministic in this case. We may use `check-random` to test the processing of a
`'send-fortune tsm`. This is illustrated by the second test using sample computations. Both `process-message` and `make-bundle` are evaluated using the
same random seed to guarantee that their results are the same. Finally, tests
using sample values also use `check-random` for `'send-fortune tsms`.

This completes the design and implementation of the distributed fortune
teller game. Make sure you run the tests and fix any typos or bugs you may
accidentally introduce. Personalize and enjoy the game!

---

6 Concentration is a card game in which all of the cards are laid face
down on a surface. At each turn a player flips two cards face up. If the
cards match the player removes them and tries again. If they do not
match the cards are flipped back down and the next player gets a turn.
Design and implement a concentration game where a player plays against
the computer and other players. The computer randomly picks two cards
to flip over when it is its turn.

---

7 A restaurant must manage its delivery drivers. A driver may request
a delivery and the server must provide one. A delivery contains a menu
item and an address. The menu item and the address may be randomly
generated, respectively, from a database of menu items and a database
of addresses. Each delivery person sees its current delivery information
on the screen.

---

19 What Have We Learned in This Chapter?

The important lessons of this chapter are summarized as follows:

- In ISL+ `random` is used to generate pseudorandom numbers.
- A deterministic function is one for which we are able to always predict the
  result of applying it to arguments.
- A nondeterministic function is one for which we are unable to predict the
  result of applying it to arguments.
- A function that uses `random` to compute its result is nondeterministic.
- A random number generator tries to maximize entropy.

- A pseudorandom number generator uses a mathematical function and a seed to generate numbers that appear random.
- Referential transparency is the property that an expression may always be substituted with its value.
- Programs that use randomness do not have referential transparency.
- Randomness has its role in computing and you must learn to use it responsibly.
- Property-based testing may be used to test functions that use randomness.
- Property-based tests may be written using `check-satisfy` in ISL+.
- Random functions may also be tested using `check-random` that provides the same seed to `random` for the two expressions tested. The expressions must request random numbers in the same order using the same ranges for corresponding requests.
- The use of randomness ought to be considered when it is important not to be able to predict a function's value.
- An infinite recursion occurs when a function fails to make progress towards termination.

Part II
Generative Recursion

Chapter 4
Introduction to Generative Recursion

In this textbook so far (and in *Animated Problem Solving*), the functions to process data of arbitrary size are designed using structural recursion. That is, a recursive call is always made with a substructure of an input. In a list-processing function a recursive call is made with the rest of the given list. In a function that processes a natural number, n, a recursive call is made with n-1. Any recursive call in a function to process a binary tree is made with either the left subtree or the right subtree. Structurally recursive programs have the property that they always make progress towards termination. In other words, every recursive call brings the input closer to satisfying the condition that stops the recursion: a list eventually becomes empty, a natural number eventually becomes 0, and a binary tree eventually becomes empty (or a leaf). If progress is always made towards termination, then it is impossible to have an infinite recursion.

In Chap. 3 the design and implementation of `generate-password` in Fig. 12 is discussed. This function brought to the forefront something new. A useful recursive call may be made without using the substructure of any input. In `generate-password` there are recursive calls that are made without the rest of any of the input lists. In other words, this function is not structurally recursive. How then is this useful? How do we know the function will terminate? It is useful because we used insight into randomness to reason that eventually all four input lists become empty. Thus, progress towards termination is not made with every recursive call but it is reasonable to assume that eventually enough recursive calls are made that make progress towards termination (i.e., all four lists being empty). We cannot, however, argue that the function will always terminate. As mentioned in Chap. 3 it is possible, although highly unlikely, that a pseudorandom number generator never generates a sequence of numbers that lead to termination. In this regard, `generate-password` is troublesome. Unless a function is nondeterministic we need to be able to argue that the functions we design always terminate. When using structural recursion a termination argument is unnecessary because an infinite recursion is impossible.

© The Author(s), under exclusive license to Springer Nature Switzerland AG 2022   81
M. T. Morazán, *Animated Program Design*, Texts in Computer Science,
https://doi.org/10.1007/978-3-031-04317-8_4

Fig. 23 Nested square images

(b) A Green Nested Squares Image.

(a) An Orange Nested Squares Image.

Fig. 24 The components of the nested square image in Fig. 23a

(a) The Bottommost Square.   **(b)** The Top Image.

20 Generating a Nested Square Image

The natural question you have now is whether or not recursion not based on
the structure of the data processed is ever useful in other settings. To answer
this let us explore writing a function to create nested square images as those
displayed in Fig. 23. Think about how these images may be created. We can
observe that the images are a composition of two images. For example, the
image in Fig. 23a may be created from the images in Fig. 24. There largest
square, displayed in Fig. 24a, is the bottommost image. Over this square we
may overlay the nested (smaller) square image displayed in Fig. 24b. Thus,
we may say the image in Fig. 23a is a recursive image because the nested
image is a (smaller) nested square image.[5] Recursive images are examples of
fractals. A fractal is a never-ending pattern across different scales.

---

[5] Recursion has been used extensively by artists throughout history. It is known as *the
Droste effect* and is named for a Dutch brand of cocoa that was advertised with an image
that contained a smaller image of itself. Centuries before this brand of cocoa existed,
the effect was used by Giotto in his *Stefaneschi Triptych*. The Dutch artist M. C. Escher
was also very successful in using this effect.

The basic idea is that from a given square image, a smaller square image is computed and processed recursively. The result of the recursive call is placed over the given square image. Observe that we are now out of the realm of structural recursion. Our design idea suggests recursively processing a smaller square image. A smaller square image is not part of structure of the given square image. If our design idea is implementable, then it becomes clear that recursion not based on the structure of the input is useful in different settings. What is used as the input to a recursive call? If you think about it carefully, a new problem has been generated. This example suggests generating a new square image to solve the problem of processing a larger square image. Recursion based on generating one or more new instances of a problem (i.e., the subproblems) and creating a solution from the solutions of the subproblems is known as *generative recursion*. It is worth noting that generative recursion subsumes structural recursion. In structural recursion the subproblems are always based on the structure of the data processed. In generative recursion the subproblems are not necessarily based on the given input's structure.

There are several important questions that must be answered when generative recursion is used. How is the recursion stopped? This is straightforward using structural recursion: the recursion stops when a nonrecursive variant of the input's datatype is received as input, for example, empty when processing a (listof X) or 0 when processing a natural number. Another important question to answer is: how are the subproblems generated? Once again, this is straightforward using structural recursion: the subcomponents of the same type are processed recursively. For example, the subtrees of a binary tree or the rest of a list are processed recursively.

Let us develop answers to these questions for generating a nested square image. First, let us address the issue of when the recursion ought to stop. Consider the limitations of the human eye. Clearly, the human eye can see a square that has a length of 100 pixels. How about a square that has a length of 2 pixels? 20 pixels? 10 pixels? 0 pixel? There is no doubt that the human eye cannot see a square with a length of 0 pixel. It is also fairly clear that when the square is too small (i.e., the length is too small), the human eye cannot distinguish it. Given that there is a limit to the sensitivity of the human eye, the recursion ought to stop when the square's length becomes too small. For this we may define a constant for when the length in pixels is too small as follows:

```
(define TOO-SMALL-LEN 20)
```

We can define sample square images that are too small and not too small as follows:

```
(define SQ1 (square   15 'outline 'blue))
(define SQ2 (square    8 'outline 'gold))
(define SQ3 (square 1000 'outline 'red))
(define SQ4 (square  800 'outline 'brown))
```

Fig. 25 Square B inside of square A

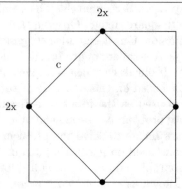

The recursion ought to stop when the length of the given square image is less than or equal to TOO-SMALL-LEN.

From a given square image how is a smaller square image, to process recursively, created? Let us call the given square A and the smaller square to be created B. By examining the nested squares in Fig. 23 we can conclude that the corners of B are at the midpoint of each of the sides of A as illustrated in Fig. 25. In Fig. 25, A has a length of 2x. We can use this observation to create the image of B. To do so B's length needs to be computed (depicted as c in Fig. 25). Observe that each side of B forms a right triangle with a corner of A. This means that the Pythagorean theorem may be used to compute c as follows:

$$x^2 + x^2 = c^2$$
$$2x^2 = c^2$$
$$\sqrt{2}x = c$$

We are still unable to create the image for B (using square) because we have no way of determining the color of a given A. For this reason A must be used to create B.

What can we do? We know that B's length is smaller than A's length. We can use our theoretical analysis above to determine what percentage c is of A's length:

$$\frac{\sqrt{2}x}{2x} \approx 0.711$$

This tells us that B's length is 71.1% of A's length. This means that A may be scaled by this factor to create a square image of the right size. Finally, observe this smaller square image needs to be rotated by 45° to create B's image.

Based on the above design idea sample expressions are written as follows:

```
;; Sample expressions for nested-squares
(define CRAZY-SQ1 SQ1)
(define CRAZY-SQ2 SQ2)
(define CRAZY-SQ3 (overlay (nested-squares
                                (rotate 45 (scale 0.711 SQ3)))
                           SQ3))
(define CRAZY-SQ4 (overlay (nested-squares
                                (rotate 45 (scale 0.711 SQ4)))
                           SQ4))
```

The first two sample expressions are the result of processing square images that have a length less than or equal to TOO-SMALL-LEN. The last two sample expressions process squares that have a length greater than TOO-SMALL-LEN by scaling and rotating the image as discussed above.

The next steps of the design recipe are to write the function's signature, purpose statement, and header. Ask yourself if that is enough for others to understand how the function achieves its purpose. Given that we are not using structural recursion it is necessary for us to explain how the answer is computed. This gives our code reviewer's an insight into our design idea. This insight is given in a *how statement*. A how statement briefly outlines how the problem is solved. For nested squares the result is:

```
;; image → image
;; Purpose: Generate nested squares image from given image
;; Assumption: Given image is a square
;; How: Overlay over the given image the nested
;;      squares image computed from using the
;;      square image obtained from scaling the
;;      given image by 0.711 and rotating
;;      it 45 degrees.
(define (nested-squares sqr-img)
```

The tests are developed in the same manner you are familiar with:

```
;; Tests using sample computations for nested-squares
(check-expect (nested-squares SQ1) CRAZY-SQ1)
(check-expect (nested-squares SQ2) CRAZY-SQ2)
(check-expect (nested-squares SQ3) CRAZY-SQ3)
(check-expect (nested-squares SQ4) CRAZY-SQ4)

;; Tests using sample values for nested-squares
(check-expect (nested-squares (square 200 'outline 'orange))
```

)

(check-expect (nested-squares (square 80 'outline 'green))

)

We note that the expressions used in the tests using sample values are those that generate the nested square images in Fig. 23.

Given that there are only two conditions that need to be distinguished, the body of the function is implemented using an if-expression. The if-expression's condition tests if the width of the given image is less than or equal to TOO-SMALL-LEN. The then-expression is obtained by abstracting over the first two sample expressions. The else-expression is obtained by abstracting over the last two sample expressions. The body of the function is:

```
(if (<= (image-width sqr-img) TOO-SMALL-LEN)
    sqr-img
    (overlay (nested-squares
                (rotate 45 (scale 0.711 sqr-img)))
             sqr-img))
```

For anyone (including ourselves) that reads our code, a natural question is whether or not the recursion terminates. We must develop a **termination argument**. A termination argument explains why a recursion will always stop. For **nested-squares**, we observe that every recursive call is made with a smaller square image. Eventually the recursive call is made with an image that has a length less than or equal to TOO-SMALL-LEN and the program terminates.

This completes the design and implementation of **nested-squares**. Run the tests and make sure they all pass.

21 The Design Recipe for Generative Recursion

An important lesson to absorb is that using generative recursion requires (usually deep) insight into a problem. For example, for **nested-squares** required us to determine that the given square image must be scaled by 0.711 and rotated by 45°. There is nothing in the structure of a square image that informs us of this. This is why a how statement is needed. Otherwise, we risk not communicating to maintainers and users of our code how a problem is

Fig. 26 The design recipe for generative recursion

1. Perform problem and data analysis.
2. Define constants for the value of sample expressions.
3. Identify and name the differences among the sample expressions.
4. Write the function's signature, purpose statement, how statement, and function header.
5. Write tests.
6. Write the function's body.
7. Write a termination argument.
8. Run the tests and, if necessary, redesign.

solved. Another important lesson to absorb is that using generative recursion requires the development of a termination argument. Otherwise, we risk any user of the code providing a valid input that leads to an infinite recursion. Can you imagine the consequences if this happened with the new release of the software you develop for a company? Do you think the next day you might be at home looking for a new job?

These new steps must be integrated into a design recipe for generative recursion. The design recipe for generative recursion is displayed in Fig. 26. For Step 1 you perform problem and data analysis. These are intrinsically intertwined because how you represent data influences how you solve a problem. Most often a solution suggested by the structure of the data suffices. Sometimes, however, it is necessary to consider other representation options and develop insights into the problem. It is not uncommon that searching for insights into a problem may reveal more than one way to solve the problem forcing us to choose among them. In this step you need to identify and define instances of the problem that are trivially solved. Outline the solution for each trivial instance. These serve as the base cases that stop the recursion. Also identify and define the nontrivial instances that must be detected. For these you need to identify how to create new problem instances (that hopefully are easier to solve) and how to combine subproblem solutions to create the solution to the problem.

Steps 2 and 3 are the same as before. Write sample expressions for trivial and nontrivial problem instances. Identify the differences among the sample expressions and choose variable names for them.

In Step 4 use the types of the differences to write the signature. Clearly state the purpose of the function and how the problem is solved. The how statement needs to give any reader of the code an idea of the insights used to solve the problem. It does not need to give a detailed explanation of everything the codes does. Finally, choose a descriptive function name and use the variable names chosen in Step 3 as parameters.

In Step 5 write tests. There must be at least one test for each trivial and nontrivial problem instance identified. Choose tests that demonstrate how the problem is solved.

Step 6 asks you to develop the function's body. This is done by abstracting over the sample expressions for each of the trivial and nontrivial problem instances. Abstracting over the expressions for an instance yields an expression for a stanza in a conditional expression.

Step 7 asks you to develop a termination argument. Sometimes this step is the most difficult one because it is not always clear that the recursion terminates. You need to reason carefully about how each recursive call makes progress towards termination. Finally, Step 8 asks you to run the tests and debug, if necessary, by reviewing your answers to the steps of the design recipe.

The design recipe suggests the template for functions using generative recursion displayed in Fig. 27. Observe that the design recipe and function template for generative recursion are not as prescriptive as their structural recursion counterparts. For example, they do not tell you that the rest of a list or the decrement of a natural number must be processed. In other words, they do not dictate what the input needs to be for a recursive call. Furthermore, the conditions that must be detected are not prescribed. The problem solver must identify the problem instances that must be detected. If a nontrivial problem instance is received as input, then the subproblems are locally defined, solved, and their solutions combined. Compare this with the template for functions on a binary tree that prescribes that the subproblems are always the left and right subtrees.

1 The following is a recursive image:

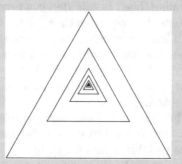

Design and implement a function to generate such an image. Personalize the triangles to your liking.

Fig. 27 The function template for generative recursion

```
(define (gen-rec-f prob-inst ...)
  (cond
    [(trivial-prob₁? prob-inst) solution for prob-inst₁]
      ⋮
    [(trivial-probₖ? prob-inst) solution for prob-instₖ]
    [else
      (local [(define genprob1 (generate-prob1 problem ...))
                ⋮
              (define genprobn (generate-probn problem ...))]
        (combine
          ... problem
          ... (gen-rec-f genprob1 ...)
              ⋮
          ... (gen-rec-f genprobn)))])))

;; Sample instances of problem
(define TRV1  ...) ... (define TRVK   ...)
(define NTRV1 ...) ... (define NTRVN ...)

;; Sample expressions for gen-rec-f
(define TRV1-VAL ...) ... (define TRVK-VAL  ...)
(define NTRV1-VAL ...) ... (define NTRVN-VAL ...)
  ⋮

;; Tests using sample computations for gen-rec-f
(check-expect (gen-rec-f TRV1  ...) TRV1-VAL)
  ⋮

(check-expect (gen-rec-f TRVK  ...) TRVK-VAL)
(check-expect (gen-rec-f NTRV1 ...) NTRV1-VAL)
  ⋮

(check-expect (gen-rec-f NTRVN ...) NTRVN-VAL)

;; Tests using sample values for gen-rec-f
(check-expect (gen-rec-f ... ...) ...)
  ⋮
```

2 A Koch curve is another example of a fractal image:

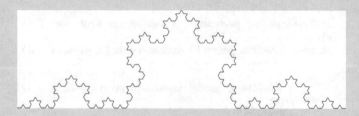

It is generated from the image of a straight line that is divided into three equal segments. At each step the middle segment is replaced by the top two sides of an equilateral triangle that have the same length as the middle segment. This results in an image with four line segments. For example, start with the following line image:

From this the following image is generated:

The process of generating a Koch curve continues by processing each of the four line segments in the above image. Design and implement a function to draw a Koch curve. Personalize the curve to your liking. HINT: Every angle in an equilateral triangle has 60°.

3 The Sierpiński triangle is a fractal image with the overall shape of an equilateral triangle:

It is named after the Polish mathematician Wacław Sierpiński. Design and implement a function to generate a Sierpiński triangle image. Personalize it to your liking.

22 All Primes ≤ n

We now turn our attention to the problem of computing all prime numbers less than or equal to n, a given natural number. The number of primes is arbitrary. Therefore, the function must return a (listof natnum). Your first thought is likely to design the function around processing n. Let us explore this design choice. If n is 0 then there are no primes to return and the answer is the empty list. If n is greater than 0, then the function must decide if n is added to the result. If n is prime then it is consed with the result of processing n-1. If n is not prime then the result is obtained by processing n-1. This design clearly suggests that there are three cases that must be distinguished: n is 0, n is prime, and n is not prime. In addition, an auxiliary predicate to determine if a given natural number is prime is needed.

To determine if n is prime there are two cases to distinguish: n < 2 and n ≥ 2. If n is less than 2 then the answer is #false because neither 0 nor 1 is prime. Otherwise, it must be determined if n is prime. How can this be done? Thinking about this carefully reveals that any natural number that divides n must be greater than or equal to 2 and less than or equal to the quotient of n and 2. This idea suggests processing the interval [2..(quotient n 2)].

Thus, an auxiliary function is needed to process this interval. This auxiliary function traverses the interval testing if n is divisible by the next number in the interval.

The function arising from the above design idea, after encapsulation of auxiliary functions, is displayed in Fig. 28. Observe that `all-primes<=n`'s body is a `cond`-expression with three stanzas (one for each condition identified in our design). As per the design idea the function returns the empty list when n is 0, a list containing n when n is prime, and a list that does not contain n when n is not prime. In addition, `all-primes<=n` locally defines the predicate `prime?` to determine if a given natural number is prime. This predicate's body is an `if`-expression that determines if n is less than 2 or not. If it is it returns `#false` given that n is not prime. Otherwise, it calls its local predicate, `any-divide?`, to process the interval `[2..(quotient n 2)]` and determine if any natural number in it divides n. The sample expressions include examples for all three conditions `all-primes<=n` must distinguish. Finally, the tests illustrate that `all-primes<=n` computes the same values as the evaluation of the sample expressions and that it works for other concrete values. Make sure to run the tests before proceeding.

Undoubtedly, you notice that the tests take a bit of time to run. Specifically, evaluating `(all-primes<=n 12K)` takes significantly longer than evaluating the function applications in the other tests. Try giving `all-primes<=n` 50,000 as input. The result (only) contains 5133 natural numbers but takes a very noticeable amount of time to compute. This may or may not be okay with you but most people need (and want) programs to be fast. If the program needs to be faster, then it is time to explore one or more different designs to determine if we can make it faster.

How else can we compute all the prime numbers that are less than or equal to n, a given natural number? Finding a different way to solve a problem may be very challenging. This is when we can benefit from insights that others may have had. Eratosthenes of Cyrene, a third-century BCE Greek mathematician, suggested using a sieving method (thus, his algorithm is popularly known as the sieve of Eratosthenes). The idea is to start with a list of natural numbers from 2 (the smallest prime number) to n. At each step, the first number in the list, i, is a prime that is added to the result and the process is repeated with the members of the rest of the list that are not multiples of i. Observe that the process is not repeated with the rest of the list, meaning that this algorithm is not based on structural recursion. It is generative recursion. When should the process stop? This may not be so clear. Let us try to figure this out by working through an example. Consider computing all the prime numbers less than or equal to n = 10. The list that contains prime number candidates is:

```
(sieve '(2 3 4 5 6 7 8 9 10))
```

One immediate observation we make is that multiples of any number greater than or equal to `(quotient n 2)` are not members of the list. For example,

Fig. 28 Computing all primes less than or equal to **n** using structural recursion

```
;; Sample natnums
(define ZERO  0)
(define ONE   1)
(define FIVE  5)
(define SIX   6)
(define SEVEN 7)
(define 12K   12000)


(define (all-primes<=n n)
  (local [;; natnum → Boolean
          ;; Purpose: Determine if given natnum is a prime
          (define (prime? n)
            (local [;; [int int] → Boolean
                    ;; Purpose: Determine if n is divisible by any number
                    ;;          in the given interval
                    (define (any-divide? low high)
                      (if (< high low)
                          #false
                          (or (= (remainder n high) 0)
                              (any-divide? low (sub1 high)))))]
              (if (< n 2)
                  #false
                  (not (any-divide? 2 (quotient n 2))))))]
    (cond [(= n 0) '()]
          [(prime? n) (cons n (all-primes<=n (sub1 n)))]
          [else (all-primes<=n (sub1 n))])))

;; Sample expressions for all-primes<=n
(define ZERO-VAL  '())
(define ONE-VAL   '())
(define FIVE-VAL  (cons FIVE (all-primes<=n (sub1 FIVE))))
(define SEVEN-VAL (cons SEVEN (all-primes<=n (sub1 SEVEN))))
(define SIX-VAL   (all-primes<=n (sub1 SIX)))
(define 12K-VAL   (all-primes<=n (sub1 12K)))

;; Tests using sample computations for all-primes<=n
(check-expect (all-primes<=n ZERO)  ZERO-VAL)
(check-expect (all-primes<=n ONE)   ONE-VAL)
(check-expect (all-primes<=n FIVE)  FIVE-VAL)
(check-expect (all-primes<=n SEVEN) SEVEN-VAL)
(check-expect (all-primes<=n 12K)   12K-VAL)

;; Tests using sample values for all-primes<=n
(check-expect (all-primes<=n 17) '(17 13 11 7 5 3 2))
(check-expect (all-primes<=n 3)  '(3 2))
```

when n = 10 there are no multiples of any number greater than 5 (i.e., the quotient of 10 and 2). This means that multiples only need to be eliminated for natural numbers in [2..(quotient n 2)]. When the first element of the list is greater than (quotient n 2), the process of identifying primes may stop.

Let us now see how the process ought to work. The process starts with:

```
(sieve '(2 3 4 5 6 7 8 9 10) 5)
```

The 5 is the limit value to stop the recursion when n = 10. We add 2 to the result and repeat the process after removing the multiples of 2. In other words:

```
(cons 2 (sieve '(3 5 7 9) 5))
```

Three is added to the result and the process is repeated after removing the multiples of 3:

```
(cons 2 (cons 3 (sieve '(5 7) 5)))
```

The process is repeated. Now, 5 is added to the result and nothing is removed because there are no multiples of 5:

```
(cons 2 (cons 3 (cons 5 (sieve '(7) 5))))
```

The process now stops because the first element of the list is greater than 5. Observe that the remaining list only contains primes (i.e., only 7 in this case) and may be returned to obtain:

```
(cons 2 (cons 3 (cons 5 '(7))))
```

As you can see, these are the primes less than or equal to 10.

We must still define how to solve the problem when n is less than 2 (i.e., 0 or 1). The solution is the empty list because there are no prime numbers less than 2.

Having completed the problem and data analysis for Step 1 of the design recipe, for Step 2 we write the following sample expressions using the same values developed for all-primes<=n:

```
;; Sample expressions for the-primes<=n
(define ZERO-VALUE  '())
(define ONE-VALUE   '())
(define FIVE-VALUE (sieve (build-list (- FIVE 1)
                                      (λ (i) (+ i 2)))
                  (quotient FIVE 2)))
(define SEVEN-VALUE (sieve (build-list (- SEVEN 1)
                                       (λ (i) (+ i 2)))
                  (quotient SEVEN 2)))
(define SIX-VALUE (sieve (build-list (- SIX 1)
                                     (λ (i) (+ i 2)))
                  (quotient SIX 2)))
```

```
(define 12K-VALUE (sieve (build-list (- 12K 1)
                                     (λ (i) (+ i 2)))
                         (quotient 12K 2)))
```

As per the design idea, if the given value is less than 2 the answer is the empty list as illustrated by the first two sample expressions. Otherwise, a function to sieve the list of numbers from 2 to the given number is called. This function is given as input the limit value to stop the sieving process.

For Step 3, observe that there are no differences when the given number is less than 2 and that there is only one difference, the given natural number, when the given natural number is greater than or equal to 2. This difference is named n. Steps 3 and 4 yield this result:

```
;; natnum → (listof natnum)
;; Purpose: Compute all primes ≤ to given natnum
(define (the-primes<=n n) ...)
```

Observe that the signature and the purpose are the same as for all-primes<=n. This is not surprising because the goal of both functions is the same. The only difference is the name of the function. A different name is chosen for this function to avoid name clashes with the previously defined all-primes<=n. There is no need for a how statement, because this function does not employ generative recursion.

The tests for Step 5 illustrate that the function computes the same value as the sample expressions and that it also works for other concrete values:

```
;; Tests using sample computations for the-primes<=n
(check-expect (the-primes<=n ZERO)  ZERO-VALUE)
(check-expect (the-primes<=n ONE)   ONE-VALUE)
(check-expect (the-primes<=n FIVE)  FIVE-VALUE)
(check-expect (the-primes<=n SEVEN) SEVEN-VALUE)
(check-expect (the-primes<=n 12K)   12K-VALUE)

;; Tests using sample values for the-primes<=n2
(check-expect (the-primes<=n 17) '(2 3 5 7 11 13 17))
(check-expect (the-primes<=n 3)  '(2 3))
```

The same input values are tested as for all-primes<=n. This drives home the point that the functions solve the same problem.

For Step 6 the expressions needed for the function's body are obtained by abstracting over the sample expressions for when the given number is less than 2 and for when it is not. Given that there are only two conditions to test an if-expression may be used as follows:

```
(if (< n 2)
    '()
    (sieve (build-list (- n 1) (λ (i) (+ i 2)))
           (quotient n 2)))
```

As observed above this function does not employ generative recursion, and, therefore, a termination argument is not required.

We now focus on developing the auxiliary function `sieve` to eliminate the nonprimes. This is the function that employs the generative recursion algorithm suggested by Eratosthenes. The input to this function must be a list of natural numbers in nondecreasing such that first element is a prime and the rest of the list does not contain a multiple of a number less than the first element. To make testing easier and to help readers of the code understand the solution, we develop samples of such a list as follows:

```
(define L1 '(7))
(define L2 '(11 13 17))
(define L3 '(5 7 11))
(define L4 '(2 3 4 5 6 7 8))
```

The sample expressions for Step 2 of the design recipe are written for both the trivial case and the nontrivial cases as follows:

```
;; Sample expressions for sieve
(define L1-VAL L1)
(define L2-VAL L2)
(define L3-VAL
       (local
         [(define new-inst
                 (filter
                  (λ (n)
                   (not (= (remainder n (first L3)) 0)))
                  (rest L3)))]
         (cons (first L3) (sieve new-inst 6))))
(define L4-VAL
       (local
         [(define new-inst
                 (filter
                  (λ (n)
                   (not (= (remainder n (first L4)) 0)))
                  (rest L4)))]
         (cons (first L4) (sieve new-inst 4))))
```

The first two sample expressions are written for lists that have a first element larger than the limit value (respectively, 4 and 9). The second two are for lists that must be recursively processed. Observe that `filter` is used to implement Eratosthenes' sieve by locally defining a new instance of the problem: a list with the multiples of the first element removed. The solution is constructed by consing the given list's first element and the result of processing the new problem instance (using the same limit value).

For Step 3 observe that there are two differences in the expressions for the nontrivial cases: the list of numbers processed and the limit value. We call these differences `lon` and `limit`. Step 4 yields:

```
;; (listof natnum) natnum → (listof natnum)
;; Purpose: Extract the prime numbers in the given list
;; Assumption:
;;    The given list of natural numbers is nonempty, its
;;    first element is prime, and contains no numbers
;;    that are divisible by a number less than the first
;;    element.
;; How: If the first list element is greater than the
;;        limit stop. Otherwise, add the first number to
;;        the result and repeat the process by removing
;;        the multiples of the first element from the rest
;;        of the given list using the same limit value.
(define (sieve lon limit) ...)
```

Observe that the assumption clearly states the conditions set on the input. The how statement summarizes our insights to solve the problem.

For Step 5 of the design recipe we write tests illustrating that the function computes the values of the sample expressions and that it works for other concrete sample values as follows:

```
;; Tests using sample computations for sieve
(check-expect (sieve L1 4) L1-VAL)
(check-expect (sieve L2 9) L2-VAL)
(check-expect (sieve L3 6) L3-VAL)
(check-expect (sieve L4 4) L4-VAL)

;; Tests using sample computations for sieve
(check-expect (sieve '(5 7) 4) '(5 7))
(check-expect (sieve '(5 7 11 13 15) 8)
              '(5 7 11 13))
```

The body of the function for Step 6 is implemented using an if-expression because there are only two cases to distinguish as follows:

```
(if  (> (first lon) limit)
     lon
     (local
       [(define new-inst
                  (filter
                    (λ (n)
                      (not (= (remainder n (first lon)) 0)))
                    (rest lon)))]
       (cons (first lon) (sieve new-inst limit))))
```

The then- and else-expressions are obtained from abstracting over the sample expressions.

Step 7 requires the development of a termination argument. This function requires a termination argument because it employs generative recursion.

Are you sure that the function always terminates? Observe two things. The first is every recursive call is made with a shorter list given that at the very least the first element of the given list is removed. The second is that with every recursive call made the first element of the list becomes larger. These observations put together mean that eventually the first element of the list becomes larger than the given limit value and the function halts.

As stated in Step 8 run the tests and make sure they all pass. This completes the design of our new function to compute a list of all the primes less than or equal to n.

A natural question to ask is: why should you care? Why should anybody care? Has anything been achieved? Our motivation to develop a new function was to speed up the program. Run the following experiment:

```
(define T3 (time (all-primes<=n 50000)))
(define T4 (time (the-primes<=n 50000)))
```

The timing data printed is the following:[6]

```
cpu time: 25968 real time: 27559 gc time: 6859
cpu time: 1359  real time: 1413  gc time: 78
```

Look at the CPU time which is expressed in milliseconds. The CPU time includes the garbage collection (gc) time. If we subtract the garbage collection time, we have that `all-primes<=n` computed the result in 19,099 ms and `the-primes<=n` computed the result in 1281 ms. This is about one order of magnitude faster. In other words, we observe a significant speedup and this is why we ought to care.

Run the experiment above multiple times. You get different timing data. This means that timing results are unreliable. They depend on the computer and the operating system used. In addition, timing data may also be different depending on how many threads are running on your machine. What is needed is complexity analysis given that abstract running time is a much better predictor of performance.

We can observe that `all-primes<=n` makes n recursive calls. For each recursive call `prime?` is called. In the worst case `prime?` makes $\frac{n}{2}$ recursive calls. This means that `all-primes<=n`'s complexity is $n * \frac{n}{2} = O(n^2)$.

For `sieve`, the function that does the work for `the-primes<=n`, we observe that the first call requires about $\frac{n}{2}$ filtering steps to remove the even numbers. The next call requires at most $\frac{n}{3}$ filtering steps to remove the remaining multiples of 3. The next call requires at most $\frac{n}{5}$ filtering steps to remove the remaining multiples of 5. We can now see the pattern. The number of steps done by `sieve` is proportional to:

$$\frac{n}{2} + \frac{n}{3} + \frac{n}{5} + \frac{n}{7} + \ldots$$

By factoring out n we obtain:

---

[6] The timing on your computer may be different.

$$n*(\tfrac{1}{2} + \tfrac{1}{3} + \tfrac{1}{5} + \tfrac{1}{7} + \ldots)$$

The series above is the harmonic progression of the sum of primes (if you have never heard of this before, that is fine). The important point is that mathematicians have proven that the above series converges to: $\log(\log(n))$. This means that the abstract running time for `sieve` is: $O(n\log(\log(n)))$, which grows much slower than $O(n^2)$. Now you truly understand why `the-primes<=n` runs much faster.

A word of caution is in order. It is not the case that generative recursion is always faster than structural recursion. Sometimes generative recursion is faster. Sometimes structural recursion is faster. Algorithmic complexity analysis and experimentation are required to draw conclusions.

4 Design and implement a program to find the first prime number greater than or equal to a given natural number greater than or equal to 2.

5 The greatest common divisor of two natural numbers, `gcd(a, b)`, is the largest natural number that evenly divides both. Assume `a > b`. Using structural recursion design and implement a function to compute `gcd(a, b)`. Use your function to compute the `gcd(101135853, 45014640)`. Are you happy with how fast your function is?

Euclid of Alexandria (323–283 BCE) observed that:

$$gcd(a,b) = \begin{cases} a & \text{if b = 0} \\ gcd(b, \text{remainder}(a, b)) & \text{otherwise} \end{cases}$$

Design and implement a function to compute `gcd(a, b)` using Euclid's algorithm. Is it faster than your solution using structural recursion. Carefully justify your answer.

6 Design and implement a function, `(next-multiple-of a b)`, that takes as input two natural numbers and returns the first natural number larger than the maximum of a and b that is a multiple of both. For example, `(next-multiple-of 8 4)` returns 16 and `(next-multiple-of 14 56)` returns 112.

7 Assume a function f(x) is greater than or equal to 0 between xlow and xhigh, where xlow ≤ xhigh. Let md be the midpoint between xlow and xhigh. The area between f(x) and the x-axis from xlow to xhigh can be approximated by adding the area of two smaller pieces: the area from xlow to md and the area from md to xhigh. If xlow and xhigh are within a small constant value, then the area can be approximated by finding the area of the rectangle whose width is the difference between xhigh and xlow and whose height is given by the minimum of f(xlow) and f(xhigh).

Design and implement a function, (integrate f xlow xhigh), that takes as input a number to number function and two numbers such that from xlow to xhigh f(x) is greater than or equal to 0, xlow ≤ xhigh, and returns the area between f(x) and the x-axis from xlow and xhigh. Use the following constant to decide if xlow and xhigh are close:

```
(define LIM 0.001)
```

Use the following as one of your tests:

```
(check-within (integrate (lambda (x) (* 3 (sqr x))) 0 10)
              1000
              0.1)
```

8 A talented but young noob to programming represents a list of three-dimensional coordinates as a list of numbers. For example,

```
'(10 7 5 8 -3 -9 99 78 -44)
```

represents the coordinates (10 7 5), (8 -3 -9), and (99 78 -44). Using this representation it is difficult for any reader of the code to understand that the above is a list of three-dimensional coordinates. Given that a three-dimensional coordinate is data of finite size, a better representation uses a structure rather than three numbers in a list. Design and implement a program that converts a given list of three-dimensional coordinates represented using numbers to a list of three-dimensional coordinates represented using structures.

9 A `2list` is a list (`listof X`) that has two elements. Design and implement a function that converts a (`listof X`) into a (`listof 2list`) when the list's length is even by merging every two elements into a `2list`. For example,

```
'(1 2 3 4 5 6 7 8)
```

is converted to

```
'((1 2) (3 4) (5 6) (7 8)).
```

23 What Have We Learned in This Chapter?

The important lessons of this chapter are summarized as follows:

- Properly using structural recursion means an infinite recursion is impossible.
- A fractal image captures a never-ending repeated pattern.
- Recursion based on generating one or more new instances of a problem (i.e., the subproblems) and creating a solution from the solutions of the subproblems is known as generative recursion.
- These questions need to be answered when using generative recursion:
  1. How is the recursion stopped?
  2. Which are trivially solved problem instances?
  3. How are the subproblems generated for problem instances that are not trivially solved?
  4. How are the solutions to the subproblems combined to create a solution for the problem?

- Using generative recursion requires developing insights into a problem.
- Using generative recursion requires writing a how statement to communicate the manner in which the problem is solved.
- Using generative recursion requires developing a termination argument.
- The design recipe for generative recursion is not as prescriptive as design recipes for programs designed using structural recursion.
- Timing results are unreliable.
- Complexity analysis is a more reliable way to judge the expected performance of a program.
- Mathematics is a powerful ally to any problem solver and programmer. Study mathematics as much as you can!
- Generative recursion is not always faster than structural recursion.

Chapter 5
Sorting

One of the most common operations in problem solving and programming is sorting. A `sorting algorithm` puts a set of elements into an order. Usually this means nonincreasing or nondecreasing order. The ordering may be, for example, numeric or lexicographical. The following list of numbers is in nondecreasing order:

```
'(-34 39 45 45 67 873 9387 9387 10000)
```

In contrast, the following list of numbers is in nonincreasing order:

```
'(987 534 532 127 87 87 3 2 1 -1 -2 -3 -3)
```

Sorting has been studied extensively to make it as efficient as possible, because it improves the efficiency of solutions to other problems (e.g., searching). The result of any sorting algorithm must satisfy two properties. The first is that the result must be *monotonic*. This means that an element is never smaller than the previous element, if it exists, when the result must be in nondecreasing order and that an element is never larger than the previous element, if it exists, when the result must be in nonincreasing order. Observe that both lists above are monotonic. The second is that the result must be a *permutation* of the input. This means that the result contains all the elements of the input and only the elements of the input in, possibly, a different order.

To explore different designs we illustrate how to sort a `(listof number)` (abbreviated `lon`). Keep in mind that the illustrated algorithms are not restricted to sorting numbers. They may be used to sort any type of data that is `ordinal`. That is, any type of data that may be ordered. To test the different algorithms the following `lon`s are defined:

```
(define LON0 '())
(define LON1 '(71 81 21 28 72 19 49 64 4 47 81 4))
(define LON2 '(91 57 93 5 16 56 61 59 93 49 -3))
(define LON3 (build-list 2500 (λ (i) (- 100000 i))))
(define LON4 (build-list 200  (λ (i) (random 100000000))))
```

© The Author(s), under exclusive license to Springer Nature Switzerland AG 2022   103
M. T. Morazán, *Animated Program Design*, Texts in Computer Science,
https://doi.org/10.1007/978-3-031-04317-8_5

Fig. 29 Insertion sorting implementation

```
;; sort: lon → lon
;; Purpose: Sort given lon in nondecreasing order
(define (insertion-sorting a-lon)
  (local [;; insert: a-num lon → lon
          ;; Purpose: To insert a num into a lon sorted in
          ;;          non-decreasing order
          (define (insert a-num a-lon)
            (cond [(empty? a-lon) (cons a-num empty)]
                  [(<= a-num (first a-lon)) (cons a-num a-lon)]
                  [else (cons (first a-lon)
                              (insert a-num (rest a-lon)))]))]
    (cond [(empty? a-lon) empty]
          [else (insert (first a-lon)
                        (insertion-sorting (rest a-lon)))])))

;; Tests using sample values for insertion-sorting
(check-expect (insertion-sorting LON0) '())
(check-expect (insertion-sorting LON1)
              (list 4 4 19 21 28 47 49 64 71 72 81 81))
(check-expect (insertion-sorting LON2)
              (list -3 5 16 49 56 57 59 61 91 93 93))
(check-expect (insertion-sorting LON3) (reverse LON3))
(check-satisfied (insertion-sorting LON4) is-sorted?)
(check-satisfied (insertion-sorting LON5) is-sorted?)
(check-expect (insertion-sorting LON6) LON6)
```

```
(define LON5 (build-list 1575 (λ (i) (random 10000000))))
(define LON6 (build-list 1575 (λ (i) i)))
```

Observe that there are sample lons for both variants. There are lons of even and odd length. There are a sorted lon (i.e., LON6) and a lon in reversed order (i.e., LON3). Finally, there are randomly generated lons to protect ourselves from any possible bias we may have when we create a lon. The important point is that we wish to be as thorough as possible when testing.

24 Insertion Sorting

You likely remember designing a function to sort a list of numbers in non-decreasing order using structural recursion. We briefly outline the design to refresh your memory. A given lon, a-lon, is tested to determine if it is empty. If it is, the empty list is returned given that there are no numbers to sort. Otherwise, the rest of a-lon is sorted and a-lon's first number is inserted into it at the right place to return a sorted list. This sorting algorithm is called insertion sorting.

To insert a given number, a-num, into a sorted list, a-lon, the list is tested to determine if it is empty. If so, the list containing only a-num is returned.

Fig. 30 Predicate to test if a `lon` is sorted

```
;; lon → Boolean
;; Purpose: Determine if given list is sorted in nondecreasing order
(define (is-sorted? L)
   (local [;; lon → Boolean
           ;; Purpose: Determine if given list is of length 1 or 2
           (define (short-lon? lst) (< (length lst) 2))]
      (or (short-lon? L)
          (and (<= (first L) (second L))
               (is-sorted? (rest L))))))

;; Tests using sample values for is-sorted?
(check-expect (is-sorted? '())      #true)
(check-expect (is-sorted? '(31))    #true)
(check-expect (is-sorted? '(3 1 9)) #false)
(check-expect (is-sorted? '(3 7 8)) #true)
```

Otherwise, a-num and a-lon's first elements are tested. If a-num is less than or equal to a-lon's first number, then a sorted list is created by adding a-num to the front of a-lon. If a-num is greater than a-lon's first number, then a sorted list is created by adding a-lon's first element to the result of inserting a-num into the rest of a-lon.

The code developed from this design idea is displayed in Fig. 29. As you can see, both insertion-sorting and insert are functions that use structural recursion. The only tests that are kept in the final version of the code are those for insertion-sorting given that insert is encapsulated. The most interesting part of the function are the tests using the randomly generated lists of numbers. Recall that we cannot predict the result of using randomness. Therefore, we cannot predict the sorted list returned by calling insertion-sorting. We use property-based testing: the value returned by insertion-sorting must be sorted in nondecreasing order.

How can we determine if a list of numbers is sorted in nondecreasing order? We observe that if a list is short (i.e., has length 0 or 1), then it is sorted in nondecreasing order. If a list is not short then it is sorted in nondecreasing order if the first number is less than or equal to the second number and the rest of the list is sorted. The predicate developed from this design idea is displayed in Fig. 30. Observe that it is based on structural recursion. The condition that tests if the given list is empty is implicitly hidden in short-lon? (the length of the empty list is less than 2). The only tests that are left after encapsulation are the tests using sample values for is-sorted?. They illustrate that the predicate works for short lists, for non-short lists that are sorted, and for non-short lists that are not sorted.

Running the tests reveals that they all pass. We shall use the same set of tests used for insertion-sorting for the other sorting functions developed in this chapter. This means that is-sorted? is needed for them.

Let us explore the performance of insertion sorting using our sample `lons`. We do so to determine if we observe any cases that make insertion sorting slow. If any such cases are detected, then we may consider designing a faster algorithm. The following table displays sample CPU running times obtained:[7]

	LON1	LON2	LON3	LON4	LON5	LON6
insertion	0	0	1953	31	15	0

We can observe that insertion sorting seems to do well for most of our sample lists. A noticeable exception is LON3, the sample list in reversed order. Why is this occurring? LON3 is the longest sample list, but not much larger than LON6. It is unlikely that the observed performance is due to the length of LON3. Think carefully about what insertion sorting is doing. Let us consider the first call:

    (insertion-sorting '(100000 ... 97501))

Given that the list is not empty this call generates the following call:

    (insert 100000 (insertion-sorting '(99999 ... 97501))

Substituting the value of the recursive call yields:

    (insert 100000 '(97501 ... 99999))

Observe that inserting 100000 requires traversing the entire list returned by the recursive call. In fact, we can observe that inserting every element of the given list requires traversing the entire sorted rest of the list. This represents the worse-case scenario for insertion sorting and explains why insertion sorting is significantly slower when given LON3.

We observe that we may derive `insertion-sorting`'s complexity from these observations. If the length of the given list is n then `insertion-sorting` is called n times. For each call, `insert` is called. As noted above, `insert` must traverse its entire input. This means that `insert` is $O(n)$ making the complexity of `insertion-sorting`: $n * O(n) = O(n^2)$.

25 Quick Sorting

The weakness of insertion sorting stems from always inserting into a sorted list, at the correct position, the given list's first element. Ask yourself: must this always be done? The British computer scientist Sir Charles Antony Richard Hoare (a.k.a. Tony Hoare)[8] thought extensively about this while

---

[7] After subtracting garbage collection time.

[8] Tony Hoare is the recipient of the 1980 Turing Award—considered the most prestigious award in Computer Science.

he was a visiting student at Moscow State University in 1959. Instead of finding the given list's first element's position after sorting the rest of the list, he suggested finding the first element's position and then sorting the remaining elements.

25.1 Problem Analysis

How can you possibly know the position of the first element before sorting the rest of the list? You cannot possibly know the index of the first element in the sorted result before sorting the rest of the elements, but you know the relative position. In the sorted result the first element, called the *pivot*, goes between the elements that are less than or equal to it and the elements that are greater than it. Assuming L = (pivot (rest L)) we can visualize this idea as follows:

```
[sorted L] = ([sorted elements <= pivot in (rest L)]
             pivot
             [sorted elements > pivot in (rest L)])
```

Observe that this suggests a divide-and-conquer algorithm. The rest of L is divided into two lists. These lists are new instances of lons that must be sorted. The sorting operation performed on L must be performed on these new instances. In other words, the new instances must be processed recursively and the sorted list must be constructed. Our visualization can be refined to:

```
(quick-sorting L)
=
(append (quick-sorting [<elements <= pivot in (rest L)])
        (cons pivot
              (quick-sorting [elements > pivot in (rest L)]))))
```

The arguments to process recursively may be obtained by filtering L. We still must identify one or more trivially solved instances that allow us to stop the recursion. Observe that the arguments for the recursive call may be empty. When the given list is empty the sorted list is empty. This is how the recursion is halted.

Observe that the design idea suggests the use of generative recursion. The recursive calls are made with new lon instances and not with part of the structure of the given list (i.e., (rest L)).

25.2 Sample Expressions and Differences

Given the above problem analysis, we may proceed with the second step of the design recipe and write sample expressions. Independently reason about

each lon subtype. When the given lon is empty, the answer is always empty.
We write the following sample expression to illustrate the processing of LONO:

```
;; Sample expressions for quick-sorting
(define LONO-VAL '())
```

When the given lon is not empty according to the problem analysis above,
it must be split into two lons: one for the elements smaller or equal to the
pivot and one for the elements larger than the pivot. Following the template
for functions using generative recursion, these two new lon instances may be
defined locally. The body of the local-expression recursively processes these
new instances and creates the result using append. The following are sample
expressions for the nonempty lon subtype:

```
(define LON1-VAL
        (local
          [(define SMALLER= (filter
                               (λ (i) (<= i (first LON1)))
                               (rest LON1)))
           (define GREATER  (filter
                               (λ (i) (> i (first LON1)))
                               (rest LON1)))]
          (append (quick-sorting SMALLER=)
                  (cons (first LON1)
                        (quick-sorting GREATER)))))
(define LON2-VAL
        (local
          [(define SMALLER= (filter
                               (λ (i) (<= i (first LON2)))
                               (rest LON2)))
           (define GREATER  (filter
                               (λ (i) (> i (first LON2)))
                               (rest LON2)))]
          (append (quick-sorting SMALLER=)
                  (cons (first LON2)
                        (quick-sorting GREATER)))))
(define LON3-VAL
        (local
          [(define SMALLER= (filter
                               (λ (i) (<= i (first LON3)))
                               (rest LON3)))
           (define GREATER  (filter
                               (λ (i) (> i (first LON3)))
                               (rest LON3)))]
          (append (quick-sorting SMALLER=)
                  (cons (first LON3)
                        (quick-sorting GREATER)))))
```

Observe that the new `lon` instances are generated using `filter` and there is no need for an auxiliary function. The result is constructed by appending the sorted numbers less than or equal to the pivot and the list that starts with the pivot and ends with the sorted numbers greater than the pivot.

There is only one difference, the list being sorted, when the given list is not empty. We name this difference `a-lon`. When the list is empty there are no differences because the answer is always the empty list. This informs us that the function only needs one parameter.

25.3 Signature, Statements, and Function Header

Step 4 of the design recipe for generative recursion is satisfied as follows:

```
;; lon → lon
;; Purpose: Sort given lon in nondecreasing order
;; How: When the given list is empty stop and return the
;;    empty list. Otherwise, place the given's list
;;    first number between the sorted numbers less than
;;    or equal to the first number and the sorted numbers
;;    greater than the first number.
(define (quick-sorting a-lon)
```

The signature clearly informs the reader that the input must be a list of numbers and the returned value is a list of numbers. The purpose statement states the overall goal of the function without delving into any design details.

The how statement briefly describes the solution in a manner consistent with the problem analysis above. It gives any reader of the code an overview of how the problem is solved by providing an outline of the design idea. Finally, for the function header a descriptive function name is chosen and the name chosen for the only difference in the sample expressions above is used as the parameter.

25.4 Tests

Step 5 asks for the development of tests. For this step we write both tests using sample computations and using sample values as follows:

```
;; Tests using sample computations for quick-sorting
(check-expect (quick-sorting LON0) LON0-VAL)
(check-expect (quick-sorting LON1) LON1-VAL)
(check-expect (quick-sorting LON2) LON2-VAL)
(check-expect (quick-sorting LON3) LON3-VAL)
```

```
;; Tests using sample values for quick-sorting
(check-satisfied (quick-sorting LON4) is-sorted?)
(check-satisfied (quick-sorting LON5) is-sorted?)
(check-expect    (quick-sorting LON6) LON6)
(check-expect    (quick-sorting '(74 83 -72 2))
                 '(-72 2 74 83))
```

Observe that all the sample lons used to test insertion-sorting are used to test quick-sorting. This makes sense because both functions are designed to solve the same problem.

In addition, there is a test with a short list that explicitly shows the expected value. Such a test is important to quickly communicate to readers of the code the goal of the function without requiring, for example, that they become familiar with is-sorted?.

25.5 Function Body

For Step 6 of the design recipe an if-expression is used because only two conditions must be distinguished: whether or not the given list is empty. The function's body is:

```
(if (empty? a-lon)
    '()
    (local [(define SMALLER= (filter
                              (λ (i) (<= i (first a-lon)))
                              (rest a-lon)))
            (define GREATER  (filter
                              (λ (i) (> i (first a-lon)))
                              (rest a-lon)))]
      (append (quick-sorting SMALLER=)
              (cons (first a-lon)
                    (quick-sorting GREATER)))))
```

The else-expression is obtained by abstracting over the last three sample expressions.

It is worth observing that good name choices for local variables allow code readers to easily associate the function's body with the description in the how statement developed. Do you think that a local variable ought to be defined for the pivot instead of having (first a-lon) inlined in the body of the local-expression?

25.6 Termination Argument

Step 7 requires that a termination argument be formulated. Observe that each recursive call is made with a `lon` that is at least one shorter than the given list. At the very least the pivot is not contained in the argument provided by either recursive call. How do we know the pivot is not contained in the argument for either recursive call? Look at how `SMALLER=` and `GREATER` are built. They are built by filtering the rest of the given `lon` and, therefore, cannot contain the pivot (i.e., the first number in the given list). Note that `SMALLER=` and `GREATER` may contain other instances of the pivot.

Given that a recursive call is always made with a shorter `lon`, we may conclude that the given list eventually becomes empty. When this happens the test in the `quick-sorting`'s body is satisfied and the function halts.

The only design step left is to run the tests. Make sure that they all pass.

25.7 Performance

A new sorting algorithm is designed and implemented, but does it perform better than insertion sorting? We may time `quick-sorting` in the same manner as `insertion-sorting` is timed. The following are sample results:

	LON1	LON2	LON3	LON4	LON5	LON6
insertion	0	0	1953	31	15	0
quick	0	0	1172	0	15	485

We first observe that quick sorting is faster on LON3 than insertion sorting. In fact, the timing measurements suggest that quick sorting is faster than insertion sorting for most sample `lon`s. The exception is LON6 (the sorted `lon`). We can further observe that for LON3 and LON6 quick sorting appears to take much more time than for other lists. Why would a sorted list and a list in reversed sorted order cause quick sorting to run slower?

25.8 Complexity Analysis

Let us try to understand these numbers by performing complexity analysis. Consider sorting a list of length n that always splits evenly. The calls generated may be visualized as follows:

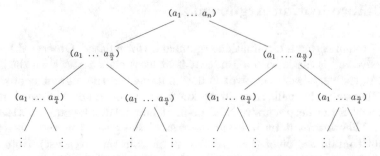

Observe that when the list always splits evenly the calls made by quick-sorting form a full binary tree. If the full binary tree were drawn, the leaves would represent all the calls made with the empty list.

Every time quick-sorting is called with a list of size k, extracting the numbers less than or equal to the pivot takes a number of operations proportional to k. Extracting the numbers greater than the pivot takes a number of operations proportional to k. Appending two lists of size $\frac{k}{2}$ takes a number of operations proportional to $\frac{k}{2}$. This means that the number of operations performed for every call to quick-sorting is proportional to k + k + $\frac{k}{2}$ = $O(k)$. This means that the number of operations performed when called with a list of size n is $O(n)$. When called with a list of size $\frac{n}{2}$ the number of operations performed is $O(\frac{n}{2})$. When called with a list of size $\frac{n}{4}$ the number of operations performed is $O(\frac{n}{4})$.

Ask yourself how many operations are performed at each level of the binary tree above. At the root, with a list of size n, $O(n)$ operations are performed. At the next level quick-sorting is called twice with a list of size $\frac{n}{2}$. This means that the number of operations performed is proportional to 2*$O(\frac{n}{2})$ = $O(n)$. At the next level quick-sorting is called four times with a list of size $\frac{n}{4}$. This means that the number of operations performed is proportional to 4*$O(\frac{n}{4})$ = $O(n)$. The pattern is clear now. At every level of the binary tree above $O(n)$ operations are performed.

To establish the abstract running time we need to know the binary tree's height (i.e., the number of levels). Starting with a list of length n, at each level the size of the list is divided by 2. How many times is n divided in order for the quotient to be 0 (i.e., the length of the list at the leaves)? Consider the problem when n = 16. We have that:

```
(quotient 16 2) = 8
(quotient  8 2) = 4
(quotient  4 2) = 2
(quotient  2 2) = 1
(quotient  1 2) = 0
```

16 may be divided by 2 5 times. Observe that 64 can be divided 2 7 times. What is the pattern? Observe that:[9]

---

[9] The notation $lg(n)$ means $log_2(n)$.

$$lg(16) + 1 = 5$$

$$lg(64) + 1 = 7$$

In general, the number of times **n** is divided by 2 to reach 0 is $lg(n) + 1$. This means that the height of the binary tree above is $O(\lg(n))$. Therefore, the abstract running time for quick sorting is $O(n * \lg(n))$. This is much better than `insertion-sorting`'s $O(n^2)$ because as **n** grows $O(n * \lg(n))$ grows slower than $O(n^2)$.

The above complexity analysis is `quick-sorting`'s best-case performance. The timing data, however, clearly suggests that when the input to `quick-sorting` is sorted or in reversed sorted order, performance degrades. Why? Let us consider the calls made when the given list is sorted:

```
(quick-sorting '(1 2 3 4))
```

This leads to the evaluation of:

```
(append (quick-sorting '())
        (cons 1
              (quick-sorting '(2 3 4)))))
```

In turn this leads to the evaluation of:

```
(append (quick-sorting '())
        (cons 2
              (quick-sorting '(3 4)))))
```

The right recursive call leads to the evaluation of:

```
(append (quick-sorting '())
        (cons 3
              (quick-sorting '(4)))))
```

The recursive call with 4 leads to the evaluation of:

```
(append (quick-sorting '())
        (cons 4
              (quick-sorting '()))))
```

Observe that the argument to the left recursive call (with the numbers less than or equal to the pivot) is always empty. This is the worst-case scenario when we hope to divide the list evenly. This means that the height of the binary tree describing the calls made to `quick-sorting` is **n** (not $\lg(n)$). This makes the abstract running time $O(n * O(n)) = O(n^2)$. This is the same abstract running time as `insertion-sorting`! This explains why `quick-sorting`'s performance is significantly worse when the input is sorted or in reversed sorted order. This analysis is the worst-case abstract running time for quick sorting.

1 Choosing the first element of the list as the pivot leads quick sorting to degrade to quadratic running time when the given list is sorted or in reversed sorted order. Instead of picking the first element of the given list as the pivot, the second largest number of among the first, the last, and the middle element of the list may be chosen as the pivot. Design and implement quick sorting picking the pivot in this manner. Does this improve performance when the given list is sorted or in reversed sorted order? Why or why not?

2 Another scenario that degrades the performance of quick sorting is when there are many repetitions of the pivot during partitioning. In such a case, the list containing the numbers less than or equal to the pivot may be much larger than the list containing the numbers greater than the pivot. To combat this problem partitioning may be done into three groups: the elements less than the pivot, the elements equal to the pivot, and the elements greater than the pivot. Design and implement quick sorting using this partitioning strategy. Does it improve performance on lists that contain many repetitions or on (long) randomly generated lists? Justify your answer.

3 Empirical evidence suggests that insertion sorting performs better than quick sorting on short lists. Design and implement quick sorting so that it uses insertion sorting when the length of the given list is at most 10. Does this strategy make quick sorting faster? Make sure to take time measurements using lists of varying sizes and varying qualities (e.g., sorted or reversed sorted order).

26 Merge Sorting

Quick sorting can be much faster than insertion sorting, but it is not always the case. When the given list is sorted or is in reversed sorted order, the performance of these two algorithms is expected to be similar: $O(n^2)$. Is there any way to always sort a list of numbers in quick sort's best case of $O(n * \lg(n))$ steps? As observed above the performance of quick sorting degrades when one of the two new `lon` instances is empty. When this occurs an empty `lon` is combined with the rest of the numbers sorted.

26.1 Problem Analysis

Ask yourself if we can guarantee that the empty list is never combined with a sorted list of numbers. In 1945 the Hungarian-American computer scientist Neumann János Lajos (better known in the English-speaking world as John von Neumann) observed that instead of starting the sorting process with a lon of length n (like done with quick sorting above), the process may start with n lons of length 1. The idea is to repeatedly merge adjacent sublists until there is a single sublist. The merging of two adjacent sublists must produce a sorted lon. Observe that this guarantees that the empty lon is never combined with a nonempty lon. The idea may be summarized as follows:

1. Convert a lon, L, of length n into a (listof lon), where each sublon has length 1.
2. Repeatedly merge adjacent sublons until the (listof lon) is of length 1.

When the (listof lon) is of length 1, it contains L sorted. This sorting algorithm is known as merge sorting. We shall follow a top-down design strategy to implement it.

26.2 The merge-sorting Function

26.2.1 Problem Analysis

Observe that only a nonempty lon may be converted to a (listof lon) with all sublons having length 1. This means that the merge-sorting function must determine if the list is empty. If the given lon is the empty list, the result is the empty list—there are no numbers to sort.

If the given list is not empty then the given list is converted into a (listof lon) in which all the elements are of length 1. Processing a (listof lon) is a different problem, and, therefore, an auxiliary function is needed. This auxiliary function must return a (listof lon) of length 1 according to the problem analysis in Sect. 26.1. The merge-sorting function returns the single element as it must be the given lon sorted.

26.2.2 Sample Expressions and Differences

Independently reason about each lon subtype. Processing the empty list, like LON0, always returns '(). We may write a sample expression to illustrate this as follows:

```
;; Sample expressions for merge-sorting
(define MS-LONO-VAL '())
```

To process a nonempty `lon` it is converted to a `(listof lon)`, with sublists of length 1, using `map`. After processing this `(listof lon)` a `(listof lon)` of length 1 is returned and its single value sublist is the value of processing a given nonempty `lon`. We write sample expressions using the same nonempty `lon`s used for `quick-sorting` as follows:

```
(define MS-LON1-VAL (first (merge-sort-helper
                            (map (λ (n) (list n)) LON1))))
(define MS-LON2-VAL (first (merge-sort-helper
                            (map (λ (n) (list n)) LON2))))
(define MS-LON3-VAL (first (merge-sort-helper
                            (map (λ (n) (list n)) LON3))))
```

The yet-to-be-written auxiliary function `merge-sort-helper` is used to process the given `lon`'s conversion into a `(listof lon)`. Why is an auxiliary function needed? An auxiliary function is needed because processing a `(listof lon)` is a different problem from processing a `lon`. Remember that processing a different type requires calling a function that processes that type.

The only difference among the sample expressions for nonempty `lon`s is the processed list. This single difference is named `a-lon`. It informs us that the function only needs one parameter.

26.2.3 Signature, Purpose, and Function Header

The signature, purpose, and function header may be written as follows:

```
;; lon → lon
;; Purpose: Sort given lon in nondecreasing order
(define (merge-sorting a-lon)
```

The signature and purpose statement are the same as those for `insertion-sorting` and `quick-sorting`. This makes sense because all three functions are designed to solve the same problem.

For the function header a descriptive function name is chosen. The single parameter is the single difference identified among the sample expressions.

26.2.4 Tests

The same tests as for `quick-sorting` are used as follows:

```
;; Tests using sample values for merge-sorting
(check-expect (merge-sorting LON0) MS-LON0-VAL)
(check-expect (merge-sorting LON1) MS-LON1-VAL)
(check-expect (merge-sorting LON2) MS-LON2-VAL)
(check-expect (merge-sorting LON3) MS-LON3-VAL)
```

```
;; Tests using sample values for merge-sorting
(check-satisfied (merge-sorting LON4) is-sorted?)
(check-satisfied (merge-sorting LON5) is-sorted?)
(check-expect    (merge-sorting LON6) LON6)
(check-expect    (merge-sorting '(74 83 -72 2))
                 '(-72 2 74 83))
```

Using the same test makes sense, once again, because merge-sorting is designed to solve the same problem.

26.2.5 Function Body

The function body is written using an if-expression to determine if the given list is empty as follows:

```
(if (empty? a-lon)
    '()
    (first (merge-sort-helper
            (map (λ (n) (list n)) a-lon))))
```

The else-expression is obtained by abstracting over the sample expressions for nonempty lons.

This completes the design of the merge-sorting function. Before running the tests the auxiliary function (and any auxiliary functions it may need) must be designed and implemented.

26.3 The merge-sort-helper Function

26.3.1 Problem Analysis

This function must repeatedly merge pairs of neighboring lons in a (listof lon) until there is a single lon left. We observe two things. First, the given (listof lon) cannot be empty. If it were empty there are no neighbors to merge and there is no (listof lon) that may be returned. Second, the halting condition for the recursion is when the length of the given (listof lon) is 1.

What if the length of the given lon is greater than 1? In this case a new (listof lon) is created by merging pairs of neighboring lons. This new (listof lon) instance must be processed recursively. Observe that this algorithm, therefore, utilizes generative recursion.

To facilitate the writing of tests the following samples (listof lon) are defined:

```
(define LOLON1 (list (list 1 2 3 4)))
(define LOLON2 (list (list -6 8 10 67)))
(define LOLON3 (list (list 1 2 3) (list -4 0 8 74) (list 5)))
(define LOLON4 (list (list 76 89 99) (list -77) (list 5 8 9)))
```

Observe that sample values for both varieties of interest are defined. The first two are of length 1. The second two are of length greater than 1.

26.3.2 Sample Expressions and Differences

There are two subtypes of (listof lon) that must be distinguished: those of length 1 and those of a larger length. Independently reason about each subtype. When the given (listof lon) has length 1, all that is required is to return it. We may write sample expressions for this case (to process LOLON1 and LOLON2) as follows:

```
;; Sample expressions for merge-sort-helper
(define MSH-LOLON1-VAL LOLON1)
(define MSH-LOLON2-VAL LOLON2)
```

The only difference among these sample expressions is the (listof lon) used.

To write the sample expressions when the given (listof lon)'s length is greater than 1, the new (listof lon) may be locally defined as suggested by the template for functions using generative recursion. The new problem instance is obtained by merging every two adjacent lons. Merging adjacent lons is a different problem and, therefore, an auxiliary function is needed. The new problem instance is given as input to merge-sort-helper. Sample expressions may be written as follows:

```
(define MSH-LOLON3-VAL
          (local [(define NEW-LOLON (merge-neighs LOLON3))]
            (merge-sort-helper NEW-LOLON)))
(define MSH-LOLON4-VAL
          (local [(define NEW-LOLON (merge-neighs LOLON4))]
            (merge-sort-helper NEW-LOLON)))
```

Observe that the sample (listof lon)s of length greater than 1 are used for these sample expressions. The needed auxiliary function to merge adjacent neighbors, merge-neighs, is yet to be designed and implemented. The only difference among these sample expressions, as before, is the (listof lon) used.

We name the only difference among the sample expressions a-lolon.

26.3.3 Signature, Statements, and Function Header

The function's signature and purpose statement are:

```
;; (listof lon) → (listof lon)
;; Purpose: Sort the numbers in the given (listof lon)
```

The signature clearly informs any reader that the input (listof lon) is used to return a (possibly different) (listof lon). The purpose statement indicates the goal of the function without explaining any details of the algorithm.

At a high level of abstraction the details of the algorithm are presented in the how statement as follows:

```
;; How: If the length of the given (listof lon) is 1 return it.
;;      Otherwise, every two neighboring lons are merged to
;;      create a new problem instance that is recursively
;;      processed.
;; Assumption: The given (listof lon) has a length greater or
;;             equal to 1 and all sublons are sorted in
;;             nondecreasing order.
```

Observe that the how statement briefly summarizes the design idea. This ought to be enough for any reader to understand what the code is doing. Although implied by the how statement the assumption statement makes explicit that the given (listof lon) cannot be empty and the sublons must be sorted. This ought to make it easier for any code reader to understand the design.

Finally, the function header is written as follows:

```
(define (merge-sort-helper a-lolon)
```

It uses a descriptive function name and the name chosen for the only difference in the sample expressions.

26.3.4 Tests

The tests using sample computations are written using the sample (listof lon)s and the constants defined for the values of the sample expressions as follows:

```
;; Tests using sample computations for merge-sort-helper
(check-expect (merge-sort-helper LOLON1) MSH-LOLON1-VAL)
(check-expect (merge-sort-helper LOLON2) MSH-LOLON2-VAL)
(check-expect (merge-sort-helper LOLON3) MSH-LOLON3-VAL)
(check-expect (merge-sort-helper LOLON4) MSH-LOLON4-VAL)
```

Observe that these tests illustrate that the function computes the value of
the sample expressions used to design it.

The tests using sample values use concrete values as follows:

```
;; Tests using sample values for merge-sort-helper
(check-expect (merge-sort-helper '((8) (7) (4)))
              '((4 7 8)))
(check-expect (merge-sort-helper '((8 9) (-87) (-4 99 678)))
              '((-87 -4 8 9 99 678)))
```

These tests help any code reader to quickly see that given valid input the
function returns the correct value.

26.3.5 Function Body

The function body uses an if-expression to distinguish if the given (listof
lon) is of length 1 or not as follows:

```
(if (= (length a-lolon) 1)
    a-lolon
    (local [(define NEW-LOLON (merge-neighs a-lolon))]
      (merge-sort-helper NEW-LOLON)))
```

The then- and else-expressions are obtained, respectively, by abstracting over
the sample expressions for (listof lon)s of length 1 and of length greater
than 1.

26.3.6 Termination Argument

Assume that the function merge-neighs terminates and works. The value
returned by merge-neighs is always shorter than a-lolon because neighboring lons are merged. This means that merge-sort-helper is always called
with a shorter (listof lon). Observe that this shorter (listof lon) is
never empty because merging neighbors in a (listof lon) of length greater
than 1 never produces an empty (listof lon). Given that the argument to
merge-sort-helper is always shorter and never length 0 we may conclude
that eventually merge-sort-helper is given a (listof lon) of length 1 and
the function halts.

Before running the tests the function merge-neighs must be designed and
implemented.

26.4 The `merge-neighs` Function

26.4.1 Problem Analysis

In order to merge two neighboring `lon`s the given (`listof lon`) must be of at least length 2. If the given (`listof lon`) is of length 0 or 1, then there are no `lon`s to merge and the answer is the given (`listof lon`).

What needs to be done if the given (`listof lon`) has length 2 or greater? The first two `lon`s need to be merged and the neighbors in the (`listof lon`) remaining after removing the first two must be merged. This may be done recursively. Observe that the input to the recursive call is not part of the structure of the given list. Therefore, this is a generative recursive algorithm.

26.4.2 Sample Expressions and Differences

There are two (`listof lon`) subtypes that must be distinguished: those of length less than 2 and those of a greater length. Independently reason about each subtype. According to the design idea, when the given (`listof lon`) has a length less than 2 the given (`listof lon`) is returned. Sample expressions for this case may be written as follows:

```
;; Sample expressions for merge-neighs
(define MN-LOLON1-VAL LOLON1)
(define MN-LOLON2-VAL LOLON2)
```

Observe that LOLON1 and LOLON2 both have a length 1, which is less than 2. The only difference between these sample expressions is the (`listof lon`) processed.

When the given (`listof lon`) has a length greater than or equal to 2, the first two `lon`s are merged. A new problem instance is locally defined and created by removing the first two elements of the given (`listof lon`). Assuming this function is named `merge-neighs`, the new problem instance is processed recursively by it. Sample expressions may be written as follows:

```
(define MN-LOLON3-VAL
          (local [(define NEW-LOLON (rest (rest LOLON3)))]
            (cons (merge (first LOLON3) (second LOLON3))
                  (merge-neighs NEW-LOLON))))
(define MN-LOLON4-VAL
          (local [(define NEW-LOLON (rest (rest LOLON4)))]
            (cons (merge (first LOLON4) (second LOLON4))
                  (merge-neighs NEW-LOLON))))
```

Observe that the new problem instance is locally defined as suggested by template for functions using generative recursion. The result of merging the first

two lons is added to the front of the (listof lon) obtained from processing the new problem instance. A new auxiliary function to merge two lons
is needed because this is a new problem that needs to be solved. The only
difference between these sample expressions is the (listof lon) processed.

There is a single difference among both sets of sample expressions: the
(listof lon) processed. This informs us that the function only needs one
parameter. We name this difference a-lolon.

26.4.3 Signature, Statements, and Function Header

The signature and purpose statements are:

```
;; (listof lon) → (listof lon)
;; Purpose: Merge every two adjacent lons in nondecreasing
;;          order
```

Observe that the signature informs the reader that from the given (listof
lon) a new (possibly different) (listof lon) is computed. The purpose
statement clearly indicates the goal of the function.

The how statement needs to, once again, outline how the problem is solved.
This may be done as follows:

```
;; How: If the given (listof lon) has a length less
;;      than 2 there are no lons to merge and the
;;      answer is the given (listof lon). Otherwise,
;;      the merging of the first two lons is added
;;      to the front of the result of processing
;;      all the remaining lons after the first two.
;; Assumption: Nested lons are in nondecreasing order
```

Observe that an assumption statement is needed. Any two lon that are
merged must be in nondecreasing order. Otherwise, the result of the merge
will not be in nondecreasing order.

The function header uses a descriptive function name and the name of the
only difference among the sample expressions:

```
(define (merge-neighs a-lolon)
```

26.4.4 Tests

The tests using sample computations use the sample (listof lon) and the
values of the sample expressions. These may be written as follows:

```
;; Tests using sample computations for merge-neighs
(check-expect (merge-neighs LOLON1) MN-LOLON1-VAL)
(check-expect (merge-neighs LOLON2) MN-LOLON2-VAL)
```

```
(check-expect (merge-neighs LOLON3) MN-LOLON3-VAL)
(check-expect (merge-neighs LOLON4) MN-LOLON4-VAL)
```

As usual, these tests inform any reader that the function correctly computes the values of the sample expressions used to define it.

The tests using sample values use concrete values to illustrate how the function works. These tests may be written as follows:

```
;; Tests using sample values for merge-neighs
(check-expect (merge-neighs '((5 8) (7 9) (-3)))
              '((5 7 8 9) (-3)))
(check-expect (merge-neighs '((2) (-9) (-3) (8 10)))
              '((-9 2) (-3 8 10)))
```

These tests illustrate that the function works for concrete (listof lon)s of odd and even lengths. They also illustrate that the function works for concrete (listof lon)s that have positive and negative numbers. Finally, the reader of the code may observe that all the elements of the concrete (listof lon)s are sorted in nondecreasing order.

26.4.5 Function Body

The function body is obtained from abstracting over the sample expressions. An if-expression is used to distinguish between a (listof lon) that has a length less than 2 and a (listof lon) that has a length greater or equal to 2. The function body is:

```
(if (< (length a-lolon) 2)
    a-lolon
    (local [(define NEW-LOLON (rest (rest a-lolon)))]
      (cons (merge (first a-lolon) (second a-lolon))
            (merge-neighs NEW-LOLON))))
```

The then-expression is obtained from abstracting over the first two sample expressions. The else-expression is obtained from abstracting over the second two sample expressions.

26.4.6 Termination Argument

The function halts if the given (listof lon) has a length less than 2. When given a (listof lon) of greater length, the first two elements are removed from it to make a recursive call. This means that the given (listof lon) eventually becomes empty if its length is even and eventually becomes a list of length 1 if its length is odd. In both cases the function terminates because the length is less than 2.

This completes the design of `merge-neighs`. Before running the tests the auxiliary function `merge` must be designed and implemented.

26.5 The `merge` Function

26.5.1 Problem Analysis

This function needs to create a sorted `lon` from two given `lons` in nondecreasing order. Given that this function receives as input at least two pieces of complex input, it is necessary to determine what the relationship is between the two inputs. Ask yourself if one input dominates the other. We can observe that this is not the case because the next number of the result may come from either input.

Ask yourself if both inputs must be processed simultaneously. This is also not the case because to build the result several numbers may be taken from one list before a number is taken from the other list.

This means that we must outline the relationship between the two given `lon`. We can observe that if the first `lon` is empty then the answer is the second `lon` because the first `lon` has no more numbers to be added to the result. Similarly, if the second `lon` is empty the answer is the first `lon`. If both `lons` are not empty then their first elements are compared. If the first element of the first `lon` is less than or equal to the first element of the second `lon`, then the first element of the first `lon` is added to the result of processing the rest of the first `lon` and the second `lon`. Otherwise, the first element of the second `lon` is added to the result of processing the first `lon` and the rest of the second `lon`.

Note that the algorithm outlined uses structural recursion. This means that a how statement and a termination argument are not required. You may, of course, include one if you like.

To make writing tests easier the following `lons` are defined:

```
(define SL1 '())
(define SL2 '(-98 -76 -8 -1))
(define SL3 '(-87 -28 -6 89))
(define SL4 '(6 7 31 87))
```

Observe that there are sample `lons` of both varieties. In addition, the nonempty `lons` are of varying lengths and contain different combinations of positive and negative numbers.

26.5.2 Sample Expressions and Differences

Problem analysis revealed that there are four conditions that must be detected:

1. The first lon is empty.
2. The second lon is empty.
3. The first element of the first lon is less than or equal to the first element of the second lon.
4. The first element of the second lon is less than the first element of the first lon.

This means that we need sample expressions for each of the above four conditions. Independently reason about each one. When one of the given lons is empty, the result is the other lon given as input. These sample expressions may be written as follows:

```
;; Sample expressions for merge
(define M-SL1-SL2-VAL SL2)
(define M-SL1-SL3-VAL SL3)
(define M-SL2-SL1-VAL SL2)
(define M-SL3-SL1-VAL SL3)
```

The first two illustrate the result when the first given lon is empty. The second two illustrate the result when the second given lon is empty.

The sample expressions for the third condition above must illustrate that the first element of the first lon is added to the result of processing the rest of the first lon and the second lon. Assuming that this function is named merge, the sample expressions may be written as follows:

```
(define M-SL2-SL3-VAL (cons (first SL2)
                           (merge (rest SL2) SL3)))
(define M-SL3-SL4-VAL (cons (first SL3)
                           (merge (rest SL3) SL4)))
```

The sample expressions for the fourth condition above must illustrate that the first element of the second lon is added to the result of processing the rest of the second lon and the first lon. The sample expressions may be written as follows:

```
(define M-SL4-SL3-VAL (cons (first SL3)
                           (merge SL4 (rest SL3))))
(define M-SL3-SL2-VAL (cons (first SL2)
                           (merge SL3 (rest SL2))))
```

The only differences among all four sets of sample expressions are the two lons processed. The function, therefore, only needs two parameters. The differences are named l1 and l2.

26.5.3 Signature, Statements, and Function Header

The signature, purpose and assumption statements, and the function header
are:

```
;; lon lon → lon
;; Purpose: Merge the given lons in nondecreasing order
;; Assumption: Given lons are in nondecreasing order
(define (merge l1 l2)
```

The assumption statement makes explicit to the user that the given lon must
be in nondecreasing order.

26.5.4 Tests

There must be tests for all four conditions discovered during problem analysis. Using the values of all the sample expressions in the tests using sample
computations guarantees that this is the case. These tests are written as
follows:

```
;; Tests using sample computations for merge
(check-expect (merge SL1 SL2) M-SL1-SL2-VAL)
(check-expect (merge SL1 SL3) M-SL1-SL3-VAL)
(check-expect (merge SL2 SL1) M-SL2-SL1-VAL)
(check-expect (merge SL3 SL1) M-SL3-SL1-VAL)
(check-expect (merge SL2 SL3) M-SL2-SL3-VAL)
(check-expect (merge SL3 SL4) M-SL3-SL4-VAL)
(check-expect (merge SL4 SL3) M-SL4-SL3-VAL)
(check-expect (merge SL3 SL2) M-SL3-SL2-VAL)
```

Observe that there are two tests for every condition identified during problem
analysis.

The tests using sample values may explicitly illustrate that the function
works for all four conditions. These may be written as follows:

```
;; Tests using sample values for merge
(check-expect (merge '() '()) '())
(check-expect (merge '() '(7 8 9)) '(7 8 9))
(check-expect (merge '(78 98) '()) '(78 98))
(check-expect (merge '(1 2 3) '(4 5 6)) '(1 2 3 4 5 6))
(check-expect (merge '(0 88) '(-5 8 17)) '(-5 0 8 17 88))
```

Observe that one of the tests illustrates what happens when both given lons
are empty. There is at least one test for each of the four conditions.

26.5.5 Function Body

The function body is written using a cond-expression with four stanzas. Each stanza corresponds to one of the conditions identified during problem analysis. The consequence expression for each stanza is obtained by abstracting over the corresponding sample expressions. This process yields:

```
(cond [(empty? l1) l2]
      [(empty? l2) l1]
      [(<= (first l1) (first l2))
       (cons (first l1) (merge (rest l1) l2))]
      [else (cons (first l2) (merge l1 (rest l2)))])
```

The consequence expression in the first stanza is obtained from abstracting over the first two sample expressions. The consequence expression in the second stanza is obtained from abstracting over the second two sample expressions. The consequence expression in the third stanza is obtained from abstracting over the fifth and sixth sample expressions. Finally, the consequence expression in the else stanza is obtained from abstracting over the last two sample expressions.

This completes the design of merge sorting. Run the tests and make sure they all pass. Once you are satisfied that all the functions work, encapsulate the auxiliary functions. Figure 31 outlines one possible encapsulation. Observe that the only missing elements are the tests for the encapsulated functions.

26.6 Performance

Does merge-sorting perform better than quick- and insertion-sorting? The CPU time for merge-sorting is added in the following table:

	LON1	LON2	LON3	LON4	LON5	LON6
Insertion	0	0	1953	31	15	0
Quick	0	0	1172	0	15	485
Merge	0	0	15	0	0	15

The data suggests two conclusions. The first is that merge sorting performs better than quick sorting on a list that is sorted (i.e., LON6) and on a list that is in reverse sorted order (i.e., LON3). The second is that on other types of lists quick sorting is faster or just as good as merge sorting.

Fig. 31 Outline of encapsulated merge sorting

```
;; lon → lon      Purpose: Sort given lon in nondecreasing order
(define (merge-sorting a-lon)
  (local [;; lon lon → lon                    Purpose: ...
          ;; Assumption: ...
          (define (merge l1 l2) ...)

          ;; (listof lon) → (listof lon)      Purpose: ...
          ;; How: ...
          ;; Assumption: ...
          (define (merge-neighs a-lolon) ...)

          ;; (listof lon) → (listof lon)      Purpose: ...
          ;; How: ...
          ;; Assumption: ...
          (define (merge-sort-helper a-lolon) ...)]
    (if (empty? a-lon)
        '()
        (first (merge-sort-helper (map (λ (n) (list n)) a-lon))))))

;; Sample expressions for merge-sorting
(define MS-LON0-VAL '())
(define MS-LON1-VAL (first (merge-sort-helper
                             (map (λ (n) (list n)) LON1))))
(define MS-LON2-VAL (first (merge-sort-helper
                             (map (λ (n) (list n)) LON2))))
(define MS-LON3-VAL (first (merge-sort-helper
                             (map (λ (n) (list n)) LON3))))

;; Tests using sample values for merge-sorting
(check-expect (merge-sorting LON0) MS-LON0-VAL)
(check-expect (merge-sorting LON1) MS-LON1-VAL)
(check-expect (merge-sorting LON2) MS-LON2-VAL)
(check-expect (merge-sorting LON3) MS-LON3-VAL)

;; Tests using sample values for merge-sorting
(check-satisfied (merge-sorting LON4) is-sorted?)
(check-satisfied (merge-sorting LON5) is-sorted?)
(check-expect    (merge-sorting LON6) LON6)
(check-expect    (merge-sorting '(74 83 -72 2)) '(-72 2 74 83))
```

26.7 Complexity Analysis

To explain the timing data observed we need to perform complexity analysis. For the call to sort n steps are taken to convert the given lon into a (listof lon).

Now let us analyze the sorting process when the given list is not empty. The first time sort is called a (listof lon) of length n is reduced to a (listof lon) of length $\frac{n}{2}$. To do so, the list is traversed in $\frac{n}{2}$ steps (two lons are removed at each step in the worst case). For each step two comparisons are needed to merge two neighboring lists of length 1. This means that the number of steps needed is proportional to $\frac{n}{2} * 2 = n$. The second time sort is called a list of length $\frac{n}{2}$ is reduced to a list of length $\frac{n}{4}$. To do so, the list is traversed in $\frac{n}{4}$ steps. For each step in the worst case four comparisons are needed to merge two neighboring lists of length 2. This occurs when list elements are taken one at a time from alternating lists. This means that the number of steps needed is proportional to $\frac{n}{4} * 4 = n$. The third time sort is called a list of length $\frac{n}{4}$ is reduced to a list of length $\frac{n}{8}$. To do so, the list is traversed in $\frac{n}{8}$ steps. In the worst case for each step eight comparisons are needed to merge two neighboring lists of length 4. This means that the number of steps needed is proportional to $\frac{n}{8} * 8 = n$. There is a clear pattern. Every time sort is called n comparisons are needed to reduce the length of the list in half.

How many times sort is called? The number of calls is proportional to the number of times n can be divided by 2 before becoming 1, which is $O(\lg(n))$. This is similar to the analysis of quick-sorting. The only difference is that for quick-sorting the length of the list had to reach 0 instead of 1.

We may therefore conclude that the abstract running time for merge-sorting is $O(n * \lg(n))$. Now we truly understand why merge sorting performs better than quick sorting when the given list is sorted or is reversed sorted order: $O(n * \lg(n))$ grows much slower than $O(n^2)$ as n gets larger. We also understand why the performance between the two is so close otherwise: both are $O(n * \lg(n))$.

---

4 The implementation of merge-sorting above starts by converting a given lon into a list of lons (or *runs*) of length 1. Clearly, any run of length 1 is sorted and may be merged with another run of length 1. It is not unreasonable, however, for a given lon to have runs of length greater than 1. This suggests that a given lon may be initially divided into runs with lengths greater than or equal to 1. For example, '(7 8 9 8 7 67 78 89 90 -2 1) may initially be converted to:

'((7 8 9) (8) (7 67 78 89 90) (-2 1))

Refactor merge-sorting to take advantage of this observation. Does this refined version run faster? When does it run much faster? Carefully justify your answers.

5 A `lon` of length `n` may be sorted by *bubbling* its largest number to the end of the list `n-1` times. A recursive call is always made with the result of bubbling the largest number to the end of the given list. For example, `'(8 56 32 25)` may be sorted in three bubbling steps as follows:

$$\text{'(56 32 25 8)} \rightarrow \text{'(32 25 \ 8 56)}$$
$$\rightarrow \text{'(25 \ 8 32 56)}$$
$$\rightarrow \text{'(8 25 32 56)}$$

Bubbling compares the first two elements. If they are in order the first element is added to the result of bubbling the rest of the list. Otherwise, the second element is added to the result of bubbling the list that contains the first element and the elements after the second one. This sorting algorithm is known as *bubble sorting*.

Design and implement bubble sorting. Compare its runtime performance and abstract running time with quick, merge, and insertion sorting.

27 What Have We Learned in This Chapter?

The important lessons of this chapter are summarized as follows:

- A sorting algorithm rearranges a set of elements into nondecreasing or nonincreasing order.
- The result of sorting must be monotonic and a permutation of the input.
- Sorting algorithms may be used on any type of data that is ordinal.
- A set to sort may be represented using a list.
- Randomness may be used to avoid bias when generating data to sort.
- Insertion sorting's abstract running time is $O(n^2)$.
- The weakness of insertion sorting stems from always inserting into a sorted list.
- Quick sorting creates a sorted set of elements by sorting the elements less than or equal to the pivot, sorting the elements greater than the pivot, and placing the pivot between these two sorted sets.
- Quick sorting is a divide-and-conquer algorithm that uses generative recursion.
- The best-case abstract running time for quick sorting is $O(n * \lg(n))$.
- The worst-case abstract running time for quick sorting is $O(n^2)$.
- Merge sorting repeatedly merges the sorted elements of a (`listof lon`) until it becomes of length 1.
- Merge sorting is an algorithm that uses generative recursion.
- The abstract running time for merge sorting is $O(n * \lg(n))$.

Chapter 6
Searching

A search problem attempts to find a value x with property P in a set S. If there is an x∈S that satisfies P, then the algorithm returns x or #true to indicate that an element that satisfies P exists in S. Otherwise, the algorithm returns #false or throws an error if appropriate.

Searching is extensively studied because it is a common operation in many subfields of human endeavors such as finding a document in the Internet, finding information in a database, finding the fastest driving route to a destination, or in artificial intelligence. For this reason there is extensive interest in making searching as fast as possible. In fact, searching is fundamental to implementing player help in the N-puzzle game. At the heart of making a good move on behalf of the player is finding a solution to the given board. Ideally, we would like to find the shortest solution to the puzzle (i.e., requiring the smallest number of moves).

To illustrate the design and implementation of different sorting algorithms, we first start with searching a (listof number). Later we use searching a tree of numbers to motivate more searching algorithms. If you do not know what a tree of numbers is, that is fine. We define it later. You are probably imagining that a tree must be similar to a binary tree and your instincts are correct. A binary tree is a tree subtype.

28 Linear Searching

Searching a (listof number) suggests using structural recursion. In all likelihood you have already designed such a function when you first studied how to solve problems involving lists. In fact, you have probably designed many functions to search different types of lists. To refresh your memory, we briefly outline the design of finding an index for an occurrence of a given number in a given (listof number). To make writing tests easier the following (listof number) instances are defined:

© The Author(s), under exclusive license to Springer Nature Switzerland AG 2022   131
M. T. Morazán, *Animated Program Design*, Texts in Computer Science,
https://doi.org/10.1007/978-3-031-04317-8_6

```
(define L0 '())
(define L1 '(88 54 4 7 87 98 -7 0 -1))
(define L2 '(9 8 7 6 5  4  3  2 1  0 -1 -2))
(define L3 (build-list 1000000 (λ (i) (random 1000000))))
(define L4 (build-list 1000000 (λ (i) i)))
```

Observe that there are instances for both (listof number) subtypes. In addition, there is a list of randomly generated numbers, L3, to protect us against any bias we may have when writing (listof number) instances, and there is, L4, a sorted (listof number). L3 and L4 are also long lists in order to force our functions to do a lot of processing.

28.1 Problem Analysis

The problem statement does not specify which index of an occurrence of a given number ought to be returned. We arbitrarily return the smallest such index. We reason about the (listof number) subtypes. If the given list is empty then the given number is not in the list. This means we are unable to return an index. This informs us that either an error may be thrown (perhaps, too drastic) or another type of value is returned (i.e., not an index into the list). We explore a design that returns a different type of value. A result is defined as follows:

```
;; A result, res, is either:
;;  1. natnum
;;  2. #false
```

The idea is that #false is returned when the given number is not in the list. This means that #false is returned when the list is empty. What if the given list is not empty? In this case the given list's first number must be compared with the given number. If they are equal then 0 is returned because this is the index of the first number. Otherwise, the rest of the list is searched for the given number. If this search returns #false then the given number is not in the given list and the answer is #false. If this search of the rest of the list returns a number, then 1 is added to it because it is an index into a list whose length is shorter by 1.

28.2 Sample Expressions and Differences

To write the sample expressions think independently about each of the four conditions identified above. Searching for any number, say 25, in the empty list ought to return #false. We may write a sample expression for this case as follows:

```
;; Sample expressions for linear-search
(define LS-L0-VAL  #false)
```

The second condition checks if the list's first number is equal to a given number. If so, the returned index is 0. For example, this occurs when searching for 88 in L1 and 9 in L2. We may write sample expressions for these as follows:

```
(define LS-L1-VAL1 0)
(define LS-L2-VAL1 0)
```

For the next two conditions the rest of the list must be searched. We may define a local variable for the result of this search and then test its value to determine which condition is being faced. The first of these conditions is when the given number is not found. This occurs, for example, when searching for −9 in L1 and 54 in L2. For these examples the following sample expressions are written:

```
(define LS-L1-VAL2
       (local
        [(define result-of-rest (linear-search -9 (rest L1)))]
        (if (false? result-of-rest)
            #false
            (add1 result-of-rest))))
(define LS-L2-VAL2
       (local
        [(define result-of-rest (linear-search 54 (rest L2)))]
        (if (false? result-of-rest)
            #false
            (add1 result-of-rest))))
```

Finally, the last condition is when the given number is found. This happens, for example, when searching for −7 in L1 and 2 in L2. In this case, 1 must be added to the index returned by searching the rest of the list. For these examples the following sample expressions are written:

```
(define LS-L1-VAL3
       (local
          [(define result-of-rest
                   (linear-search -7 (rest L1)))]
         (if (false? result-of-rest)
             #false
             (add1 result-of-rest))))
(define LS-L2-VAL3
       (local
          [(define result-of-rest
                   (linear-search  2 (rest L2)))]
         (if (false? result-of-rest)
             #false
             (add1 result-of-rest))))
```

We can observe that in the sample expressions for each condition, there are two differences: the number searched for and the list searched. This means that our function to perform linear searching requires two parameters. We name these differences, respectively, `a-num` and `a-lon`.

28.3 Signature, Purpose, and Function Header

From the previous step we know that there are two parameters: the first is a number and the second is a `lon`. The purpose statement briefly summarizes the goal of the function: in this case to return the index of the first occurrence of the given number or `#false`, that is, to return a `res` instance. Finally, we choose a descriptive function name, `linear-search`, and use the names of the differences in the sample expressions as the parameters in the function header. The result of these steps is:

```
;; number lon → res
;; Purpose: Return the index of the first occurrence of
;;          the given number if it is a member of the
;;          given list. Otherwise, return #false
(define (linear-search a-num a-lon)
```

28.4 Tests

The tests using sample computations illustrate that the function computes the same values obtained from evaluating the sample expressions. They are written as follows:

```
;; Tests using sample computations for linear-search
(check-expect (linear-search 25 L0) LS-L0-VAL)
(check-expect (linear-search 88 L1) LS-L1-VAL1)
(check-expect (linear-search  9 L2) LS-L2-VAL1)
(check-expect (linear-search -9 L1) LS-L1-VAL2)
(check-expect (linear-search 54 L2) LS-L2-VAL2)
(check-expect (linear-search -7 L1) LS-L1-VAL3)
(check-expect (linear-search  2 L2) LS-L2-VAL3)
```

Observe that the same concrete values used in a given sample expression are used to call the function in the corresponding test.

For the tests using sample values we may use `check-satisfied` in conjunction with, L3, the list of randomly generated numbers. A predicate that tests the properties of the `res` returned is needed. This predicate may check that the returned `res` is either `#false` or an index into L3 for the number searched for. In addition, we may write tests using short concrete list and our

long sorted list illustrating both possible outcomes. The tests using sample
values are:

```
;; Tests using sample values for linear-search
(check-satisfied
 (linear-search 100 L3)
 (λ (a-res) (or (false? a-res)
                (= (list-ref L3 a-res) 100))))
(check-expect (linear-search 2 '(1 2 3)) 1)
(check-expect (linear-search 5 '(1 2 3)) #false)
(check-expect (linear-search 2000000 L4) #false)
(check-expect (linear-search 998999  L4) 998999)
```

28.5 Function Body

The function's body uses a cond-expression to distinguish among the four
cases identified by the problem analysis above. The consequence expression
for each stanza is obtained by abstracting over the sample expressions for
each case. The result for this step of the design recipe is:

```
(cond [(empty? a-lon) #false]
      [(= a-num (first a-lon)) 0]
      [else
       (local
         [(define result-of-rest
                  (linear-search a-num (rest a-lon)))]
         (if (false? result-of-rest)
             #false
             (add1 result-of-rest)))])
```

28.6 Performance and Complexity

We have implemented a function to search a lon. How well do you think it
performs? We can measure the CPU running time by running the following
experiments:

```
(define LSL0 (time (linear-search 83333 L0)))
(define LSL1 (time (linear-search 0 L1)))
(define LSL2 (time (linear-search 8 L2)))
(define LSL3 (time (linear-search (first L3) L3)))
(define LSL4 (time (linear-search 2000000 L4)))
```

The first three experiments are on short lists and it is expected for the function to perform well. The fourth experiment measures the best-case perfor-

mance when the number searched for is the first number in the list. In this case the list is not traversed beyond the first number. The fifth experiment measures the worst-case performance when the number searched for is not in the list. In this case the entire list must be searched. The following table displays a sampling of CPU running times in milliseconds (after subtracting garbage collection time):

	L0	L1	L2	L3	L4
linear-search	0	0	0	0	1359

Remember that measured CPU running times may vary every time you run the experiments and may vary when using different computers. When you run the experiments on your computer, you may get different CPU times. On short lists the function performs well as expected. It also performs well in its best-case scenario. In the worst-case scenario we see a significant rise in actual running time.

The observed performance may be explained by determining the abstract running time. In the best case `linear-search` is called once making the abstract running time $O(k)$, where k is a constant. Observe that the size of the list is irrelevant. In the worst case `linear-search` must compare the given number with every element in the list. This means that `linear-search` is called n+1 times, where n is the number of elements in the list. In the worst case, therefore, `linear-search` is $O(n)$. Observe that the worst-case abstract running time is proportional to a linear polynomial (n has degree 1). This is why it is called linear search.

29 Binary Search

Chapter 5 suggests that the performance of searching may be improved by first sorting. We turn our focus to exploring this idea. Intuitively, this is likely to make sense to you. For example, consider looking for a word in a dictionary. Do you start the search with the first word starting with "a" and check every word until you find the word or reach the last word starting with "z"? You probably do not. Instead, you probably open the dictionary in the middle and decide whether or not the word you are searching for is on the opened page. If so, you look at its definition. If not, you decide to search for the word in either the first or second half. The process is repeated with the chosen half until the word is found or the chosen half is empty.

Observe that you never search both halves for the word. This means that at each step half of the remaining dictionary is eliminated from the search. Compare this with a linear search that eliminates a single word at each step. This suggests that if a set is sorted, then it can be divided into two subsets:

one that does not need to be searched and one that needs to be searched. The search continues until the desired element is found or the subset that needs to be searched is empty (indicating that the element searched for is not in the set). Given that the sorted set is always divided into two to continue the search, this algorithm is known as `binary search`. Let us explore this idea in the context of finding an index for an instance of a given number in a given list of numbers.

29.1 The `binary-search` Function

The goal is to search a sorted `lon` for an index that stores a given number. To implement binary search the ability to split the given list into its two halves is necessary. How can this be done? One approach is to extract the elements in the first half and extract the elements in the second half. Observe that such an approach makes the search $O(n)$ because the entire list must be traversed—precisely what we wish to avoid!

If you think carefully about searching a dictionary, all the elements in the two halves are never extracted. Instead, a decision is made as to which half to explore. If the first half is chosen, the words from the beginning of the dictionary to the word before the middle word are searched. If the second half is chosen, the words starting with the word after the middle word to the last word in the dictionary are searched.

29.1.1 Problem Analysis

Observe that if the words in the dictionary were numbered the middle word's index is computable. If the index of the first word is 0 and the index of the last word is `n-1`, then the index of the middle word is given by:

$$\text{mid-index} = \frac{0 + (n-1)}{2}$$

This suggests that if the elements of a sorted set are numbered, then searching may be done by processing an interval. The interval for the first half is `[0..(mid-index - 1)]` and the interval for the second half is `[(mid-index + 1)..(n - 1)]`.

The elements of a sorted `lon` are numbered by the valid indices into the list. If the list is of length `n`, then the interval of valid indices is `[0..(n - 1)]`. The `lon` defined by this interval must be searched for the given number. This means that the problem of searching a sorted `lon` can be cast as an interval-processing problem.

To facilitate the writing of sample expressions and tests, the following sorted `lon`s, based on the `lon`s used to design `linear-searching`, are defined:

```
(define L1S (sort L1 <))
(define L2S (sort L2 <))
(define L3S (sort L3 <))
```

29.1.2 Sample Expressions and Differences

Processing a lon by processing an interval means that an auxiliary function
to process an interval is needed. This function's job is to call the interval-
processing function with the correct interval. It does not process the given
lon, and, therefore, the same thing must be done regardless of the given lon.

The auxiliary function needs the number searched for, the valid indices
interval, and the lon. If this auxiliary function is named bin-search, sample
expressions may be written as follows:

```
;; Sample expressions for binary-search
(define BS-L0-VAL  (bin-search 25 0 (sub1 (length L0))  L0))
(define BS-L1-VAL1 (bin-search 88 0 (sub1 (length L1S)) L1S))
(define BS-L2-VAL1 (bin-search  9 0 (sub1 (length L2S)) L2S))
(define BS-L1-VAL2 (bin-search -9 0 (sub1 (length L1S)) L1S))
(define BS-L2-VAL2 (bin-search 54 0 (sub1 (length L2S)) L2S))
(define BS-L1-VAL3 (bin-search -7 0 (sub1 (length L1S)) L1S))
(define BS-L2-VAL3 (bin-search  2 0 (sub1 (length L2S)) L2S))
```

There are two differences among the sample expressions: the number
searched for and the sorted list. This means that this function only needs
two parameters. We name the differences a-num and a-lon.

29.1.3 Signature, Statements, and Function Header

The differences in the sample expressions tell us that the inputs are a number
and a list of numbers. The returned value is a res. Observe that this means
that the signature is the same as linear-search. This makes sense because
this function is designed to solve the same problem. Therefore, the purpose
statement is the same. This function, however, assumes that the given lon
is sorted in nondecreasing order. The function header uses a function name
that suggests the purpose of the function and the parameters are the names
chosen for the differences in the sample expressions. The result of the next
steps of the design recipe is:

```
;; number lon → res
;; Purpose: Return the index of the given number if it
;;          is a member of the given list. Otherwise,
;;          return #false
;; Assumption: The given lon is sorted in nondecreasing
;;             order
(define (binary-search a-num a-lon)
```

A how statement is not required because the problem analysis does not suggest this function uses generative recursion.

29.1.4 Tests

The tests using sample computations are written with the same numbers to search for as the corresponding tests for linear-search. These tests, however, are written with the sorted version of the lists used for linear-search. The tests that illustrate that the function computes the values of the sample expressions are:

```
;; Tests using sample computations for binary-search
(check-expect (binary-search 25 L0)  BS-L0-VAL)
(check-expect (binary-search 88 L1S) BS-L1-VAL1)
(check-expect (binary-search  9 L2S) BS-L2-VAL1)
(check-expect (binary-search -9 L1S) BS-L1-VAL2)
(check-expect (binary-search 54 L2S) BS-L2-VAL2)
(check-expect (binary-search -7 L1S) BS-L1-VAL3)
(check-expect (binary-search  2 L2S) BS-L2-VAL3)
```

The tests using sample computations are also essentially the same as those used for linear-search. To test L3 (the randomly generated lon), however, its sorted version is used. The tests are:

```
;; Tests using sample values for binary-search
(check-satisfied
 (binary-search 100 L3S)
 (λ (a-res) (or (false? a-res)
               (= (list-ref L3 a-res) 100))))
(check-expect (binary-search 2 '(1 2 3)) 1)
(check-expect (binary-search 5 '(1 2 3)) #false)
(check-expect (binary-search 2000000 L4) #false)
(check-expect (binary-search 998999  L4) 998999)
```

29.1.5 Function Body

The function body is obtained by abstracting over the sample expressions. The body of the function is:

```
(bin-search a-num 0 (sub1 (length a-lon)) a-lon)
```

Observe that the interval given to bin-search only contains valid indices into a-lon.

A termination argument is not required because this function does not use generative recursion. The only design recipe step left is running the tests

and, if necessary, debugging. Running the tests must wait until `bin-search`
is designed and implemented.

29.2 The `bin-search` Function

29.2.1 Problem Analysis

This function searches a given list by traversing a given interval. The interval
is the range of indices into the list that may still contain an instance of the
number searched for. Independently reason about each interval subtype. If
the interval is empty then the number is not in the list and the answer is
`#false`.

   If the interval is not empty, then the list element corresponding to the
middle index in the given interval is compared with the number searched for.
If they are equal the middle index is returned as the answer. If they are not
equal then a decision must be made as to which new interval to search. If
the number searched for is less than the number at the middle index, then
the first half of the interval must be searched. If the number searched for is
greater than the number at the middle index, then the second half of the
interval must be searched. Observe that a new instance of the problem, an
interval that is not a substructure of the given interval, is created for the
half to be searched. Therefore, the proposed algorithm is based on generative
recursion.

29.2.2 Sample Expressions and Differences

Sample expressions need to be written for the four conditions identified during
problem analysis:

1. The interval is empty.
2. The middle index list element equals the given number.
3. The middle index list element is greater than the given number.
4. The middle index list element is less than the given number.

Independently reason about each condition. If the given interval is empty,
then the answer is always `#false`. Sample expressions for when the given
interval is empty are:

```
;; Sample expressions for bin-search
(define BINS-LO-VAL1  #false)
(define BINS-L3S-VAL1 #false)
```

   If the given interval is not empty, then the middle index must be computed.
This value may be locally defined. When the middle index element is equal

to the given number, the middle index is returned. Sample expressions for searching L1S for 7 and for 3 in the interval [3..7] in L2S may be written as follows:

```
(define BINS-L1S-VAL1
        (local [(define mid-index (quotient (+ 0  8) 2))]
          mid-index))
(define BINS-L2S-VAL1
        (local [(define mid-index (quotient (+ 3 7) 2))]
          mid-index))
```

When the middle index element is greater than the given number, the first half of the interval must be searched. The first half on the interval is from its low end to the middle index minus 1. Sample expressions to search L1S for 0 and L2S for −6 may be written as follows:

```
(define BINS-L1S-VAL2
        (local [(define mid-index (quotient (+ 0 8) 2))]
          (bin-search  0 0 (sub1 mid-index) L1S)))
(define BINS-L2S-VAL2
        (local [(define mid-index (quotient (+ 0 11) 2))]
          (bin-search -6 0 (sub1 mid-index) L2S)))
```

When the middle index element is less than the given number, the second half of the interval must be searched. The second half on the interval is from the middle index plus 1 to its high end. Sample expressions to search L1S for 90 and L2S for 8 may be written as follows:

```
(define BINS-L1S-VAL3
        (local [(define mid-index (quotient (+ 0 8) 2))]
          (bin-search  90 (add1 mid-index)  8 L1S)))
(define BINS-L2S-VAL3
        (local [(define mid-index (quotient (+ 0 11) 2))]
          (bin-search  8 (add1 mid-index) 11 L2S)))
```

There are two differences in the sample expressions when the middle index list element equals the given number: the given interval's low and high ends. We name these differences low and high.

There are four differences among the sample expressions when the middle index list element is not equal to the given number: the number searched for, the interval's low and high ends, and the list to search. We name the number and list differences, respectively, a-num and a-lon. In total, the function needs four parameters because there is a total of four differences among the sample expressions.

29.2.3 Signature, Statements, and Function Header

The signature for this function specifies the type of each of the differences
among the sample expressions. These are a number, an interval with a low
end greater than or equal to 0 and with a high end greater than or equal to -1,
and a lon. The function returns a res just as expected by binary-search.
The purpose is to return an index for the given number in the given list or
return #false. The how statement briefly summarizes the design obtained
from problem analysis. Finally, there are two assumptions. First, the given list
is sorted in nondecreasing order. Second, all the indices in the given interval
are valid for the given list. The result of these design recipe steps is:

```
;; number [int>=0..int>=-1] lon → res
;; Purpose: Return an index for the given number if it
;;          is a member of the given list. Otherwise,
;;          return #false.
;; How: If the given interval is empty the given number
;;   is not in the given list and return #false. Otherwise,
;;   compute the middle index and return it if the given
;;   list has the given number at that index. If not
;;   search either the first or the second half of the
;;   given interval.
;; Assumption: The given lon is sorted in nondecreasing
;;   order and the given interval only contains valid
;;   indices into the given lon.
(define (bin-search a-num low high a-lon)
```

29.2.4 Tests

The tests using sample computations must illustrate that the function computes the same value as the evaluation of the sample expressions. For each
sample expression write a test. Make sure that the arguments provided to
the function are those used in the sample expressions. The tests using sample
computations are:

```
;; Tests using sample computations for bin-search
(check-expect (bin-search 65 0 -1 L0)  BINS-L0-VAL1)
(check-expect (bin-search -9 5  4 L3S) BINS-L3S-VAL1)
(check-expect (bin-search  7 0  8 L1S) BINS-L1S-VAL1)
(check-expect (bin-search  3 3  7 L2S) BINS-L2S-VAL1)
(check-expect (bin-search  0 0  8 L1S) BINS-L1S-VAL2)
(check-expect (bin-search -6 0 11 L2S) BINS-L2S-VAL2)
(check-expect (bin-search 90 0  8 L1S) BINS-L1S-VAL3)
(check-expect (bin-search  8 0 11 L2S) BINS-L2S-VAL3)
```

The tests using sample values use property-based testing with L3S. In addition, short lists are used to illustrate the function works properly with concrete values. The tests using sample values are:

```
;; Tests using sample values for bin-search
(check-satisfied
  (bin-search 100 0 (sub1 10000) L3S)
  (λ (a-res) (or (false? a-res)
                 (= (list-ref L3S a-res) 100))))
(check-expect (bin-search 2 0 2 '(1 2 3)) 1)
(check-expect (bin-search 5 0 5 '(1 2 3 4 6 7)) #false)
```

29.2.5 Function Body

An if-expression is used to distinguish between an empty and nonempty interval. The sample expressions for processing an empty interval tell us that the result is #false. The sample expressions for processing a nonempty interval tell us that the middle index must always be computed. This value may be locally defined (once) for all three conditions. The body of the local-expression is a conditional that distinguishes among the three conditions when the interval is not empty. The sample expressions for when the middle index element equals the given number inform us that the result is the middle index. Abstracting over the sample expressions for when the middle index element is greater than the given number informs us that the interval to recursively search is from low to one less than the middle index. Abstracting over the remaining sample expressions informs us that the interval to recursively search is from one more than the middle index to high. The body of the function is:

```
(if (< high low)
    #false
    (local [(define mid-index (quotient (+ low high) 2))]
      (cond
        [(= (list-ref a-lon mid-index) a-num) mid-index]
        [(> (list-ref a-lon mid-index) a-num)
         (bin-search a-num low (sub1 mid-index) a-lon)]
        [else
          (bin-search a-num (add1 mid-index) high a-lon)])))
```

Take a minute to appreciate the elegance of a well-designed solution. Most readers of the code are likely to understand the solution. Run the tests and make sure they all pass.

29.3 Termination Argument

The function halts when either the given interval is empty or when the middle index element is equal to the given number. Whenever `bin-search` is called, a new interval of half the size is generated and recursively processed. This means that with every recursive call the interval is getting smaller. Eventually either the middle index element is equal to the given number or the interval becomes empty and the function halts.

29.4 Performance and Complexity

To explore the performance of our binary search implementation, we can time its performance using the sorted sample `lon`s. For the sorted randomly generated list, L3S, the search is done for L3's first element. Recall that this is the best-case scenario for `linear-search`. For the sorted list, L4, the search is done for a number larger than any element in L4 (as done for `linear-search`). Recall that this is the worst-case scenario for `linear-search`. These experiments may be executed by making the following definitions:

```
(define BSL0 (time (binary-search 83333 L0)))
(define BSL1 (time (binary-search 0 L1S)))
(define BSL2 (time (binary-search 8 L2S)))
(define BSL3 (time (binary-search (first L3) L3S)))
(define BSL4 (time (binary-search 2000000 L4)))
```

Sample CPU times after subtracting, if any, garbage collection time are:

	L0	L1	L2	L3	L4
linear-search	0	0	0	0	1359
binary-search	0	0	0	31	218

Observe that for short lists (i.e., L0–L2) both programs perform equally well. The test that uses linear search's best-case scenario illustrates that linear search performs better than binary search. This is something you likely expected. It may be surprising to you, however, that linear search performs better by very little. Binary search proves to be very competitive. Searching for a number that is not in the given `lon`, on the other hand, illustrates that binary search is much faster than linear search. This suggests that our efforts to improve searching performance have been successful. Why is binary search so competitive when facing linear search's best-case scenario? Why is binary search so much better when facing linear search's worst-case scenario?

To explain these numbers let us explore the abstract running time for binary search. We look to establish the abstract running time of `bin-search` because it does all the work for `binary-search`. Recall that for `linear-search` the best running time is $O(k)$ and the worst-case running time is $O(n)$. What is the best running time for `binary-search`? It is when a recursive call is not made, that is, when the given interval is empty or the middle index element equals the given number. The number of operations in both cases is constant. In other words, they do not depend on, n, the size of the list. The best-case abstract running time for `bin-search`, therefore, is $O(k)$. This is the same as the best-case running time for `linear-search`. Why exactly is `linear-search` a little faster in the experiment using L3S? Observe that `linear-search` finds the number in L3 only testing one list element. On the other hand, `bin-search` needs to split the interval several times before finding the number. This explains why `linear-search` performs slightly better.

1 Run a new experiment comparing linear search and binary search. Search for the middle element of L4. Which performs better? Why?

The worst-case scenario for `bin-search` occurs when the given number is not in the given `lon`. This is when the interval must be split the most. In the worst case how many times is the interval be split in half? If the list has n elements, then we know that the maximum number of times the interval can be split in half is proportional to $O(\lg(n))$. How many operations are done for every recursive call? At a glance it seems that in the worst case part of the list must be traversed twice (using `list-ref`) making the number of operations proportional to $2n = O(n)$. This would make `bin-search`'s complexity $O(n * \lg(n))$. This is worse than `linear-search`'s worst-case $O(n)$ operations.

Why then do we observe that `bin-search` is faster for the experiments with L4? One explanation may be that the constant of proportionality for `linear-search` is large enough that a much longer list must be processed to observe `linear-search` as faster. Another possible explanation is that our assumption about `list-ref` is wrong. Maybe in ISL+ `list-ref` is an $O(k)$ operation and not $O(n)$. If so, this means that in the worst case the number of operations performed for every recursive call is proportional to $2k = O(k)$. This would make `bin-search`'s complexity $O(\lg(n))$. If so, this is much better than $O(n)$ and explains why we observe `bin-search` performing much better.

This suggests a provocative thought. Can binary search be implemented such that we can establish its complexity is $O(\lg(n))$ and not depend on how `list-ref` is implemented? Think about this. We shall explore binary search again.

2 Eliminate repeated expressions in `bin-search` by using a local variable. Why is this a good idea?

3 Is the comparison performed between linear and binary searching fair? Observe that when the given list is sorted linear searching can also be optimized. If the number reached in the list is greater than the number searched for, the search may stop. Why? Design and implement a `linear-search` function that takes advantage of this observation. Compare its performance with binary search.

4 In the implementations above linear searching returns the smallest index that contains the given number and binary search returns any index that contains the given number. Design and implement a function that uses binary search to find an index that contains the given number and then uses a linear search to find the smallest index that contains the given number. Compare the performance of this new function with that of `linear-search`. When is it faster or slower?

30 Trees

Linear search and binary search work well when data is represented using a linear data type such as a list, a natural number, or an interval. As you know not all data types are linear. A binary tree is a nonlinear data type. To search a binary tree the left subtree and the right subtree may both need to be searched. If we have a binary search tree, then only one of the subtrees must be searched. Binary trees are straightforward to search because a node always has two subtrees (or children).

The set of binary trees is a subtype of `tree`. A tree is a nonlinear data structure in which every node has an arbitrary number of subtrees (or children). The top node is called the root of the tree and does not have a parent. All other nodes have a single parent. A tree is defined as follows:

```
;; A (treeof X) is either:
;;   1. '()
;;   2. (make-node X (listof node))

(define-struct node (val subtrees))
```

Note that the children (or subtrees) of a `node` are represented as a list of `nodes`. There can be 0 or more children. Further observe that we have mutually recursive data definitions. To easily visualize this the templates for

Fig. 32 Templates for functions to process a `(treeof X)`

```
#| TEMPLATE FOR FUNCTIONS ON A (treeof X)
;;  Sample (treeof X)
(define TOX0 '())     (define TOX1 (make-node ... ...)) ...
;; (treeof X) ... → ...      Purpose:
(define (f-on-tox a-tox ...)
  (if (empty? a-tox) ... (f-on-node a-tox ...)))
;; Sample expressions for f-on-tox
(define TOX0-VAL ...)        (define TOX1-VAL ...) ...
;; Tests using sample computations for f-on-tox
(check-expect (f-on-tox TOX0 ...) TOX0-VAL)
(check-expect (f-on-tox TOX1 ...) TOX1-VAL) ...
;; Tests using sample values for f-on-tox
(check-expect (f-on-tox ... ...) ...) ...

TEMPLATE FOR FUNCTIONS ON A node
;; Sample nodes
(define NODE0 (make-node ... ...)) ...
;; node ... → ...       Purpose:
(define (f-on-node a-node ...)
  (...(f-on-X (node-val a-node ...)
  ... (f-on-lonode (node-subtrees a-node) ...)))
;; Sample expressions for f-on-node
(define NODE0-VAL ...) ...
;; Tests using sample computations for f-on-node
(check-expect (f-on-node NODE0 ...) NODE0-VAL) ...
;; Tests using sample values for f-on-node
(check-expect (f-on-node ... ...) ...) ...

TEMPLATE FOR FUNCTIONS ON A (listof node)
;; Sample (listof node)
(define LONODE0 '())      (define LONODE1 ...) ...
;; a-lonode ... → ...     Purpose:
(define (f-on-lonode a-lonode ...)
  (if (empty? a-lonode)
        ...
        ... (f-on-node (first a-lox) ...) ... (f-on-lonode (rest a-lox)) ...))
;; Sample expressions for f-on-lonode
(define LONODE0-VAL ...)      (define LONODE1-VAL ...) ...
;; Tests using sample computations for f-on-lonode
(check-expect (f-on-lox LONODE0 ...) LONODE0-VAL)
(check-expect (f-on-lox LONODE1 ...) LONODE1-VAL) ...
;; Tests using sample values for f-on-lonode
(check-expect (f-on-lonode ... ...) ...) ...                    |#
```

functions on a tree, on a node, and a list of nodes are displayed in Fig. 32. The mutually recursive function calls are highlighted in red. To process a tree a node-processing function is needed. To process a node a (listof node)-processing function is needed. To process a (listof node) a node-processing function is needed. This informs us that to process a tree we need three functions. Of these, two call each other (i.e., are mutually recursive).

How is such a nonlinear data type searched? To explore this problem we define the following sample nodes and trees (of numbers):

```
(define NODE10   (make-node 10  '()))
(define NODE3    (make-node  3  '()))
(define NODE87   (make-node 87  '()))
(define NODE-5   (make-node  -5 '()))
(define NODE0    (make-node   0 '()))
(define NODE66   (make-node  66 '()))
(define NODE44   (make-node  44 '()))
(define NODE47   (make-node  47 '()))
(define NODE850 (make-node 850 (list NODE10 NODE3)))
(define NODE235 (make-node 235 (list NODE87 NODE-5 NODE0)))
(define NODE23  (make-node  23 (list NODE44 NODE47)))
(define NODE-88 (make-node -88 (list NODE23)))
(define NODE600 (make-node
                      600 (list NODE850 NODE235 NODE66 NODE-88)))
(define T0 '())
(define T1 NODE10)
(define T2 NODE600)
```

Given that typing deep trees is a long, tedious, error-prone, and bias-prone process, it is best to write a function to create nonempty trees. To protect ourselves against any bias, we develop a function to create a tree of random natural numbers with a maximum given depth.

This function may be designed using structural recursion on a natural number. We define the following constants to generate a random root value and a random number for the number of subtrees:

```
(define RANDOM-NUM-RANGE 1000000)
(define MAX-NUM-SUBTREES 10)
```

If the given depth, d, is 0 then a tree with a random root number and no subtrees is created. If d is greater than 0, then a tree with a random root number and a random number of subtrees, each with a maximum depth of d-1, is created.

Sample expressions for a random tree of depth 0 are:

```
;; Sample expressions for make-tonatnum
(define TON0
        (local
          [(define root-val (random RANDOM-NUM-RANGE))]
          (make-node root-val '())))
(define TON0-2
        (local
          [(define root-val (random RANDOM-NUM-RANGE))]
          (make-node root-val '())))
```

The value at the root is locally defined. Observe that there are no differences among these sample expressions.

Sample expressions for a tree of depth greater than 0 are:

```
(define TON1
        (local
           [(define root-val (random RANDOM-NUM-RANGE))]
           (make-node
            root-val
            (build-list (random MAX-NUM-SUBTREES)
                        (λ (i)
                          (make-tonatnum (sub1 1)))))))
(define TON2
        (local
           [(define root-val (random RANDOM-NUM-RANGE))]
           (make-node
            root-val
            (build-list (random MAX-NUM-SUBTREES)
                        (λ (i)
                          (make-tonatnum (sub1 2)))))))
```

The value at the root of the tree is also a locally defined. The number of subtrees is random. Observe that the only difference is the maximum depth of the tree built. This informs us that the function only needs one parameter. We name this difference **d**.

The signature, purpose statement, and function header are written as follows:

```
;; natnum → (treeof number)
;; Purpose: Create a random tree of numbers of the given
;;          maximum depth
(define (make-tonatnum d)
```

Given that randomness is used to generate the trees, property-based testing is utilized. If the given tree is of depth 0, then the root value must be an integer greater than or equal to 0 and the list of subtrees must be empty. The tests using sample computations for a depth of 0 are:

```
;; Tests using sample computations for make-tonatnum
(check-satisfied TON0-1 (λ (t)
                         (and (integer? (node-val t))
                              (>= (node-val t) 0)
                              (empty? (node-subtrees t)))))
(check-satisfied TON0-2 (λ (t)
                         (and (integer? (node-val t))
                              (>= (node-val t) 0)
                              (empty? (node-subtrees t)))))
```

If the depth of the given tree is 1, then the root value must be an integer greater than or equal to 0. The list of subtrees must have a length less than or equal to the maximum number of subtrees allowed. Each subtree, if any, must have a root value greater than or equal to 0 and an empty list of subtrees. A test using sample computations for a tree of depth 1 is:

```
(check-satisfied
TON1
(λ (t) (and (integer? (node-val t))
            (>= (node-val t) 0)
            (< (length (node-subtrees t)) MAX-NUM-SUBTREES)
            (and (andmap (λ (n)
                           (and (integer? (node-val n))
                                (>= (node-val t) 0)))
                         (node-subtrees t))
                 (andmap
                   (λ (n) (empty? (node-subtrees n)))
                   (node-subtrees t)))))))
```

Tests using sample values are written calling the function or by explicitly creating nodes for shallow trees. The following are sample tests for trees of depth 0:

```
;; Tests using sample values for make-tonatnum
(check-satisfied
  (make-tonatnum 0)
  (λ (t) (and (integer? (node-val t))
              (>= (node-val t) 0)
              (empty? (node-subtrees t)))))
(check-satisfied
  (make-node 7 '())
    (λ (t) (and (integer? (node-val t))
                (>= (node-val t) 0)
                (empty? (node-subtrees t)))))
```

The function's body is obtained by abstracting over the sample expressions. Observe that for both varieties of a natural number, a random root value is locally defined. This may be done before the given natural number is tested. The body of the function is:

```
(local [(define root-val (random RANDOM-NUM-RANGE))]
    (cond  [(= d 0) (make-node root-val '())]
           [else
             (make-node root-val
                        (build-list
                         (random MAX-NUM-SUBTREES)
                         (λ (i) (make-tonatnum (sub1 d)))))]))
```

Run the tests and make sure they all pass. We may now define a sample tree of arbitrary depth, say 7, as follows:

```
(define T3 (make-tonatnum 7))
```

This tree is also used to test the tree searching programs developed.

5 How do we write tests for trees of depth greater than 1? One possibility is to check that the depth of the tree returned by `make-tonatnum` is less than or equal to the maximum depth given as input. Design and implement a function, `tox-depth`, that takes as input a tree and that computes its depth. Use your function to test trees of a depth greater than 1 as follows:

```
(check-satisfied T3 (λ (t) (<= (tox-depth t) 7)))
(check-satisfied (make-tonatnum 5)
                 (λ (t) (<= (tox-depth t) 5)))
```

31 Depth-First Search

Consider the problem of determining if a given number is a member of a given (`treeof number`). A linear traversal cannot be done because a tree is not a linear data structure. We now explore this problem.

31.1 Problem Analysis

It is certainly the case that the root value may be the number that is searched for. If it is the answer is `#true`. This provides us a condition for stopping the search process.

What if the root value is not the number searched for? In this case the number may be in the first subtree. If so, then the answer is `#true`. What if it is not in the first subtree? This is where things get interesting. After a failed search of the first subtree, it is necessary to *backtrack* (up the tree) to search the rest of the siblings. The process is repeated for each subtree until one contains the number searched for or there are no more siblings to search. If any of the siblings contains the number searched for, the answer is `#true`. If none of the subtrees contain this number, then the answer is `#false`. Observe that the search may also stop when there are no more subtrees to search. This is known as *depth-first search*. In depth-first search an avenue (like a subtree) is searched before any other search avenues (like other subtrees).

31.2 Sample Expressions and Differences

To determine if a given tree contains a given number, independently reason about each tree subtype. If the tree is empty then the given number is not found in the given tree. If the given tree is not empty, then a `node` must be searched (as suggested by the template for functions on a tree). Given that we are writing a predicate we can dispense with the `if`-expression by observing that a given number is in the given tree if the given tree is not empty and the given number is contained in the given nonempty tree (i.e., `node`). Assuming that the function to search a node is named `node-dfs-contains?`, we write sample expressions as follows:

```
;; Sample expressions for ton-dfs-contains?
(define T0-DFS-VAL (and (not (empty? T0))
                        (node-dfs-contains? 77 T1)))
(define T1-DFS-VAL (and (not (empty? T1))
                        (node-dfs-contains? 33 T1)))
(define T2-DFS-VAL (and (not (empty? T2))
                        (node-dfs-contains? 23 T2)))
(define T3-DFS-VAL (and (not (empty? T3))
                        (node-dfs-contains? 45 T3)))
```

Observe that there are two differences among the sample expressions: the number that is searched for and the tree that is searched. This confirms that the function only needs two parameters that we call `a-num` and `a-ton`.

31.3 Signature, Purpose, and Function Header

The two differences among the sample expressions are a number and a tree. This gives us part of the signature. The returned value is a Boolean. This completes the signature. The purpose statement needs to summarize the problem solved. The function header needs a descriptive function name and two parameters. These steps of the design recipe yield:

```
;; number (treeof number) → Boolean
;; Purpose: Determine if the given number is in the given tree
(define (ton-dfs-contains? a-num a-ton)
```

31.4 Tests

The tests using sample computations illustrate that the function computes the same values as the sample expressions:

```
;; Tests using sample computations for ton-dfs-contains?
(check-expect (ton-dfs-contains? 77 T0) T0-DFS-VAL)
(check-expect (ton-dfs-contains? 33 T1) T1-DFS-VAL)
(check-expect (ton-dfs-contains? 23 T2) T2-DFS-VAL)
(check-expect (ton-dfs-contains? 45 T3) T3-DFS-VAL)
```

The tests using sample values illustrate how the function works using concrete values:

```
;; Tests using sample values for ton-dfs-contains?
(check-satisfied (make-node
                  307759
                  (list (make-node 816392 '())
                        (make-node 153333 '())
                        (make-node 684270 '())))
                 (λ (t) (ton-dfs-contains? 153333 t)))

(check-satisfied (make-node
                  307759
                  (list (make-node 816392 '())
                        (make-node 153333 '())
                        (make-node 684270 '())))
                 (λ (t) (not (ton-dfs-contains? 6561 t))))
```

31.5 The Function Body

The function body is obtained by abstracting over the sample expressions. The answer to this step of the design recipe is:

```
(and (not (empty? a-ton))
     (node-dfs-contains? a-num a-ton))
```

This completes the design and implementation of ton-dfs-contains?. Before running the tests the auxiliary function must be designed and implemented.

31.6 The node-dfs-contains? Function

31.6.1 Problem Analysis

This function must implement a depth-first search of a nonempty tree (i.e., a node). A node contains the given number if it is the root value or if any subtree contains the given value. The former may be determined by comparing the given number and the root value of the given tree.

As suggested by the template for functions on a `node`, the latter must be determined by calling a function to process a list. This function, however, must be mutually recursive with `node-dfs-contains?` and must stop when a subtree that contains the given number is found. That is, it should process as many subtrees as necessary (not all of them if possible). Stopping when *any* subtree meets a condition (e.g., containing the given number) suggests `or`ing the results for each subtree as they are processed. Recall that the evaluation of arguments in an `or`-expression stops when one of the expressions evaluates to `#true` and the rest of the subexpressions are not evaluated. Thus, `or`ing the results for each subtree gives us exactly what is needed to implement a depth-first search.

31.6.2 Sample Expressions

Testing if the root value is equal to the given number is easily done using `=`. Testing if any subtree has the given number by `or`ing results without testing every subtree in a list may be done using `ormap`. Recall that `ormap` uses `or` to combine results. Therefore, it stops when one of the subtrees contains the given number. Observe that in this case `ormap` is the list-processing function that is suggested in the template for `node`-processing functions. The sample expressions are:

```
;; Sample expressions for node-dfs-contains?
(define NODE10-VAL1 (or (= 33 (node-val NODE10))
                        (ormap (λ (t)
                                 (node-dfs-contains? 33 t))
                               (node-subtrees NODE10))))
(define NODE10-VAL2 (or (= 10 (node-val NODE10))
                        (ormap (λ (t)
                                 (node-dfs-contains? 10 t))
                               (node-subtrees NODE10))))
(define NODE600-VAL (or (= -5 (node-val NODE600))
                        (ormap (λ (t)
                                 (node-dfs-contains? -5 t))
                               (node-subtrees NODE600))))
```

There are two differences among the sample expressions: the number that is searched for and the `node` that is searched. This confirms that the function only needs two parameters that we call `a-num` and `a-node`.

31.7 Signature, Purpose, and Function Definition

As you develop expertise you may be able to perform the steps of the design recipe in a different order. We try our hand at specializing the definition template before writing tests. Two parameters and abstraction over the sample expressions are needed to specialize the definition template as follows:

```
;; number node → Boolean
;; Purpose: Determine if given node contains given number
(define (node-dfs-contains? a-num a-node)
  (or (= a-num (node-val a-node))
      (ormap (λ (t) (node-dfs-contains? a-num t))
             (node-subtrees a-node))))
```

Observe that, indeed, `node-dfs-contains?` and the λ-expression are mutually recursive based on the structure of a `node` and a `(listof node)`. This informs us that a how statement and a termination argument are not required.

31.7.1 Tests

Writing tests is the last step we need to complete. The tests using sample computations illustrate that the function, when given the concrete values used in the sample expressions, returns the same value as the evaluation of the sample expressions. These tests are:

```
;; Tests using sample computations for node-dfs-contains?
(check-expect (node-dfs-contains? 33 NODE10)   NODE10-VAL1)
(check-expect (node-dfs-contains? 10 NODE10)   NODE10-VAL2)
(check-expect (node-dfs-contains? -5 NODE600) NODE600-VAL)
```

Observe that the tests cover both possible values returned.

Tests using sample values use short trees to test if `node-dfs-contains?` is or is not satisfied. The tests are:

```
;; Tests using sample values for node-dfs-contains?
(check-satisfied (make-node 31
                            (list (make-node 45 '())
                                  (make-node 31 '())
                                  (make-node  7 '())))
                 (λ (t) (node-dfs-contains? 31 t)))
(check-satisfied (make-node 67
                            (list (make-node 45 '())
                                  (make-node 31 '())
                                  (make-node  7 '())))
                 (λ (t) (not (node-dfs-contains? 87 t))))
```

This completes the design and implementation of `ton-dfs-contains?`. Run and make sure all the tests pass.

31.8 Performance and Complexity

To illustrate the performance of `ton-dfs-contains?` we time three searches using T3. The first is a search for the number in the first subtree five levels down. The second is a search for the root value of the last subtree. The third is a search for a number that is not in the tree. The expressions for the experiments are:

```
(time
 (ton-dfs-contains?
  (node-val
   (first
   (node-subtrees
     (first
      (node-subtrees
       (first
        (node-subtrees
         (first
          (node-subtrees
           (first
            (node-subtrees
             (first (node-subtrees T3)))))))))))))
   T3))

(time
 (ton-dfs-contains?
  (list-ref (map (λ (t) (node-val t)) (node-subtrees T3))
            (sub1 (length (node-subtrees T3))))
  T3))

(time (ton-dfs-contains? -8 T3))
```

Before running the experiments make sure the randomly created T3 has a height of at least 5. The following is a sampling of CPU times (after subtracting garbage collection time):

	Experiment$_1$	Experiment$_2$	Experiment$_3$
DFS	0	156	671

Depth-first search is very fast when the number searched for is in the first subtree. This is due to not having to search most of the tree. The program is slower when several subtrees must be searched like in the second experiment. In this experiment, given the timing for the first experiment, it is unlikely that the number is found in the first subtree. It is unfortunate that the search is slower given that the number searched for is at a depth of only 1 in the tree. The worst performance is seen when the entire tree is searched like for the third experiment. This is the worst-case scenario for depth-first search.

To determine the abstract running time of depth-first search, we define V as the set of nodes in the tree and E as the set of edges in the tree (an edge connects a parent with one child). Observe that in the worst case (when the given number is not in the given tree), all the root values must be compared with the given number and all the edges must be traversed to reach every node. This makes the work done by a depth-first search of a tree proportional to, |V|, the number of nodes and, |E|, the number of edges. If we define n = |V| + |E| then the abstract running time is $O(n)$. That is, it is a linear-time algorithm.

6 Design and implement a program to find the largest number in a (`treeof number`) using depth-first search.

7 Design and implement a program using depth-first search that takes as input a (`treeof posn`) and that returns a list of all the `posn`s in the first quadrant.

32 Breadth-First Search

The experiments in the previous subsection revealed that depth-first search's performance is disappointing when the number searched for is at a shallow level in the tree. Why search multiple subtrees when the number may be found only a few levels away from the root? This suggests that a tree be traversed level by level instead of by subtrees.

32.1 Problem Analysis for `ton-bfs-contains?`

To explore a tree level by level the root values of all siblings at level h must be explored before any values at a higher level. Think carefully about how this can be done. The first number to check during the search is the root value because it has the lowest depth. If the search must continue, then the first values that need to be checked are the root values of its children. If necessary the process continues with grandchildren and so on. This may be achieved by keeping the trees that need to be traversed in a `first-in first-out` (FIFO) order. To start the given tree is stored in a FIFO manner. If the root value is not equal to the given number, then all the children are added to the set of trees that may still need to be searched in a FIFO manner. This process repeats itself until the given number is found or the set of trees to search is empty.

The natural question to ask is: how are trees kept in FIFO order? Clearly, this must be data of arbitrary size because the number of trees that may still be searched is arbitrary. A data structure that keeps its elements in FIFO order is called a `queue`.

32.1.1 Queues

Before continuing with the steps of the design recipe, we discuss and implement queues. You have dealt with queues throughout your life. When you get in line to pay at a supermarket, you are in a queue. The first person in line is the first to pay. The second in line is the second to pay and so on. The persons in line keep themselves in FIFO order. This is why skipping the line is not cool!

How can we implement a queue? Given that it is data of arbitrary size the queue may be represented using a list. Let us explore this idea. The data definition is:

A (queueof X) is a (listof X)

This may seem silly. Why is a new data definition needed if a queue is a list? It is important to be careful in our reasoning here. The answer is that the interfaces for a list and a queue are not the same. Recall that an interface are the operations valid on some type of data. For a list the interface includes `empty?`, `first`, and `rest`. You know how these functions work. For a queue we define the following interface:

qempty?   This function tests if the given queue is empty.
qfirst   This function returns the first element of the queue.
enqueue   This function adds a set of elements to the end of the queue.
dequeue   This function removes the first element from the queue.

To have the benefit of a queue these four operations must be implemented.

32.1.2 The Implementation of `qempty?` and `qfirst`

A queue is empty if the list used to represent it is empty. Therefore, we may define the empty queue and implement the `qempty?` predicate as follows:

```
(define E-QUEUE '())

(define qempty? empty?)

;; Tests for qempty?
(check-expect (qempty? '())      #true)
(check-expect (qempty? '(a b c)) #false)
```

Extracting the first element of a queue can only be performed if the queue is not empty. If the queue is empty an error is thrown. If a queue is not empty then the first element of the list used to represent it is returned. This queue operation is implemented as follows:

```
;; (qof X) → X throws error
;; Purpose: Return first X of the given queue
(define (qfirst a-qox)
  (if (qempty? a-qox)
      (error "qfirst applied to an empty queue")
      (first a-qox)))

;; Tests for qfirst
(check-error  (qfirst '())
                "qfirst applied to an empty queue")
(check-expect (qfirst '(a b c)) 'a)
```

Observe this implementation choice means that any elements added to the queue must be added to the end of the list that represents it. In this manner, the elements are kept in FIFO order.

32.1.3 The Implementation of enqueue and dequeue

The function to add elements takes as input a list of elements and a queue. As noted above, the new elements must be added to the end of the list to maintain all elements in FIFO order. This is akin to a few people getting in line at a register in a supermarket. The function to add elements is implemented as follows:

```
;; (listof X) (qof X) → (qof X)
;; Purpose: Add the given list of X to the given
;;          queue of X
(define (enqueue a-lox a-qox) (append a-qox a-lox))

;; Tests for enqueue
(check-expect (enqueue '(8 d) '()) '(8 d))
(check-expect (enqueue '(d) '(a b c)) '(a b c d))
(check-expect (enqueue '(6 5 4) '(7)) '(7 6 5 4))
```

An element may only be removed from a nonempty. If the given queue is not empty, then its sub-queue, without the first element, is returned. This is akin to the first person in the register line at a supermarket paying and leaving. This function may be implemented as follows:

```
;; (qof X) → (qof X) throws error
;; Purpose: Return the rest of the given queue
(define (dequeue a-qox)
  (if (qempty? a-qox)
      (error "dequeue applied to an empty queue")
      (rest a-qox)))

;; Tests for qfirst
(check-error  (dequeue '())
              "dequeue applied to an empty queue")
(check-expect (dequeue '(a b c)) '(b c))
```

32.2 Sample Expressions and Differences for ton-bfs-contains?

A given number can only be in a given tree if the tree is not empty. If the tree is empty the answer is always #false. A sample expression to illustrate this is:

```
;;; Sample expressions for ton-bfs-contains?
(define T0-BFS-VAL #false)
```

If the tree is not empty the search is performed by placing the tree in a queue and calling an auxiliary function to search trees in the given queue. Assuming the auxiliary function is named bfs-helper, the sample expressions for this case may be written as follows:

```
(define T1-BFS-VAL (bfs-helper
                     33
                     (enqueue (list T1) E-QUEUE)))
(define T2-BFS-VAL (bfs-helper
                     23
                     (enqueue (list T2) E-QUEUE)))
(define T3-BFS-VAL (bfs-helper
                     45
                     (enqueue (list T3) E-QUEUE)))
```

Observe that there are only two differences among the sample expressions: a number and a tree. This confirms that the auxiliary function only needs two parameters. We name these differences a-num and a-qton.

32.3 Tests for `ton-bfs-contains?`

The tests using sample computations are written using the concrete values in the sample expressions. The number used to test searching the empty tree, T0, is arbitrary because the answer is always #false. The tests using sample computations are:

```
;;; Tests using sample computations for ton-bfs-contains?
(check-expect (ton-bfs-contains? 77 T0) T0-BFS-VAL)
(check-expect (ton-bfs-contains? 33 T1) T1-BFS-VAL)
(check-expect (ton-bfs-contains? 23 T2) T2-BFS-VAL)
(check-expect (ton-bfs-contains? 45 T3) T3-BFS-VAL)
```

The tests using sample values use short trees to illustrate both possible outcomes of the function. These tests are:

```
;;; Tests using sample values for ton-dfs-contains?
(check-satisfied (make-node 307759
                       (list (make-node 816392 '())
                             (make-node 153333 '())
                             (make-node 684270 '())))
             (λ (t)
                (ton-bfs-contains? 153333 t)))
(check-satisfied (make-node 307759
                       (list (make-node 816392 '())
                             (make-node 153333 '())
                             (make-node 684270 '())))
             (λ
                (t) (not (ton-bfs-contains? 6561 t)))))
```

32.4 Function Definition for `ton-bfs-contains?`

The remaining steps of the design recipe, as always, build on the results of previous steps. The input types in the signature and the function parameters come from the differences in the sample expressions. The returned type in the signature comes from problem analysis. An if-expression is needed to distinguish between (treeof X) subtypes. The then-expression is always #false as outlined to develop the sample expressions. Finally, the else-expression is obtained by abstracting over sample expressions. The remaining steps of the design recipe yield:

```
;; number (treeof number) → Boolean
;; Purpose: Determine if the given number is in the
;;          given tree
(define (ton-bfs-contains? a-num a-ton)
  (if (empty? a-ton)
      #false
      (bfs-helper a-num (enqueue (list a-ton) E-QUEUE))))
```

The design and implementation of `ton-bfs-contains?` is complete. Before running the tests the auxiliary function must be designed and implemented.

32.5 Problem Analysis for `bfs-helper`

If the given queue is empty the given number is not found and the answer is `#false`. If the given queue is not empty, then the number may be the root value of the first tree in the queue, may be found in any of the rest of the trees in the queue, or may be found in any of the subtrees of the first tree in the queue. The trees that may still be searched, therefore, are the rest of the trees in the queue and the subtrees of the first tree in the queue.

To process the new set of trees a new queue is needed. This new queue is built by dequeuing the first element in the queue and enqueuing the children of the first tree in the queue. This means that the algorithm uses generative recursion.

To facilitate the writing of sample expressions and tests using sample computations, the following sample (qof (treeof natnum)) is defined:

```
(define QTON0 '())
(define QTON1 (list T1))
(define QTON2 (list T2 T1))
```

32.6 Sample Expressions and Differences for `bfs-helper`

Based on the problem analysis above, the given number is in the tree if the queue is not empty and either the given number equals the root value of the first tree in the queue or the given number is in any of the other trees in the queue or in any subtree of the first tree in the queue. This suggests using **and** and **or** to write the sample expressions as follows:

```
;; Sample expressions for bfs-helper
(define QTON0-VAL
  (and (not (qempty? QTON0))
       (or (= 89 (node-val (qfirst QTON0)))
```

```
                    (local
                      [(define newq (enqueue
                                      (node-subtrees (qfirst QTON0))
                                      (dequeue QTON0)))]
                        (bfs-helper 89 newq)))))
(define QTON1-VAL
  (and (not (qempty? QTON1))
       (or (= 99 (node-val (qfirst QTON1)))
           (local
              [(define newq (enqueue
                              (node-subtrees (qfirst QTON1))
                              (dequeue QTON1)))]
                (bfs-helper 99 newq)))))
(define QTON2-VAL
  (and (not (qempty? QTON2))
       (or (= 47 (node-val (qfirst QTON2)))
           (local
              [(define newq (enqueue
                              (node-subtrees (qfirst QTON2))
                              (dequeue QTON2)))]
                (bfs-helper 47 newq)))))
```

Observe that the new problem instance (i.e., the new queue) is locally defined
as suggested by the template for functions using generative recursion. Further
observe that for the call to `bfs-helper` the trees are kept in FIFO order.

The only differences among the sample expressions are a number and a
queue. This informs us that the function only needs two parameters. We call
these difference, respectively, `a-num` and `a-ton`.

32.7 Tests for `bfs-helper`

The tests using sample computations are written using the values found in
the sample expressions and the values of these expressions. The number used
to search the empty queue is arbitrary given that the result is always `#false`.
The tests using sample computations are:

```
;; Tests using sample computations for bfs-helper
(check-expect (bfs-helper 89 QTON0) QTON0-VAL)
(check-expect (bfs-helper 99 QTON1) QTON1-VAL)
(check-expect (bfs-helper 47 QTON2) QTON2-VAL)
```

The tests using sample values are written with short queues containing shallow trees. There is a test for each possible Boolean result. These tests are:

```
;; Tests using sample values for bfs-helper
(check-expect (bfs-helper
                31
                (list (make-node 768 '()))
              #false)
(check-expect (bfs-helper
                78
                (list (make-node 768 '())
                  (make-node
                    90
                    (list (make-node 1 '())
                          (make-node 78 '())))))
              #true)
```

32.8 Signature, Statements, and Function Definition for bfs-helper

The function processes a number and a queue containing trees of natural numbers and returns a Boolean. This follows from the differences in the sample expressions and from problem analysis. The purpose is to search for the given number in the given queue. The how statement summarizes how the problem is solved. It outlines the halting conditions and how the process is repeated with a new queue. The function header is written using a descriptive function name and the names for the differences in the sample expressions. Finally, the function body is obtained by abstracting over the sample expressions. These remaining steps of the design recipe yield:

```
;; number (qof (treeof number)) → Boolean
;; Purpose: Search the trees in the given queue for the
;;          given number.
;; How: If the queue is empty or if the root value of
;;   the first tree in the queue equals the given number
;;   then stop. Otherwise, search for the number in a
;;   queue that contains all but the first tree in the
;;   given queue and the subtrees of the first tree in
;;   the given queue.
(define (bfs-helper a-num a-qton)
  (and (not (qempty? a-qton))
       (or (= a-num (node-val (qfirst a-qton)))
```

```
(local
  [(define newq (enqueue
                   (node-subtrees (qfirst a-qton))
                   (dequeue a-qton)))]
  (bfs-helper a-num newq)))))
```

This completes `ton-bfs-contains?`'s design and implementation. Make sure all the tests pass when you run them.

32.9 Performance and Complexity

To illustrate `ton-bfs-contains?`'s runtime performance, use the same experiments as those used for `ton-dfs-contains?`. The expressions for the experiments are:

```
(time
  (ton-bfs-contains?
   (node-val
    (first
     (node-subtrees
      (first
       (node-subtrees
        (first
         (node-subtrees
          (first
           (node-subtrees
            (first
             (node-subtrees
              (first (node-subtrees T3)))))))))))))
    T3))

(time
  (ton-bfs-contains?
   (list-ref (map (λ (t) (node-val t)) (node-subtrees T3))
             (sub1 (length (node-subtrees T3))))
   T3))
```

```
(time (ton-bfs-contains? -8 T3))
```

The CPU time after subtracting any garbage collection time is displayed in the following table:

	Experiment$_1$	Experiment$_2$	Experiment$_3$
DFS	0	156	671
BFS	281	0	36531

We can observe that breadth-first search is slower when the number searched for is deep in the first subtree. This is explained by observing that breadth-first search explores all subtrees level by level doing more work than depth-first search. Depth-first search only explores one subtree allowing it to find the given number faster. In contrast, breadth-first search is faster when the given number is shallow in one of the trees (e.g., the root value of the last subtree). Breadth-first search does not spend time searching the entire subtrees before moving on to the next subtree like depth-first search. Thus, breadth-first search is able to find the number faster. In the worst-case scenario (when the given number is not in the given tree), we observe that depth-first search is faster. To explain this observed behavior, let us look at the abstract running time.

Recall that `ton-dfs-contains?`'s abstract running time is $O(n)$, where n = |V| + |E|, V is the set of nodes, and E is the set of edges. For breadth-first search in the worst case (when the given number is not in the given tree), all the root values must be compared with the given number and all the edges must be traversed to reach every node. Every node, v, is visited (not searched) multiple times: every time a set of nodes is added to the queue while v is in the queue. How many times is v visited while in the queue? The answer is `MAX-NUM-SUBTREES` given that in the worst case v is the last sibling and remains in the queue until the children of all its siblings are added to the queue. This makes the abstract running time $O(\texttt{MAX-NUM-SUBTREES} * |V|+|E|) = O(\texttt{MAX-NUM-SUBTREES} * n) = O(n)$. Breadth-first search has the same complexity as depth-first search. Why then is breadth-first search slower than depth-first search in the worst-case scenario? The reason, as you can observe, is the constant of proportionality is larger for breadth-first search.

8 Design and implement a program to find the largest number in a (`treeof number`) using breadth-first search.

9 Design and implement a program using breadth-first search that takes as input a (`treeof posn`) and that returns a list of all the `posn`s in the first quadrant.

10 Design and implement a function that searches a (`treeof X`) for a given X and that returns the smallest depth it occurs at.

11 Design and implement a function that traverses a (treeof string) and that returns the string obtained by appending all the strings in the given tree.

12 Implement a function to determine if a (treeof natnum) has a repeated natnum.

33 What Have We Learned in This Chapter?

The important lessons of this chapter are summarized as follows:

- A search problem attempts to find a value x with property P in a set S.
- The worst-case scenario for linear search is having to traverse all the elements in the set searched.
- The complexity of linear search is $O(n)$.
- Binary search processes an ordered set.
- Binary search repeatedly halves the search space until the element searched for is found or the search space becomes empty.
- The worst-case scenario for binary search is when the element searched for is not in the set searched.
- The complexity of binary search is $O(\lg(n))$.
- A tree is a nonlinear data structure in which every node has an arbitrary number of subtrees (or children).
- Binary tree is a tree subtype.
- Random generation of test data protects problem solvers from bias.
- In depth-first search an avenue, like a subtree, is exhaustively searched before any other search avenues, like the siblings of a subtree, are considered.
- Backtracking refers to the ability to take a step back and search other avenues when a search avenue fails.
- The complexity of depth-first search is $O(n)$.
- In breadth-first search all search avenues are explored simultaneously moving one step at a time in each search avenue.
- The complexity of breadth-first search is $O(n)$.

Chapter 7
N-Puzzle Version 2

Section 16 explores a refinement to the N-puzzle game in which the help button makes a random move for the player. Using randomness to make a move for the player is a poor choice for two reasons. The first is that we cannot convincingly argue that the puzzle can be solved in a reasonable amount of time. In fact, a pseudo number generator may never generate a sequence of numbers to make the moves to WIN. The second is that we have no idea if a random move is a useful move. If a move is made for the player, it ought to be a move that brings the player one step closer to solving the puzzle. Swapping the empty tile space with, for example, the 5 tile repeatedly 20 times in a row is certainly not bringing the player closer to solving the puzzle.

To make sure a useful move is made on behalf of the player, the puzzle needs to be solved by our program before making a move. The questions that need to be answered, therefore, are what a solution is and how a solution can be represented. A solution is a sequence of moves that start with a given board and end in WIN. For example, consider the player requesting help when the board is:

A solution to the puzzle consists of two moves. This solution may be visualized as follows:

© The Author(s), under exclusive license to Springer Nature Switzerland AG 2022   169
M. T. Morazán, *Animated Program Design*, Texts in Computer Science,
https://doi.org/10.1007/978-3-031-04317-8_7

It is important to note that the above is one solution of many. Another solution to the puzzle is:

1	2	3	1	2	3	1	2	3	1	2	3	1	2	3
4		6	4	5	6	4	5	6	4	5	6	4	5	6
7	5	8	7		8		7	8	7		8	7	8	

Clearly the first solution is better because it is shorter. Therefore, we may argue that the shortest solution ought to be found. At first, however, we focus on finding a solution. A later refinement of the game may focus on finding the best solution.

Before redesigning and implementing `make-move`, think carefully about how `process-key` ought to be tested. All tests written for N-puzzle version 1 in Sect. 16 should still pass. However, given that `make-move` is not yet designed, it is impossible to predict what possible solution is used to return the next `world`. Tests using an explicit value for `process-key`'s expected value when given HKEY are added after designing and implementing `make-move`.

34 Design and Implementation of `make-move`

To redesign `make-move` the functions that are local to `process-vk` need to be moved to the global level. If this is done then tests may be written for `make-move` as part of the design process. Once `make-move` is thoroughly tested with success, all these functions may be re-encapsulated.

34.1 Problem Analysis

The implementation of `make-move` needs to be updated to find the move to make. This move must be part of a solution to the puzzle for a given `world`. The first step is to decide how a solution shall be represented. From the examples above we may conclude that a solution is data of arbitrary size. Given the linear nature of a solution, the empty tile space is moved from one element in the solution to the next, a list seems to be a natural fit. Specifically, we can use a (`listof world`). Given a valid board (one that may be reached from WIN by making 0 or more moves), a solution always exists. That is, there are always sequences of moves that take us from the given board to WIN. This informs us that there is no reason for this function to declare a failed search.

If the given `world` is WIN no moves need to be made. Therefore, the given world may be returned. Put differently, given WIN and having `make-move`

return WIN is equivalent to not making a move. If the given `world` is not
WIN then reason carefully about what a solution is. A solution starts with
the given board and ends with WIN. This means that a solution in this case
must have at least two boards. The second `world`, w_2, in the solution must be
a successor of the given `world` by making one move. Therefore, `make-move`
returns w_2.

We now understand that the next move is the second `world` in a (`listof`
`world`) that is a solution. Finding the solution is a different problem from
making a move. Therefore, it ought to be solved by a different function. The
auxiliary function needs the starting `world` and is independently designed.

The following sample `worlds` are defined to aid in writing sample expressions and tests:

```
;; Sample worlds
(define WRLD1 (make-world 1 2 3
                          4 5 6
                          7 0 8))

(define WRLD2 (make-world 1 0 3
                          4 2 6
                          7 5 8))
```

34.2 Sample Expressions and Differences

Based on our problem analysis the answer is the given world when it is equal
to WIN. We can write a sample expression for this condition using WIN as
follows:

```
;; Sample expressions for make-move
(define MM-WIN-VAL   WIN)
```

If the given world is not WIN then a solution must be found. As per our
problem analysis, the solution is found by an auxiliary function and its second
`world` is returned as the answer. We may write sample expressions using
WRLD1 and WRLD2 as follows:

```
(define MM-WRLD1-VAL (second (find-solution WRLD1)))
(define MM-WRLD2-VAL (second (find-sol-solution WRLD2)))
```

The name `find-solution` is used for the auxiliary function given that it
describes the purpose of the function.

Observe that the only difference among the sample expressions is the `world`
processed. We name this difference `a-world`.

34.3 Signature, Purpose, and Function Header

Based on the differences among the sample expression, this function only needs one parameter. The type of this parameter is `world`. Problem analysis informed us that the return type is `world`. The purpose of the function is to make a move for the player. The function header is written using, `make-move`, the chosen function name and the chosen parameter name. These observations yield the following results for the next steps of the design recipe:

```
;; world → world
;; Purpose: Make a move for the player
(define (make-move a-world)
```

34.4 Tests

The tests using sample computations test the value returned by `make-move` by giving it as input the values used in the sample expressions. The expected values are the constants defined for the sample expressions. The tests are written as follows:

```
;; Tests using sample computations for make-move
(check-expect (make-move WIN)  MM-WIN-VAL)
(check-expect (make-move WRLD1) MM-WRLD1-VAL)
(check-expect (make-move WRLD2) MM-WRLD2-VAL)
```

How are tests using sample values written for `make-move`? This presents a challenge because our problem analysis does not specify how `find-solution` processes the neighbors of the empty tile's `bpos`. Given that starting from any valid board a solution exists, we do know that only one of the successors of the given world needs to be processed. Let us assume (for now) that `find-solution` processes the first neighbor of the empty tile's `bpos` as listed in `neighbors`. This means that a solution starting with a board that has the empty tile space in position 4 has as its second element the board obtained

Fig. 33 Partial view of the search space for a solution

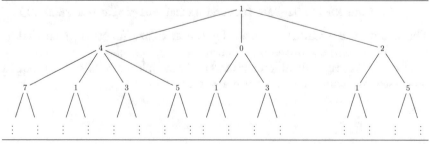

by moving the empty tile space to position 7 (7 is the first neighbor listed for position 4 in `neighbors`). Similarly, a solution starting with a board that has the empty tile space in position 5 has as its second element the board obtained by moving the empty tile space to position 2. Based on these observations the following tests are written:

```
;; Tests using sample values for make-move
(check-expect (make-move (make-world 1 2 3
                                     4 0 6
                                     7 5 8))
              (make-world 1 2 3
                          4 5 6
                          7 0 8))
(check-expect (make-move (make-world 1 2 3
                                     4 5 0
                                     7 8 6))
              (make-world 1 2 0
                          4 5 3
                          7 8 6))
```

34.5 Function Body

The function body is written using an `if`-expression to distinguish between getting `WIN` and getting another `world` as input. When the given `world` is `WIN` the given `world` is returned. The else-expression is obtained by abstracting over the second and third sample expressions. The body of the function is:

```
(if (equal? a-world WIN)
    a-world
    (second (find-solution a-world)))
```

This completes the design and implementation of `make-move`. Before running the tests the auxiliary function `find-solution` must be designed and implemented.

35 Design and Implementation of `find-solution`

35.1 Problem Analysis

This function must find a solution to the puzzle starting from a given world. Observe that a solution is a list that starts with the given board and ends with a solution that starts from one of the successors of the given board. As you can see already the process of finding a solution is recursive. When does the search for a solution terminate? All solutions terminate when the given board is WIN. In this case a list containing WIN is returned because to reach WIN no moves need to be made.

What if the given board is not WIN? In this case a solution must be found from one of the successors of the given board. How is this done? To answer this let us examine the search space for a solution. The search space is all possible sequences of moves starting with the given world. Figure 33 displays a partial visualization of the search space starting with a `world` that has the empty tile space at a `bpos` = 1. Observe that the search space is a tree rooted at the `world` that has the empty tile space at `bpos` = 1. At level 1 we have the successors of the root `world` (i.e., the `world`s with the empty tile space at `bpos` = 4, 0, and 2) in the order that they are listed in `neighbors`. At level 2 we have the successors of the `world` where the blank space is at `bpos` = 4 (i.e., the `world`s with the empty tile space at `bpos` = 7, 1, 3, and 5), at `bpos` = 0 (i.e., the `world`s with the empty tile space at `bpos` = 1 and 3), and at `bpos` = 2 (i.e., the `world`s with the empty tile space at `bpos` = 1 and 5) in the order that they appear in `neighbors`. Further levels of the tree are built in the same manner.

The search space being a tree is good news because we know how to search a tree. We can either perform a depth-first search or a breadth-first search. For this version of the game, let us explore using depth-first search. We assume that the given world is a valid board. If the given `world` is WIN the solution is a list that only contains the given `world`. If it is not WIN then the path that starts with the first successor of the given `world` as listed in `neighbors` is used to build the solution. Our job is greatly simplified because backtracking is not required given that a solution may be found starting from any valid board.

Observe that the described algorithm recursively performs a search with a new instance of the problem (i.e., a new board that is a successor of the given board). This clearly means that this function uses generative recursion. Therefore, a how statement and a termination argument are required as part of the design process.

35.2 Sample Expressions and Differences

When given WIN, as per the problem analysis, this function must always return a list containing the given `world`. The sample expression for this case is:

```
;; Sample expressions for find-solution
(define FS-WIN-VAL (list WIN))
```

If the given `world` is not `WIN` then, as suggested by the template for functions using generative recursion, a new instance of the problem is locally defined. In this case `map` is used to compute all the successors of the given board and the first of these is the new problem instance used by depth-first search. There is no need to implement backtracking because a solution starting at the new problem instance exists. That is, it suffices to search the first subtree to find a solution. Sample expressions are written as follows:

```
(define FS-WRLD1-VAL
  (local
    [(define first-child
             (first (map
                      (λ (neigh)
                        (swap-empty WRLD1 neigh))
                      (list-ref neighbors
                                (blank-pos WRLD1)))))]
    (cons WRLD1 (find-solution first-child))))

(define FS-WRLD2-VAL
  (local
    [(define first-child
             (first (map
                      (λ (neigh)
                        (swap-empty WRLD2 neigh))
                      (list-ref neighbors
                                (blank-pos WRLD2)))))]
    (cons WRLD2 (find-solution first-child))))
```

As you can see, the first successor is used to search for a solution and the rest of the successors are ignored. There is no backtracking implemented.

The only difference among the sample expressions is the `world` processed. We name this difference `a-world`.

35.3 Signature, Statements, and Function Header

This function, based on the differences among the sample expressions, takes as input a world and returns, based on the problem analysis, a (`listof world`). The purpose is to return a solution to the puzzle. That is, the purpose is to return a sequence of moves from the given board to `WIN`. The solution is created using the given `world` and the solution starting from the first successor of the given `world`. The function header is written using the descriptive function name and the descriptive name chosen for the only difference among the sample expressions. The next steps of the design recipe yield:

```
;; world → (listof world)
;; Purpose: Return sequence of moves from given world
;;          to WIN
;; How: The solution is built using the given world
;;      and the solution found starting from the
;;      first successor of the given world.
(define (find-solution a-world)
```

35.4 Tests

The tests using sample computations give find-solution the worlds used in the sample expressions. They test that the value returned by find-solution is the same as the value obtained from evaluating the sample expressions. The tests are:

```
;; Tests using sample computations for find-solution
(check-expect (find-solution WIN)   FS-WIN-VAL)
(check-expect (find-solution WRLD1) FS-WRLD1-VAL)
(check-expect (find-solution WRLD2) FS-WRLD2-VAL)
```

The tests using sample values require explicit solutions. This is most easily done by tracing by hand short solutions obtained using depth-first search. For example, given:

the solution starts with this world. By examining neighbors we see that the first neighbor of the empty tile space listed is 7. Therefore, the next board in the solution is:

The first neighbor of bpos = 7 listed in neighbors is 8. Thus, the next world in the solution is:

Observe that this is WIN and, therefore, a solution has been found. The first test below corresponds to this example. The second test below is developed in a similar fashion.

```
;; Tests using sample values for find-solution
(check-expect (find-solution (make-world 1 2 3
                                         4 0 6
                                         7 5 8)))
             (list (make-world 1 2 3
                               4 0 6
                               7 5 8)
                   (make-world 1 2 3
                               4 5 6
                               7 0 8)
                   (make-world 1 2 3
                               4 5 6
                               7 8 0)))

(check-expect (find-solution (make-world 1 0 3
                                         4 2 6
                                         7 5 8)))
             (list (make-world 1 0 3
                               4 2 6
                               7 5 8))
                   (make-world 1 2 3
                               4 0 6
                               7 5 8)
                   (make-world 1 2 3
                               4 5 6
                               7 0 8)
                   (make-world 1 2 3
                               4 5 6
                               7 8 0)))
```

35.5 Function Body

The body of the function uses an `if`-expression to distinguish WIN from other worlds. The then-expression always returns a list with the given world as exemplified by the first sample expression. The else-expression is obtained by abstracting over the second and third sample expressions. The body of the function is:

```
(if (equal? a-world WIN)
    (list a-world)
    (local
      [(define first-child
         (first (map
                  (λ (neigh)
                    (swap-empty a-world neigh))
                  (list-ref neighbors
                            (blank-pos a-world)))))]
      (cons a-world (find-solution first-child))))
```

This completes `find-solution`'s design and implementation. Observe that the tests written for `make-move` do not have to be updated because `find-solution` processes the first neighbor of the empty tile's `bpos` as listed in `neighbors`.

35.6 Termination Argument

We need to develop a termination argument for `find-solution` given that it uses generative recursion. Every time this function is recursively called, it is given a successor of the given board as input. Since a solution that starts with any valid board always exists, eventually the given successor is `WIN` and the function halts.

Before running the tests we shall add tests for `process-key`.

36 New Tests for `process-key`

Given that now there is an implementation of `make-move` we are able to write tests for `process-key` when given `HKEY` as input. The world returned by `process-key` is always a successor of the given board. Specifically, it is the successor obtained by moving the empty tile space to the first `bpos` listed in `neighbors` for the empty tile space's `bpos` in the given world. Consider, for example, the following world:

1	2	3
4	5	6
7		8

The `bpos` for the empty tile space is 7. The first neighbor of 7 listed in
`neighbors` is 8. Therefore, the `world` returned by processing the above `world`
and `HKEY` is:

1	2	3
4	5	6
7	8	

This example is captured in the first test below. The second test is developed
in the same manner.

```
(check-expect (process-key (make-world 1 2 3
                                       4 5 6
                                       7 0 8)
                           HKEY)
              (make-world 1 2 3
                          4 5 6
                          7 8 0))
(check-expect (process-key (make-world 2 3 0
                                       1 5 6
                                       4 7 8)
                           HKEY)
              (make-world 2 0 3
                          1 5 6
                          4 7 8))
```

This completes the redesign of `process-key`. Before proceeding make sure
to run the tests.

37 A Bug: Infinite Recursion

When you run the tests you immediately discover that there is at least one
test that does not halt. In fact, the second new test for `process-key` above
contains the following call:

```
(process-key (make-world 2 3 0
                         1 5 6
                         4 7 8)
             HKEY)
```

This call results in an infinite recursion. An infinite recursion is a bug that
prevents a program from returning a value because it never terminates. How
is this possible in the program developed if we have a termination argument?

It turns out that we have done sloppy work and did not think carefully
about the termination argument. The termination argument above claims

Fig. 34 Partial trace of (`find-solution` (`make-world` 2 3 0 1 5 6 4 7 8))

```
(find-solution (make-world 2 3 0 1 5 6 4 7 8))
→ (find-solution (make-world 2 0 3 1 5 6 4 7 8))
→ (find-solution (make-world 2 5 3 1 0 6 4 7 8))
→ (find-solution (make-world 2 5 3 1 7 6 4 0 8))
→ (find-solution (make-world 2 5 3 1 7 6 4 8 0))
→ (find-solution (make-world 2 5 3 1 7 0 4 8 6))
→ (find-solution (make-world 2 5 0 1 7 3 4 8 6))
→ (find-solution (make-world 2 0 5 1 7 3 4 8 6))
→ (find-solution (make-world 2 7 5 1 0 3 4 8 6))
→ (find-solution (make-world 2 7 5 1 8 3 4 0 6))
→ (find-solution (make-world 2 7 5 1 8 3 4 6 0))
→ (find-solution (make-world 2 7 5 1 8 0 4 6 3))
→ (find-solution (make-world 2 7 0 1 8 5 4 6 3))
→ (find-solution (make-world 2 0 7 1 8 5 4 6 3))
→ (find-solution (make-world 2 8 7 1 0 5 4 6 3))
→ (find-solution (make-world 2 8 7 1 6 5 4 0 3))
→ (find-solution (make-world 2 8 7 1 6 5 4 3 0))
→ (find-solution (make-world 2 8 7 1 6 0 4 3 5))
→ (find-solution (make-world 2 8 0 1 6 7 4 3 5))
→ (find-solution (make-world 2 0 8 1 6 7 4 3 5))
→ (find-solution (make-world 2 6 8 1 0 7 4 3 5))
→ (find-solution (make-world 2 6 8 1 3 7 4 0 5))
→ (find-solution (make-world 2 6 8 1 3 7 4 5 0))
→ (find-solution (make-world 2 6 8 1 3 0 4 5 7))
→ (find-solution (make-world 2 6 0 1 3 8 4 5 7))
→ (find-solution (make-world 2 0 6 1 3 8 4 5 7))
→ (find-solution (make-world 2 3 6 1 0 8 4 5 7))
→ (find-solution (make-world 2 3 6 1 5 8 4 0 7))
→ (find-solution (make-world 2 3 6 1 5 8 4 7 0))
→ (find-solution (make-world 2 3 6 1 5 0 4 7 8))
→ (find-solution (make-world 2 3 0 1 5 6 4 7 8))
                        ⋮
```

that since a solution that starts with any valid board always exists, eventually the successor given as input to `find-solution` is WIN and the function halts. Although a solution does exist starting with any given valid board, it is not the case that depth-first search eventually provides `find-solution` with WIN as input. Figure 34 displays a trace of the calls generated by the second new test for `process-key`. Observe that the `world` given to `find-solution` is the same in the first and in the last call displayed. Given that depth-first search always picks the same successor given the same input, the cycle of calls repeats itself forever and the function never halts.

An important lesson to take away is that termination arguments are extremely important. Despite our efforts to carefully design the solution to providing help to the player, there is an infinite recursion. This type of bug is not something you can test for because the program never returns a value. It would be nice to be able to write a test as the following:

```
(check-expect (halts? find-solution
                      (make-world 2 3 0 1 5 6 4 7 8))
              #true)
```

The predicate `halts?` returns `#true` if the given function halts on the given input. Otherwise, it returns `#false`. Determining if a given arbitrary program halts on a given arbitrary input is called *the halting problem*. Alas, `halts?` does not and cannot exist. As you shall learn in an Automata Theory and Formal Languages course the halting problem is unsolvable. Alas, there is no general algorithm that can tell us that if a generative recursive program halts on a given input. This means that problem solvers using generative recursion must carefully craft termination arguments to establish that generative recursive functions terminate.

Another important lesson to take away is that an infinite recursion bug does not always manifest itself. A test for `process-key` revealed the infinite recursion bug but the tests for `find-solution` did not reveal the bug. This is why thorough testing of programs that use generative recursion is so important. The bug could have been revealed by testing `find-solution`, for example, as follows:

```
(define WRLD3 (make-world 2 3 0
                          1 5 6
                          4 7 8))


(define FS-WRLD3-VAL
  (local
    [(define first-child
             (first (map
                     (λ (neigh)
                       (swap-empty WRLD3 neigh))
                     (list-ref neighbors
                               (blank-pos WRLD3)))))]
    (cons WRLD3 (find-solution first-child))))

(check-expect (find-solution WRLD3) FS-WRLD3-VAL)
```

Our quest to find a solution to the problem of providing the player with help must continue. Any ideas on how to solve this problem?

1 Consider adding backtracking to `find-solution`. Does this resolve the infinite recursion bug?

2 Redesign `find-solution` to randomly choose a neighbor for moving the empty tile space instead of always picking the first neighbor. Does this solve the infinite recursion outlined above? Is this a good solution to the problem of providing help to the user? Justify your answer.

3 Consider the following data definition:

    A directed acyclic graph with an end node, dage, is either:
      1. empty
      2. (cons (make-node symbol (listof symbol)) dage),
    where the symbol is the node's name and the (listof symbol)
    are the node's neighbors.

For every **dage**:

1. There is an outgoing edge between a node and each of its neighbors.
2. There is a single node, called the end node, that has no neighbors.
3. There is a single node, the start node, that has no incoming edges.
4. The set of edges do not form any cycles.
5. There is at least one path from every node to the end node.

The following is an example of a **dage**:

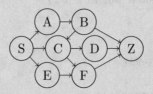

The start node is S and the end node is Z. Observe that the graph does not contain cycles and that there is a path from every node to Z.

Design and implement a function using depth-first search to find the path from a given node to the end node in a given **dage**.

38 What Have We Learned in This Chapter?

The important lessons of this chapter are summarized as follows:

- Sometimes tests using a concrete expected value cannot be written until auxiliary functions are designed and implemented.
- A search space is the set of all possible values that may or may not contain the value searched for.
- When a search space is a tree, either depth-first or breadth-first search may be used.

- Backtracking is not always required for a depth-first search.
- An infinite recursion is a bug that prevents a program from ever returning a value.
- Tests for the result of infinite recursion are never completed.
- Determining if a given arbitrary program halts on a given arbitrary input is called the halting problem.
- The halting problem is unsolvable.
- An infinite recursion bug does not always manifest itself.
- Termination arguments for and through testing of programs that use generative recursion are essential.

Chapter 8
N-Puzzle Version 3

Chapter 7 revealed that depth-first search may get caught in an infinite loop if a search generates the same problem instance more than once. The infinite recursion arises because depth-first search explores a single search path. This means that either multiple search paths must be explored simultaneously or repeatedly exploring the same problem instance must be avoided. We explore a design based on the former because we know how to explore multiple paths in a tree simultaneously. Recall that breadth-first search explores all possible paths. This is accomplished by maintaining a queue of the paths that still need to be explored.

Our goal is to redesign `make-move` to perform a breadth-first search instead of a depth-first search. As in the previous chapter, `make-move` and its auxiliary functions must not be encapsulated inside `process-vk` during the design process. After `make-move` is implemented and testing gives us confidence that it works, all these functions may be re-encapsulated.

39 The Design of `make-move`

39.1 Problem Analysis

The purpose is to solve the puzzle and based on that solution return the next world. If the given `world` is WIN, no moves are needed, and the given `world` is returned. As done with depth-first search, if the given `world` is not WIN, then a solution must be computed. This solution is computed using breath-first search and must have at least two `world`s in it. The move made is the second `world` in the solution.

A solution is represented as was done for depth-first search. That is, a solution is a (`listof world`). This list starts with the given `world` and ends with WIN.

© The Author(s), under exclusive license to Springer Nature Switzerland AG 2022   185
M. T. Morazán, *Animated Program Design*, Texts in Computer Science,
https://doi.org/10.1007/978-3-031-04317-8_8

39.2 Sample Expressions and Differences

Whenever `make-move` receives `WIN` as input, it returns the given world. A
sample expression for processing `WIN` is:

```
;; Sample expressions for make-move
(define MM-WIN-VAL   WIN)
```

If the given `world` is not `WIN`, then the second `world` in a solution is
the move returned. The problem of finding a solution is different from the
problem of making a move. Therefore, an auxiliary function is needed to find
a solution. As per the problem analysis, this solution is searched for using
breadth-first search. Breadth-first search requires a queue of paths that need
to be explored to find a solution. That is, it requires a queue of (`listof`
`world`) to search for a solution. Initially, there is only one known path, and
it only contains the given `world`. Sample expressions using `WRLD1` and `WRLD2`
are:[10]

```
(define MM-WRLD1-VAL (second (find-solution-bfs
                                (enqueue (list (list WRLD1))
                                         E-QUEUE))))
(define MM-WRLD2-VAL (second (find-solution-bfs
                                (enqueue (list (list WRLD2))
                                         E-QUEUE))))
```

Observe that the search for the solution starts with a queue that contains a
single path. Be clear as to why this single path is placed in a list. Recall the
signature for `enqueue`:

```
(listof X) (qof X)  →  (qof X)
```

For our purposes `X` is a path. That is, `X` is a (`listof world`). This is why
the single path in the above sample expressions is placed inside a list.

The only difference among the sample expressions is the `world` processed.
Therefore, `make-move` only requires one parameter. We name this difference
`a-world`.

39.3 Signature, Purpose, and Function Header

As observed in the previous subsection, the input is a `world`. As per the
problem analysis, the returned value is a `world`. The purpose is to make a
move for the player. The function header is written using the chosen function
name and the chosen parameter name. The results of the next steps of the
design recipe are:

---

[10] `WRLD1` and `WRLD2` are defined in Sect. 34.1.

Fig. 35 Visualization of paths explored by breadth-first search

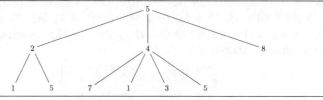

```
;; world → world
;; Purpose: Make a move for the player
(define (make-move a-world)
```

39.4 Tests

The tests using sample computations illustrate that the value of the sample expressions is the same as the value returned by the function when given the `worlds` used in the sample expressions. The tests using sample computations are:

```
;; Tests using sample computations for make-move
(check-expect (make-move WIN)    MM-WIN-VAL)
(check-expect (make-move WRLD1) MM-WRLD1-VAL)
(check-expect (make-move WRLD2) MM-WRLD2-VAL)
```

To write tests using sample values, it is necessary to determine which solution is returned by `find-solution-bfs`. This may be done by drawing the part of the search space explored by breadth-first search until a solution is returned. Consider starting the search with the `world` for this image:

1	2	3
4	5	
7	8	6

Observe that the empty tile space is at `bpos = 5`. Figure 35 displays a visualization of the part of the search space explored by breadth-first search. The tree displays the `bpos` of the empty tile space for each world generated. At the root, the empty tile space is at `bpos = 5`. Given that the root is not `WIN`, the 3 successor worlds of the root are generated, and, therefore, there are now three paths to explore: (5 2), (5 4), and (5 8). Breadth-first search examines the first path and determines `WIN` has not been reached. New paths are added using the successors of 2. The paths to explore now are: (5 4), (5 8), (5 2 1), and (5 2 5). The process is repeated. After determining that the moves in (5 4) have not reached WIN, the paths to explore are (5 8), (5 2 1), (5 2 5), (5 4 7), (5 4 1), (5 4 3), and (5 4 5). At the next iteration, breadth-first search determines that the path (5 8) has reached WIN, and the following path is returned:

1	2	3		1	2	3
4	5			4	5	6
7	8	6		7	8	

This informs us that make-move returns:

1	2	3
4	5	6
7	8	

This result is captured by the first test using sample values below. The second test is developed in the same manner.

```
;; Tests using sample values for make-move
(check-expect (make-move (make-world 1 2 3
                                     4 5 0
                                     7 8 6))
              (make-world 1 2 3
                          4 5 6
                          7 8 0))

(check-expect (make-move (make-world 1 2 3
                                     4 0 6
                                     7 5 8))
              (make-world 1 2 3
                          4 5 6
                          7 0 8))
```

39.5 Function Body

The function's body uses an if-expression to determine if the given world is WIN. If so the given world is returned as done in the first sample expression. The else-expressions is obtained by abstracting over the remaining sample expressions. The function's body is:

```
(if (equal? a-world WIN)
    a-world
    (second (find-solution-bfs
              (enqueue (list (list a-world)) E-QUEUE)))))
```

This completes `make-moves`'s design and implementation. Before running the tests, the auxiliary function must be designed and implemented.

40 The Design of `find-solution-bfs`

40.1 Problem Analysis

The purpose is to find a solution to the puzzle using breadth-first search given a queue of paths to explore. Recall that each path is a (`listof world`). We assume that the given queue nonempty. This can be guaranteed by making sure `make-move` calls this function with an nonempty queue (which it does) and that new paths are always added to the queue when a recursive call is made. This is also straightforward to guarantee given that new paths are constructible using the successors of the last `world` in a path. Therefore, it is not necessary to test if the given queue is empty in this function.

It is necessary to first determine if the first path in the queue has reached `WIN`. If so the first path is returned. To determine if `WIN` has been reached, the last `world` in the path is compared to `WIN`.

If the first path has not reached `WIN`, then the successors of the last world in the first path are used to create new paths. Each new path is created by adding one of these successors to the first path. We must determine where to add the successor. There are two obvious choices: the front or the end of the list. Adding to the front is done using `cons`, and adding to the end is done using `append`. Of these, `cons` is the faster operation, and we explore this design choice here. Note that adding a successor to the front of an existing path means two things: first, that the paths are kept in reversed order (i.e., the starting `world` is at the end of the list) and, second, the last `world` in each path is the first `world` in the (`listof world`) used to represent the path.

After creating the new paths, the first path is removed from the given queue, and the new paths are added to the queue. The search process is repeated using the new queue.

To facilitate the development of sample expressions and tests using sample computations, the following sample (`qof (listof world)`) are defined:

```
;; Sample (qof (listof world))
(define QLOW1 (enqueue (list (list WIN)) E-QUEUE))'
```

```
           (define QLOW2 (enqueue (list (list WIN
                                               (make-world 1 2 3
                                                           4 5 0
                                                           7 8 6)))
                                  E-QUEUE))

           (define QLOW3 (enqueue (list (list (make-world 1 2 0
                                                           4 5 3
                                                           7 8 6)
                                              (make-world 1 2 3
                                                           4 5 0
                                                           7 8 6))
                                        (list (make-world 1 2 3
                                                           4 0 5
                                                           7 8 6)
                                              (make-world 1 2 3
                                                           4 5 0
                                                           7 8 6))
                                        (list (make-world 1 2 3
                                                           4 5 6
                                                           7 8 0)
                                              (make-world 1 2 3
                                                           4 5 0
                                                           7 8 6)))
                                  E-QUEUE))

           (define QLOW4 (enqueue (list (list (make-world 1 2 3
                                                           0 5 6
                                                           4 7 8)
                                              (make-world 1 2 3
                                                           4 5 6
                                                           0 7 8))
                                        (list (make-world 1 2 3
                                                           4 5 6
                                                           7 0 8)
                                              (make-world 1 2 3
                                                           4 5 6
                                                           0 7 8)))
                                  E-QUEUE))
```

Each path in the queues above is in reversed order. The last world in the list
is the first world in the path, and the first world in the list is the last world
in the path.

40.2 Sample Expressions and Differences

If the last world in the queue's first path is WIN, then a solution has been found, and the first path reversed is returned. Sample expressions for this case are written using QLOW1 and QLOW2 as follows:

```
;; Sample expressions for find-solution-bfs
(define FS-QLOW1-VAL
        (local [(define first-path (qfirst QLOW1))]
          (reverse first-path)))


(define FS-QLOW2-VAL
        (local [(define first-path (qfirst QLOW2))]
          (reverse first-path)))
```

Observe that the use of a local variable helps make it easier to understand the code. Compare the first sample expression above with its alternative:

```
(reverse (qfirst QLOW1))
```

Do you agree that use of a local variable makes the code more readable? Always keep in mind that one of the primary goals of a program is to communicate how a problem is solved.

If the last world in the queue's first path is not WIN, then a new queue must be created with the new paths generated from the first path. This queue is the new problem instance and, as suggested by the template for functions using generative recursion, is defined locally. To compute the new paths, the first world of the first path in the queue is needed. The successors of this world are computed, and each is added to the first path to create new paths. To continue the search, the first path is removed from the queue, and the new paths are added. Sample expressions using QLOW3 and QLOW4 are:

```
(define FS-QLOW3-VAL
   (local [(define first-path  (qfirst QLOW3))
           (define first-world (first first-path))
           (define successors
                   (map (λ (neigh)
                          (swap-empty first-world neigh))
                        (list-ref neighbors
                                  (blank-pos first-world))))
           (define new-paths (map (λ (w)
                                     (cons w first-path))
                                   successors))
           (define new-q (enqueue new-paths (dequeue QLOW3)))]
     (find-solution-bfs new-q)))
```

```
(define FS-QLOW4-VAL
  (local [(define first-path (qfirst QLOW4))
          (define first-world (first first-path))
          (define successors
                  (map (λ (neigh)
                          (swap-empty first-world neigh))
                       (list-ref neighbors
                                 (blank-pos first-world))))
          (define new-paths (map (λ (w)
                                    (cons w first-path))
                                 successors))
          (define new-q (enqueue new-paths (dequeue QLOW4)))]
    (find-solution-bfs new-q)))
```

Observe that each element needed or computed is defined as a separate local variable to better communicate how the problem is solved. Compare the first sample expression above with this version that does not make use of local variables:

```
(find-solution-bfs
  (enqueue (map (λ (w)
                   (cons w (qfirst QLOW4)))
                (map (λ (neigh)
                        (swap-empty (first (qfirst QLOW4))
                                    neigh))
                     (list-ref
                      neighbors
                      (blank-pos (first (qfirst QLOW4))))))
           (dequeue QLOW4)))
```

The point should now be clear. Local variables not only allow for multiple uses of an expression's value but also make communicating how a problem is solved more effective. Do not be afraid to use local variables.

Observe that the third and fourth sample expressions have a recursive call to find-solution-bfs. The argument is always a new queue obtained from removing the first path and adding new paths. This new queue is not part of the structure of the given queue. Therefore, this function uses generative recursion. As such, a how statement and a termination argument are required.

The only difference among the sample expressions is the (qof (list world)) processed. This confirms that this function only needs one parameter. We name this difference a-qlow.

40.3 Signature, Statements, and Function Header

The previous steps of the design recipe inform us the input is a (qof (listof world)) and that the output is a (listof world). The purpose is to return a sequence of moves solving the puzzle. The problem is solved by examining the last world in the first path of the given queue. If it is WIN, then the first path is returned given that the puzzle is solved. Otherwise, a new queue is created by removing the first path and adding the paths obtained by adding the successors of the last world in the first path to the first path. Finally, the function header is written using the chosen function and parameter names. The results of the next steps of the design recipe are:

```
;; (qof (listof world)) → (listof world)
;; Purpose: Return sequence of moves to WIN
;; How: If the first world in the first path of
;;      of the given queue is WIN then return
;;      the reverse of the first path. Otherwise,
;;      continue the search with a new queue
;;      obtained by removing the first path and
;;      adding paths that have a successor of the
;;      first world of the first path added to
;;      the first path.
(define (find-solution-bfs a-qlow)
```

40.4 Tests

The tests using sample computations illustrate that the function computes the same value as the evaluation of the sample expressions. The queue in each sample expression is the only input to the function. These tests are:

```
;; Tests using sample computations for find-solution
(check-expect (find-solution-bfs QLOW1) FS-QLOW1-VAL)
(check-expect (find-solution-bfs QLOW2) FS-QLOW2-VAL)
(check-expect (find-solution-bfs QLOW3) FS-QLOW3-VAL)
(check-expect (find-solution-bfs QLOW4) FS-QLOW4-VAL)
```

To write tests using sample values, paper and pencil traversals of the search space may be performed. This is the approach taken to write such tests for make-move. If you think about what breadth-first search returns, however, you realize that it returns the path that reaches WIN first. This means that this occurrence of WIN is at the lowest depth in the search tree. In other words, it is the shortest solution. We have designed an algorithm to find the best solution to the N puzzle. Given this observation, we can write tests using sample values and using the solution with minimum number of moves. These tests using sample values are:

```
;; Tests using sample values for find-solution
(check-expect (find-solution-bfs
                (list (list (make-world 0 2 3
                                        1 5 6
                                        4 7 8))))
              (list
               (make-world 0 2 3
                           1 5 6
                           4 7 8)
               (make-world 1 2 3
                           0 5 6
                           4 7 8)
               (make-world 1 2 3
                           4 5 6
                           0 7 8)
               (make-world 1 2 3
                           4 5 6
                           7 0 8)
               (make-world 1 2 3
                           4 5 6
                           7 8 0)))


(check-expect (find-solution-bfs
                (list (list (make-world 1 2 3
                                        4 6 0
                                        7 5 8))))
              (list
               (make-world 1 2 3
                           4 6 0
                           7 5 8)
               (make-world 1 2 3
                           4 0 6
                           7 5 8)
               (make-world 1 2 3
                           4 5 6
                           7 0 8)
               (make-world 1 2 3
                           4 5 6
                           7 8 0)))
```

40.5 Function Body

The function's body is written using an `if`-expression to determine if the
first path in the queue has reached `WIN`. The then-expression is obtained
by abstracting over the first two sample expressions. The else expression is
obtained by abstracting over the second two sample expressions. Observe
that all the sample expressions define a local variable for the first path in
the queue. This variable may be locally defined once for both branches of
the `if`-expression. Further observe that the first world of the first path is
needed by the second two sample expressions and is needed by the test of the
`if`-expression. Instead of extracting it twice, it may also be locally defined
once for both uses. Based on these observations, the function's body is:

```
(local [(define first-path  (qfirst a-qlow))
        (define first-world (first first-path))]
   (if (equal? first-world WIN)
       (reverse first-path)
       (local
         [(define successors
                  (map (λ (neigh)
                         (swap-empty first-world neigh))
                       (list-ref neighbors
                                 (blank-pos first-world))))
          (define new-paths (map (λ (w)
                                   (cons w first-path))
                                 successors))
          (define new-q (enqueue new-paths
                                  (dequeue a-qlow)))]
         (find-solution-bfs new-q))))
```

40.6 Termination Argument

When the first path's first `world` in the given queue is `WIN` `find-solution-bfs` halts. For each recursive call, one path is taken one step down in the
search tree, and the new paths to this tree level are added to the queue.
Recall that a queue keeps its elements in `FIFO` order. This means that shorter
paths are processed before longer paths. This guarantees that all existing
paths reaching the search tree's level `h` are tested to determine if they are a
solution (i.e., the first world is `WIN`) before any path that reaches level `h + 1`.
Given that a solution exists starting from any valid `world`, eventually, one of
the paths at some height `h` reaches `WIN`, and the function terminates. Observe
that this occurs even though infinite-length paths with loops (i.e., repeated
worlds) are explored. These infinite-length paths are only explored until the
shortest solution is found.

This completes the design and implementation of `find-solution-bfs` and of `make-move`. Before running the tests, make sure to include the following test for `process-key` that led to the discovery that using depth-first search may result in an infinite recursion:

```
(check-expect (process-key (make-world 2 3 0
                                       1 5 6
                                       4 7 8)
              HKEY)
      (make-world 2 0 3
                  1 5 6
                  4 7 8))
```

Barring any typos or syntax errors you may have all the tests pass. Hurray!

41 Performance

It is tremendously satisfying to have solved the problem of offering help to the player. As problem solver, however, we must always ask ourselves if the implementation offers acceptable performance or if further refinements are desirable. To this end, run the game with the following initial `world`:

Do not make any moves and simply request help. What do you notice?

Providing help takes a relatively long time. Why? Perhaps, it was a fluke because the computer was very busy with other tasks? To test this hypothesis, we may run the following timing experiment several times:

```
(time (find-solution-bfs (make-world 1 3 8 5 2 0 4 6 7)))
```

Here are the timing results in milliseconds (after subtracting any garbage collection time) for five executions of the experiment:

Execution time
32,734
33,250
32,546
33,625
33,906

As you may see, it is unlikely that the sluggish response to a help request is a fluke. All five experiments yield similar timings with an average of about 33 seconds. You would imagine that the solution must be very long given that it takes about 33 seconds to compute. In fact, the solution only has 11 moves:

```
(list
  (make-world 1 3 8 5 2 0 4 6 7)
  (make-world 1 3 0 5 2 8 4 6 7)
  (make-world 1 0 3 5 2 8 4 6 7)
  (make-world 1 2 3 5 0 8 4 6 7)
  (make-world 1 2 3 5 6 8 4 0 7)
  (make-world 1 2 3 5 6 8 4 7 0)
  (make-world 1 2 3 5 6 0 4 7 8)
  (make-world 1 2 3 5 0 6 4 7 8)
  (make-world 1 2 3 0 5 6 4 7 8)
  (make-world 1 2 3 4 5 6 0 7 8)
  (make-world 1 2 3 4 5 6 7 0 8)
  (make-world 1 2 3 4 5 6 7 8 0))
```

This is likely to be very surprising to you. Why does it take so long?

To answer this question, let us approximate the number of paths that exists in a full tree of height h. A full tree of height h means that all the empty subtrees are at nodes at height h. Observe that the minimum number of neighbors a bpos has is 2. This means that a lower bound for the number of paths in a tree of height h is the number of paths in a binary tree of height h. The number of paths in a full binary tree of height h is equal to the number of leaves (i.e., nodes without children). We may generalize a formula from the following table:

h	Number of paths
0	$1 = 2^h$
1	$2 = 2^h$
2	$4 = 2^h$
3	$8 = 2^h$
4	$16 = 2^h$
⋮	⋮

As you can see, an invariant property for all the rows of the above table is that:

```
num-paths(h) = 2^h
```

This is an exponential function which means that the number of paths in the queue grows exponentially. Clearly, limiting our analysis to a search space that has the shape of a binary tree is a gross under approximation of the number of paths in the queue. Nonetheless, the point is made that the number

of paths generated that must be explored grows exponentially. This is what
makes breadth-first search slow. Exhaustively searching all possible paths
takes time. For the timing experiment above, there are 98,499 paths in the
queue when the solution is found. That is, indeed, a lot of paths to generate
and explore.

We must face the music. There is nothing worse than a slow video game.
Our search for a solution to providing help to the player needs to continue.
We have a solution, but we need a faster more efficient solution. We can see
that both depth-first and breadth-first search suffer from the same problem:
the repetition of worlds in paths. In depth-first search, repeated worlds lead
to infinite recursion. For breadth-first search, consider a move that takes the
w_1 to w_2. One of the neighbors of w_2 is w_1. This means that the new path
generated that has w_1 as the last board will explore all the paths generated
by the original w_1 that led to w_2. In other words, in the search tree, a subtree
rooted at w_1 is repeated. Therefore, in breadth-first search, repeated worlds
lead to repeatedly exploring copies of the same subtree in the search tree.
These observations suggest that worlds that have been encountered need
to be remembered in order not to explore them again. How can functions
remember?

---

1 A hacker looks at your `find-solution-bfs` function and suggests that
it is silly to keep the paths in a queue because longer solutions are likely
closer to `WIN` and should be explored first. The hacker suggests the following `find-solution-bfs` implementation:

```
;; (listof (listof world)) → (listof world)
(define (find-solution-bfs a-lolow)
  (local [(define first-path (qfirst a-lolow))
          (define first-world (first first-path))]
      (if (equal? first-world WIN)
          (reverse first-path)
          (local
            [(define successors
                      (map (λ (neigh)
                             (swap-empty first-world neigh))
                           (list-ref neighbors
                                     (blank-pos first-world))))
             (define new-paths (map (λ (w)
                                      (cons w first-path))
                                    successors))
             (define new-lolow (append new-paths
                                        (rest a-qlow)))]
            (find-solution-bfs new-q)))))
```

Does this work? Try it out and explain your answer.

2 The function `find-solution-bfs` always creates a new path for every successor. Instead, a new path may be added only for successors that are not already members of the first path. Redesign `find-solution-bfs` using this observation. Does this improve or worsen performance? Justify your answer.

3 Exercise 3 in Chap. 7 defines a `dage`. Design and implement a function using breadth-first search to find the path from a given node to the end node in a given `dage`.

42 What Have We Learned in This Chapter?

The important lessons of this chapter are summarized as follows:

- Breadth-first search simultaneously explores all paths in the search tree.
- Local expressions can make communicating how a problem is solved easier.
- Breadth-first search returns, if it exists, the answer that has the lowest depth in the search tree.
- Test for breadth-first search may be developed by tracing how the search tree is traversed.
- Test for breadth-first search may be developed by testing the known solution with the smallest depth in the search tree.
- Data representation influences the choice of functions used in a program.
- The use of a queue guarantees that shorter paths in the search tree are explored before longer paths.
- Breadth-first search is not caught in an infinite loop due to repetitions.
- Once a problem is solved, always ask yourself if it offers acceptable performance.
- Run a timing experiment multiple times to reduce the probability that the result observed happened by chance.
- The performance of breadth-first search degrades as it traverses deeper into the search tree given that the number of paths grows exponentially.
- Repetitions in the search tree cause an infinite recursion using depth-first search and degrade the performance of breadth-first search by forcing the exploration of subtree copies.

Part III
Accumulative Recursion

Chapter 9
Accumulators

Chapter 8 ended with a question to ponder: How can functions remember? This chapter addresses this issue. When one asks how can a function remember, one must also know *what* a function needs to remember. Remembering, of course, is quite natural in every day activities, and we know what to remember. For example, when we go to the supermarket, we remember the groceries that we must buy, and when you go to the bank to withdraw money from the ATM machine, you remember how much money to withdraw. To go to the grocery store, you can memorize the items to buy, or you write down a list of the items to buy. To withdraw money from an ATM machine, you memorize a natural number for the amount to withdraw, or you write down the natural number (e.g., as a 100 or "one hundred"). Why do you memorize or write down data (or if you like information)? Clearly, the answer is because you will need the data to solve a problem. Put differently, you do not want to suffer from *loss of knowledge* that is useful to solve a problem.

Observe that in the examples above you either memorize or write down the data to remember. This means you are storing the data to remember in brain cells or on paper. Programs, of course, do not have access to brain cells nor paper to store data. So, where can programs store data that needs to be remembered? As illustrated by the examples above, the data that is stored, a list or a natural number, may vary from one problem to another. You already know that programs store values that may vary from one problem instance to another in variables. Therefore, programs can remember data by using variables. Variables that help a program or a function remember data are called *accumulators*. To add one or more accumulators to a function, it is necessary to clearly identify what value the accumulator stores and how the accumulator is exploited. Clearly identifying what an accumulator stores is done by developing an *accumulator invariant*. An accumulator invariant is an assertion that must always be true about the variable when a function is called. Identifying how the accumulator is exploited is done by explaining how the accumulator is used during the computation.

© The Author(s), under exclusive license to Springer Nature Switzerland AG 2022   203
M. T. Morazán, *Animated Program Design*, Texts in Computer Science,
https://doi.org/10.1007/978-3-031-04317-8_9

Accumulators may be added as parameters to functions that use structural or generative recursion. A function is designed and implemented using the appropriate design recipe. If you recognize that a function may benefit from one or more accumulators, then add the necessary accumulators to the function, and develop an accumulator invariant for each. When may a function benefit from an accumulator? There are two common scenarios. When a function is based on structural recursion and the result of a recursive call is input to another function, consider using an accumulator. When a function is based on generative recursion and you understand that the function may fail to produce a result, like `find-solution` in Chap. 7, consider using an accumulator. Using accumulators with functions based on generative recursion is harder because it requires deep insight into why a function may go into an infinite recursion. There are other situations in which the use of an accumulator may be considered, but the most common cases are the two outlined. Recursion that uses accumulators is called *accumulative recursion*.

43 Running Totals

Consider the problem of computing the running totals of a list of numbers. The running total for the ith element of the list is the sum of all the elements up to and including the ith element. In other words, the sum of all the list elements in the index interval [0..i]. Running totals are used by businesses that manage an inventory. For example, if the given `lon` represents the number of items sold each day, a business may track the total number of items sold up to a given date.

43.1 Problem Analysis for `lon-running-totals`

Assume that the given list is called `a-lon`. The first running total is the sum that includes the first number in `a-lon`. The second running total is the sum that includes the first two numbers in `a-lon`. The third running total is the sum that includes the first three numbers in `a-lon`. In general, the kth running total is the sum that includes the first k numbers in `a-lon`. Observe that the number of elements in the sum starts at 1 and increases by 1 for the next running sum. This suggests traversing the interval [0..(sub1 (lenght a-lon))] to compute the running totals.

Traversing an interval is a different problem from traversing a list. Therefore, an auxiliary function is needed. To simplify writing sample expressions and tests, the following sample `lon`s are defined:

```
(define L0 '())
(define L1 (list 1 2 3 4 5 6))
(define L2 (build-list 2500 (λ (n) (random 100000))))
```

43.2 Sample Expressions and Differences for `lon-running-totals`

To compute the running totals of a given lon, the interval to traverse always starts at 0 and ends at 1 less than the length of the given lon. The following are the sample expressions using the defined sample lons:

```
;; Sample expressions for lon-running-totals
(define LRS-L0 (lon-running-totals-helper
              L0
              0
              (sub1 (length L0))))

(define LRS-L1 (lon-running-totals-helper
              L1
              0
              (sub1 (length L1))))

(define LRS-L2 (lon-running-totals-helper
              L2
              0
              (sub1 (length L2))))
```

Observe that the auxiliary function, `lon-running-totals-helper`, to traverse an interval is always called. This auxiliary function is designed and implemented after we are done implementing `lon-running-totals`.

The only difference among the sample expressions is the lon processed. We name this difference a-lon.

43.3 Signature, Function Definition, and Tests for `lon-running-totals`

The only input is a lon, and the output is a lon. The purpose is to return a list of running totals for the given list. The header of the function uses a descriptive function name and the chosen parameter name. The body of the function is obtained by abstracting over the sample expressions. The results of these steps of the design recipe are:

```
;; lon → lon
;; Purpose: Return list of running totals for the
;;          given lon
(define (lon-running-totals a-lon)
  (lon-running-totals-helper a-lon
                            0
                            (sub1 (length a-lon))))
```

The tests using sample computations must illustrate that the function computes the same values as the evaluation of the sample expressions. The tests using sample values must illustrate that a list of running totals is computed given a concrete list. The tests are the following:

```
;; Tests using sample computations for lon-running-totals
(check-expect (lon-running-totals L0) LRS-L0)
(check-expect (lon-running-totals L1) LRS-L1)
(check-expect (lon-running-totals L2) LRS-L2)

;; Tests using sample values for lon-running-totals
(check-expect (lon-running-totals '(-1 0 1)) '(-1 -1 0))
(check-expect (lon-running-totals '(-5 2 4 0))
                                  '(-5 -3 1 1))
```

Before running the tests, the auxiliary function to process an interval must be designed and implemented.

43.4 Problem Analysis for `lon-running-totals-helper`

Assuming that the given interval only contains valid indices into the given list, we must decide how to process the interval. Given that the sum of the first k numbers is needed for each index in the same order as the indices, the easiest approach is to process the interval from low end, `low`, to, `high`, the high end. If the given interval is empty, then there are no sums to compute, and the answer is the empty list. If the given interval is not empty, the sum of the numbers indexed by `[0..low]` is added to the front of the list obtained by processing the rest of the interval.

Computing the sum of the numbers indexed by `[0..low]` is a different problem from computing a list of running totals. Therefore, an auxiliary function is needed. This auxiliary function traverses the interval `[0..low]` to compute the needed sum.

43.5 Sample Expressions and Differences for `lon-running-totals-helper`

The answer is always the empty list when the given interval is empty. A sample expression, processing L0 from 0 to -1, to illustrate this case is:

```
;; Sample expressions for lon-running-totals-helper
(define LORSH-L0-5  '())
```

When the given interval is not empty, an auxiliary function to compute the next running total is called with the given list and the interval [0..low]. This sum is added to the front of the list obtained from processing the rest of the interval. Sample expressions for the running totals for L1 given [0..5] and for L2 given [75..2499] are:

```
(define LORSH-L1-0  (cons (lon-sum L1 0 0)
                          (lon-running-totals-helper
                           L1
                           (add1 0)
                           5)))
```

```
(define LORSH-L2-75 (cons (lon-sum L2 0 75)
                          (lon-running-totals-helper
                           L2
                           (add1 75)
                           2499)))
```

The differences among the sample expressions are the list and the interval processed. We name these differences a-lon, low, and high.

43.6 Signature, Function Definition, and Tests for lon-running-totals-helper

The function processes a lon and an interval (of indices into to the lon). It returns a list of running totals assuming the interval only contains valid indices into the given lon. The function header is written using the chosen function and parameter names. The body of the function is written using an if-expression, as suggested by the template for functions on an interval, to distinguish the interval subtypes. The then-expression is the empty list as illustrated by the first sample expression. The else-expression is obtained by abstracting over the second and third sample expressions. The result of these steps of the design recipe is:

```
;; lon [int..int] → lon
;; Purpose: Return list of running totals for the
;;               given list and interval.
;; Assumption: The given interval contains only
;;               valid indices into the given list
(define (lon-running-totals-helper a-lon low high)
  (if (> low high)
      '()
```

```
(cons (lon-sum a-lon 0 low)
      (lon-running-totals-helper
       a-lon
       (add1 low)
       high))))
```

The remaining step is to write the tests. The tests using sample computations are written using the values used to develop the sample expressions and the variables defined for the values of the sample expressions. The tests using sample values use short lists to illustrate that a list of running totals is returned by the function. The tests are:

```
;; Tests using sample computations for
;;    lon-running-totals-helper
(check-expect (lon-running-totals-helper L0 0 -1)
              LORSH-L0-5)
(check-expect (lon-running-totals-helper L1 0 5)
              LORSH-L1-0)
(check-expect (lon-running-totals-helper L2 75 2499)
              LORSH-L2-75)

;; Tests using sample values for lon-running-totals-helper
(check-expect
  (lon-running-totals-helper
    '(-2 -1 0 1 2)
    0
    4)
  '(-2 -3 -3 -2 0))
(check-expect
  (lon-running-totals-helper
    '(50 25 -40)
    1
    2)
  '(75 35))
```

Before running the tests, the auxiliary function to sum the list's first low + 1 elements must be designed and implemented.

43.7 The lon-sum Function

The problem of summing the list elements indexed by a given interval is solved using structural recursion on an interval. The result of following the steps of the design recipe is:

```
;; lon [int..int] → lon
;; Purpose: Return the list element sum for the
;;          given interval
;; Assumption: The given interval only contains valid
;;               indices into the given lon
(define (lon-sum a-lon low high)
  (if (> low high)
      0
      (+ (list-ref a-lon high)
         (lon-sum a-lon low (sub1 high))))))

;; Sample expressions for lon-sum
(define SFN-L0-VAL 0)
(define SFN-L1-VAL (+ (list-ref L1 3)
                      (lon-sum L1 1 (sub1 3))))
(define SFN-L2-VAL (+ (list-ref L2 99)
                      (lon-sum L2 0 (sub1 99))))

;; Tests using sample computations for lon-sum
(check-expect (lon-sum L0 0 -1) SFN-L0-VAL)
(check-expect (lon-sum L1 1  3) SFN-L1-VAL)
(check-expect (lon-sum L2 0 99) SFN-L2-VAL)

;; Tests using sample values for lon-sum
(check-expect (lon-sum '(10 20 30 40) 0 1) 30)
(check-expect (lon-sum '(0 1 2 3 4 5) 0 5) 15)
```

1 Verify that the steps of the design recipe have been successfully completed for lon-sum. Does anything need to be changed or refined?

2 Refactor lon-sum to process the interval from low to high. Does this have an impact on performance?

44 Running Totals Using an Accumulator

44.1 Problem Analysis

Observe that the solution obtained from designing using structural recursion does a lot of repetitive work. Let L = '(1 2 3 4 5). The following table illustrates the duplicated work done by lon-running-totals-helper:

low	New Running Total Computed
0	(+ 1 0)
1	(+ 1 2 0)
2	(+ 1 2 3 0)
3	(+ 1 2 3 4 0)
4	(+ 1 2 3 4 5 0)

At each step, the computation of the previous running total is repeated. For example, to compute the new running total value when low = 3, the running total computed in the previous row in the table (when low = 2) is repeated. Would you compute the running totals like this if you did not have the benefit of a computer? The answer is that you would not. Instead of recomputing a previous running total, you would remember this value and use it to compute the next running total. When low = 3, for example, you would remember that the running total for low = 2 is 6 and then add 4 to it to obtain the new running total value.

This analysis suggests that computing running totals may benefit from using an accumulator to store the previous running total. At the beginning, the running total starts at 0 given that none of the list's elements have been added. We may refactor lon-running-totals to call an auxiliary function that processes the given list using an accumulator with an initial value of 0.

44.2 Sample Expressions and Differences for lon-running-totals-v2

To compute a given lon's running totals, an auxiliary function is called with the given lon and an initial accumulator value of 0. Sample expressions using the sample lons are:

```
;; Sample expressions for lon-running-totals2
(define LRS2-L0 (lon-running-totals-helper-v2 L0 0))
(define LRS2-L1 (lon-running-totals-helper-v2 L1 0))
(define LRS2-L2 (lon-running-totals-helper-v2 L2 0))
```

The only difference among the sample expressions is the list processed. We call this difference a-lon.

44.3 Function Definition for lon-running-totals-v2

This function is a refactoring of lon-running-totals. As such, it has the same signature and purpose. The function header is written using a new descriptive name and the name chosen for the difference in the sample expressions. The body of the function is obtained by abstracting over the sample expressions. The results of the next steps of the design recipe are:

```
;; lon → lon
;; Purpose: Return the list of running totals for the
;;          given lon
(define (lon-running-totals-v2 a-lon)
  (lon-running-totals-helper-v2 a-lon 0))
```

44.4 Tests for lon-running-totals-v2

Given that this is a refactoring of lon-running-totals, the same tests using sample values are used (just changing the name of the function called). The tests using sample computations are written using the values used in and variables for the values of the sample expressions. The tests are:

```
;; Tests using sample computations for lon-running-totals2
(check-expect (lon-running-totals-v2 L0) LRS2-L0)
(check-expect (lon-running-totals-v2 L1) LRS2-L1)
(check-expect (lon-running-totals-v2 L2) LRS2-L2)

;; Tests using sample values for lon-running-totals2
(check-expect (lon-running-totals-v2 '(-1 0 1))
              '(-1 -1 0))
(check-expect (lon-running-totals-v2 '(-5 2 4 0))
              '(-5 -3 1 1))
```

Before running the tests, the function to process the given lon must be designed and implemented.

44.5 Problem Analysis for lon-running-totals-helper-v2

If the given list is empty, there are no more running totals to compute, and the empty list is the answer. If the given list is not empty, then the next running total is obtained by adding the first list element to the accumulator. This value is both the next value to add to the result and the new value of the accumulator. As part of the result, it is added to the front of the lon obtained from processing the rest of the list. Observe that we have identified how to exploit the accumulator: at each step, it is used to compute the next running total.

We must also clearly identify the value that is stored in the accumulator by developing an accumulator invariant. To do so, it is useful to think of the list given by `lon-running-totals-v2` as divided in two parts: the processed part and the unprocessed part. Let us examine at table that traces the values of these two parts and the accumulator for L = `'(1 2 3 4 5)`:

Processed	Unprocessed	Accumulator
`'()`	`(1 2 3 4 5)`	0
`(1)`	`(2 3 4 5)`	1
`(1 2)`	`(3 4 5)`	3
`(1 2 3)`	`(4 5)`	6
`(1 2 3 4)`	`(5)`	10
`(1 2 3 4 5)`	`'()`	15

Ask yourself what is true about the accumulator at each step captured by the table. More specifically, how is the value stored in the accumulator related to the other values in the table. We can observe that:

```
Sum of L's elements =
   Accumulator + Sum of L's unprocessed elements
```

is true for every step. This is an invariant property that must be maintained by our solution. We can more concisely state the accumulator invariant as:

```
Accumulator = Sum of L's processed elements
            = the previous running total
```

Note that the accumulator invariant is true when `lon-running-totals-helper-v2` is called by `lon-running-totals-v2`. We can confirm this by plugging in values:

```
Accumulator = the previous running total
          0 = the previous running total
          0 = 0
```

The last substitution follows from observing that the previous running total must be 0 because no elements have been processed when `lon-running-totals-v2` calls `lon-running-totals-helper-v2`.

44.6 Sample Expressions and Differences for `lon-running-totals-helper-v2`

When the given `lon` is empty, the answer is always the empty list regardless of the value of the accumulator. We can capture this in the following sample expression to process L0 when the accumulator is 0:

```
;; Sample expressions for lon-running-totals-helper-v2
(define LRTHV2-L0-0 '())
```

When the given list is not empty, the new accumulator is computed by
adding the first number in the given lon to it. This value may be locally
defined. It is added to the front of the lon obtained from processing the rest
of the given lon and is used as the accumulator for the recursive call. Sample
expressions for processing L1 with a given accumulator equal to 0 and for
processing the rest of L2 with a given accumulator equal to the first element
of L2:

```
(define LRTHV2-L1-0
        (local [(define new-accum (+ (first L1) 0))]
          (cons new-accum
                (lon-running-totals-helper-v2
                 (rest L1) new-accum))))

(define LRTHV2-L2-5
        (local [(define new-accum (+ (first (rest L2))
                                     (first L2)))]
          (cons new-accum
                (lon-running-totals-helper-v2
                 (rest (rest L2)) new-accum))))
```

Observe that the values provided as arguments to the call to lon-running-
totals-helper-v2 make the accumulator invariant true.

There are two differences among the sample expressions: the lon processed
and the value of the accumulator. We name these differences a-lon and acc.

44.7 Signature, Statements, and Function Header for
lon-running-totals-helper-v2

The inputs to this function are a lon to process and a number as an accumulator. According to problem analysis, a lon is returned. The purpose is to
return a lon containing the given list's running totals given an accumulator
containing the previous running total. In addition to the purpose statement,
the accumulator invariant is written to clearly communicate the design to
any reader of the code. The function header is written using a descriptive
function name and the chosen names for the differences among the sample
expressions. The next steps of the design recipe yield:

```
;; lon number → lon
;; Purpose: Return the list of running totals for the
;;             given lon and given previous running total.
;; Accumulator Invaraint: acc = previous running total
(define (lon-running-totals-helper-v2 a-lon acc)
```

44.8 Tests for `lon-running-totals-helper-v2`

The tests using sample computations illustrate that the evaluation of the
sample expressions and calling the function with values used to develop the
sample expressions yield the same results. These tests are:

```
;; Tests using sample computations for
;;    lon-running-totals-helper-v2
(check-expect (lon-running-totals-helper-v2 L0 0)
              LRTHV2-L0-0)
(check-expect (lon-running-totals-helper-v2 L1 0)
              LRTHV2-L1-0)
(check-expect (lon-running-totals-helper-v2 (rest L2)
                                            (first L2))
              LRTHV2-L2-5)
```

The tests using sample values illustrate that the function works for concrete values. Short lists are used to easily communicate that running totals
starting with the given accumulator value are returned. These tests are:

```
;; Tests using sample values for
;;    lon-running-totals-helper-v2
(check-expect (lon-running-totals-helper-v2 '(1 2 3)  0)
              '(1 3 6))
(check-expect (lon-running-totals-helper-v2
                (rest (rest '(10 4 5 6)))
                14)
              '(19 25))
```

44.9 Function Body for `lon-running-totals-helper-v2`

The body of the function uses an `if`-expression to distinguish the list subtype.
The then-expression is the same as the first sample expression. The else-
expression is obtained by abstracting over the remaining sample expressions.
The body of the function is:

```
(if (empty? a-lon)
    '()
    (local [(define new-accum (+ (first a-lon) acc))]
      (cons new-accum
            (lon-running-totals-helper-v2
              (rest a-lon)
              new-accum))))
```

This completes the design and implementation of the function to compute running totals using an accumulator. Run the tests and make sure they all pass.

45 Performance and Complexity Analysis

We have two solutions to compute running totals. Is there any reason to prefer one over another? To start answering this question, we perform a small empirical study using L2. We chose L2 because it is long and should not suffer from any bias given that it is lon generated using randomness. The following experiments were executed five times:

```
(time (lon-running-totals    L2))
(time (lon-running-totals-v2 L2))
```

The following table displays the CPU times in milliseconds obtained (after subtracting, if any, garbage collection time):

	lon-running-totals	lon-running-totals-v2
Run 1	21, 406	0
Run 2	21, 563	0
Run 3	21, 860	0
Run 4	13, 562	15
Run 5	14, 031	0

The empirical data shows some variation, but it clearly suggests that using an accumulator has made the solution significantly faster. The average CPU time decreased from about 18.5 seconds without using an accumulator to 3 milliseconds when using an accumulator.

To explain such an impressive performance improvement, we examine each solution's abstract running time. The function lon-running-totals-helper is called n + 1 times in the worst case, where n is the size of the list given to lon-running-totals. This means that the number of times it is called is $O(n)$. For n of those calls lon-sum is called. In the worst case, the function lon-sum is called n + 1 times. This makes the calls to lon-sum $O(n)$. Thus, the complexity of lon-running-totals is $O(n) * O(n) = O(n^2)$.

The function lon-running-totals-helper-v2 is called n + 1 times in the worst case, where n is the size of the list given to lon-running-totals-v2. For each of those calls, a constant number of operations are performed (i.e., empty?, +, cons, and rest). This makes the number of operations performed by lon-running-totals-v2 $O(k * n) = O(n)$. The complexity of the solution has been reduced from quadratic to linear. This explains the impressive performance improvement.

3 Design and implement a function to compute the running maximums for a (listof lon). The following test illustrates how the function works:

```
(check-expect (running-maxes '((1 4 3)
                               (87 26 54 31 90)
                               (78 77 21  9 -5)
                               ( 0  4 100 8 -10)))
              '(4 90 90 100))
```

4 Consider the following function to reverse a list:

```
;; (listof X) → (listof X)
;; Purpose: To reverse the given list
(define (rev L)
  (if (empty? L)
      '()
      (append (rev (rest L)) (list (first L)))))

;; Tests
(check-expect (rev '()) '())
(check-expect (rev '(1 2 3 4 5)) '(5 4 3 2 1))
(check-random
  (rev (build-list 1500 (λ (i) (random 100000))))
  (reverse (build-list 1500 (λ (i) (random 100000)))))
```

Observe that the result of the recursive call is input to append. Refactor the function to use accumulative recursion. Does it have an impact on performance? Justify your answer.

5 Design and implement a function using accumulative recursion that takes as input a (listof posn) and that returns the number of posns whose x and y values are the same.

6 Design and implement a function using accumulative recursion that finds the longest string in a (listof string).

7 Design and implement a function using accumulative recursion to compute n^2 by adding the first n odd natural numbers.

Fig. 36 A sample graph with 8 nodes and 12 edges

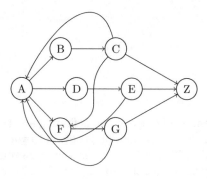

8 Design and implement a function using accumulative recursion that takes as input a nonempty binary search tree of numbers and a number in the binary search tree and that returns the path of 'lefts and 'rights followed to reach the number. The following test illustrates how the function works:

```
(check-expect (find-path '(50 (25 (15 10 17)
                                   (35 30 38))
                               (75 (65 55 70)
                                   (90 81 99)))
                         30)
              '(left right left))
```

46 Finding a Path in a Directed Graph

A directed graph is a representation of a relation or of a map. Every graph has a finite set of nodes and arrows. Each arrow connects two nodes. The tip of an arrow indicates the destination node. A global positioning system (GPS), for example, may represent maps containing cities and roads as a graph. Each node in the graph represents a city, and each edge represents a direct road between two cities. Figure 36 displays a graph that has 8 nodes and 13 edges. The finite set of edges is:

A B C D E F G Z

The finite set of edges is:

```
(A B) (A D) (A F)
(B C)
(C F) (C Z)
(D E)
(E A) (E Z)
(F G)
(G A) (G Z)
```

A common problem involving a graph is finding a path between two nodes. An answer to this problem, for example, is given to you every time you enter an address into a GPS. The start point is your location, and the end point is the address your wish to get to. How is this done? Solving this problem is our next challenge.

46.1 Data Analysis

In order to solve a problem about a graph, we need a representation for a graph. That is, we need to perform data analysis and develop a data definition for a graph. There are many possible representations of a graph. We shall use an *adjaceny list* representation. In an adjacency list representation, a graph is a list of nodes. Every node has a name and a list of the names of its neighbors following outgoing edges.

For our purposes, the data definition of a node is:

```
#|
A node is a structure, (make-node symbol (listof symbol)),
where the symbol is the node's name and the
(listof symbol) is a list of the names of the node's
neighbors on outgoing edges.
|#
```

The design recipe asks us to define samples of every data definition. The following are sample nodes:

```
;; Nodes for G1
(define NODEA (make-node 'A '(B D F)))
(define NODEB (make-node 'B '(C)))
(define NODEC (make-node 'C '(Z)))
(define NODED (make-node 'D '(E)))
(define NODEE (make-node 'E '(Z)))
(define NODEF (make-node 'F '(G)))
(define NODEG (make-node 'G '(Z)))
(define NODEZ (make-node 'Z '()))
```

```
;; Nodes for G2
(define NODEC2 (make-node 'C '()))

;; Nodes for G3
(define NODEC3 (make-node 'C '(A F Z)))
(define NODEE3 (make-node 'E '(A Z)))
(define NODEG3 (make-node 'G '(A Z)))
```

As suggested by the comments, these nodes are used to build sample graphs. The design recipe also asks us to develop a function template for all data definitions. The following is the template for functions on a node:

```
#| Template for functions on a node

node ... → ...
Purpose:
(define (f-on-node a-node ...)
  ...(node-name a-node)...(node-neighs a-node)...)

;; Sample expressions for f-on-node
(define NODEA-VAL ...)
        ⋮

;; Tests using sample computations for f-on-node
(check-expect (f-on-node NODEA ...) NODEA-VAL)
        ⋮

;; Tests using sample values for f-on-node
(check-expect (f-on-node ... ...) ...)
        ⋮
|#
```

A graph contains an arbitrary number of nodes. A list is a natural fit to represent a graph. The data definition for a graph is:

```
#| A graph is a nonempty (listof node). |#
```

The following are sample graphs:

```
(define G1 (list NODEA NODEB NODEC NODED
                 NODEE NODEF NODEG NODEZ))

(define G2 (list NODEA NODEB NODEC2 NODED
                 NODEE NODEF NODEG  NODEZ))

(define G3 (list NODEA  NODEB NODEC3 NODED
                 NODEE3 NODEF NODEG3 NODEZ))
```

The last sample graph, G3, corresponds to the graph in Fig. 36. The template
for functions on a graph is:

```
#| Template for functions on a graph

graph ... → ...
Purpose:
(define (f-on-graph a-graph ...)
  (if (empty? (rest a-graph))
      (f-on-node (first a-graph) ...)
      (...(f-on-node (first a-graph)...)...
       ...(f-on-graph (rest a-graph)...)...)))

;; Sample expressions for f-on-graph
(define FONG-G1-VAL ...)
(define FONG-G2-VAL ...)
(define FONG-G13-VAL ...)
                    .
                    .
                    .

;; Tests using sample computations for f-on-graph
(check-expect (f-on-graph G1 ...) FONG-G1-VAL)
(check-expect (f-on-graph G2 ...) FONG-G2-VAL)
(check-expect (f-on-graph G3 ...) FONG-G3-VAL)
                    .
                    .
                    .

;; Tests using sample values for f-on-graph
(check-expect (f-on-graph ... ...) ...)
                    .
                    .
                    .
|#
```

9 Rewrite the data definition for a graph to explicitly list the graph
subtypes, and draw G1 and G2.

Finally, observe that a path between two nodes may or may not exist. For
example, in Fig. 36, there is a path, F → G → A, from F to A, and there is
no path from Z to D. This means there are path subtypes. The following data
definition is used to represent a path:

```
#|
A path is either:
  1. (listof symbol)
  2. 'no-path
|#
```

10 Develop sample **paths** and a template for functions on a path.

46.2 Design and Implementation of `find-path`

46.2.1 Problem Analysis

To find a path in a given graph, the starting and ending nodes' are needed. We can observe that a path from **start** to **end**, if it exists, starts with **start** and then contains a path from an outgoing neighbor of **start** to **end**. This clearly suggests that the given graph must be traversed to find such a path or to determine that such a path does not exist. How can a graph be traversed?

A graph is not a linear data structure given that a node may have an arbitrary number of outgoing neighbors. In Fig. 36, for example, Z has 0 outgoing neighbors, and C has 3 outgoing neighbors. This is similar to the number of subtrees a node in a tree may have. As studied in Chap. 6, a nonlinear data structure may be traversed using depth-first search or breadth-first search. Without loss of generality, we explore a design based on depth-first search.

Recall that depth-first search completely explores a path in the search space before exploring any other paths. As we learned in Chap. 7, we must be careful about repetitions in the search space to avoid an infinite recursion. Is this an issue when searching for a path in a graph using depth-first search? Consider finding a path from A to Z in G3 (i.e., the graph displayed in Fig. 36). You can clearly see that there is a path from A to Z. In fact, there are many paths from A to Z. We only need to find one of these paths. The steps for the path search using a depth-first approach may be outlined as follows:

```
path from A to Z = A → path from one in (B D F) to Z
                 = A → path from B to Z
                 = A → B → from one in (C) to Z
                 = A → B → path from C to Z
                 = A → B → C → from one in (A F Z)
                 = A → B → C → path from A to Z
                   ⋮
```

Alas, falling into an infinite recursion is an issue when traversing a graph using depth-first search.

How can we prevent an infinite recursion? Observe that the problem arises because a path from a node already visited, A, is used in the search again. This suggests that a depth-first search may benefit from an accumulator used to remember the nodes that have been visited during a search. If a node has been visited during a search, it is not used to find a path again. This analysis suggests that an auxiliary function that has an accumulator as an additional parameter is needed. This accumulator stores the names of the nodes visited. At the beginning of the search, this accumulator is empty because no nodes have been visited.

46.2.2 Sample Expressions and Differences

As outlined during problem analysis, this function calls an auxiliary function with the given graph, the given node names, and an empty accumulator. This is captured by the following sample expressions:

```
;; Sample expressions for find-path
(define FP-AZ-G1 (find-path-acc G1 'A 'Z '()))
(define FP-AZ-G2 (find-path-acc G2 'C 'Z '()))
(define FP-AZ-G3 (find-path-acc G3 'A 'Z '()))
```

Observe that there are expressions for a successful search (the first and third) and for a failed search (the second).

There are three differences: the graph to search, symbol for the starting node, and a symbol for the destination node. We call these differences: a-graph, start, and end. Observe that we give the auxiliary function called a descriptive name.

46.2.3 Signature, Purpose, and Function Definition

The input types are the types of the three differences in the sample expressions, and the returned type is a path as established by data and problem analysis. The purpose is to find a path in the given graph between the node named as the first given symbol and the node named as the second given symbol. The header is written using a descriptive function name and the descriptive parameter names chosen for the differences in the sample expressions. We assume that nodes with the given names exist in the graph. Finally, the body of the function is obtained by abstracting over the sample expressions. These steps of the design recipe yield:

```
;; graph symbol symbol → path
;; Purpose: Find a path between nodes with the given names
;;          in the given graph
;; Assumption: Given node names are in the given graph
(define (find-path a-graph start end)
  (find-path-acc a-graph start end '()))
```

46.2.4 Tests

The tests using sample computations are written using the values used in the sample expressions and the variables defined for the value of the sample expressions. They illustrate that the function evaluates to the same value as the sample expressions. These tests are:

```
;; Test using sample computations for find-path
(check-expect (find-path G1 'A 'Z) FP-AZ-G1)
(check-expect (find-path G2 'C 'Z) FP-AZ-G2)
(check-expect (find-path G3 'A 'Z) FP-AZ-G3)
```

Observe that finding a path from A to Z in G3 should not generate an infinite recursion.

The tests using sample values are written to illustrate, using a concrete value, that the function computes the correct **path**. Care must be taken to determine the proper expected value because there may be multiple paths between two nodes in a graph. If so, the expected value must be the **path** found by depth-first search. In G1, for example, there is no path from Z to A. This is captured by the following test:

```
;; Test using sample values for find-path
(check-expect (find-path G1 'Z 'A) 'no-path)
```

In G2 there is only one path from F to Z. A depth-first search goes from F to its only neighbor G. From G it moves to its only neighbor Z. This is captured by the following test:

```
(check-expect (find-path G2 'F 'Z) '(F G Z))
```

As a third test in this suite, we use the example from the problem analysis that illustrated that an infinite recursion is a concern: finding a path from A to Z in G3 (the graph displayed in Fig. 36). Depth-first search moves from A to its first neighbor B and then onto B's only neighbor C. At this point in the computation, A and B have been visited. From C depth-first search moves to F given that C's first neighbor, A, has been visited. The search then moves to G followed by Z. This is captured by the following test:

```
(check-expect (find-path G3 'C 'Z) '(A B C F G Z))
```

Observe that the accumulator is used to not fall into an infinite recursion. This is how the accumulator is exploited by **find-path-acc**. Note that the above test illustrates that the function does not find the shortest path between two nodes.

46.3 Design and Implementation of `find-path-acc`

46.3.1 Problem Analysis

This function must use a depth-first search to find a path in the given graph starting at the node named as the first given name, say node I, to the node, say J, named as the second given name without going through any of the nodes named as any element in the accumulated list of visited names. A node is visited if its neighbors are part of the search. We can informally state that the accumulator invariant is:

```
Accumulator = nodes whose neighbors are part of the search
```

Initially, the invariant is true because `find-path` provides the empty list as its value and there are no nodes whose neighbors are part of the search.

If the given node names are the same, then there is a path between them that only contains the given name. For example, the path from A to A is (A). Observe that this path does not go through any nodes that have a name included in the accumulator.

If the given node names are not equal, then I's unvisited neighbors are computed, and a search for a path from any of these neighbors to J is performed. The unvisited neighbors are computed using the accumulator of visited node names to filter I's neighbors. If a path from one of I's unvisited neighbors to J does not exist, then there is no path from I to J, and the answer is `'no-path`. If there is a path, p, from one of I's neighbors to J, then the path from I to J is obtained by adding I to the front of p.

Finding a path from one of I's unvisited neighbors to J is a different problem from finding a path from I to J. Therefore, an auxiliary function that processes the list of neighbors is needed. In the worst case, the auxiliary function calls `find-path-acc` for each of I's neighbors. This informs us that these functions are mutually recursive and that the auxiliary function needs the value of the accumulator, if for no other reason, to call `find-path-acc`.

46.3.2 Sample Expressions and Differences

When the given names match, then, regardless of the given `graph` and the given accumulator, the answer is a path that only contains that one name. This is illustrated by the following sample expression to search for a path from A to A in G1 when the accumulator is empty:

```
;; Sample expressions for find-path-acc
(define FPACC-AA-G1 (list 'A))
```

If the names do not match then the new value for the visited node names (i.e., the new accumulator value), the unvisited neighbors from the starting node and the result of searching for a path from any of these neighbors may be locally defined. The new visited nodes have the starting node added to it given that its neighbors become part of the search. The unvisited neighbors are computed using the new accumulator value to filter the starting node's neighbors. Observe that the name of the starting node is included in the filtering because the start node may be its own neighbor (i.e., there is an edge from the starting node to itself). A path from any neighbor is computed by calling an auxiliary function to process the list of unvisited neighbors. This function needs the given graph, the unvisited neighbors, the name of the end node, and the accumulator containing the nodes not to revisit. The nodes not to revisit are the nodes in the accumulator and the starting node given that its neighbors are made part of the search when the auxiliary function is called. If searching for a path from any of the neighbors is 'no-path, then the answer is 'no-path. Otherwise, the starting name is added to the front of the path from any of the neighbors to the ending node. The following sample expressions illustrate this idea by searching for a path from A to Z in G1 with C visited and from Z to B in G3 with no nodes visited:

```
(define FPACC-AZ-G1
        (local [(define new-visited (cons 'A '(C)))
                (define start-unvisited-neighs
                        (filter
                          (λ (s) (not (member? s new-visited)))
                          (node-neighs
                            (first
                              (filter
                                (λ (n) (eq? (node-name n) 'A))
                                G1)))))
                (define path-from-neigh
                        (find-path-from-neighbors
                          G1
                          start-unvisited-neighs
                          'Z
                          new-visited))]
          (if (eq? path-from-neigh 'no-path)
              'no-path
              (cons 'A path-from-neigh)))))

(define FPACC-ZB-G3
        (local [(define new-visited (cons 'Z '()))
                (define start-unvisited-neighs
                        (filter
                          (λ (s) (not (member? s new-visited)))
                          (node-neighs
                            (first
                              (filter
                                (λ (n) (eq? (node-name n) 'Z))
                                G1)))))
```

```
                    (define path-from-neigh
                        (find-path-from-neighbors
                         G1
                         start-unvisited-neighs
                         'B
                         new-visited))]
                (if (eq? path-from-neigh 'no-path)
                    'no-path
                    (cons 'Z path-from-neigh))))
```

Observe that the accumulator is exploited to filter the neighbors of the starting node. Further, observe that the starting node's name is added to the
accumulator when the auxiliary function is called. For the reason indicated
above, this is the correct course of action in order to maintain the accumulator
invariant.

The differences among the sample expressions are the given graph, the
given node names, and the given accumulator. We name these differences
a-graph, start, end, and visited.

46.3.3 Signature, Purpose, Invariant, and Function Header

The types of the four inputs are determined by differences among the sample
expressions. The return type and purpose are determined as part of problem
analysis. The signature and purpose statement are:

```
;; graph symbol symbol (listof symbol) → path
;; Purpose: Find a path between the given node names in
;;          the given graph without going through any
;;          visited neighbors
```

As part of the design when using accumulative recursion, there must be an invariant for each accumulator. In this example, there is only one accumulator:
visited. The accumulator invariant is:

```
;; Accumulator Invariant:
;; visited = nodes whose neighbors are part of the search
```

We also assume that the given node names are part of the given graph. The
assumption statement is:

```
;; Assumption: Given node names are in the given graph
```

The function header is written using the chosen descriptive function name
and the chosen descriptive name for the differences among the sample expressions. The function header is:

```
(define (find-path-acc a-graph start end visited)
```

46.3.4 Tests

The tests using sample computations illustrate that the values of the sample expressions are the same as the values returned by the function when given the values used to write the sample expressions. The tests are:

```
;; Test using sample computations for find-path-acc
(check-expect (find-path-acc G1 'A 'A '())  FPACC-AA-G1)
(check-expect (find-path-acc G1 'A 'Z '(C))  FPACC-AZ-G1)
(check-expect (find-path-acc G3 'Z 'B '())  FPACC-ZB-G3)
```

The tests using sample values illustrate the answers returned by the function using concrete values. For G2, a path from A to Z without going through B and D moves from A to F to G and finally to Z. For G3, a path from F to Z without going through G does not exist. These examples are used to write the following tests:

```
;; Test using sample values for find-path-acc
(check-expect (find-path-acc G2 'A 'Z '(B D))
              (list 'A 'F 'G 'Z))
(check-expect (find-path-acc G3 'F 'Z '(G)) 'no-path)
```

46.3.5 Function Body

The function body uses an if-expression to determine if the given names match. The then-expression returns a list containing only the matching name as illustrated by the first sample expression. Without loss of generality, a list containing end is created. The else-expression is obtained by abstracting over the second and third sample expressions. The body of the function is:

```
(if (eq? start end)
    (list end)
    (local
      [(define start-unvisited-neighs
         (filter
           (λ (s) (not (member? s visited)))
           (node-neighs
             (first
               (filter (λ (n)
                         (eq? (node-name n) start))
                       a-graph)))))
       (define path-from-neigh
         (find-path-from-neighbors
           a-graph
           start-unvisited-neighs
           end
           (cons start visited)))]
```

```
(if (eq? path-from-neigh 'no-path)
    'no-path
    (cons start path-from-neigh))))
```

This completes find-path-acc's design and implementation. Before running the tests, find-path-from-neighbors's design and implementation must be completed.

46.4 Design and Implementation of find-path-from-neighbors

46.4.1 Problem Analysis

The purpose of this function is to find a path in the given graph from a node whose name is in the given list of neighbor names to the end node with the given name without going through any node whose name is in the given accumulator. This is done using depth-first search with backtracking. Backtracking is needed because there may not be a way to get to the end node from every neighbor. Based on find-path-acc's design and implementation, we may assume that all the given neighbors and the end node are in the given graph and that none of the given neighbors are in visited. The latter is a safe assumption because find-path-acc filters out any neighbor in the accumulator.

If the neighbor list is empty, then a path to the end node does not exist, and the answer is 'no-path. If the neighbor list is not empty, then the path from the first neighbor to the end node is determined. This is done by calling, find-path-acc, a function to find a path between two nodes. The given graph and end node name are passed unchanged. The first neighbor is the argument for start. The accumulator is also passed unchanged because finding the path from the first neighbor does not add any nodes to the search. If there is a path of node names from the first neighbor to the end node, then this path is returned as the path from any neighbor to the end node. If the path from the first neighbor to the end node is 'no-path, then backtracking is necessary to explore the possible paths from the rest of the neighbors. This is accomplished by recursively processing the rest of the neighbors.

46.4.2 Sample Expressions and Differences

As per the problem analysis, the answer is 'no-path when the list of neighbor names is empty. This is captured, for example, by the following sample expression to search for a path to 'A in G1 with an empty list of neighboring names and an empty accumulator:

```
;; Sample Expressions for find-path-from-neighbors
(define FPN-ZA-G1 'no-path)
```

If the list of neighbor names is not empty, then a local variable is defined for the **path** from the first neighbor to the end node. This is accomplished by calling **find-path-acc** with the given graph, the first neighbor's node name, the given end node name, and the given accumulator. If the returned **path** is not 'no-path, then it is returned as the answer. Otherwise, backtracking is performed with a recursive call that is given the same graph, the rest of the neighbor names, the same end node name, and the same accumulator. The following sample expressions search for a path in G2 from the neighbors of A to Z with A visited and in G3 from the neighbors of F to A with F visited:

```
(define FPN-AZ-G2
        (local [(define path-from-first
                        (find-path-acc
                         G2
                         (first '(B D F))
                         'Z
                         '(A)))]
            (if (not (eq? path-from-first 'no-path))
                path-from-first
                (find-path-from-neighbors G2
                                          (rest '(B D F))
                                          'Z
                                          '(A)))))
(define FPN-FA-G3
        (local [(define path-from-first
                        (find-path-acc
                         G3
                         (first '(E))
                         'A
                         '(F)))]
            (if (not (eq? path-from-first 'no-path))
                path-from-first
                (find-path-from-neighbors
                 G3
                 (rest '(E))
                 'A
                 '(F)))))
```

The differences among the sample expressions are the graph, the list of neighbor names, the end node name, and the list of visited node names. We name these differences: a-graph, neighs, end, and visited.

46.4.3 Signature, Purpose, Invariant, and Function Header

The input types are graph, (listof symbol), symbol, and (listof symbol).
The return type is path. The purpose is to find a path from any of the
given node names to the given end node name without going through any of
the nodes represented in the given visited list. The accumulator invariant is
the same as for find-path-acc. That is, an accumulator invariant does not
change among mutually recursive functions. The assumptions are that all the
given node names are in the given graph and that none of the given neighbors
have been visited. The function header is written using the descriptive names
chosen for the function and for the differences among the sample expressions.
The next steps of the design recipe produce:

```
;; graph (listof symbol) symbol (listof symbol) → path
;; Purpose: Find a path from any neighbor to the given
;;          node in the given graph without going through
;;          any visited neighbors
;; Accumulator Invariant:
;;   visited = nodes whose neighbors are part of the search
;; Assumptions: Given neighbors and node name are in the
;;                    given graph
;;                    None of the given neighbors are in visited
(define (find-path-from-neighbors a-graph neighs end visited)
```

46.4.4 Tests

To illustrate that the function produces the same values as the evaluation
of the sample expressions, the concrete values used to develop the sample
expressions are given as input to the function. These tests are:

```
;; Tests using sample computations for find-path-from-neighbors
(check-expect (find-path-from-neighbors G1 '()       'A '())
              FPN-ZA-G1)
(check-expect (find-path-from-neighbors G2 '(B D E) 'Z '(A))
              FPN-AZ-G2)
(check-expect (find-path-from-neighbors G3 '(E)       'A '(E))
              FPN-FA-G3)
```

The tests using sample values require us to determine the path returned
by depth-first search. In G1 there is not path from the neighbors of B to E that
does not go through B. In G3, the path from the neighbors of F to C without
going through F goes through G (the first unvisited neighbor of F), A the first
unvisited neighbor of G, B (the first unvisited neighbor of A), and C (the first
unvisited neighbor of B). These examples are captured by the following tests:

```
;; Tests using sample values for find-path-from-neighbors
(check-expect (find-path-from-neighbors G1 '(C) 'E '(B))
              'no-path)

(check-expect (find-path-from-neighbors G3 '(G) 'C '(F))
              '(G A B C))
```

46.4.5 Function Body

The function body uses an if-expression to determine if the list of neighbor names is empty. If so, the first sample expression informs us that the then-expression is 'no-path. The else-expression is obtained by abstracting over the second and third sample expressions. The body of the function is:

```
(if (empty? neighs)
    'no-path
    (local [(define path-from-first
                    (find-path-acc a-graph (first neighs) end visited))]
       (if (not (eq? path-from-first 'no-path))
           path-from-first
           (find-path-from-neighbors a-graph
                                     (rest neighs)
                                     end
                                     visited))))
```

46.5 Termination Argument

The mutual recursion between find-path-acc and find-path-from-neighbors is based on finding a path from the neighbors of a node. A different start node is explored every time find-path-acc is called. This program, therefore, is based on generative recursion and requires a termination argument.

We can observe that find-path-acc is never called with the same start node name because this name is placed in the accumulator to prevent following a loop to it. This means that any path explored does not contain repeated nodes and depth-first search is not caught in an infinite loop due to cycles in the given graph. As the path explored gets larger, the names in the accumulator increase. This means one of two things. Either the neighbors of the start node are all visited or the end node is reached. In both cases, the program terminates.

This concludes the design and implementation of the solution to the problem of finding a path in a graph. Run the tests and make sure they all pass.

11 Section 41 suggests that breadth-first search may repeat a search. For example, finding a path from A to Z in the graph displayed in Fig. 36 starts with a single path (A) in the queue. Processing the first path in the queue removes the first path and places the new (reversed) paths in the queue to make it:

    ((B A) (D A) (F A))

Processing the first path in the queue makes the queue:

    (D A) (F A)) (C B A)

Processing the first path in the queue makes the queue:

    (F A) (C B A) (E D A)

Processing the first path in the queue makes the queue:

    (C B A) (E D A) (G F A)

Processing the next path in the queue leads to repetition:

    (E D A) (G F A) (A C B A) (F C B A) (Z C B A)

Observe that the third path in the queue, ending with A, means that breadth-first may again search all the (sub-)paths starting at A. This repetition is inefficient.

Searching for a path in a graph using breadth-first search can benefit from an accumulator that remembers the nodes whose successors are already part of the search. This accumulator may be used to avoid the repetition outlined. Design and implement a program to find a path in a graph using breadth-first search that does not re-explore paths starting at any node.

47 Revisiting Insertion Sorting

Section 24 discusses the design and implementation of insertion sorting. The (unencapsulated) developed functions are:

```
;; insert: a-num lon → lon
;; Purpose: To insert a num into a lon sorted in
;; non-decreasing order
(define (insert a-num a-lon)
  (cond [(empty? a-lon) (cons a-num '())]
        [(<= a-num (first a-lon)) (cons a-num a-lon)]
        [else (cons (first a-lon)
                    (insert a-num (rest a-lon)))]))
```

```
;; sort: lon → lon
;; Purpose: Sort given lon in nondecreasing order
(define (insertion-sorting a-lon)
  (cond [(empty? a-lon) '()]
        [else (insert (first a-lon)
                      (insertion-sorting (rest a-lon)))]))
```

Observe that in both functions, the result of a recursive call is input to another function. This suggests that these functions may benefit from the use of accumulators. Our goal is to redesign these functions to exploit accumulators.

To facilitate the writing of sample expressions and tests the sample lists, LON0-LON6, defined at the beginning of Chap. 5 are used. In addition, the following sorted lists are defined:

```
(define LON7 '(1 2 3 4 5))
(define LON8 '(-10 -5 0 5 10))
```

47.1 The Redesign of insert

47.1.1 Problem Analysis

Let us start with refactoring insert. This function traverses the given sorted list to find the position of the given number. As the search progresses, a new list is built. Observe that this list may be accumulated as the list traversal progresses. The traversed elements may be kept sorted. At each step the next element of the sorted list is added to the accumulator. In essence, the accumulator is a copy of the processed sublist. Table 3 illustrates the design idea. The process of adding the first number in the sorted list to the accumulator continues until the position of the given number is found or the sorted list is empty. In Table 3 the process stops because the position of 5 has been found.

If the sorted list is empty, then the given number is larger than all the numbers in the accumulator, and the answer is obtained by adding the given number at the end of the accumulator. If the given number is less than or equal to the first number in the sorted list (like in the last line in Table 3), then the given number's place is in the front of the sorted list. The answer is constructed by appending the accumulator and the consing of the given number and the sorted list. If the given number is greater than the first number in the sorted list, then the rest of the sorted list is processed recursively, and the first element of the sorted list is added to the end of the accumulator.

To develop the accumulator invariant, ask yourself what is true for each row in the table displayed in Table 3. You can observe that the accumulator contains all the processed numbers in a nondecreasing order. This alone, however, is not enough to establish that the returned value is sorted when

number	Unprocessed list	Accumulator
5	(-4 1 3 4 8)	'()
5	(1 3 4 8)	'(-4)
5	(3 4 8)	'(-4 1)
5	(4 8)	'(-4 1 3)
5	(8)	'(-4 1 3 4)

Table 3: Table illustrating inserting using an accumulator

the given number is less than or equal to the first number in the given sorted list. For example, consider the following list:

```
L = '(1 2 3 40 50)
```

Assume that the following values are stored in the variables for `insert-accum`:

```
a-num = 35
a-slon = '(50)
  acc = '(1 2 3 40)
```

You can observe that the accumulator contains the processed numbers in nondecreasing order and that 35 is less than 50. Let us examine the appending of the accumulator and the list with the number and the remaining part of the sorted list:

```
(append '(1 2 3 40)
        (cons 35 '(50)))
= '(1 2 3 40 35 50)
```

Clearly, the result is not sorted. This means we need a stronger accumulator invariant. You may argue that the above scenario should never happen because 35 is less than 40. That is an example of *dynamic reasoning* or reasoning about what happens as the program runs. It turns out that this type of reasoning is error-prone and unreliable. You need to engage in *static reasoning* or reasoning solely about the values of the variables.

Ask yourself what else is invariant about the accumulator for every row in Table 3. There must be something invariant that does not allow the above scenario to occur. Observe that for every row, all the elements of the accumulator are less than the given number. Maintaining this invariant property guarantees that the above scenario never occurs. This makes the accumulator invariant:

```
Accumulator = traversed numbers in nondecreasing order
            ∧
∀i (list-ref i accum) < a-num, where i is a valid
                              index into accum
```

The invariant has two components that are connected using **and** (denoted by ∧). The second part states that all numbers in `accum` are less than `a-num`. The symbol ∀ means **for all**.

47.1.2 Sample Expressions and Differences

Inserting a number into an empty sorted list means that the answer is built by appending the given number to the accumulator. Sample expressions are:

```
;; Sample expressions for insert-accum
(define INSERTACC-LON0 (append '()        (list 10)))
(define INSERTACC-EXMP (append '(5 6 7) (list 20)))
```

The first sample expression above is for inserting 10 into an empty sorted list when the accumulator is empty. The second sample expression above is for inserting 20 into an empty sorted list when the accumulator contains 5, 6, and 7.

When the given number is less than or equal to the first number in the sorted list, the answer is built by appending the accumulator and the list containing the given number and the sorted list. This is the case, for example, when inserting 0 into LON7 with an empty accumulator and when inserting -2 into LON8 after traversing its first two elements. The sample expressions capturing these two examples are:

```
(define INSERTACC-LON7 (append '() (cons 0 LON7)))
(define INSERTACC-LON8 (append
                          '(-10 -5)
                          (cons -2 (rest (rest LON8)))))
```

When the given number is greater than the first number in the sorted list, the answer is built by recursively processing the rest of the sorted list and adding the first element of the sorted list to the end of the accumulator. This is the case when inserting 7 into LON7 with an empty accumulator and when inserting 8 into LON8 after its first two elements have been traversed. The following sample expressions capture these examples:

```
(define INSERTACC-LON7-2
        (insert-accum
          7
          (rest LON7)
          (append '() (list (first LON7)))))

(define INSERTACC-LON8-2
        (insert-accum
          8
          (rest '(0 5 10))
          (append '(-10 -5)
                    (list (first '(0 5 10)))))))
```

The differences among the sample expressions are a number to insert and two lons for the sorted list and the accumulator. We name these differences: a-num, a-slon, and accum.

47.1.3 Signature, Statements, and Function Header

The function's signature is written using the types of the differences among
the sample expressions and the return type identified in problem analysis.
The purpose is to return a sorted list that only includes the given number
and all the elements of the given sorted list.

We explicitly state the accumulator invariant and the assumption that the
list being inserted into is sorted in nondecreasing order. These steps of the
design recipe yield:

```
;; number lon lon → lon
;; Purpose: To insert the given number in the given
;;          sorted lon
;; Accumulator Invariant:
;;  accum = traversed numbers in nondecreasing order AND
;;  For all i (list-ref i accum) < a-num, where i is a
;;    valid index into accum
;; Assumption: a-slon is sorted in nondecreasing order
(define (insert-accum a-num a-slon accum)
```

47.1.4 Tests

Writing the tests using sample computations requires giving the function the
values used to write the sample expressions and making the expected values
the respective variable defined for each sample expression. The tests are:

```
;; Tests using sample computations for insert-accum
(check-expect (insert-accum 10 '()  '())
              INSERTACC-LON0)
(check-expect (insert-accum 20 '()  '(5 6 7))
              INSERTACC-EXMP)
(check-expect (insert-accum  0 LON7 '())
              INSERTACC-LON7)
(check-expect (insert-accum -2
                           (rest (rest LON8))
                           '(-10 -5))
              INSERTACC-LON8)
(check-expect (insert-accum  7 LON7 '())
            INSERTACC-LON7-2)
(check-expect (insert-accum  8
                           (rest (rest LON8))
                           '(-10 -5))
            INSERTACC-LON8-2)
```

The tests using sample values use concrete values to illustrate how the
function works. We write three such tests: one inserting a number into the

empty sorted list when the accumulator is empty, one inserting a number into a non-empty sorted list when the accumulator is empty, and one inserting a number into a partially traversed list. The tests are:

```
;; Tests using sample values for insert-accum
(check-expect (insert-accum 23 '()   '())
              '(23))
(check-expect (insert-accum 31 '(50 50)   '())
              '(31 50 50))
(check-expect (insert-accum 87 '(50 78 90)   '(20 30))
              '(20 30 50 78 87 90))
```

47.1.5 Function Body

The function body is obtained by abstracting over the sample expressions for each of the three conditions that may be encountered. The result of this abstraction step is:

```
(cond [(empty? a-slon) (append accum (list a-num))]
      [(<= a-num (first a-slon))
       (append accum (cons a-num a-slon))]
      [else (insert-accum a-num
                          (rest a-slon)
                          (append accum (list (first a-slon))))])
```

This completes `insert-accum`'s design and implementation. Run the tests and make sure that they all pass.

47.2 The Redesign of `insertion-sorting`

47.2.1 Problem Analysis

Insertion sorting repeatedly inserts a list element into a sorted list. The structurally recursive function above first sorts the rest of the list and then inserts the first element. Does it have to be done in this order? Think about this carefully. Instead of sorting the rest of the list first and then inserting the first element, the traversed elements may be accumulated in nondecreasing order. If the given list is empty, then the answer is the accumulator because all elements are traversed and accumulated in nondecreasing order. If the given list is not empty, then the first list element is inserted into the accumulator, and the rest of the list is processed recursively.

Table 4 illustrates the sorting process. At the beginning, no list elements have been traversed, and, therefore, the accumulator is empty. For the next step, the first element, 7, is removed from the list and inserted into the

Unprocessed list	Accumulator
(7 9 1 8 6)	'()
(9 1 8 6)	'(7)
(1 8 6)	'(7 9)
(8 6)	'(1 7 9)
(6)	'(1 7 8 9)
()	'(1 6 7 8 9)

Table 4: Table illustrating insertion sorting using an accumulator

accumulator. This process is repeated for every step until the sorted list is empty. Observe that when the sorted list is empty, the accumulator contains all the elements traversed, and they are sorted in nondecreasing order.

Table 4 may be used to develop the accumulator invariant. Ask yourself what is true about the accumulator at each step (i.e., for each row). It may be tempting to state the invariant as follows:

```
Accumulator = The sorted list in nondecreasing order
```

Although the elements in the accumulator are sorted in nondecreasing order, this assertion is only true for the final step. For the other steps, the accumulator does not contain all the elements that need to be sorted, and, therefore, it is not always the sorted list. These observations help us hone in on the accumulator invariant. The accumulator is not all elements sorted, but the traversed elements sorted. We may state the accumulator invariant as follows:

```
Accumulator = Traversed elements in nondecreasing order
```

Observe that the given list contains the elements to traverse. When it is empty, it means that all elements have been traversed, and, therefore, all elements are in the accumulator in nondecreasing order. This informs us that the accumulator has the value that satisfies the purpose and returning the accumulator is the correct value to return.

47.2.2 Sample Expressions and Differences

When the sorted list is empty, the accumulator is the answer. To sort LON0, the accumulator invariant tells us that accumulator must be empty. After processing LON6 (a sorted list in nondecreasing order), the accumulator invariant tells us that accumulator must be LON6. The following sample expressions capture these examples:

```
;; Sample expressions for insertion-sorting-accum
(define INSALON0-VAL '())
(define INSALON6-VAL LON6)
```

When the sorted list is not empty, the answer is obtained by inserting its first element into the accumulator and recursively process the rest of the list.

Inserting into the accumulator is done by calling `insert-accum`. Sorting LON1 inserts its first element into the accumulator to make the recursive call. The same is done to sort LON4. The following sample expressions capture these examples:

```
(define INSALON1-VAL (insertion-sorting-accum
                      (rest LON1)
                      (insert-accum (first LON1) '() '())))
 (define INSALON4-VAL (insertion-sorting-accum
                      (rest LON4)
                      (insert-accum (first LON4) '() '())))
```

There are two differences among the sample expressions: the `lon` to sort and the accumulator `lon`. We call these differences `a-lon` and `accum`.

47.2.3 Signature, Purpose, Invariant, and Function Header

The input types are identified by the differences among the sample expressions. The return type and the purpose are identified by problem analysis. The accumulator invariant is identified using Table 4. Finally, the function header is written using the chosen descriptive function name and parameter names. The next design recipe steps yield:

```
;; lon lon → lon
;; Purpose: Sort the first given lon in nondecreasing order
;; Accumulator Invariant:
;;   accum = traversed elements in nondecreasing order
(define (insertion-sorting-accum a-lon accum)
```

47.2.4 Tests

The tests using sample computations are written by providing the function the values used to develop the sample expressions and the variables defined for the values of the sample expressions. These tests are:

```
;; Tests using sample computations for
;;   insertion-sorting-accum
(check-expect (insertion-sorting-accum LON0 '())
              INSALON0-VAL)
(check-expect (insertion-sorting-accum '() LON6)
              INSALON6-VAL)
(check-expect (insertion-sorting-accum LON1 '())
              INSALON1-VAL)
(check-expect (insertion-sorting-accum LON4 '())
              INSALON4-VAL)
```

The tests using sample values illustrate the result of sorting a concrete list with no elements traversed and a concrete list that has been partially traversed. For the second test, the first three elements of '(8 1 9 3 1 8) have been traversed. Observe that the accumulator's value makes the invariant true. The tests are:

```
;; Tests using sample values for insertion-sorting-accum
(check-expect (insertion-sorting-accum '(3 1 8) '())
              '(1 3 8))
(check-expect (insertion-sorting-accum '(3 1 8) '(1 8 9))
              '(1 1 3 8 8 9))
```

47.2.5 Function Body

The function body uses an if-expression to distinguish between lon subtypes. The then-expression is obtained by abstracting over the first two sample expressions. The else-expression is obtained by abstracting over the second two sample expressions. The function body is:

```
(cond [(empty? a-lon) accum]
      [else
       (insertion-sorting-accum
         (rest a-lon)
         (insert-accum (first a-lon) accum '()))])
```

47.3 Performance and Complexity Analysis

We have a new insertion sorting implementation. Has anything been gained by using accumulators? To answer this question, we gather empirical data using LON5. The following experiments are executed five times:

```
(time (insertion-sorting       LON5)))
(time (insertion-sorting-accum LON5 '()))
```

The following table displays the CPU times in milliseconds obtained (after subtracting, if any, garbage collection time):

	Structural Recursion	Accumulative Recursion
Run 1	1203	6844
Run 2	1515	7701
Run 3	1375	6422
Run 4	1375	8687
Run 5	1375	7859

The empirical data strongly suggests that the version using structural recursion is significantly faster. Alas, using accumulators has made insertion sorting slower.

Why is the implementation using structural recursion faster? Does the implementation using accumulators have a worse abstract running time? We know from Sect. 24 that `insertion-sorting`'s complexity is $O(n^2)$. What is `insertion-sorting-accum`'s complexity?

In the worst case, `insert-accum` is called n + 1 times to traverse the entire given sorted list of size n. For each call but the last, the accumulator is traversed by `append` to add a number to its end. In the worst case, the accumulator has size n. This makes `insert-accum`'s complexity $O((n{+}1) * (n{+}1)) = O(n^2)$.

To sort a `lon` of length n `insertion-sorting-accum` is called n + 1 times. For each call but the last `insert-accum` is called. This yields a complexity of $O(n * O(n^2)) = O(n^3)$. This is a worse abstract running time than using structural recursion and explains the empirical results observed.

An important lesson to take away is that using accumulative recursion is not always faster. Experimentation is required to determine the impact of accumulators on performance. Another important lesson to take away is that redesigning a function may make its abstract running time worse.

The most important skill you need to develop is determining accumulator invariants. This is likely the most difficult step when designing accumulative recursive functions. It is, however, time well invested. Studies have shown that problem-solvers that take the time to determine accumulator invariants tend to write more bug-free and understandable code.

---

12 Observe that `insertion-sorting-accum` changes the interface for anyone using insertion sorting. Instead of simply providing the `lon` to sort, the `lon` to sort and the value of the accumulator must be provided. This exposes the implementation to users of `insertion-sorting-accum`. It is desirable not to change the interface for users. Design and implement a function that only takes as input a `lon` and uses `insertion-sorting-accum` as an auxiliary function to sort the given list in nondecreasing order.

13 The developed accumulator invariant for `insert-accum` is:

```
accum = traversed numbers in nondecreasing order
        ∧
∀i (list-ref i accum) < a-num,
  where i is a valid index into accum
```

By keeping the accumulator in nondecreasing order, it must be traversed every time the function is called to append a number to its end. Redesign `insert-accum` using the following accumulator invariant:

```
accum = traversed numbers in nonincreasing order
        ∧
∀i (list-ref i accum) < a-num,
  where i is a valid index into accum
```

Does this design improve performance or the abstract running time? Carefully justify your answers.

14 In Sect. 26, the function `merge-neighs` is designed and implemented. Redesign this function to use an accumulator for the merged sublists. Does the use of accumulators have an impact on performance?

48 What Have We Learned in This Chapter?

The important lessons of this chapter are summarized as follows:

- Accumulators are variables used to avoid loss of knowledge.
- To add one or more accumulators to a function, it is necessary to develop an accumulator invariant to clearly identify what value the accumulator stores.
- An accumulator invariant is an assertion about an accumulator that must hold when a function is called.
- Problem-solving using accumulators requires identifying how the accumulators are exploited.
- Accumulators may be added to functions based on structural or generative recursion.
- Recursion that employs accumulators is called accumulative recursion.
- Consider using an accumulator when a function is based on structural recursion and the result of a recursive call is input to another function.
- Consider using an accumulator when a function is based on generative recursion and you understand that the function may fail to produce a result.

- Using accumulative recursion may reduce or increase the abstract running time of a function.
- A graph may be represented as an adjacency list in which each node has a list of neighbors.
- An accumulator invariant does not change among mutually recursive functions.
- A stronger accumulator invariant is needed when the invariant is insufficient to establish that the correct value is returned.
- Accumulative recursion is not always faster.
- Developing accumulator invariants may be the hardest part of designing programs using accumulators.
- Studies have shown that problem-solvers that take the time to determine accumulator invariants develop better programs.

Chapter 10
N-Puzzle Versions 4 and 5

In Chap. 7 we discovered that using depth-first search to find a solution to the N-puzzle problem may fall into an infinite recursion. This occurs because depth-first search may get stuck repeatedly visiting the same worlds. That is, it gets stuck in a path that has a loop. This problem was solved in Chap. 8 by using breadth-first search to find a solution. Breadth-first search, however, repeatedly searches for solutions starting from the same world. In other words, the successors of a world, w_1, are repeatedly used to generate new paths even if they are already part of the search process. A consequence, for example, a loop on w_1, is repeatedly explored.

The experience gained in Chap. 9 suggests that finding a solution for the N-puzzle problem may benefit from using accumulators. An accumulator may be used to remember the worlds whose successors are part of the search. The number of successors is data of arbitrary size, and a list may be used to represent them. If a successor of a world is already part of the search, then it is not used to generate new paths. For depth-first search, this means that backtracking is needed to search for a different solution. As a consequence, depth-first search does not fall into an infinite recursion. For breadth-first search, this means that not all paths in the search space are explored. The exploration of a path with a repeated node is discontinued.

49 N-Puzzle Version 4

Our first goal is to improve the use of depth-first search in finding a solution to the N-puzzle problem. To this end, the program for N-puzzle version 2 (in Chap. 7) is refined. The function make-move is refactored to call find-solution with an initial accumulator value. This means that find-solution must be redesigned to exploit the accumulator and maintain the accumulator invariant. In addition, the test that led to discovering that using depth-first search may lead to an infinite recursion:

© The Author(s), under exclusive license to Springer Nature Switzerland AG 2022 245
M. T. Morazán, *Animated Program Design*, Texts in Computer Science,
https://doi.org/10.1007/978-3-031-04317-8_10

```
(check-expect (process-key (make-world 2 3 0
                                        1 5 6
                                        4 7 8)
                           HKEY)
              (make-world 2 0 3
                          1 5 6
                          4 7 8))
```

is added to the test suite. If we are successful, the test above will pass instead of leading to an infinite recursion.

If the player presses HKEY, the function make-move is called. When the world given to make-move is not WIN, find-solution is called. This call must now include the initial value of the accumulator. Given that the successors of no board are part of the search, the initial value of the accumulator is '(). This means that make-move may be refactored to:

```
;; world → world
;; Purpose: Make a move for the player
(define (make-move a-world)
  (if (equal? a-world WIN)
      a-world
      (second (find-solution a-world '()))))
```

Observe that the only difference is an argument for the initial accumulator value given to find-solution. Refactoring make-move means, of course, that the tests do not change, but the sample expressions must be updated to provide '() to find-solution. The refined sample expressions are:

```
;; Sample expressions for make-move
(define MM-WIN-VAL   WIN)
(define MM-WRLD1-VAL (second (find-solution WRLD1 '())))
(define MM-WRLD2-VAL (second (find-solution WRLD2 '())))
```

49.1 The Design and Implementation of find-solution

49.1.1 Problem Analysis

This function receives as input a world and the list of worlds that have been visited (i.e., whose successors are part of the search). The successors of the given world must be filtered to eliminate those that are already visited. The process continues by finding a solution from any of the remaining successors. Finding a solution from a set of successor worlds is a different problem from finding a solution from a world. Therefore, an auxiliary function is needed to perform this search.

Let us use `visited` to refer to the accumulated list of worlds whose children are part of the search. The above analysis informs us that the accumulator invariant is:

```
visited = list of worlds whose successors are part of
          the search
```

The accumulator is exploited to determine which successors of the given world need to be added to the search for a solution.

If the solution returned from searching the successors is `'no-solution`, then a solution that does not go through the visited worlds does not exists, and the answer is `'no-solution`. Otherwise, the solution is obtained by adding the given world to the front of the solution returned by searching for a solution from any of the successors.

49.1.2 Sample Expressions and Differences

If the given world is WIN, then the answer is always the list containing WIN. Sample expressions to process WIN and an empty accumulator and to process WIN and a nonempty accumulator equal to (list WRLD1 WRLD2) are:

```
;; Sample expressions for find-solution
(define FS-WIN-VAL  (list WIN))
(define FS-WIN-VAL2 (list WIN))
```

If the given world is not WIN, then we may locally define a variable for the unvisited successors and for the solution found from any unvisited successor. If there is no solution from any of the unvisited successors, then there is no solution for the given world that does not go through a visited world. If there is a solution using any of the unvisited successors, then the solution for the given world is constructed by adding the given world to the front of the solution from any unvisited successor. To keep in the spirit of our new design we name of the auxiliary function to search for a path from any successor `find-solution-from-any-succ`. We may write sample expressions to find a solution starting at WRLD1 with no visited worlds and to find a solution starting from a successor of WRLD2 with only WRLD2 visited as follows:

```
(define FS-WRLD1-VAL
        (local
          [(define succs
                  (filter
                    (λ (w) (not (member? WRLD1 '())))
                    (map (λ (neigh)
                             (swap-empty WRLD1 neigh))
                         (list-ref
                           neighbors
                           (blank-pos WRLD1)))))]
```

```
               (define solution-from-any-succ
                 (find-solution-from-any-succ
                   succs
                   (cons WRLD1 '()))))]
           (if (eq? solution-from-any-succ 'no-solution)
               'no-solution
               (cons WRLD1 solution-from-any-succ))))

(define FS-WRLD2-VAL
   (local
      [(define succ
          (filter
             (λ (w) (not (member? w (list WRLD2))))
             (map (λ (neigh)
                     (swap-empty
                        (make-world 1 3 0
                                    4 2 6
                                    7 5 8)
                          neigh))
                  (list-ref
                    neighbors
                    (blank-pos
                      (make-world 1 3 0
                                  4 2 6
                                  7 5 8)))))))
       (define solution-from-any-succ
         (find-solution-from-any-succ
           succs
           (cons (make-world 1 3 0
                             4 2 6
                             7 5 8)
                 (list WRLD2))))]
      (if (eq? solution-from-any-succ 'no-solution)
          'no-solution
          (cons (make-world 1 3 0
                            4 2 6
                            7 5 8)
                solution-from-any-succ))))
```

Observe that the differences among the sample expressions are the given world and the given (listof world) for the accumulator. We name these differences a-world and visited.

49.1.3 Signature, Statements, and Function Header

The accumulator's type, (listof world), is added as an input to the signature. The purpose is to return a sequence of moves that does not go through any of the worlds in the given accumulator. The how-statement briefly outlines the design idea based on depth-first search and exploiting the accumulator. The accumulator invariant is stated to help any reader understand the program. The chosen variable name, visited, for the accumulator is added to the function header. These observations lead to:

```
;; world (listof world) → (listof world)
;; Purpose: Return a sequence of moves to WIN that does
;;            not go through worlds in the accumulator.
;; How: The solution is built using the given world
;;      and the first successor found by depth-first
;;      search that leads to WIN without exploring
;;      successors of the given world that are in
;;      the accumulator.
;; Accumulator Invariant
;;   visited = list of worlds whose children are part of
;;             the search
(define (find-solution a-world visited)
```

49.1.4 Tests

The tests using sample computations illustrate that the function returns the same value as the evaluation of the sample expressions when provided with the same concrete values used to write the sample expressions. The tests are:

```
;; Tests using sample computations for find-solution
(check-expect (find-solution WIN '())
              FS-WIN-VAL)
(check-expect (find-solution WIN (list WRLD1 WRLD2))
              FS-WIN-VAL2)
(check-expect (find-solution WRLD1 '())
              FS-WRLD1-VAL)
(check-expect (find-solution
                (make-world 1 3 0
                            4 2 6
                            7 5 8)
                (list WRLD2))
              FS-WRLD2-VAL)
```

We use the same tests using sample values as those in Sect. 35.4. The only difference is that '() is provided as the initial value for the accumulator. The tests are:

```
;; Tests using sample values for find-solution
(check-expect (find-solution (make-world 1 2 3
                                          4 0 6
                                          7 5 8)
                             '())
              (list (make-world 1 2 3
                                4 0 6
                                7 5 8)
                    (make-world 1 2 3
                                4 5 6
                                7 0 8)
                    (make-world 1 2 3
                                4 5 6
                                7 8 0)))

(check-expect (find-solution (make-world 1 0 3
                                         4 2 6
                                         7 5 8)
                             (list WRLD2))
              (list
               (make-world 1 0 3
                           4 2 6
                           7 5 8)
               (make-world 1 2 3
                           4 0 6
                           7 5 8)
               (make-world 1 2 3
                           4 5 6
                           7 0 8)
               (make-world 1 2 3
                           4 5 6
                           7 8 0)))
```

49.1.5 Function Body

The function's body uses an if-expression to determine if the given world is
WIN. The then-expression is obtained by abstracting over the first two sample
expressions. The else-expression is obtained by abstracting over the second
two sample expressions. The function body is:

```
(if (equal? a-world WIN)
    (list a-world)
    (local
      [(define succs
         (filter (λ (w)
                   (not (member? w accum)))
```

```
                    (map (λ (neigh)
                          (swap-empty a-world neigh))
                      (list-ref
                        neighbors
                        blank-pos a-world)))))
        (define solution-from-any-succ
              (find-solution-from-any-succ
                succs
                (cons a-world visited)))]
      (if (eq? solution-from-any-succ 'no-solution)
          'no-solution
          (cons a-world solution-from-any-succ))))
```

49.2 The `find-solution-from-any-succ` Design and Implementation

49.2.1 Problem Analysis

This function searches for a solution by traversing the given list of successor worlds using depth-first search without going through any world in the accumulator. If the given list of successor worlds is empty, then there is no solution, and the answer is 'no-solution. If the first successor is WIN, then there is no need to make any moves, and the solution is the list containing WIN.

If there are still successors to explore and the first successor is not WIN, then a search for a solution is performed with the first successor and the given accumulator by calling find-solution. Nothing needs to be added to the accumulator because no new successors have been added to the search. If this search returns a sequence of moves, then the solution is constructed by adding the first successor to it. If the search returns 'no-solution, then backtracking must take place. The search continues using the rest of the given successors and a new accumulator. Why is a new accumulator needed? Observe that the successors of the first given successor have been explored by the call to find-solution. This means that they are already part of the search process and should not be searched again because we already know they did not lead to a solution. Therefore, the first successor is added to the accumulator to process the rest of the successors.

49.2.2 Sample Expressions and Differences

Problem analysis reveals three conditions, and all three require sample expressions for computing the answer. The answer is always 'no-solution when the given successor list is empty. Sample expressions to illustrate this condition may be written for an empty successor list and either an empty visited list or a visited list containing A-WRLD as follows:

```
;; Sample expressions for find-solution-from-any-succ
(define FSFAS-EMPSUCCS1 'no-solution)
(define FSFAS-EMPSUCCS2 'no-solution)
```

When the first successor is WIN, the answer is always a list containing WIN. This occurs, for example, when the successor list only contains WIN, and the visited list is empty. This is an easy sample expression to develop, but we ought to be more thorough using an example a little more complex. Consider finding a solution starting with the following board:

1	2	3
4	5	6
7		8

This `world` is added to the accumulator when its successors:

1	2	3		1	2	3		1	2	3
4	5	6		4		6		4	5	6
7	8			7	5	8			7	8

are given as input to `find-solution-from-any-succ`. Observe that the successors appear in the same order defined by `neighbors` (the neighbors of bpos = 7 are `'(list 8 4 6)`). The first successor is WIN, and, therefore, the solution is the list containing WIN. The sample expressions for both examples are the same:

```
(define FSFAS-WIN1 (list WIN))
(define FSFAS-WIN2 (list WIN))
```

To simplify the writing of a test using the second sample expression, the following variables are defined:

```
(define SUCCS-WIN2 (list WIN
                        (make-world 1 2 3
                                    4 0 6
                                    7 5 8)
                        (make-world 1 2 3
                                    4 5 6
                                    0 7 8)))

(define ACCUM-WIN2 (list (make-world 1 2 3
                                     4 5 6
                                     7 0 8)))
```

Any sample expression for the third condition requires a nonempty successor list that does not start with WIN. For example, the following world:

1	2	3
4		6
7	5	8

has the following successors:

1	2	3	1		3	1	2	3	1	2	3
4	5	6	4	2	6		4	6	4		6
7		8	7	5	8	7	5	8	7	5	8

Once again care is taken to list the successors in the order determined by neighbors. A sample expression may use the above successors and an accumulator that has the starting world above. To simplify writing a sample expression, the following variables for the successors and the accumulator are defined:

```
(define SUCCS-WRLD1 (list (make-world 1 2 3
                                      4 5 6
                                      7 0 8)
                          (make-world 1 0 3
                                      4 2 6
                                      7 5 8)
                          (make-world 1 2 3
                                      0 4 6
                                      7 5 8)
```

```
                    (make-world 1 2 3
                                4 6 0
                                7 5 8)))

(define VISITED1 (list (make-world 1 2 3
                                   4 0 6
                                   7 5 8)))
```

A sample expression may also be developed for when a move has been made. Consider an accumulator with the following worlds:

The search has made a move from bpos = 3 to, its first neighbor in neighbors, bpos = 0. There is only one unvisited successor for bpos = 0:

To simplify writing a sample expression, the following variables for the successor and the accumulator are defined:

```
(define SUCCS-WRLD2 (list (make-world 2 0 3
                                      1 5 6
                                      4 7 8)))

(define VISITED2 (list (make-world 0 2 3
                                   1 5 6
                                   4 7 8)
                       (make-world 1 2 3
                                   0 5 6
                                   4 7 8)))
```

The sample expressions are written by locally defining a variable for the result of searching for a solution using the first successor. If the result of this search is not 'no-solution, then it is returned. Otherwise, the function backtracks and continues the search with the rest of the successors and with a new accumulator obtained by adding the first successor to the existing accumulator. The sample expressions are:

```
(define FSFAS-SUCC1
       (local
        [(define solution-from-first-succ
                (find-solution (first SUCCS-WRLD1)
                               VISITED1))]
          (if (not (eq? solution-from-first-succ
                        'no-solution))
              solution-from-first-succ
              (find-solution-from-any-succ
               (rest SUCCS-WRLD1)
               (cons (first SUCCS-WRLD1)
                     VISITED1)))))

(define FSFAS-SUCC2
   (local [(define solution-from-first-succ
                   (find-solution (first SUCCS-WRLD2)
                                  VISITED2))]
          (if (not (eq? solution-from-first-succ
                        'no-solution))
              solution-from-first-succ
              (find-solution-from-any-succ
               (rest SUCCS-WRLD2)
               (cons (first SUCCS-WRLD2)
                     VISITED2)))))
```

There are two differences among the sample expressions. They are both a (listof world). One is for the successors, and the other is for the accumulated visited worlds. We name these differences succs and visited.

49.2.3 Signature, Statements, and Function Header

The input types are two (listof world), and the output is a (listof world). The purpose statement summarizes the design idea of finding a solution from any successor without going through any visited world. The accumulator invariant is stated to help any reader better understand how the problem is solved. The next steps of the design recipe yield:

```
;; (listof world) (listof world) → (listof world)
;; Purpose: Find a solution from any world in the first
;;          given list without going through any world
;;          in the second given list.
;; Accumulator Invariant:
;;   visited = list of worlds whose successors are part
;;             of the search
(define (find-solution-from-any-succ succs visited)
```

49.2.4 Tests

The tests using sample computations provide `find-solution-from-any-succ` the values employed to design the sample expressions. The expected value is always the corresponding variable defined for the value of the sample expression. In this manner, we illustrate that the function correctly computes the values of the sample expressions. These tests are:

```
;; Tests using sample computations for
;; find-solution-from-any-succ
(check-expect (find-solution-from-any-succ '() '())
              FSFAS-EMPSUCCS1)
(check-expect (find-solution-from-any-succ
               '()
               (list A-WRLD))
              FSFAS-EMPSUCCS2)

(check-expect (find-solution-from-any-succ
               (list WIN)
               '())
              FSFAS-WIN1)
(check-expect (find-solution-from-any-succ
               SUCCS-WIN2
               ACCUM-WIN2)
              FSFAS-WIN2)

(check-expect (find-solution-from-any-succ
               SUCCS-WRLD1
               VISITED1)
              FSFAS-SUCC1)
(check-expect (find-solution-from-any-succ
               SUCCS-WRLD2
               VISITED2)
              FSFAS-SUCC2)
```

Writing tests using sample values requires determining the solution the function ought to return after a series of moves has been made. In the first test below, a solution is searched for after moving the empty tile space from `bpos` = 5 to `bpos` = 2 (the first neighbor of 5 listed in `neighbors`). The expected value is obtained by exploring the first neighbor as listed in `neighbors` of each successive board. The same approach is used to develop the second test without any moves having been made. The tests are:

```
;; Tests using sample values for find-solution-from-any-succ
(check-expect (find-solution-from-any-succ
                (list (make-world 1 0 3
                                  4 2 6
                                  7 5 8))
                      (list (make-world 1 3 0
                                        4 2 6
                                        7 5 8)
                            (make-world 1 3 6
                                        4 2 0
                                        7 5 8)))
              (list
                (make-world 1 0 3
                            4 2 6
                            7 5 8)
                (make-world 1 2 3
                            4 0 6
                            7 5 8)
                (make-world 1 2 3
                            4 5 6
                            7 0 8)
                (make-world 1 2 3
                            4 5 6
                            7 8 0)))

(check-expect (find-solution-from-any-succ
                (list (make-world 1 0 3
                                  4 2 6
                                  7 5 8))
                      '())
              (list
                (make-world 1 0 3
                            4 2 6
                            7 5 8)
                (make-world 1 2 3
                            4 0 6
                            7 5 8)
                (make-world 1 2 3
                            4 5 6
                            7 0 8)
                (make-world 1 2 3
                            4 5 6
                            7 8 0)))
```

1 Develop a test using sample values in which the search for a solution starts after two moves have been made.

49.2.5 Function Body

The function body uses a `cond`-expression to distinguish among the three cases identified. The solution when the list of successors is empty is obtained from abstracting over the first two sample expressions. The solution when the first successor is `WIN` is obtained from abstracting over the second two sample expressions. Finally, the default expression is obtained from abstracting over the last two sample expressions. The function body is:

```
(cond
    [(empty? succs) 'no-solution]
    [(equal? (first succs) WIN) (list WIN)]
    [else
     (local [(define solution-from-first-succ
                (find-solution (first succs) visited))]
       (if (not (eq? solution-from-first-succ
                     'no-solution))
           solution-from-first-succ
           (find-solution-from-any-succ
            (rest succs)
            (cons (first succs) visited))))])
```

49.3 Termination Argument

We establish that the accumulator invariant is maintained in order to develop a termination argument. This means convincingly arguing that both `find-solution` and `find-solution-from-any-succ` maintain the accumulator invariant.

Consider the two calls to `find-solution` in the program. The first is made from `make-move` with an empty accumulator. Clearly, the accumulator invariant is true because the successors of no `world` are part of the search. The second is from `find-solution-from-any-succ`. This call is made with an unvisited successor and the unchanged list of accumulated visited `worlds`. The accumulator invariant is maintained given that no new successor `worlds` are part of the search.

Now consider the two calls to `find-solution-from-any-succ` in the program. The first is from `find-solution`. This call is made with a list of unvisited successors and an accumulator that contains all the `worlds` whose successors are part of the search including its given `world`. The second is a recursive call in `find-solution-from-any-succ`. This call is made with a list of unvisited successors and an accumulator that contains all the `world`s whose successors are part of the search including the `world` that failed to produce a solution without going through a visited `world`. Both calls, therefore, maintain the accumulator invariant.

The fact that the invariant is maintained means two things. The first is that `find-solution` can never loop back to the same `world` when building a solution and, therefore, fall into an infinite recursion on a path that contains a loop. The second is that `find-solution-from-any-succ` will not repeat a failed search starting from the given `world`. Given that there is a solution from all valid worlds, that there cannot be any repeated nodes in a solution being built, and that failed searches cannot be repeated, we have that eventually `find-solution` gets WIN as input and the program terminates.

This completes the design and implementation of finding a solution using depth-first search and accumulators. Run the tests and make sure they all pass. When you run the tests, be patient as it may take a few minutes.

2 Consider the following call with an invalid board:

```
(find-solution (make-world 1 2 3
                           4 5 6
                           8 7 0)
               '())
```

What happens? Carefully explain your answer. You may find it useful to first consider what happens with this call:

```
(find-solution (make-world 1 2 3
                           4 5 6
                           8 7 0)
               (list (make-world 1 2 3
                                 4 5 6
                                 8 0 7)
                     (make-world 1 2 3
                                 4 5 0
                                 8 7 6)))
```

50 N-Puzzle Version 5

In this section N-Puzzle Version 3 from Chap. 8 is refined. This refinement introduces an accumulator to reduce the amount of work done by `find-solution-bfs`.

50.1 Problem Analysis

In Sect. 41, we observed that for breadth-first search, the number of paths in the queue grows exponentially. The repetition of worlds in solutions being constructed means that breadth-first search, in essence, explores the same paths in the search tree repeatedly. Consider a queue that has the following paths after making one move:

$(w_1 \ w_0)$
$(w_2 \ w_0)$
$(w_3 \ w_0)$
$(w_4 \ w_0)$

There are four paths being explored by breadth-first search. Let us assume that w_1 is not WIN. After generating new paths from the first path, the queue becomes:

$(w_2 \ w_0)$
$(w_3 \ w_0)$
$(w_4 \ w_0)$
$(w_5 \ w_1 \ w_0)$
$(w_0 \ w_1 \ w_0)$
$(w_6 \ w_1 \ w_0)$

Observe that the next to last path reverses the first move from w_0 to w_1. From this point on, this path generates the same successors as w_0 initially does. That is, the subtree in the search tree rooted at w_0 with w_1 and w_0 as ancestors is the same as the search tree rooted at w_0. Certainly, there is a shorter solution than the one obtained by following w_0 in the next to last path. That shorter solution is obtained by eliminating the loop on w_0. This shorter solution is actually found by breadth-first search first. Therefore, it makes little sense to explore the paths generated by the next to last path in the queue.

An accumulator can be added to `find-solution-bfs` (from Chap. 8) to remember the worlds whose successors are already part of the search. This accumulator is used to reduce the number of new paths generated. Only successors not in the accumulator are used to generate new paths. For the example above, the new queue is:

$(w_2 \; w_0)$
$(w_3 \; w_0)$
$(w_4 \; w_0)$
$(w_5 \; w_1 \; w_0)$
$(w_6 \; w_1 \; w_0)$

Observe that the path that reverses the first move is not generated. It is not generated because w_0 is remembered in the accumulator.

The accumulator is data of arbitrary size. It is implemented as a (listof world).

50.2 Sample Expressions and Differences

We refine the sample expressions used in Chap. 8 to exploit and create a new accumulator when necessary. The sample expressions for when the first world of the queue's first path is WIN do not need to be changed because the answer is still the list containing WIN. They remain as:

```
;; Sample expressions for find-solution-bfs
(define FS-QLOW1-VAL
   (local [(define first-path (qfirst QLOW1))]
     (reverse first-path)))

(define FS-QLOW2-VAL
   (local [(define first-path (qfirst QLOW2))]
     (reverse first-path)))
```

The sample expressions for when the first world of the queue's first path is not WIN need to generate new paths only after filtering out successors that are in the accumulator and need to update the accumulator to recursively process the new queue. To this end the given accumulator is exploited to filter the successors of the first world in the first path, and the new accumulator is constructed by adding this first world to the front of the given accumulator. The tests from Chap. 8 using QLOW3 and QLOW4 are updated, respectively, to use the following initial queues:

```
(list (make-world 1 2 3          (list (make-world 1 2 3
                 4 5 0                           4 5 6
                 7 8 6))                         0 7 8))
```

The accumulator for each test contains the world used to generate the new paths of length 2 found in the respective queues. The new sample expressions are:

```
(define FS-QLOW3-VAL
  (local
    [(define first-path (qfirst QLOW3))
     (define first-world (first first-path))
     (define successors
             (filter
               (λ (w)
                 (not (member?
                         w
                         (list (make-world 1 2 3
                                           4 5 0
                                           7 8 6)))))
               (map (λ (neigh)
                      (swap-empty first-world neigh))
                    (list-ref
                      neighbors
                      (blank-pos first-world)))))
     (define new-paths (map (λ (w) (cons w first-path))
                            successors))
     (define new-q (enqueue new-paths (dequeue QLOW3)))]
    (find-solution-bfs
      new-q
      (cons first-world
            (list (make-world 1 2 3
                              4 5 0
                              7 8 6))))))

(define FS-QLOW4-VAL
  (local
    [(define first-path (qfirst QLOW4))
     (define first-world (first first-path))
     (define successors
             (filter
               (λ (w)
                 (not (member?
                         w
                         (list (make-world 1 2 3
                                           4 5 6
                                           0 7 8)))))
               (map (λ (neigh)
                      (swap-empty first-world neigh))
                    (list-ref
                      neighbors
                      (blank-pos first-world)))))
     (define new-paths (map (λ (w)
                              (cons w first-path))
                            successors))
```

```
          (define new-q (enqueue new-paths (dequeue QLOW4)))]
       (find-solution-bfs
         new-q
         (cons first-world
               (list (make-world 1 2 3
                                  4 5 6
                                  0 7 8)))))))
```

The differences among the sample expressions are a (qof (listof world)) (for the paths) and a (listof world) for the worlds whose successors are part of the search. We name these differences a-qlow and visited.

50.3 Signature, Statements, and Function Header

The function's signature must now include, (listof world), the accumulator's type. The purpose statement must reflect the design idea motivating the accumulator's use. The accumulator invariant needs to be stated to make the code readable to others. Finally, the function header must now have two parameters, not one, for the differences among the sample expressions. The next steps of the design recipe yield:

```
;; (qof (listof world)) (listof world) → (listof world)
;; Purpose: Return sequence of moves to WIN
;; How: If the first path's first world is WIN then return
;;       the reverse of the first path. Otherwise, continue the
;;       search with:
;;          1. a new queue obtained by removing the first
;;             path and adding paths constructed using the
;;             unvisited successors of the first path's first
;;             world and the first path.
;;          2. an accumulator obtained by adding the first
;;             path's first world to the given accumulator.
;; Accumulator Invariant:
;;    visited = worlds whose successors are part of the search
(define (find-solution-bfs a-qlow visited)
```

50.4 Tests

The tests using sample computations are refined by adding the queue values used to write the sample expressions as an argument to the function. The refined tests are:

```
;; Tests using sample computations for find-solution
(check-expect (find-solution-bfs QLOW1 '()) FS-QLOW1-VAL)
(check-expect (find-solution-bfs QLOW2 '()) FS-QLOW2-VAL)
(check-expect (find-solution-bfs QLOW3
                              (list (make-world 1 2 3
                                                4 5 0
                                                7 8 6)))
              FS-QLOW3-VAL)
(check-expect (find-solution-bfs QLOW4
                              (list (make-world 1 2 3
                                                4 5 6
                                                0 7 8)))
              FS-QLOW4-VAL)
```

The tests using sample values are written using an initial queue and an accumulator for which we know there is a short solution. This requires writing out the search tree to determine the path ordering based on **neighbors**. The first test below illustrates how the function works using a queue with a single path and an empty accumulator (no moves made towards the solution). The solution requires four moves. The second test below illustrates how the function works using a queue containing the four paths generated after making one move using a **world** where the empty tile space is in **bpos = 4** (the center position in the board). The accumulator contains the board used to generate the four paths in the queue value. The solution requires three moves. The tests are:

```
;; Tests using sample values for find-solution
(check-expect (find-solution-bfs
                (list (list (make-world 0 2 3
                                        1 5 6
                                        4 7 8)))
                '())
                (list
                  (make-world 0 2 3
                              1 5 6
                              4 7 8)
                  (make-world 1 2 3
                              0 5 6
                              4 7 8)
```

```
                    (make-world 1 2 3
                                4 5 6
                                0 7 8)
                    (make-world 1 2 3
                                4 5 6
                                7 0 8)
                    (make-world 1 2 3
                                4 5 6
                                7 8 0)))

(check-expect (find-solution-bfs
                    (list (list (make-world 1 2 3
                                            4 5 6
                                            7 0 8)
                                (make-world 1 2 3
                                            4 0 6
                                            7 5 8))
                          (list (make-world 1 0 3
                                            4 2 6
                                            7 5 8)
                                (make-world 1 2 3
                                            4 0 6
                                            7 5 8))
                          (list (make-world 1 2 3
                                            0 4 6
                                            7 5 8)
                                (make-world 1 2 3
                                            4 0 6
                                            7 5 8))
                          (list (make-world 1 2 3
                                            4 6 0
                                            7 5 8)
                                (make-world 1 2 3
                                            4 0 6
                                            7 5 8)))
                    (list (make-world 1 2 3
                                      4 0 6
                                      7 5 8)))
               (list
                 (make-world 1 2 3
                             4 0 6
                             7 5 8)
                 (make-world 1 2 3
                             4 5 6
                             7 0 8)
```

```
(make-world 1 2 3
            4 5 6
            7 8 0)))
```

50.5 Function Body

The function's body, as in Chap. 8, uses a conditional to determine if the first world in the reversed first path in the queue is or is not WIN. The then-expression is obtained by abstracting over the first two sample expressions. The else-expression is obtained by abstracting over the last two sample expressions. As done in Chap. 8, we observe that the first path and the first path's first world are needed more than once, and a local variable is defined for each. The function's body is:

```
(local [(define first-path (qfirst a-qlow))
        (define first-world (first first-path))]
  (if (equal? first-world WIN)
     (reverse first-path)
     (local
       [(define successors
                (filter
                 (λ (w)
                   (not (member? w visited)))
                 (map (λ (neigh)
                        (swap-empty first-world neigh))
                      (list-ref
                       neighbors
                       (blank-pos first-world)))))
        (define new-paths (map (λ (w)
                                 (cons w first-path))
                               successors))
        (define new-q (enqueue new-paths
                               (dequeue a-qlow)))]
       (find-solution-bfs new-q (cons first-world visited)))))
```

50.6 Termination Argument

The termination argument is, as expected, similar to the termination argument presented in Sect. 40.6. Observe that if there is a solution with a loop (i.e., a repeated world), then there is a shorter solution that does not traverse the loop. This means that a path in the search tree that has a loop may safely be discarded from the search and that from any valid board there is

a loopless solution. When the first path's first `world` in the given queue is
`WIN` `find-solution-bfs` halts. For each recursive call, one path is taken one
step down the search tree using only unvisited successors to avoid following
paths with loops. The new paths to this tree level are added to the queue
in order to keep them in `FIFO` order. This means that shorter loopless paths
are processed before longer loopless paths. This guarantees that all loopless
paths reaching the search tree's level h are tested to determine if they are
a solution before any path that reaches level h + 1. Given that a loopless
solution exists starting from any valid `world`, eventually, a path reaching the
search tree's height k contains `WIN`, and the function terminates.

51 Complexity and Performance

We now have four proposed implementations for the N puzzle game: two
using depth-first search (one of which does not work from Chap. 7) and two
implementations using breadth-first search. The question we need to answer
is which should we favor? Our first instinct is to compare the complexity of
the three working versions. Let T_1, T_2, and T_3 be the partial search subtrees
explored, respectively, by breadth-first search without an accumulator from
Chap. 8 (BFS), depth-first search with an accumulator (DFSA), and breadth-
first search with an accumulator (BFSA). Let h be the height of the tallest
among T_1, T_2, and T_3, and let T_i be the full search subtree of height h. We
define n as the number of edges and number of nodes in T_i. In the worst
case, all three working implementations must traverse T_i in its entirety. Such
a traversal visits each node and each edge exactly once. This means each
algorithm performs $O(n)$ steps to complete the traversal. For each of these
steps, BFS performs $O(3n)$ steps (two `map` and one `enqueue` operations),
DFSA performs $O(2n)$ steps (one `map` and one `filter` operations), and BFSA
performs $O(4n)$ steps (two `map`, one `filter`, and one `enqueue` operations).
Therefore, all three solutions have the same complexity: $O(n^2)$.

Complexity analysis did not reveal any implementation having a superior
abstract running time. In such cases, an empirical study is required. We may
measure running time to try to discern if any implementation is best. To do
so, run the following timing experiments using the same starting `worlds` with
each implementation five times:

BFS:
```
1: (time (find-solution-bfs
         (list (list (make-world 1 3 8 5 2 0 4 6 7)))))
2: (time (find-solution-bfs
         (list (list (make-world 0 2 3 1 5 6 4 7 8)))))
3: (time (find-solution-bfs
         (list (list (make-world 4 1 3 7 2 6 0 5 8)))))
4: (time (find-solution-bfs
         (list (list (make-world 1 2 3 0 5 6 4 7 8)))))
```

	Run 1	Run 2	Run 3	Run 4	Run 5	Average	Solution length
BFS 1	32,438	32,281	32,938	32,078	32,422	32,481.4	12
BFS 2	0	0	0	0	0	0	5
BFS 3	15	0	0	0	0	3	7
BFS 4	0	0	0	0	0	0	4
DFSA 1	352,032	351,187	349,938	350,891	351,703	351,150.2	26282
DFSA 2	328	328	312	343	328	327.8	1109
DFSA 3	0	0	0	0	0	0	7
DFSA 4	7704	7953	8047	7172	7140	7603.2	5680
BFSA 1	843	984	1031	953	985	959.2	12
BFSA 2	15	0	0	15	0	6	5
BFSA 3	15	0	0	0	0	3	7
BFSA 4	0	0	0	0	0	0	4

Table 5: CPU times in milliseconds for finding a solution

```
DFSA:
  1: (time (find-solution (make-world 1 3 8 5 2 0 4 6 7) '()))
  2: (time (find-solution (make-world 0 2 3 1 5 6 4 7 8) '()))
  3: (time (find-solution (make-world 4 1 3 7 2 6 0 5 8) '()))
  4: (time (find-solution (make-world 1 2 3 0 5 6 4 7 8) '()))

BFSA:
  1: (time (find-solution-bfs
             (list (list (make-world 1 3 8 5 2 0 4 6 7))) '()))
  2: (time (find-solution-bfs
             (list (list (make-world 0 2 3 1 5 6 4 7 8))) '()))
  3: (time (find-solution-bfs
             (list (list (make-world 4 1 3 7 2 6 0 5 8))) '()))
  4: (time (find-solution-bfs
             (list (list (make-world 1 2 3 0 5 6 4 7 8))) '()))
```

For each implementation, the world in the first experiment is the one from Sect. 41 that led to the discovery that breadth-first search may be slow. The remaining starting worlds were chosen because they have relatively short solutions.

Table 5 presents CPU times (minus garbage collection time) obtained, the average execution time for each experiment, and the length of the solution found. The most salient feature is that except for DFSA 3 breadth-first search finds a significantly shorter solution. This explains why, for corresponding experiments, both implementations using breadth-first search are significantly faster than DFSA 1, DFSA 2, and DFSA 4: depth-first search is going much deeper in the search tree to find a solution. In other words, the subtree explored by depth-first search is significantly taller. For the one exception, DFSA 3, depth-first search is faster (ever so slightly) on average and never worse than either breadth-first implementation. Observe that depth-first search explores the search tree to the same depth as breadth-first search. This suggests that there are conditions under which depth-first search is as fast or faster than breadth-first search. For example, this occurs when depth-first search finds a solution by following the first neighbor of each input `world` without encountering a `world` twice. In contrast, breadth-first search is tied up searching all possible paths.

The performance between breadth-first search with and without an accumulator is very similar. They are essentially the same except for `BFS 1` and `BFSA 1` (the case that led to our discovery that `BFS` can be slow). `BFSA 1` is significantly faster. The average CPU time is reduced from about 32 seconds to just under 1 second. How is this explained? As mentioned in Sect. 41, there are 98,499 paths in the queue when the solution is found by `BFS`. There are 603 paths in the queue when the solution is found by `BFSA`. Clearly, `BFSA` is exploring significantly fewer paths through the search tree, and this explains why it is significantly faster. It is worth noting that the savings are enough to render the 3n versus 4n factor discovered by the complexity analysis above inconsequential. In other words, the cost of maintaining and exploiting an accumulator paid off in our experiments.

In this chapter, we have made some progress. Depth-first search always finds a solution and can be faster under certain conditions. Breadth-first search is faster under other conditions. This suggests a tantalizing question: Is there a way to combine these two searching algorithms to get the best of both? The goal is to find a short solution like breadth-first search by exploring fewer paths in the search tree like depth-first search.

---

3 The `find-solution-bfs`'s implementation using an accumulator always adds a `world` to the front of the accumulator. A hacker casually comments that this is silly because for the first path, the first `world` in the accumulator will be repeated before the first `world` in the first path. For example, consider following values for the first path and the accumulator:

```
first path  = (w3 w2 w1 w0)
accumulator = (w2 w1 w0)
```

For the first `world` in the first path, w_3, w_2 is a successor, and w_3 is not. Therefore, w_2 is repeated before w_3 as a potential successor to create new paths. The hacker suggests keeping the first `world` of the accumulator as the first `world` in the new accumulator and making the first `world` of the first path the second `world` in the accumulator. Is the hacker right? Will this improve `BFSA`'s performance? Implement the suggested change, and run the experiments again to justify your answer.

4 A different hacker from the previous problem suggests that a new `world` ought to be added to the end, not the front, of the accumulator. Is this hacker right? Will this improve `BFSA`'s performance. Implement this change, and run the experiments again to justify your answer.

52 What Have We Learned in This Chapter?

The important lessons of this chapter are summarized as follows:

- Accumulators may be used to fix an infinite recursion bug.
- Accumulators may be used to reduce the amount of searching done.
- Establishing that an accumulator invariant is maintained can be helpful in developing a termination argument.
- When complexity analysis fails to reveal that there is an implementation with a lower abstract running time, an empirical study is needed.
- Depth-first search may need to traverse the search tree deeper than breadth-first search.
- Depth-first search can be faster than breadth-first search.
- Breadth-first search can be faster than depth-first search.
- Searching less does not always lead to faster searches.
- Exploiting and maintaining an accumulator may have a negative impact on performance.

Chapter 11
Iteration

Recursive functions are a form of iteration. That is, they repeatedly perform the same evaluation using different values until a condition is met. Recursion is how we have implemented iteration. A recursive function may contain one or more *delayed operations*. This is the case when functions are designed using structural recursion. A delayed operation is a function application that cannot be evaluated until the evaluation of a different function call is finished (e.g., a recursive call). This means that the delayed operation and the values it needs must be remembered to complete the computation. That is, the evaluation of the program requires an accumulator to remember the delayed operations and the needed values. This may have an impact on performance. Allocating memory to remember needed values takes time. Calling a function (i.e., like a recursive call) and returning from said call to finish a delayed operation also takes time.

We have studied accumulators as a mechanism to solve the loss of knowledge problem. Accumulators may also be used to make program evaluation more efficient. In essence, accumulators may be used to reduce or eliminate delayed operations. The idea is to use one or more accumulators to remember a partially computed value that is used to finish the computation.

Consider, for example, the program to compute the factorial of a given natural number n. Recall that n factorial, n!, is 1 if n is 0 and otherwise is the product of n and (n - 1)!. The program in Fig. 37 computes n! and is designed using structural recursion on a natural number. Observe that it contains a delayed operation: *. Applying * to its arguments must be delayed until (fact (sub1 n)) is evaluated. This means that the value of n and the function to apply, *, must be remembered in order to finish the program's evaluation. We may visualize the computation of 6! as follows:

```
(fact 6) = (* 6 (fact 5))
         = (* 6 (* 5 (fact 4)))
         = (* 6 (* 5 (* 4 (fact 3))))
         = (* 6 (* 5 (* 4 (* 3 (fact 2)))))
         = (* 6 (* 5 (* 4 (* 3 (* 2 (fact 1))))))
```

© The Author(s), under exclusive license to Springer Nature Switzerland AG 2022   271
M. T. Morazán, *Animated Program Design*, Texts in Computer Science,
https://doi.org/10.1007/978-3-031-04317-8_11

Fig. 37 The program to compute n! based on structural recursion

```
;; natnum → natnum
;; Purpose: Compute the factorial of the given natural number
(define (fact n)
  (if (= n 0)
      1
      (* n (fact (sub1 n))))))

;; Sample expressions for fact
(define F0  1)
(define F5  (* 5 (fact (sub1 5))))
(define F10 (* 10 (fact (sub1 10))))

;; Tests using sample computations for fact
(check-expect (fact 0)  F0)
(check-expect (fact 5)  F5)
(check-expect (fact 10) F10)

;; Tests using sample values for fact
(check-expect (fact 2)  2)
(check-expect (fact 6)  720)
```

```
= (* 6 (* 5 (* 4 (* 3 (* 2 (* 1 (fact 0)))))))
= (* 6 (* 5 (* 4 (* 3 (* 2 (* 1 1))))))
= (* 6 (* 5 (* 4 (* 3 (* 2 1)))))
= (* 6 (* 5 (* 4 (* 3 2))))
= (* 6 (* 5 (* 4 6)))
= (* 6 (* 5 24))
= (* 6 120)
= 720
```

Observe that at each step in the trace, the value of n and *, the delayed function, must be remembered. This is why we see a "bump" in the trace. This indicates that more memory is required at each step to store information for delayed operations until n is 0. After this point, the delayed operations start to be executed, and the "bump" is reduced. When all the delayed operations are executed, the value of the computation, 720, is returned.

As discussed in Chap. 9, using an accumulator ought to be considered when a function is based on structural recursion, and the result of a recursive call is input to another function. Such is the case for fact. The partial product so far may be stored in an accumulator to eliminate the delayed operation. The program in Fig. 38 is the result of introducing an accumulator and encapsulation. Observe that there are no delayed operations in the program. The result of fact2 is the result of fact-accum. There is no delayed operation. Inside fact-accum there are no delayed operations for the recursive call. That is, the recursive call is fact-accum's final action. When the final action of a function is a function call, we say that it is a *tail call*. When said call

Fig. 38 The program to compute n! based on accumulative recursion

```
;; natnum → natnum
;; Purpose: Compute the factorial of the given natural number
(define (fact2 n)
  (local [;; natnum natnum → natnum
          ;; Purpose: Compute the factorial of the first
          ;;             given natural number
          ;; Accumulator invariant
          ;;    accum = the product of the natural numbers in [k+1..n]
          (define (fact-accum n accum)
            (if (= n 0)
                accum
                (fact-accum (sub1 n) (* n accum))))]
    (fact-accum n 1)))

;; Tests using sample values for fact2
(check-expect (fact2 0)   1)
(check-expect (fact2 5)   120)
(check-expect (fact2 10) 3628800)
(check-expect (fact2 2)   2)
(check-expect (fact2 6)   720)
```

is a recursive call, we say that the function is *tail recursive*. Tail-recursive functions may be evaluated without having to remember values needed or functions to execute in the future of the computation. Let us visualize the evaluation of 6! using fact2:

```
(fact2 6) = (fact-accum 6   1)
          = (fact-accum 5   6)
          = (fact-accum 4  30)
          = (fact-accum 3 120)
          = (fact-accum 2 360)
          = (fact-accum 1 720)
          = (fact-accum 0 720)
          = 720
```

Observe that there is no "bump" in the trace of the program. This is because there are no delayed operations. Computing factorial may be done using a constant amount of memory: two variables. In general, tail-recursion is considered an efficient form of iteration because programs may be evaluated using a constant number of variables. The only memory required is the memory needed to store the values of the variables. No time is required to finish a delayed operation after a tail call.

Naturally, we may ask if fact2 is faster than fact. To determine this, we use the following benchmarks:

```
(time (fact  20000)))
(time (fact2 20000)))
```

The following table displays the CPU times obtained (after subtracting, if any, garbage collection time) for five executions of the benchmarks:

	Run 1	Run 2	Run 3	Run 4	Run 5	Average
fact	516	484	515	485	485	497
fact2	609	610	593	594	594	600

Alas, `fact` is slightly faster. On average `fact` is 103 milliseconds faster. This is, indeed, surprising. After all, `fact2` does not have to make a recursive call and come back to finish a delayed operation. Does this mean that tail-recursion is not an efficient form of iteration? The answer is an unequivocal no. One benchmark is not enough to reach such a conclusion. We must be more thorough in our exploration of tail-recursion. Computing factorial may be the proverbial exception to the rule. Perhaps, the `ISL+` interpreter is able to perform optimizations that give `fact` an ever so slight edge over `fact2`. We must determine if any such optimizations always make the tail-recursive programs we write less efficient.

We explore the conversion of list-folding operations into tail-recursive form. A list-folding operation traverses a given list to combine (i.e., fold) its values into an answer. At each step a list element is used to the computation of the needed answer.

53 List-Folding Operations from the Left

The most natural way to process a list is from left to right or, put differently, from its first element to its last element. A list-folding function designed using structural recursion always traverses the entire list and provides the result of the recursive call as input to another function. This makes them good candidates for using an accumulator. We explore two problems: summing a list of numbers and reversing a (`listof X`).

53.1 Summing a List of Numbers

53.1.1 Problem Analysis

Figure 39 displays a program to sum the elements of a given `lon` designed using structural recursion. Observe that the result of the recursive call is input to `+`. The application of `+` to its arguments is, therefore, a delayed operation. Our goal is to introduce an accumulator to eliminate the delayed operation.

Fig. 39 Summing a `lon` using structural recursion

```
;; Sample lons
(define ELON '())
(define LON1 '(6 4 9 4 2))
(define LON2 '(-10 0 7 -20))

;; (listof number) → number
;; Purpose: Add the numbers in the given lon
(define (sum-lon a-lon)
  (if (empty? a-lon)
      0
      (+ (first a-lon)
         (sum-lon (rest a-lon)))))

;; Sample expressions for sum-lon
(define SUM-ELON 0)
(define SUM-LON1 (+ (first LON1)
                    (sum-lon (rest LON1))))
(define SUM-LON2 (+ (first LON2)
                    (sum-lon (rest LON2))))

;; Tests using sample computations for sum-lon
(check-expect (sum-lon ELON) SUM-ELON)
(check-expect (sum-lon LON1) SUM-LON1)
(check-expect (sum-lon LON2) SUM-LON2)

;; Tests using sample values for sum-lon
(check-expect (sum-lon '(1 2 3 4)) 10)
(check-expect (sum-lon '(7 31 8)) 46)
```

Instead of delaying a + application for each recursive call, an accumulator may be used to remember the sum of list elements so far. Assuming the accumulator is named `accum`, the proposed accumulator invariant is:

`accum = the sum of list elements so far`

Initially `accum` must be 0 because no list elements have been added. At each step the first number in the given list is folded into `accum`.

When the given list of numbers is empty, the accumulator contains the completed sum, and it is returned as the value of the function. This is how the accumulator is exploited. When the list of numbers is not empty, a recursive call is made with the rest of the list, and the first list element is folded into the accumulator using +.

53.1.2 Refactoring `sum-lon`

The function `sum-lon` is refactored to call an auxiliary function that takes as input the given list and the initial accumulator value of 0. Figure 40 displays

Fig. 40 The refactored `sum-lon` using an accumulator

```
;; (listof number) → number
;; Purpose: Add the numbers in the given lon
(define (sum-lon2 a-lon)
  (sum-lon-accum a-lon 0))

;; Sample expressions for sum-lon2
(define SUM2-ELON (sum-lon-accum ELON 0))
(define SUM2-LON1 (sum-lon-accum LON1 0))
(define SUM2-LON2 (sum-lon-accum LON2 0))

;; Tests using sample computations for sum-lon2
(check-expect (sum-lon2 ELON) SUM2-ELON)
(check-expect (sum-lon2 LON1) SUM2-LON1)
(check-expect (sum-lon2 LON2) SUM2-LON2)

;; Tests using sample values for sum-lon2
(check-expect (sum-lon2 '(1 2 3 4)) 10)
(check-expect (sum-lon2 '(7 31 8)) 46)
```

the refactored code. The name of the function and the name of the variables for the value of the sample expressions are changed in order to allow you to have both versions of `sum-lon` reside in the same ISL+ file. The only real differences, therefore, between Figs. 39 and 40 are the body of the function and the sample expressions.

53.1.3 `sum-lon-accum`'s Sample Expressions and Differences

To write the sample expressions, we use the same sample `lon`s defined in Fig. 39. The answer is always the accumulator when the given `lon` is `ELON`. For example, processing `ELON` and 0 means the answer is 0, and processing `ELON` after traversing `'(10 6 4)` means the answer is 20. Sample expressions for these are written as follows:

```
;; Sample expressions for sum-lon-accum
(define SUMACCUM-ELON1 0)
```

```
(define SUMACCUM-ELON2 20)
```

If the given list is not empty, a recursive call with the rest of the given list and a new accumulator value obtained from adding in the given list's first number is needed. To process `LON1` the accumulator must be 0. The needed call is made with the rest of `LON1` and `LON1`'s first element added to 0 (i.e., the accumulator). After processing `LON2`'s first element, the accumulator must be equal to `LON2`'s first element. The needed call is made with the sublist starting with `LON2`'s third element and the adding of `LON2`'s second element to the accumulator. Sample expressions may be written as follows:

```
(define SUMACCUM-LON1 (sum-lon-accum
                       (rest LON1)
                       (+ (first LON1) 0)))

(define SUMACCUM-RLON2 (sum-lon-accum
                        (rest (rest LON2))
                        (+ (second LON2) (first LON2))))
```

The only differences among the sample expressions are a list of numbers and a number. We name these differences a-lon and accum.

53.1.4 Signature, Statements, and Function Header for sum-lon-accum

The function takes as input the differences among the sample expressions, a lon and a number, and returns a number. The purpose is to add all the elements of the given lon into the given accumulator. The accumulator invariant is stated to help any code reader understand the solution to the problem and the role of the accumulator. Finally, the function header is written using the names chosen for the function and the differences among the sample expressions. The next steps of the design recipe yield:

```
;; (listof number) number → number
;; Purpose: Add the numbers in the given lon to the
;;          given accumulator
;; Accumulator invariant
;;   accum = sum of list elements so far
(define (sum-lon-accum a-lon accum)
```

53.1.5 Tests for sum-lon-accum

The tests using sample expressions illustrate that the function computes the values of the sample expressions. They are written by providing the function the values used to design the sample expressions. These tests are:

```
;; Tests using sample computations for sum-lon-accum
(check-expect (sum-lon-accum ELON 0)   SUMACCUM-ELON1)
(check-expect (sum-lon-accum ELON 20) SUMACCUM-ELON2)
(check-expect (sum-lon-accum LON1 0)   SUMACCUM-LON1)
(check-expect (sum-lon-accum (rest LON2) (first LON2))
              SUMACCUM-RLON2)
```

The tests using sample values illustrate how the function works using concrete values. For example, processing a lon that contains the numbers 1–5 with an accumulator of 0 evaluates to 10, and processing a lon containing

7, 31, and 8 with an accumulator of 0 evaluates to 46. Tests are written as follows:

```
;; Tests using sample values for sum-lon-accum
(check-expect (sum-lon-accum '(1 2 3 4)  0) 10)
(check-expect (sum-lon-accum '(7 31 8)   0) 46)
```

53.1.6 sum-lon-accum's Function Body

The function body uses an if-expression to distinguish among lon subtypes. The then-expression is obtained by abstracting over the first two sample expressions. The else-expression is obtained by abstracting over the second two sample expressions. The body of the function is:

```
(if (empty? a-lon)
      accum
      (sum-lon-accum
        (rest a-lon)
        (+ (first a-lon) accum)))
```

Observe that the function is tail-recursive. That is, it does not have any delayed operations.

53.1.7 Performance

We have two solutions to compute the sum of a list of numbers. One contains a delayed operation and other is tail-recursive. Has anything been gained by using an accumulator? To answer this question, we perform an empirical study. Why?

1 What is the complexity of sum-lon? What is the complexity of sum-lon2?

We define the following list and experiments to gather empirical data:

```
(define L (build-list 1000000 (λ (i) (random 100000))))

(time (sum-lon L)))
(time (sum-lon2 L)))
```

We use a large list to truly discern any difference in performance. Each experiment is executed five times. The obtained CPU times (after subtracting garbage collecting time) and the average of the five runs are displayed in the following table:

	Run 1	Run 2	Run 3	Run 4	Run 5	Average
sum-lon	344	390	328	329	312	340.6
sum-lon2	297	313	297	328	297	306.4

Observe that **sum-lon2**, the tail-recursive version, is always faster. That is, we see a positive impact on performance by using an accumulator. To compare the averages, we may use their *relative difference*. The relative difference is a means to compare two numbers taking into account their sizes. It is a unitless ratio that uses one of the measurements as a reference value and informs us by how much the measurements are proportionally different. Relative difference is defined as follows:

$$\frac{x - x_{reference}}{x_{reference}}$$

If the relative difference is positive, then the reference performs better. Otherwise, the reference's performance is inferior.

Using **sum-lon2**'s average as the reference measurement, we obtain a relative difference that is approximately 0.11. This informs us that the tail-recursive version is about 11% faster. That is, the reference would need to perform 11% worse for the measurements to be the same. This is a significant improvement in performance.

53.2 Reversing a List

As a second example of folding a list from the left, we consider reversing a list of **X**. For example, reversing '(d c b a) yields '(a b c d). Figure 41 displays the code developed using a design based on structural recursion. Observe that **append** is a delayed operation. Our goal is to redesign **rev-lox** to exploit an accumulator and eliminate the delayed operation.

53.2.1 Problem Analysis

Consider how the program in Fig. 41 reverses the list '(d c b a):

```
  (rev-lox '(d c b a)
= (append
    (rev-lox '(c b a))
    (list 'd))
= (append
    (append
      (rev-lox '(b a))
      (list 'c))
    (list 'd))
```

Fig. 41 Reversing a list using structural recursion

```
(define ELOX '())
(define LOX1 '(d c b a))
(define LOX2 '(99 #true "Hi!"))

;; (listof X) → (listof X)
;; Purpose: Reverse the given list
(define (rev-lox a-lox)
  (if (empty? a-lox)
      '()
      (append (rev-lox (rest a-lox)) (list (first a-lox)))))

;; Sample expressions for rev-lox
(define REV-ELOX '())
(define REV-LOX1 (append (rev-lox (rest LOX1))
                         (list (first LOX1))))
(define REV-LOX2 (append (rev-lox (rest LOX2))
                         (list (first LOX2))))

;; Tests using sample computations for rev-lox
(check-expect (rev-lox ELOX) REV-ELOX)
(check-expect (rev-lox LOX1) REV-LOX1)
(check-expect (rev-lox LOX2) REV-LOX2)

;; Tests using sample values for rev-lox
(check-expect (rev-lox '(1 2 3 4 5))
              '(5 4 3 2 1))
(check-expect (rev-lox '(red white blue))
              '(blue white red))
```

```
= (append
    (append
      (append
        (rev-lox '(a))
        (list 'b))
      (list 'c))
    (list 'd))
= (append
    (append
      (append
        (append
          (rev-lox '())
          (list 'a))
        (list 'b))
      (list 'c))
    (list 'd))
= (append
    (append
      (append
```

```
            (append
             '()
             (list 'a))
            (list 'b))
          (list 'c))
        (list 'd))
= (append
    (append
      (append
        (list 'a)
        (list 'b))
      (list 'c))
    (list 'd))
= (append
    (append
      (list 'a b)
      (list 'c))
    (list 'd))
= (append
    (list 'a b c)
    (list 'd))
= (list 'a b c d)
```

After the last recursive call is made, a list element is added to the end of the partially computed result. For example, c is added to the end of (list 'a b).

Instead of delaying the append operation as each list element is encountered, it may be added to an accumulator that stores the reverse of the list traversed so far. Initially, the accumulator is '() given that none of the list is traversed. If the list is '() then the entire list has been traversed, and the accumulator is returned. Otherwise, a recursive call is made with the rest of the given list and an accumulator that has the first element of the given list added to the front of the given accumulator. Observe that in this manner, the list elements are kept in reversed order as the list is traversed. The following table illustrates the process:

a-lox	accum
(d c b a)	'()
(c b a)	(d)
(b a)	(c d)
(a)	(b c d)
()	(a b c d)

Observe that for each step (i.e., row in the table above) we have the following invariant property:

```
accum = the list of traversed elements reversed
```

Fig. 42 Reversing a list using an accumulator

```
;; (listof X) → (listof X)
;; Purpose: Reverse the given list
(define (rev-lox2 a-lox)
  (rev-lox-accum a-lox '()))


;; Sample expressions for rev-lox2
(define REV2-ELOX (rev-lox-accum ELOX '()))
(define REV2-LOX1 (rev-lox-accum LOX1 '()))
(define REV2-LOX2 (rev-lox-accum LOX2 '()))


;; Tests using sample computations for rev-lox2
(check-expect (rev-lox2 ELOX) REV2-ELOX)
(check-expect (rev-lox2 LOX1) REV2-LOX1)
(check-expect (rev-lox2 LOX2) REV2-LOX2)


;; Tests using sample values for rev-lox2
(check-expect (rev-lox2 '(1 2 3 4 5))
              '(5 4 3 2 1))
(check-expect (rev-lox2 '(red white blue))
              '(blue white red))
```

When a-lox is '() all the list elements have been traversed, and the accumulator is the reversed list.

Based on the above problem analysis, rev-lox from Fig. 41 may be refactored to call an auxiliary function with the given list and the initial accumulator value '(). The result of this refactoring is displayed in Fig. 42. The function name and the names of the variables for the values of the sample expressions are refined so that both versions of the program may exist in the same file. The only significant differences are the sample expressions and the function body that now call the auxiliary function rev-lox-accum.

53.2.2 Sample Expressions and Differences for rev-lox-accum

When the given list is empty, the accumulator is returned. This is how the accumulator is exploited. When ELOX is processed, the accumulator must be '() and the accumulator is returned as the value of the function. Consider having processed '(red white blue). The given list is empty and the accumulator, '(blue white red), is returned as the value of the function. Sample expressions for these examples are:

```
;; Sample expressions for rev-lox-accum
(define SUMACCUM-ELOX1 '())
(define SUMACCUM-ELOX2 '(blue white red))
```

When the given list is not empty, a recursive call is made with the rest of the list and an accumulator obtained by adding the first element of the

given list to the given accumulator. The sample expressions for processing
LOX1 and for processing the rest of LOX2 are:

```
(define SUMACCUM-LOX1 (rev-lox-accum
                        (rest LOX1)
                        (cons (first LOX1) '())))
(define SUMACCUM-RLOX2 (rev-lox-accum
                         (rest (rest LOX2))
                         (cons (first (rest LOX2))
                               (list (first LOX2)))))
```

Observe that there are no delayed operations.

The only differences among the sample expressions are the given (listof
X) to reverse and the given (listof X) for the accumulator. We name these
differences a-lox and accum.

53.2.3 rev-lox-accum's Signature, Statements, and Function Header

The function takes two (listof X) as input and returns a (listof X). The
purpose is to reverse the first given list. The accumulator invariant is stated
to make sure any reader understands that the accumulator is used to hold
the partially reversed list during the reversing process. The function header is
written using the chosen function name and the chosen parameter names for
the differences among the sample expressions. The results of the next steps
of the design recipe are:

```
;; (listof X) → (listof X)
;; Purpose: Reverse the first given list
;; Accumulator invariant:
;;   accum = the list of traversed elements reversed
(define (rev-lox-accum a-lox accum)
```

53.2.4 Tests for rev-lox-accum

The tests using sample computations are written with the values used to
design the sample expressions and the corresponding variables for said expressions. These tests are:

```
;; Tests using sample computations for rev-lox-accum
(check-expect (rev-lox-accum ELOX '())
              SUMACCUM-ELOX1)
(check-expect (rev-lox-accum ELOX '(blue white red))
              SUMACCUM-ELOX2)
(check-expect (rev-lox-accum LOX1 '())
              SUMACCUM-LOX1)
```

```
(check-expect (rev-lox-accum (rest LOX2)
                             (list (first LOX2)))
              SUMACCUM-RLOX2)
```

The tests using sample values illustrate how a list is reversed using concrete values without first showing the expressions used to compute the expected value. Sample tests are:

```
;; Tests using sample values for rev-lox-accum
(check-expect (rev-lox-accum '(1 2 3 4) '())
              '(4 3 2 1))
(check-expect (rev-lox-accum '(#false #true)  '())
              '(#true #false))
```

53.2.5 Function Body for `rev-lox-accum`

The function body uses an `if`-expression to distinguish among the subtypes of a (`listof X`). The then-expression is obtained by abstracting over the first two sample expressions, and the else-expression is obtained by abstracting over the second two sample expressions. The body of the function is:

```
(if (empty? a-lox)
    accum
    (rev-lox-accum (rest a-lox) (cons (first a-lox) accum)))
```

53.2.6 Performance

To determine if either implementation to reverse a list is superior, the following experiments using a list of length 50000 are executed 5 times:

```
(define L (build-list 50000 (λ (i) (random 100000))))

(time (rev-lox  L)))
(time (rev-lox2 L)))
```

The CPU times obtained are displayed in the following table:

	Run 1	Run 2	Run 3	Run 4	Run 5	Average
rev-lox	12172	12313	12187	12562	11829	12212.6
rev-lox2	15	15	15	0	0	9

The data clearly suggest that using an accumulator has a tremendous impact on performance. Using the average CPU time for `rev-lox2` as the reference measurement yields a relative difference of 1355.95. This informs us that for the experiments executed on average, the version using an accumulator is about 1357 times faster.[11]

---

[11] Observe that $(+ 9 (* 9 1355.95)) = 12212.55$.

Such a dramatic impact on performance suggests that the use of an accumulator has done much more than simply eliminate the delayed operations. Let us look at the abstract running time of each implementation. We can observe that `rev-lox` is called n + 1 times where n is the length of the given list. The number of calls is $O(n)$. For each call except the last `append` is called which we know is $O(n)$. This means that the complexity of `rev-lox` is $O(n * n) = O(n^2)$. Observe that `rev-lox-accum` is also called n + 1 times making the number of calls $O(n)$. In contrast, however, for each call except the last, a `rest`, a `first`, and a `cons` are executed. For each call the complexity is $O(3)$. This means that the complexity of `rev-lox-accum` is $O(3 * n) = O(n)$. This explains why the performance of `rev-lox-accum` is so superior.

2 Design and implement a tail-recursive function to find the maximum in a nonempty list of numbers.

3 Design and implement a tail-recursive function to count the number of times a given symbol occurs in a given list of symbols.

4 Design and implement a tail-recursive function to compute the length of a (`listof X`).

5 Design and implement a tail-recursive function that implements `andmap`.

6 Design and implement a tail-recursive function to convert a list of numbers in nonincreasing order into a list with the same elements in nondecreasing order.

7 Design and implement a tail-recursive function to add the odd numbers in a list of numbers.

54 List-Folding Operations from the Right

List-folding from the left works well when list elements may be folded into the result (i.e., the accumulator) in the reversed order used by structural

Fig. 43 Computing the lengths of strings using structural recursion

```
(define ELOSTR '())
(define LOSTR1 '("a" "b" "c"))
(define LOSTR2 '("Program" "design" "is" "awesome!"))

;; (listof string) → (listof natnum)
;; Purpose: Return the lengths of the strings in the given
;;          list of strings
(define (lengths-lostr a-lostr)
  (if (empty? a-lostr)
      '()
      (cons (string-length (first a-lostr))
            (lengths-lostr (rest a-lostr)))))

;; Sample expressions for lengths-lostr
(define LENS-ELOSTR '())
(define LENS-LOSTR1 (cons (string-length (first LOSTR1))
                         (lengths-lostr (rest  LOSTR1))))
(define LENS-LOSTR2 (cons (string-length (first LOSTR2))
                         (lengths-lostr (rest  LOSTR2))))

;; Tests using sample computations for lengths-lostr
(check-expect (lengths-lostr ELOSTR) LENS-ELOSTR)
(check-expect (lengths-lostr LOSTR1) LENS-LOSTR1)
(check-expect (lengths-lostr LOSTR2) LENS-LOSTR2)

;; Tests using sample values for lengths-lostr
(check-expect (lengths-lostr '("I" "love" "invariants."))
              '(1 4 11))
(check-expect (lengths-lostr '("Accumulators" "Rock!"))
              '(12 5))
```

recursion. For example, when reversing a list, the last element appended by
`rev-lox` to the result is the first element of the given list. In contrast, when
reversing a list, `rev-lox2` first adds the first given list element to the result.

Sometimes processing list elements in the reversed order followed by structural recursion yields the wrong result. It is, therefore, necessary to process
list elements in the same order as structural recursion, that is, from right to
left. Other times an operation is associative, and it may be natural to follow
a design that processes list elements from right to left. In this section we
explore two problems whose solutions are designed by processing elements
from right to left. The first is computing the length of every string in a list
of strings. The second revisits summing a list of numbers.

54.1 Computing String Lengths from a List of Strings

Given a list of strings, we need to compute the lengths of the strings. Clearly, the answer's type is a list of natural numbers. In the resulting list, the order in which the numbers appear matters. The first length ought to correspond to the first length, the second length ought to correspond to the second list, and so on.

Figure 43 displays the solution obtained using a design based on structural recursion. At each step, the length of the first string in the given list is added to the result. Observe that `cons` in `lengths-lostr` is a delayed operation. Our goal is to introduce an accumulator to render the function tail-recursive.

54.1.1 Problem Analysis

An accumulator may be used to store the string lengths of the traversed part of the list. An auxiliary function that takes the accumulator as an additional input may be used. Initially, the accumulator must be `'()` given that none of the list of strings has been traversed.

We need to be careful about the list provided to the auxiliary function, because the order in which lengths are added to the accumulator matters. If we give the auxiliary function the given list of strings as input, every new length must be added to the end of the accumulator. This means that `append` must be used. Using `append` would result in a solution that is $O(n^2)$: n steps to traverse the list and for each step $O(n)$ for `append`. This situation is reminiscent of the problem faced with `rev-lox` where `append`'s use increased the complexity of the solution.

Can we avoid using `append`? This would require giving the auxiliary function a list that allowed for each length to be added to the front of the accumulator. Instead of providing the given list of strings to the auxiliary function, we can provide the given list of strings reversed. In this manner, the auxiliary function processes the given list from right to left and may add the next length to the front of the accumulator. Observe that the resulting lengths are in reversed order from the reversed list provided to the auxiliary function which is the right order for the given list of strings. For example, we can illustrate the idea as follows:

```
    (lengths-lostr2 '("Oct" "31" "2352"))
  = (lengths-lostr-accum '("2352" "31" "Oct") '())
  = (lengths-lostr-accum '("31" "Oct") '(4))
  = (lengths-lostr-accum '("Oct") '(2 4))
  = (lengths-lostr-accum '() '(3 2 4))
  = '(3 2 4)
```

At each step, the auxiliary function adds the first string's length to the front of the accumulator, and there is no need to use `append`. When the list given

Fig. 44 Computing the lengths of strings using accumulative recursion

```
;; (listof string) → (listof natnum)
;; Purpose: Return the lengths of the strings in the given
;;          list of strings
(define (lengths-lostr2 a-lostr)
  (lengths-lostr-accum (reverse a-lostr) '()))

;; Sample expressions for lengths-lostr2
(define LENS2-ELOSTR (lengths-lostr-accum (reverse ELOSTR) '()))
(define LENS2-LOSTR1 (lengths-lostr-accum (reverse LOSTR1) '()))
(define LENS2-LOSTR2 (lengths-lostr-accum (reverse LOSTR2) '()))

;; Tests using sample computations for lengths-lostr2
(check-expect (lengths-lostr2 ELOSTR) LENS2-ELOSTR)
(check-expect (lengths-lostr2 LOSTR1) LENS2-LOSTR1)
(check-expect (lengths-lostr2 LOSTR2) LENS2-LOSTR2)

;; Tests using sample values for lengths-lostr2
(check-expect (lengths-lostr '("I" "love" "invariants.")) '(1 4 11))
(check-expect (lengths-lostr '("Accumulators" "Rock!")) '(12 5))
```

to the auxiliary function is empty, the accumulator is returned. It contains the string lengths in the right order for `lengths-lostr2`. From the example above, we can state that the accumulator invariant is (assuming the accumulator is called `accum`):

```
accum = traversed list string lengths in reversed order
```

Based on our problem analysis, we may refactor `lengths-lostr` to call an auxiliary function that takes an accumulator as an additional input. The result of this refactoring is displayed in Fig. 44. The only significant changes are found in the body of the function and in the sample expressions that now call the auxiliary function with the reversed given list. The function and variable name changes are solely done to allow both versions, `lengths-lostr` and `lengths-lostr2`, to exist in the same ISL+ file.

Note that the given list is reversed to call the auxiliary function. This is an $O(n)$ operation that is not performed by the program in Fig. 43. Is this operation costly enough to wipe out any gains from eliminating delayed operations? Empirical data is needed to answer this question.

54.1.2 Sample Expressions and Differences for
`lengths-lostr-accum`

Whenever the given list is empty, the answer is the accumulator. To process an empty (`listof string`), the accumulator must be `'()` and returned. After processing `'("c" "b" "a")`, the accumulator must be `'("1" "1" "1")` and returned. Sample expressions for when the given list is empty are:

```
;; Sample expressions for lengths-lostr-accum
(define LACC2-ELOSTR1 '())
(define LACC2-ELOSTR2 '("1" "1" "1"))
```

When the given list is not empty, a recursive tail-call is needed with the rest of the given list and the length of the first string in the given list added to the front of the given accumulator. To process LOSTR1, the recursive call is made with the rest of LOSTR1 and with LOSTR1's first string's length added to the empty accumulator. To process the rest of LOSTR2, the recursive call is made with the rest of the rest of LOSTR2 and with the length of the second string in LOSTR2 added to the accumulator that contains the length of the first string in LOSTR2. The sample expressions are:

```
(define LACC2-LOSTR1 (lengths-lostr-accum
                        (rest LOSTR1)
                         (cons (string-length (first LOSTR1))
                              '())))
(define LACC2-LOSTR2 (lengths-lostr-accum
                        (rest (rest LOSTR2))
                         (cons (string-length (second LOSTR2))
                              (list (first LOSTR2)))))
```

Do not be confused by these sample expressions. LOSTR1 and LOSTR2 are used here as sample lists that are already reversed.

There are two differences among the sample expressions: the given (listof string) and the given (listof natnum) for the accumulator. We name these differences a-lostr and accum.

54.1.3 Signature, Statements, and Function Header for lengths-lostr-accum

The function takes as input a (listof string) and a (listof natnum) and returns a (listof natnum). The purpose is to return a list of string lengths in reversed order from the given list of strings. The accumulator invariant helps explain the function's design to any reader or maintainer of the code. The function header is written using the descriptive function and parameter names. The next steps of the design recipe result in:

```
;; (listof string) (listof natnum) → (listof natnum)
;; Purpose: Return the lengths of the strings in the given
;;          list of strings in reversed order
;; Accumulator invariant:
;;   accum = traversed list string lengths in reversed order
(define (lengths-lostr-accum a-lostr accum)
```

54.1.4 Tests for `lengths-lostr-accum`

The tests using sample computations are written using the values used to design the sample expressions and the variables defined for their values. These tests are:

```
;; Tests using sample computations for lengths-lostr-accum
(check-expect (lengths-lostr-accum ELOSTR '())
              LACC2-ELOSTR1)
(check-expect (lengths-lostr-accum ELOSTR '("1" "1" "1"))
              LACC2-ELOSTR2)
(check-expect (lengths-lostr-accum LOSTR1 '())
              LACC2-LOSTR1)
(check-expect (lengths-lostr-accum (rest LOSTR2)
                                   (list (first LOSTR2)))
              LACC2-LOSTR2)
```

The tests using sample values use concrete values to illustrate how the function works without exhibiting how the answer is computed. The sample expressions below follow the lead of the corresponding tests for `lengths-lostr2`:

```
;; Tests using sample values for lengths-lostr-accum
(check-expect (lengths-lostr-accum
                 '("invariants." "love" "I")
                 '())
              '(1 4 11))
(check-expect (lengths-lostr-accum
                 '("Rock!" "Accumulators")
                 '())
              '(12 5))
```

54.1.5 Function Body for `lengths-lostr-accum`

The body of the function uses an `if`-expression to distinguish the (`listof string`) subtypes. The then-expression is obtained by abstracting over the first two sample expressions. The else-expression is obtained by abstracting over the second two sample expressions. The function body is:

```
(if (empty? a-lostr)
    accum
    (lengths-lostr-accum
      (rest a-lostr)
      (cons (string-length (first a-lostr)) accum))))
```

54.1.6 Performance

It is time to determine if the introduction of an accumulator has a positive or negative impact on performance. The following experiments are executed 5 times:

```
(define L (build-list
           50000
           (λ (i)
             (generate-password (+ 10 (random 20))))))

(time (lengths-lostr  L)))
(time (lengths-lostr2 L)))
```

The list of strings is built using `generate-password` designed in Sect. 17. Recall that a password must have at least length 10, and that is why 10 is added to a random length in [0..19]. The CPU times obtained from the experiments (with garbage collection time subtracted) and their average are displayed in the following table:

	Run 1	Run 2	Run 3	Run 4	Run 5	Average
lengths-lostr	78	78	109	62	47	74.8
lengths-lostr2	78	63	47	78	78	68.8

At a first glance, there is no clear winner here. Sometimes `lengths-lostr` is faster (runs 4–5), and sometimes `lengths-lostr2` is faster (runs 1–3). If we use `lengths-lostr2`'s average CPU time as the reference measurement, the relative difference is approximately 0.087. This would suggest that `lengths-lostr` is about 8% faster on average. We must, however, be careful of *outliers*. An outlier measurement is one that is significantly larger or smaller than the rest of the measurements. In other words, it is an atypical measurement. Such measurements may have a disproportional impact on the average of a set of measurements. A large outlier inflates the average and a small outlier deflates the average. Statisticians suggest removing outliers from the data set when measurements are not entirely reliable (as is the case for timing data).

In the data collected, 47 and 109 may be considered outliers given that they are significantly smaller and larger than the rest of the measurements. If we remove them from the data set, the average for `lengths-lostr` becomes approximately 72.6, and the average for `lengths-lostr2` becomes approximately 74.25. As you can see, this suggests a very small performance gap between the two implementations. The relative difference between the average running times becomes approximately -0.02. This suggests that `lengths-lostr` is ever so slightly faster on average, but given the unreliability of timing measurements, the conclusion to reach is that there is no discernable difference in the running times. Certainly, reversing the list in `lengths-lostr2` does not have a significant impact on performance.

Fig. 45 Summing a list of numbers from right to left

```
;; (listof number) → number
;; Purpose: Add the numbers in the given list of numbers
(define (sum-lon3 a-lon)
  (sum-lon-accum (reverse a-lon) 0))

;; Sample expressions for sum-lon3
(define SUM3-ELON (sum-lon-accum (reverse ELON) 0))
(define SUM3-LON1 (sum-lon-accum (reverse LON1) 0))
(define SUM3-LON2 (sum-lon-accum (reverse LON2) 0))

;; Tests using sample computations for sum-lon3
(check-expect (sum-lon3 ELON) SUM3-ELON)
(check-expect (sum-lon3 LON1) SUM3-LON1)
(check-expect (sum-lon3 LON2) SUM3-LON2)

;; Tests using sample values for sum-lon3
(check-expect (sum-lon3 '(1 2 3 4)) 10)
(check-expect (sum-lon3 '(7 31 8)) 46)
```

54.2 Summing a List of Numbers Revisited

Summing a list of numbers is an associative operation. If RL = (reverse L), then this means that:

(sum-lon L) = (sum-lon RL)   when L = '()

```
  (+ (first L)  (sum-lon (rest L)))
= (+ (first RL) (sum-lon (rest RL)))   when L ≠ '()
```

These equations inform us that summing a list of numbers may be done from left to right or from right to left.

To sum a list of numbers from right to left, all that is needed is to refactor sum-lon2 from Fig. 40. Instead of passing a-lon to the auxiliary function, (reverse a-lon) is passed. The refactored code is displayed in Fig. 45. The only significant differences are the body and sample expressions that reverse the list to process. The changes to the function and variable names are made so that all solutions may reside in the same ISL+ file.

There are no changes required for sum-lon-accum. This function continues to fold the given list's elements into the accumulator from left to right.

We compare the performance of this new solution to sum a list of numbers with our previous versions by running the same experiments. Adding the obtained measurements to the table from Sect. 53.1.7 yields:

	Run 1	Run 2	Run 3	Run 4	Run 5	Average
sum-lon	344	390	328	329	312	340.6
sum-lon2	297	313	297	328	297	306.4
sum-lon3	308	312	313	313	328	314.8

The table suggests that reversing the list has a small impact on performance. On average `sum-lon3` is faster than `sum-lon` suggesting that using an accumulator still has a positive impact on performance but not as accentuated as that obtained from `sum-lon2`. Using `sum-lon2`'s average running time as the reference measurement against `sum-lon3`'s average running time, we observe a relative difference of approximately 0.027. This suggests that the price paid to reverse the list is about 3%. The lesson to derive is that it is better to avoid reversing the list whenever possible.

8 Design and implement a tail-recursive function that implements `ormap`.

9 Design and implement a tail-recursive function that implements `map`.

10 Design and implement a tail-recursive function that implements `filter`.

11 Design and implement a tail-recursive function to append the strings in a list of strings. The following test ought to pass:

```
(check-expect (append-lostr '("Hi " "there" "!"))
              "Hi There!")
```

12 Design and implement a tail-recursive function to scale a given list of numbers by a given number.

55 Functional Abstraction

The functions `sum-lon2` and `rev-lox2` developed to fold a list from left to right using an accumulator are very similar. The functions `sum-lon3` and `lengths-lostr2`, developed to fold a list from right to left using an accumulator, are also very similar. This means they are good candidates for abstraction to reduce their size and to make writing any similar functions easier in the future.

Recall the design recipe for abstracting over functions:

1. Compare and mark the differences in the bodies of the functions.
2. Define the abstract function that takes as additional input the differences.

Fig. 46 Encapsulated left to right processing functions

```(define (sum-lon2 a-lon)```
  ```(local```
   ```[(define```
     ```(sum-lon-accum a-lon accum)```
     ```(if (empty? a-lon)```
       ```accum```
       ```(sum-lon-accum```
        ```(rest a-lon)```
        ```(+ (first a-lon)```
          ```accum))))]```
    ```(sum-lon-accum a-lon 0)))```
	```(define (rev-lox2 a-lox)```
	  ```(local```
	   ```[(define```
	     ```(rev-lox-accum a-lox accum)```
	     ```(if (empty? a-lox)```
	       ```accum```
	       ```(rev-lox-accum```
	        ```(rest a-lox)```
	        ```(cons (first a-lox)```
	          ```accum))))]```
	    ```(rev-lox-accum a-lox '())))```

(a) Encapsulated sum-lon2.	**(b)** Encapsulated rev-lox2.

3. Refactor the functions abstracted over to use the abstract function.

We use this design recipe to abstract over the similar functions developed in this chapter.

56 Abstraction over Left to Right Accumulating Folding Functions

Figure 46 displays the encapsulated functions developed that fold a list from left to right. Figure 46(a) displays the encapsulated sum-lon2, and Fig. 46(b) displays the encapsulated rev-lox2. Placed side by side in this manner, it becomes clear that the functions are almost identical. There are two differences among them. The first is the base value given to the auxiliary function. For sum-lon2, this value is 0, and for rev-lox2, this value is '(). The second is the function used to compute the new value of the accumulator. This function takes as input a list value and an accumulator. For sum-lon2, this function is +, and for rev-lox2, this function is cons.

56.1 The Abstraction

The abstract function inherits its structure from the functions abstracted over. To develop the abstract function, we first determine the signature for the auxiliary function. The type of the given list to traverse may vary. Therefore, a generic type is needed: (listof X). The returned value's type may also vary and must be a generic type: Y. Given that the auxiliary function returns

Fig. 47 Abstract function for folding a list from left to right

```
;; Y (X Y → Y) (listof X) → Y
;; Purpose: Fold the given list from left to right using the given
;;          initial accumulator value and given combinator function.
(define (fold-from-left base comb a-lox)
  (local [;; (listof X) Y arrow Y
          ;; Purpose: Fold the list values from left to right into
          ;;          the given accumulator.
          ;; Accumulator invariant:
          ;;    accum = Y value for traversed list elements so far
          (define (aux-f a-lox accum)
            (if (empty? a-lox)
                accum
                (aux-f
                  (rest a-lox)
                  (comb (first a-lox) accum))))]
    (aux-f a-lox base)))
```

the accumulator, its type is Y. We can now write the signature, purpose, accumulator invariant, and header for the auxiliary function as:

```
;; (listof X) Y → Y
;; Purpose: Fold the list values from left to right into
;;          the given accumulator.
;; Accumulator invariant:
;;    accum = Y value for traversed list elements so far
(define (aux-f a-lox accum)
```

Observe that the purpose statement only specifies the generic behavior of the function and that the accumulator invariant now refers to the accumulator's generic type.

We can now develop the signature for the generic function. The base value and the list to traverse are given as input to the auxiliary function. This means that, respectively, their types are Y and (listof X). The function to compute the new accumulator value takes as input a list element and the accumulator and returns an accumulator values. This means its type is (X Y →Y). The abstract function returns the value of the auxiliary function. Therefore, the return type for the auxiliary function is Y. We can now write the signature, purpose, accumulator invariant, and function header as:

```
;; Y (X Y → Y) (listof X) → Y
;; Purpose: Fold the given list from left to right using
;;          the given initial accumulator value and given
;;          combinator function.
(define (fold-from-left base comb a-lox)
```

Observe that once again the purpose statement is a generic description of what the function does. Finally, fold-from-left's body is obtained by abstracting over the expressions in the bodies of sum-lon2 and rev-lox2, and

Fig. 48 Refactored sum-lon2 and rev-lox2 to use abstract function

```
;; (listof number) → number
;; Purpose: Add the numbers in the given lon
(define (sum-lon4 a-lon) (fold-from-left 0 + a-lon))


;; Sample expressions for sum-lon4
(define SUM5-ELON (fold-from-left 0 + ELON))
(define SUM5-LON1 (fold-from-left 0 + LON1))
(define SUM5-LON2 (fold-from-left 0 + LON2))

;; Tests using sample computations for sum-lon4
(check-expect (sum-lon4 ELON) SUM4-ELON)
(check-expect (sum-lon4 LON1) SUM4-LON1)
(check-expect (sum-lon4 LON2) SUM4-LON2)

;; Tests using sample values for sum-lon4
(check-expect (sum-lon4 '(1 2 3 4)) 10)
(check-expect (sum-lon4 '(7 31 8)) 46)


;; (listof X) → (listof X)
;; Purpose: Reverse the given list
(define (rev-lox3 a-lox) (fold-from-left '() cons a-lox))

;; Sample expressions for sum-lon3
(define REV3-ELON (fold-from-left '() cons ELOX))
(define REV3-LON1 (fold-from-left '() cons LOX1))
(define REV3-LON2 (fold-from-left '() cons LOX2))

;; Tests using sample computations for rev-lox3
(check-expect (rev-lox3 ELOX) REV5-ELON)
(check-expect (rev-lox3 LOX1) REV5-LON1)
(check-expect (rev-lox3 LOX2) REV5-LON2)

;; Tests using sample values for rev-lox3
(check-expect (rev-lox3 '(1 2 3 4 5))
              '(5 4 3 2 1))
(check-expect (rev-lox3 '(red white blue))
              '(blue white red))
```

aux-f's body is obtained by abstracting over the expressions in the bodies of sum-lon2's and rev-lox2's auxiliary functions. The result of the first two steps of the design recipe for abstraction is displayed in Fig. 47.

The final step is to refactor the functions abstracted over. These functions must call the abstract function with the appropriate base value and combinator function to update the accumulator. The refactored functions are displayed in Fig. 48. The function name and variable name changes are only done so that these new versions of the solution may reside in the same ISL+ file as the previous solutions.

Take a minute to appreciate the conciseness and elegance of the refactored functions. Any problem that may be solved by folding a value into an accumulator by traversing a list from left to right may be written using `fold-from-left`. This is the power of abstraction. In fact, this abstraction is so powerful and useful that ISL+ has an abstract function to fold a list from left to right: `foldl`. It takes as input the same types of value as `fold-from-left` but in a different order. The signature for `foldl` is:

   (X Y → Y) Y (listof X) → Y

This means we can write the function definitions for `sum-lon2` and `rev-lox2` as follows:

```
(define (sum-lon5 a-lon) (foldl + 0 a-lon))

(define (rev-lox3 a-lox) (foldl cons '() a-lox))
```

56.2 Performance

To explore the abstraction's performance to sum a list of numbers `sum-lon5` is used as a benchmark. The same experiments as with the previous three versions of the solution are executed to yield:

	Run 1	Run 2	Run 3	Run 4	Run 5	Average
sum-lon	344	390	328	329	312	340.6
sum-lon2	297	313	297	328	297	306.4
sum-lon3	308	312	313	313	328	314.8
sum-lon5	15	15	15	15	15	15

We can observe that the CPU times are significantly better for `sum-lon5`. Given that `sum-lon2` and `sum-lon5` perform the same operations in the same order, it is bewildering why there is such an improvement in performance. The answer is that programming languages like ISL+ highly optimize their abstract functions and, therefore, run faster than the code we have developed. Our `sum-lon2` does not enjoy all the optimizations that `sum-lon5` enjoys by using `foldl`.

To explore the abstraction's performance to reverse a list `rev-lox3` is used as a benchmark. The same experiments as with the previous two versions of the solution are executed to yield:

	Run 1	Run 2	Run 3	Run 4	Run 5	Average
rev-lox	12172	12313	12187	12562	11829	12212.6
rev-lox2	15	15	15	0	0	9
rev-lox3	0	0	0	0	0	0

Fig. 49 Encapsulated right to left processing functions

```
(define (sum-lon2 a-lon)
  (local
   [(define
     (aux-f a-lon accum)
     (if (empty? a-lon)
         accum
         (aux-f
          (rest a-lon)
          (+ (first a-lon)
             accum))))]
   (aux-f (reverse a-lon) 0)))
```

(a) Encapsulated sum-lon2.

```
(define (lengths-lostr2 a-lostr)
  (local
   [(define
     (aux-f a-lostr accum)
     (if (empty? a-lostr)
         accum
         (aux-f
          (rest a-lostr)
          (cons (string-length
                 (first a-lostr))
                accum))))]
   (aux-f (reverse a-lostr) '())))
```

(b) Encapsulated lengths-lostr2.

Fig. 50 Abstract function for folding a list from right to left

```
;; Y (X Y → Y) (listof X) → Y
;; Purpose: Fold the given list from right to left using
;;          the given initial accumulator value and given
;;          combinator function.
(define (fold-from-right base comb a-lox)
  (local [;; (listof X) Y → Y
          ;; Purpose: Fold the list values from right to
          ;;          left into the given accumulator.
          ;; Accumulator invariant:
          ;;    accum = Y value for traversed list elements so far
          (define (aux-f a-lox accum)
            (if (empty? a-lox)
                accum
                (aux-f (rest a-lox) (comb (first a-lox) accum))))]
    (aux-f (reverse a-lox) base)))
```

Once again, we see that the function using the abstraction yields the best CPU times. As with sum-lon5, this occurs because of optimizations done to foldl done by the developers of ISL+.

57 Abstraction Over Right to Left Accumulating Folding Functions

Figure 49 displays the encapsulated functions developed that fold a list from right to left. Figure 49a displays another encapsulated version of sum-lon2, and Fig. 49b displays the encapsulated lengths-lostr2. It immediately becomes clear that these functions are very similar and good candidates for abstraction.

Following the steps of the design recipe for abstraction yields the abstract function displayed in Fig. 50. This abstraction is so powerful and useful that ISL+ also has an abstract function to fold a list from right to left: `foldr`. It takes as input the same types of value as `fold-from-right` but in a different order. The signature for `foldr` is:

```
(X Y → Y) Y (listof X) → Y
```

We can refactor the function definitions in Fig. 49 to use `foldr`. The refactoring of `sum-lon2` yields a function similar to `sum-lon5`:

```
(define (sum-lon6 a-lon) (foldr + 0 a-lon))
```

The `lengths-lostr2`'s refactoring requires slightly more care because a function is applied to the first element of the list before it is folded into the accumulator. Where should this function be placed in the version using `foldr`? Observe that the combinator function's signature given to `foldr` (and for that matter `foldl`) states its input is of type X. That is, it is an element of the given list. This means that any function that is applied to a list element must be part of the combinator function. The combinator function, therefore, must apply the needed function before adding a value to the front of the accumulator. We may define the combinator function using a λ-expression. The `lengths-lostr2`'s refactoring yields:

```
(define (lengths-lostr3 a-lostr)
  (foldr (λ (a-str acc)
           (cons (string-length a-str) acc))
         '()
         a-lostr))
```

Observe that `string-length` is applied to the given string before adding it to the front of the accumulator.

How well does `foldr` perform? We run the same experiments using `sum-lon6` as done for the other solutions to summing a list a numbers. The obtained measurements are added to our running table:

	Run 1	Run 2	Run 3	Run 4	Run 5	Average
sum-lon	344	390	328	329	312	340.6
sum-lon2	297	313	297	328	297	306.4
sum-lon3	308	312	313	313	328	314.8
sum-lon5	15	15	15	15	15	15
sum-lon6	78	78	32	47	78	47

We can observe that using ISL+'s abstract function to fold from the right performs significantly better than the solutions using structural recursion and accumulative recursion. The version using `foldl` always performs slightly better. This is expected because folding a list from the right requires a little more work than folding a list from the left. These results strengthen our previous observation that whenever possible a list ought to be folded from the left.

The following table contains the measurement obtained from running the experiments to compute the lengths of strings using `lengths-lostr3`:

	Run 1	Run 2	Run 3	Run 4	Run 5	Average
lengths-lostr	78	78	109	62	47	74.8
lengths-lostr2	78	63	47	78	78	68.8
lengths-lostr3	15	0	0	0	0	3

We observe the same pattern as with other benchmarks. Using ISL+'s built-in abstract function yields significantly superior performance.

In conclusion, we have seen that accumulators provide significant gains in performance for list folding operations. This stems from the fact that the functions using accumulators are tail-recursive. That is, they are intended to be efficient iteration. A word of caution is necessary here. Not all programming languages implement tail-recursive programs efficiently. When you program in other programming languages, you must inform yourself if tail-recursion is optimized and run empirical experiments when performance is important. Another important lesson is that many programming languages optimize built-in functions. Therefore, more often than not, it is better to use a function provided by the programming language (like `foldl` and `foldr`) than to write our own. This is not to say that it is impossible for you to write a more efficient function than one provided by the programming language. If you need better performance, write your own function, and conduct empirical experiments to determine if anything is gained from its use. It is certainly true, nonetheless, that when an abstraction is not provided by the programming language, then you must write your own.

13 Design and implement functions using `foldl` or `foldr` to:

1. Implement `map`.
2. Implement `filter`
3. Implement `ormap`
4. Implement `andmap`
5. Find the shortest string in a nonempty list of strings.
6. Compute the product of the numbers in a list of numbers.

14 Design and implement function to implement `fold-from-right` using `foldl`.

15 Using `foldl` or `foldr`, design and implement function to determine if all the elements in a given (`listof` X) are the equal.

16 Using `foldl` or `foldr`, design and implement function to make a copy of a given (`listof X`).

58 What Have We Learned in This Chapter?

The important lessons of this chapter are summarized as follows:

- Iteration is the process of repeatedly performing the same evaluation using different values until a condition is met.
- A delayed operation is a function application that cannot be evaluated until the evaluation of a different function call is finished.
- Delayed operations may have a negative impact on performance.
- Accumulators may be used to make program evaluation more efficient by eliminating delayed operations.
- A tail call is a function call for which there are no delayed operations.
- A tail-recursive program only has tail calls.
- Tail-recursion is considered an efficient form of iteration because no memory beyond the declared variables is needed.
- A list fold traverses a given list to combine its values.
- Relative difference is a ratio used to determine how much measurements are proportionally different.
- Using accumulators may reduce abstract running time.
- List-folding from the left works well when list elements may be folded into the result in the reversed order used by structural recursion.
- Sometimes it is necessary or natural to process list elements from right to left.
- An outlier measurement is one that is significantly larger or smaller than the rest of the measurements that may disproportionably affect the average of the data set.
- Statisticians suggest removing outliers from the data set when measurements are not entirely reliable.
- When a list folding operation is associative, it may be implemented by processing the list left to right or right to left.
- Abstract list-folding functions require a function to update the accumulator, an initial value for the accumulator, and the list to traverse.
- `foldl` and `foldr` are efficiently implemented abstract functions to fold the values in a given list into an accumulator, respectively, from left to right and from right to left.

Chapter 12
N-Puzzle Version 6

In Chap. 10, the N-Puzzle is solved using depth-first search and breadth-first search. We discovered that both may be used to find a solution and that both benefit from the use of an accumulator. Depth-first search's attractive feature is that it only explores one path in the search tree giving it the potential for speed. Only exploring only one path, as we discovered, may also hinder its performance because it must search deep in the search tree to find a solution. Breadth-first search's attractive feature is that it always explores the search tree to the minimum depth possible. This, as we discovered, means that it always finds the shortest solution but may be slow due to having to track too many paths in the search tree.

In essence, depth-first search explores a single path in the search tree, and breadth-first search explores all paths in the search tree. Neither strategy makes an effort to intelligently decide which paths to explore. In this chapter, we explore a design strategy based on trying to intelligently decide which path to further explore. It combines depth-first search and breadth-first search by only exploring the paths with the best potential to quickly lead to a solution. Instead of blindly exploring only one path like depth-first search or blindly exploring all paths like breadth-first search, our new design shall (attempt to) pick the best path to explore at each step. All paths explored are remembered like breadth-first search, but only the path with the best potential is further explored. A path may be explored as long as it is judged to be the best path to explore giving the algorithm a depth-first-like quality: explore a single path while it is the best path to explore. If the path being explored at some point is no longer judged to be the best path to explore, the algorithm backtracks and explores a different path. This algorithm is commonly used in the field of artificial intelligence and is called the *A* search algorithm*. The algorithm uses a *heuristic function* (or simply a heuristic) to guide the search. A heuristic is a function that ranks the alternatives in a search. The heuristic is used to choose among potential search paths to further explore. The path with the best heuristic value is explored at each step. A*, therefore, is a *best-first search*

© The Author(s), under exclusive license to Springer Nature Switzerland AG 2022 303
M. T. Morazán, *Animated Program Design*, Texts in Computer Science,
https://doi.org/10.1007/978-3-031-04317-8_12

algorithm. The expectation is that by exploring fewer paths than breadth-first search, convergence to a solution is faster.

A word of caution is appropriate. A heuristic may not always converge to a solution faster. In fact, it may not converge to a solution. This is especially common when the heuristic is a rule of thumb based solely on "real-world" experience without any rigorous theoretical analysis. Rigorous analysis and empirical experimental analysis are needed to guarantee that a heuristic converges to a solution and that its use makes the search faster.

We shall refine the program from Sect. 50 that utilizes breadth-first search to find a solution. Recall that this program utilizes a queue to represent the paths generated that still may be searched and represents an accumulator as a list of `worlds`. The accumulator is used to reduce, when possible, the number of new paths generated.

59 The Manhattan Distance Heuristic

To develop a heuristic for a problem, we need to develop insight into the problem just as an insight must be developed to use generative recursion. For the N-puzzle, we need to approximate how many moves are needed to solve it. If we can approximate the number of moves needed to solve the puzzle, then every time the search needs to continue, the path with the smallest number of approximate moves may be chosen to create new paths.

Consider a single tile in the N-puzzle. We may ask ourselves what is the minimum number of moves required to place the tile in its final position as specified by `WIN`. This number is called the distance of the tile to its correct position. For instance, consider the following `world`:

2	5	3
4		1
7	8	6

The distance of each tile to its correct position in `WIN` is displayed in the following table:

Tile	Distance
1	3
2	1
3	0
4	0
5	1
6	1
7	0
8	0

The distance of tile 3 is 0 because it is in its final position. The distance for tile 1 is 3 because at least three moves are needed to place it in its final position: two moves on the horizontal axis and one on the vertical axis.

The *Manhattan distance* of a world is the sum of all the tile distances. For the world above, we have:

```
manhattan distance = 3 + 1 + 0 + 0 + 1 + 1 + 0 + 0
                   = 6
```

The Manhattan distance suggests that at least six moves are needed to solve the puzzle. We can use the Manhattan distance as an approximation for the number of moves required to solve the puzzle. Observe that the Manhattan distance is an optimistic prediction. That is, it is always less than or equal to the minimum number of actual moves needed to solve the puzzle.

Figure 51 displays a function to compute the Manhattan distance of a given world. The design adds the distances of the eight board positions by calling the auxiliary function sum-distances. The function sum-distances is designed using structural recursion on natural numbers. For each board position, the distance of its tile value to the tile's position in WIN is added to the result. If the board position contains the empty tile space, then 0 is added to the result. The distance is computed by adding the absolute values of the row and of the column differences between the given board positions. The board position's row is given by its quotient with 3, and its column is given by its remainder with 3. Finally, a given tile value's board position in WIN is 8 if it is the empty tile value (i.e., 0) and the tile value minus 1 otherwise. The tests illustrate that the Manhattan distance is correctly computed for a few sample world instances.

1 Redesign sum-distances to eliminate its delayed operation.

2 The function tile-value is written multiple times in the program for the N-Puzzle game. Eliminate the repetitions by having a single copy that is in scope for all functions that use it.

Fig. 51 Function to compute a world's Manhattan distance

```
;; world → natnum
;; Purpose: Compute the Manhattan distance for the given world
(define (manhattan-distance a-world)
  (local [;; bpos → natnum
          ;; Purpose: Sum the tile distances in a-world
          (define (sum-distances a-bpos)
            (local [;; world bpos → bval
                    ;; Purpose: Return the given bpos' bval
                    (define (tile-value a-bpos)
                      (cond [(= a-bpos 0) (world-t0 a-world)]
                            [(= a-bpos 1) (world-t1 a-world)]
                            [(= a-bpos 2) (world-t2 a-world)]
                            [(= a-bpos 3) (world-t3 a-world)]
                            [(= a-bpos 4) (world-t4 a-world)]
                            [(= a-bpos 5) (world-t5 a-world)]
                            [(= a-bpos 6) (world-t6 a-world)]
                            [(= a-bpos 7) (world-t7 a-world)]
                            [else (world-t8 a-world)]))
                    ;; tval → bpos
                    ;; Purpose: Return WIN bpos for the given tval
                    (define (final-bpos a-tval)
                      (if (= a-tval 0) 8 (sub1 a-tval)))
                    ;; bpos → natnum  Purpose: Return bpos' row
                    (define (get-row a-bpos) (quotient a-bpos 3))
                    ;; bpos → natnum  Purpose: Return bpos' column
                    (define (get-col a-bpos) (remainder a-bpos 3))
                    ;; bpos bpos → natnum Purpose: Return distance
                    (define (distance bpos1 bpos2)
                      (if (= (tile-value bpos1) 0)
                          0
                          (+ (abs (- (get-row bpos1) (get-row bpos2)))
                             (abs (- (get-col bpos1)
                                     (get-col bpos2))))))
                    (define win-bpos (final-bpos
                                       (tile-value a-bpos)))]
              (if (= a-bpos 0)
                  (distance a-bpos win-bpos)
                  (+ (distance a-bpos win-bpos)
                     (sum-distances (sub1 a-bpos))))))]
    (sum-distances 8)))

;; Test using sample values for manhattan-distance
(check-expect (manhattan-distance WIN)      0)
(check-expect (manhattan-distance A-WRLD) 4)
(check-expect (manhattan-distance (make-world 4 1 2 7 0 3 8 5 6)) 8)
```

60 Problem Analysis

The goal is to explore the most promising paths first. In this manner, promising paths are explored faster (i.e., in a depth-first-like manner), but all paths generated may be explored if necessary to guarantee that a solution is found. The best path is the path with the smallest Manhattan distance. Given this, the paths may not be stored in a queue because they are no longer accessed in a FIFO manner. The best path may not be the path that was first placed in the queue. Therefore, the generated paths are stored in a (listof (listof world)). The previously defined sample queues are recast as sample (listof (listof world)):

```
;; Sample (listof (listof world))
(define LLOW1 (list (list WIN)))
(define LLOW2 (list (list WIN
                   (make-world 1 2 3
                               4 5 0
                               7 8 6))))
(define LLOW3 (list (list (make-world 1 2 0
                               4 5 3
                               7 8 6)
                     (make-world 1 2 3
                               4 5 0
                               7 8 6))
               (list (make-world 1 2 3
                               4 0 5
                               7 8 6)
                     (make-world 1 2 3
                               4 5 0
                               7 8 6))
               (list (make-world 1 2 3
                               4 5 6
                               7 8 0)
                     (make-world 1 2 3
                               4 5 0
                               7 8 6))))

(define LLOW4 (list (list (make-world 1 2 3
                               0 5 6
                               4 7 8)
                     (make-world 1 2 3
                               4 5 6
                               0 7 8))
               (list (make-world 1 2 3
                               4 5 6
                               7 0 8)
```

```
(make-world 1 2 3
             4 5 6
             0 7 8))))
```

Given that queues were implemented using lists, the only difference is the names used. The new variable names closely reflect what they represent.

An accumulator to remember the worlds whose successors are part of the search is still needed. Like with breadth-first search, this accumulator is used to reduce the number of paths generated. The role of the accumulator is unchanged, and its representation remains the same as a (listof world). The accumulator invariant also remains unchanged:

```
;; Accumulator Invariant:
;;   visited = worlds whose successors are part of the search
```

At each step, the best path is extracted from the given (listof (listof world)). If the first world of the best path is WIN, then the reverse of the best path is returned.[12] Otherwise, a recursive call is made with a new set of paths and a new accumulator. The new set of paths contains the paths in the given (listof (listof world)) with the best path removed and the new paths generated using each successor not in the accumulator of the best path's first world. Each new path is obtained by adding an unvisited successor to the best path. The new accumulator is obtained by adding the best path's first world to the given accumulator. Observe that generative recursion is employed, and, therefore, a termination argument is necessary.

The above problem analysis allows us to refactor make-move. The required changes are straightforward. This function must now find a solution using an auxiliary function that implements the A* algorithm. The sample expressions when the world is not WIN must also use this function. The refactored sample expressions and function definition are:

```
;; world → world
;; Purpose: Make a move for the player
(define (make-move a-world)
  (if (equal? a-world WIN)
      a-world
      (second (find-solution-a* (list (list a-world))
                                '()))))


;; Sample expressions for make-move
(define MM-WIN-VAL WIN)
(define MM-WRLD1-VAL (second (find-solution-a*
                              (list (list WRLD1))
                              '())))
```

---

[12] Recall that the paths are stored in reversed order.

```
(define MM-WRLD2-VAL (second (find-solution-a*
                              (list (list WRLD2))
                              '()))))
```

Observe that the auxiliary function is now called find-solution-a*, and it takes a (listof (listof world)), not a (qof (listof world)), as input. The initial value of the accumulator remains the same, '(), given that the successors of no worlds have been used to generate new paths. No changes need to be made to the tests.

61 Sample Expressions and Differences for find-solution-a*

The natural tendency is to refactor the sample expressions for find-solution-bfs to use the sample (listof (listof world))s defined above. We must, however, keep this natural tendency in check. Why? Simply stated, the use of breadth-first search and the use of A* may produce different solutions for the same problem. This means that they may work differently for some inputs. Thus, careful analysis is required rather than a blind refactoring of the sample expressions.

Before refactoring the sample expressions we need to establish how the path with the best (i.e., smallest) Manhattan distance is found. The given (listof (listof world)) must be traversed, and for each first world in each path, its Manhattan distance is computed. The first path with the smallest Manhattan distance is chosen as the best path. This analysis suggests traversing the list from left to right. We know from Sect. 53 that a list may be traversed and a value accumulated using foldl. The value accumulated is the path with the minimum Manhattan distance so far. Given that there is a solution starting from every valid board, A* is guaranteed to find solution which implies that the given (listof (listof world)) is never empty. This means that foldl may traverse the rest of the given (listof (listof world)) using the first path as the accumulator's initial value. Sample expressions for when the best path's first world is WIN may be written as follows:

```
;; Sample expressions for find-solution-a*
(define FS-LLOW1-VAL
  (local
    [(define best-path
       (foldl
         (λ (p accum)
           (if (< (manhattan-distance (first p))
                  (manhattan-distance (first accum)))
```

```
                             p
                          accum))
                 (first LLOW1)
                 (rest  LLOW1)))]
      (reverse best-path)))

 (define FS-LLOW2-VAL
   (local
     [(define best-path
              (foldl
                (λ (p accum)
                  (if (< (manhattan-distance (first p))
                         (manhattan-distance (first accum)))
                      p
                      accum))
                (first LLOW2)
                (rest  LLOW2)))]
      (reverse best-path)))
```

Observe that the same initial set of paths used for find-solution-bfs are
used here. That is, LLOW1 is used instead of QLOW1, and LLOW2 is used instead
of QLOW2. This is not surprising because if the first queue path has WIN as
its first world, then this is the leftmost world with the smallest Manhattan
distance in the respective (listof (listof world)).

We now turn our attention to sample expressions for when the first world
of the best path is not WIN. We would like to refactor the following sample
expression for find-solution-bfs to use LLOW3:

```
 (define FS-QLOW3-VAL
   (local [(define first-path (qfirst QLOW3))
           (define first-world (first first-path))
           (define successors
             (filter (λ (w)
                       (not (member?
                             w
                             (list (make-world 1 2 3
                                               4 5 0
                                               7 8 6)))))
                (map (λ (neigh)
                       (swap-empty first-world neigh))
                     (list-ref
                      neighbors
                      (blank-pos first-world)))))
           (define new-paths (map (λ (w)
                                    (cons w first-path))
                                  successors))
```

```
                (define new-q (enqueue new-paths
                                    (dequeue QLOW3)))]
         (find-solution-bfs new-q
                     (cons first-world
                           (list (make-world 1 2 3
                                              4 5 0
                                              7 8 6))))))
```

Observe, however, that the best path in QLOW3 has WIN as its first world. Therefore, LLOW3 cannot be used to write a sample expression for when the best path does not start with WIN.

We need to design a sample expression using new values for when the best path's first world is not WIN. For this we may pick a world that may be solved in a small number of steps. For example, consider solving the following puzzle:

Its successors are:

Observe that the successors do not include WIN. Based on this we may define a (listof (listof world)) with three paths:

```
(define LLOW5 (list (list (make-world 1 5 2
                                      4 0 3
                                      7 8 6)
                          (make-world 1 0 2
                                      4 5 3
                                      7 8 6))
                    (list (make-world 0 1 2
                                      4 5 3
                                      7 8 6)
```

```
                              (make-world 1 0 2
                                          4 5 3
                                          7 8 6))
                     (list (make-world 1 2 0
                                       4 5 3
                                       7 8 6)
                           (make-world 1 0 2
                                       4 5 3
                                       7 8 6))))
```

LLOW5 along with an accumulator containing the single world above may be
used to design a sample expression for find-solution-a*. LLOW5's best path
is determined using foldl as was done for LLOW1 and LLOW2. The best path's
first world's successors are computed by filtering out any successors in the
accumulator and then mapping swap-empty. The new paths are constructed,
using map, by adding each successor to the front of the best path. The new
(listof (listof world)) is constructed by removing the best path and
appending the new paths, and the new accumulator is constructed by adding
the best path's first world to the front of the accumulator. Finally, the puzzle is solved by calling find-solution-a* with the new (listof (listof
world)) and the new accumulator. The sample expression for this example is:

```
(define FS-LLOW5-VAL
  (local
   [(define best-path
            (foldl
             (λ (p accum)
               (if (< (manhattan-distance (first p))
                      (manhattan-distance (first accum)))
                   p
                   accum))
             (first LLOW5)
             (rest  LLOW5)))
    (define first-world (first best-path))
    (define successors
            (map (λ (neigh)
                   (swap-empty first-world neigh))
                 (filter
                  (λ (w)
                    (not (member?
                          w
                          (list (make-world 1 0 2
                                            4 5 3
                                            7 8 6)))))
                  (list-ref neighbors
                            (blank-pos first-world)))))
```

```
(define new-paths (map (λ (w)
                         (cons w best-path))
                       successors))
(define new-llow (append (remove best-path LLOW5)
                         new-paths))]
(find-solution-a* new-llow
                  (cons first-world
                        (list (make-world 1 0 2
                                          4 5 3
                                          7 8 6))))))
```

LLOW4 may be used to design a sample expression for when the best path's
first world is not WIN because none of its paths have WIN as the first world.
For LLOW4 the same local values as for LLOW5 are computed. The sample
expression is:

```
(define FS-LLOW4-VAL
  (local
    [(define best-path
       (foldl
         (λ (p accum)
           (if (< (manhattan-distance (first p))
                  (manhattan-distance (first accum)))
               p
               accum))
         (first LLOW4)
         (rest LLOW4)))
     (define first-world (first best-path))
     (define successors
       (filter
         (λ (w)
           (not (member? w
                         (list (make-world 1 2 3
                                           4 5 6
                                           0 7 8)))))
         (map (λ (neigh)
                (swap-empty first-world neigh))
              (filter (λ (w)
                        (not (member?
                              w
                              (list (make-world 1 2 3
                                                4 5 6
                                                0 7 8)))))
                      (list-ref neighbors
                                (blank-pos first-world))))))
```

```
(define new-paths (map (λ (w)
                         (cons w best-path))
                       successors))
(define new-llow (append (remove best-path LLOW4)
                         new-paths))]
(find-solution-a* new-llow
                  (cons first-world
                        (list (make-world 1 2 3
                                          4 5 6
                                          0 7 8))))))
```

There are two differences among the sample expressions. The first is the
(listof (listof world)) used for the generated paths. The second is the
(listof world) used for the accumulator. We name these differences a-llow
and visited. The name of the accumulator is chosen to not cause any confu-
sion with the accumulator used by foldl in the sample expressions. We say
that a world is visited if its successors are part of the search.

62 Signature, Statements, and Function Header

The signature is defined by the differences' types found in the sample expressions, (listof (listof world)) and (listof world), and the return
type, (listof world), for a solution. The purpose is to return a solution
to the given world. That is, to return a sequence of moves to WIN. For a
function using generative recursion, recall that a how-statement is required.
The how-statement summarizes that if the best path's first world is WIN,
then the puzzle is solved, and the reversed best bath is returned. Otherwise,
the search continues with the given paths except the best path and the new
paths generated using the unvisited successors of the best path's first world
and with a new accumulator that has the best path's first world and the
given accumulator. The accumulator invariant is stated to make its purpose
clear. The function header is written using the chosen function name and
the names chosen for the differences among the sample expressions. The next
steps of the design recipe yield:

```
;; (listof (listof world)) (listof world) → (listof world)
;; Purpose: Return sequence of moves to WIN
;; How: If the best path's first world is WIN then return
;;      the reverse of the best path. Otherwise, continue
;;      the search with:
;;         1. a new list of paths is obtained by removing the
;;            best path and adding paths constructed using
;;            the unvisited successors of the best path's
;;            first world and the best path.
```

```
;;            2. an accumulator obtained by adding the best
;;               path's first world to the given accumulator.
;; Accumulator Invariant:
;;   visited = worlds whose successors are part of the search
(define (find-solution-a* a-llow visited)
```

63 Tests for find-solution-a*

The tests using sample computations provide the values used to design the sample expressions as input to find-solution-a* and use the variables defined for the value of the sample expressions as the expected values. They illustrate that the function computes the values of the sample expressions. The tests are:

```
;; Tests using sample computations for find-solution-a*
(check-expect (find-solution-a* LLOW1 '()) FS-LLOW1-VAL)
(check-expect (find-solution-a* LLOW2 '()) FS-LLOW2-VAL)
(check-expect (find-solution-a*
               LLOW4
               (list (make-world 1 2 3
                                 4 5 6
                                 0 7 8)))
               FS-LLOW4-VAL)
(check-expect (find-solution-a*
               LLOW5
               (list (make-world 1 0 2
                                 4 5 3
                                 7 8 6)))
               FS-LLOW5-VAL)
```

3 Write a sample expression and test using LLOW3 for when the best path's first world is WIN.

To write the tests using sample values, we examine the corresponding tests written for find-solution-bfs in Sect. 50. Observe that for neither test, the best path has WIN as its first world. This means that both may be used as nontrivial tests for find-solution-a*. Given that a queue for find-solution-bfs is implemented as a (listof (listof world)), the only change needed is to make the called function find-solution-a*. The tests using sample values are:

```
;; Tests using sample values for find-solution-a*
(check-expect
  (find-solution-a*
    (list (list (make-world 0 2 3 1 5 6 4 7 8)))
    '())
  (list
    (make-world 0 2 3 1 5 6 4 7 8)
    (make-world 1 2 3 0 5 6 4 7 8)
    (make-world 1 2 3 4 5 6 0 7 8)
    (make-world 1 2 3 4 5 6 7 0 8)
    (make-world 1 2 3 4 5 6 7 8 0)))

(check-expect
  (find-solution-a*
    (list (list (make-world 1 2 3 4 5 6 7 0 8)
                (make-world 1 2 3 4 0 6 7 5 8))
          (list (make-world 1 0 3 4 2 6 7 5 8)
                (make-world 1 2 3 4 0 6 7 5 8))
          (list (make-world 1 2 3 0 4 6 7 5 8)
                (make-world 1 2 3 4 0 6 7 5 8))
          (list (make-world 1 2 3 4 6 0 7 5 8)
                (make-world 1 2 3 4 0 6 7 5 8)))
    (list (make-world 1 2 3 4 0 6 7 5 8)))
  (list
    (make-world 1 2 3 4 0 6 7 5 8)
    (make-world 1 2 3 4 5 6 7 0 8)
    (make-world 1 2 3 4 5 6 7 8 0)))
```

64 Function Body for find-solution-a*

The body of the function locally defines variables for the best path and for the
best path's first world because they are needed multiple times. The local-
expression's body uses an if-expression to determine if the best path's first
world is WIN. The then-expression is obtained by abstracting over the first
two sample expressions. The else-expression is obtained by abstracting over
the second two sample expressions. The body of the function is:

```
(local [(define best-path
          (foldl
            (λ (p accum)
              (if (< (manhattan-distance (first p))
                     (manhattan-distance (first accum)))
                  p
                  accum))
```

```
                        (first a-llow)
                        (rest a-llow)))
             (define first-world (first best-path))]
   (if (equal? first-world WIN)
       (reverse best-path)
       (local
         [(define successors
                   (filter
                    (λ (w)
                     (not (member? w visited)))
                    (map
                     (λ (neigh)
                      (swap-empty first-world neigh))
                     (list-ref neighbors
                               (blank-pos first-world)))))
          (define new-paths (map (λ (w)
                                   (cons w best-path))
                                 successors))
          (define new-llow (append (remove best-path
                                           a-llow)
                                   new-paths))]
         (find-solution-a* new-llow
                           (cons first-world visited)))))
```

65 Termination Argument

In the worst case, just like breadth-first search, the A* algorithm exhaustively traverses all paths rooted at a given world once. This exhaustive search is guaranteed because the successors of each world encountered are only used to create new paths and the path used to create them is eliminated from the search. That is, the search for a solution continues only with the new paths created. Every new path is explored if and when it has the smallest Manhattan distance. Given that there is a solution from every (valid) world with the smallest Manhattan distance, eventually, a path reaches WIN, and the process halts.

66 Performance

We have new implementation for solving the N-puzzle problem, and as responsible computer scientists, we must ask ourselves has anything been gained? Which implementation should be recommended? In Sect. 51, we saw

	Run 1	Run 2	Run 3	Run 4	Run 5	Average	Solution length
DFSA 1	352,032	351,187	349,938	350,891	351,703	351,150.2	26282
DFSA 2	328	328	312	343	328	327.8	1109
DFSA 3	0	0	0	0	0	0	7
DFSA 4	7704	7953	8047	7172	7140	7603.2	5680
BFSA 1	843	984	1031	953	985	959.2	12
BFSA 2	15	0	0	15	0	6	5
BFSA 3	15	0	0	0	0	3	7
BFSA 4	0	0	0	0	0	0	4
BFSA* 1	0	0	0	0	0	0	12
BFSA* 2	0	0	0	0	0	0	5
BFSA* 3	0	0	0	0	0	0	7
BFSA* 4	0	0	0	0	0	0	4

Table 6: CPU times for finding a solution using A*

that breadth-first search using an accumulator is generally faster than depth-first search using an accumulator. Furthermore, we observed that the solution found by breadth-first search is also never longer than the solution found by depth-first search.

Table 6 displays the obtained CPU times (minus any garbage collection time) for the A* algorithm (BFSA*) for the same experiments used in Sect. 51. We can immediately observe that BFSA* is always faster or just as fast as both DFSA and BFSA. The CPU times for BFSA* illustrate that BFSA* can converge quickly on a solution like DFSA 3. The CPU times of and the lengths of the solutions found by BFSA* illustrate that BFSA* finds the shortest solution faster than BFSA. Why is this the case? To answer this, we may look at the number of paths being explored when a solution is found. Let us examine BFSA 1 versus BFSA* 1 (the experiment with the largest performance gap between the two). As mentioned in Sect. 51, there are 603 paths in the queue when the solution is found by BFSA 1. When BFSA* 1 finds a solution, there are 14 paths in the given (listof (listof world)). BFSA* is searching fewer paths and, therefore, finds a solution faster. BFSA* does not invest as much effort as BFSA searching paths that are not promising. This illustrates that the heuristic implemented, the Manhattan distance, is an effective heuristic that reduces the amount of work done to find a solution which makes the search faster.

4 The expression for `new-llow`'s local definition in `find-solution-a*` is:

>   (append (remove best-path a-llow) new-paths)

A hacker observes that `(remove best-path a-llow)` is usually longer than `new-paths` and suggests that the program will be faster if the expression for `new-llow`'s local definition is changed to:

>   (append new-paths (remove best-path a-llow))

The hacker argues that the program will be faster because `append` traverses the shorter list instead of the longer list.

Consider finding a solution for:

2		3
4	5	1
7	8	6

The length of the solution is 14 when using the original definition for `new-llow`. The length of the solution is 32 when using the hacker's suggestion. Why is the hacker's suggestion a bad idea? Why is the solution found longer?

5 Carefully argue that the implementation of A* in this chapter finds the shortest solution.

6 For the BFSA* 1 experiment, does A* explore more than one path, or does it always extend one path until it finds a solution? Illustrate your answer by tracing the steps performed by the algorithm.

7 A simpler heuristic to solve the N-puzzle is the number of misplaced tiles. Consider the following `world`:

1	8	
4	3	2
5	7	6

The value of the heuristic function is 6 because six tiles are misplaced. Remember that we do not include the empty tile space in the heuristic. Redesign `find-solution-a*` to use this heuristic instead of the Manhattan distance. At each step, the path that is further searched is the one with the smallest heuristic value. Does this new heuristic perform better? Why or why not?

67 What Have We Learned in This Chapter?

The important lessons of this chapter are summarized as follows:

- The A^* search algorithm combines breadth-first and depth-first search.
- A^* further explores the best path generated first.
- A heuristic function ranks the paths generated and is used to pick the best path that is further explored by the A^* algorithm.
- To develop a heuristic for a problem, we need to develop insight into the problem.
- A^* can converge quickly on a solution like depth-first search using an accumulator.
- A^* is guaranteed to find a solution if it exists just like breadth-first search.
- A^* can have a profound impact on performance.
- A heuristic is effective if it reduces the amount of work done to find a solution.

Chapter 13
Continuation-Passing Style

Chapter 11 explored how to use accumulators to make programs tail-recursive. That is, we studied how to make iteration more efficient by eliminating delayed operations. We observed that if there is a function call to a programmer-defined g in an argument position for a call to f, then f is a delayed operation. Such a scenario means that the program must make the call to g and remember to return to complete the call to f. The information that must be remembered is *control information*. Control information is used by an ISL+ program to determine what to evaluate next. This is why we see a "bump" in the trace of a program as described in Chap. 11. An accumulator is used to eliminate the need to remember control information.

In Chap. 11, however, only functions with a single function call in an argument position were studied (e.g., fact, sum-lon, and lengths-lostr). A natural question that arises is how are delayed operations eliminated when there is more than one function call in an argument position. Consider, for example, the following function for quick sorting developed in Sect. 25:

```
(define (quick-sorting a-lon)
  (if (empty? a-lon)
      '()
      (local [(define SMALLER= (filter
                                (λ (i) (<= i (first a-lon)))
                                (rest a-lon)))
              (define GREATER  (filter
                                (λ (i) (> i (first a-lon)))
                                (rest a-lon)))]
        (append (quick-sorting SMALLER=)
                (cons (first a-lon)
                      (quick-sorting GREATER))))))
```

There are two calls to quick-sorting in an argument position for append. Evaluating a call to quick-sorting with a nonempty list means that three steps are needed:

© The Author(s), under exclusive license to Springer Nature Switzerland AG 2022   321
M. T. Morazán, *Animated Program Design*, Texts in Computer Science,
https://doi.org/10.1007/978-3-031-04317-8_13

1. Evaluate (quick-sorting SMALLER=)
2. Evaluate (cons (first a-lon) (quick-sorting GREATER))
3. Evaluate append

To perform the first step, the program must remember that once (quick-sorting SMALLER=) is evaluated, it still needs to evaluate the second argument to append and evaluate the call to append. To perform the second step, the program must remember the result of the first step and remember that once (quick-sorting GREATER) is evaluated, it still needs to evaluate the call to append. To perform the third step, the program calls append with the remembered value obtained from Step 1 and the value obtained from Step 2.

It is difficult to see how an accumulator may be introduced to remember a partial result using append because two recursive calls must be resolved to evaluate append. This situation is different from the one faced when eliminating sum-lon's delayed operation in Sect. 53. In that case it is straightforward to see that the first element of the given lon may be added to a partial sum so far. How can the delayed operations be eliminated from quick-sorting?

68 Accumulating Control

To answer the question above think carefully about the steps needed to evaluate a call to quick-sorting with a nonempty list. At each step, control information must be remembered. In other words, control information must be accumulated. To finish the computation, the result obtained from one or more previous steps and control information are used to finish the computation. Consider sorting '(5 8 2 9 1 8 4):

```
   (quick-sort '(5 8 2 9 1 8 4))
 = (append (quick-sorting '(2 1 4))
           (cons 5 (quick-sorting '(8 9 8))))
```

Let us assume (quick-sorting '(2 1 4)) is evaluated first, and let us call this value ssm (for sorted smaller). How is the computation completed? The expression that needs to be evaluated becomes:

```
   (append ssm (cons 5 (quick-sorting '(8 9 8))))
```

This expression is obtained by substituting (quick-sorting '(2 1 4)) with its value. We can observe that there still is a function call in an argument position. Therefore, control information must once again be accumulated to finish the computation after (the second) call to quick-sorting. Let us name the value of this call sgr (for sorted greater). Now, the expression that must be evaluated becomes:

```
   (append ssm (cons 5 sgr))
```

At this point `append` may be called and its value returned.

Observe that the evaluation described above is an iteration. If there are no function calls in an argument position return the value of the expression. If there is a function call in an argument position:

1. Evaluate a function call in an argument position.
2. Use the value obtained to evaluate a specialized expression to complete the computation.

This suggests that a computation may be divided into two parts. The first evaluates a function call in an argument position. The second part is a function. This function takes as input an intermediate result (like the value of (`quick-sorting` '(2 1 4))), and its body is an expression specialized by substituting the evaluated function call with the function's parameter. This function, in essence, knows how to finish the computation and is called a *continuation*. A continuation is a function that accumulates all the control information needed to complete a computation.

Let us consider quick sorting a list of numbers using a continuation. This means that the sorting function must now take an additional input: the continuation to finish the computation. It is important to realize that a computation can only be finished by the continuation. This means that instead of returning a value, the function must pass the returned value to the continuation. It is also important to determine the initial value of the continuation. When an evaluation is started, like (`quick-sort` '(5 8 2 9 1 8 4)), the continuation only needs to return the value of the expression. This means that the continuation is a function that simply returns its input:

```
(define (endk v) v)
```

Consider sorting the empty list. Given that the list is empty `quick-sorting` returns '(). To finish the computation using a continuation, '() is given as input to the continuation. For example:

```
(quick-sorting/k '() endk) = (endk '())
```

Now consider sorting a nonempty list:

```
(quick-sorting/k '(5 8 2 9 1 8 4) endk) = ???
```

Intuitively, we would like to apply the continuation, `endk`, to the result of `append` as follows:

```
(endk (append (quick-sorting '(2 1 4))
              (cons 5 (quick-sorting '(8 9 8)))))
```

This would defeat our purpose because the expression is not in *tail-form*. That is, it has delayed operations. Specifically, the two calls to `quick-sorting` must be evaluated before the calls to `append` and `endk` may be evaluated. We need to refactor the expression to eliminate the function calls in an argument position. Let us start with the first call to `quick-sorting`. If we evaluate (quick-sorting '(2 1 4)), first then we need a new continuation that knows how to end the computation once the value of this call to quick-sorting is known. This new continuation is a function that takes as input the value of (quick-sorting '(2 1 4)). Its body is obtained by substituting (quick-sorting '(2 1 4)) with the new continuation's parameter. This yields:

```
  (quick-sorting/k '(5 8 2 9 1 8 4) endk)
= (quick-sorting/k
    '(2 1 4)
    (λ (ssm)
      (endk (append ssm
                    (cons 5 (quick-sorting '(8 9 8)))))))
```

Observe that the first call to quick-sorting is now in tail position. That is, it is no longer a function call in an argument position. Take a minute to digest what we have just done. Observe that the expression above is explicitly forcing DrRacket to first compute the value of sorting '(2 1 4). This is accomplished by growing the control context, that is, by creating a new continuation to finish the computation. This means that function calls in an argument position grow the control context.

Our job is not done because in the body of the continuation, there is a function call, (quick-sorting '(8 9 8)), in an argument position. This means that the control context grows, and we need a new continuation to put this call to quick-sorting in tail-position. We shall refactor the continuation's body. The call to quick-sorting is made with a new continuation that takes as input the value obtained from sorting '(8 9 8). The body of this new continuation is obtained by substituting (quick-sorting '(8 9 8)) with the continuation's parameter. This yields:

```
  (quick-sorting/k '(5 8 2 9 1 8 4) endk)
= (quick-sorting/k
    '(2 1 4)
    (λ (ssm)
      (quick-sorting/k '(8 9 8)
                       (λ (sgr)
                         (endk (append ssm (cons 5 sgr)))))
```

We assume that calling ISL+ built-in functions, like append and cons, does not grow the control context. This means that the body of the new continuation is in tail-form. That is, our job is done because there are no delayed operations.

To obtain the refactored version of quick-sorting, we only need to observe that the above transformation may be done with any given lon and any given continuation. That is, the transformation is not dependent on any concrete values. The refactored quick-sorting function is:

```
;; lon (lon → lon) → lon
;; Purpose: Sort given lon in nondecreasing order
(define (quick-sorting/k a-lon k)
  (if (empty? a-lon)
      (k '())
      (local [(define SMALLER= (filter
                                (λ (i)
                                  (<= i (first a-lon)))
                                (rest a-lon)))
              (define GREATER  (filter
                                (λ (i)
                                  (> i (first a-lon)))
                                (rest a-lon)))]
        (quick-sorting/k
         SMALLER=
         (λ (ssm)
           (quick-sorting/k
            GREATER
            (λ (sgr)
              (k (append
                  ssm
                  (cons (first a-lon) sgr)))))))))))
```

We say that the function is in *continuation-passing style* (CPS). A function is in CPS if the control context is passed as an argument in the form of a continuation, and it ends by passing the continuation a value. Observe that in CPS style `quick-sorting` has been *linearized* (or *serialized*). First the numbers less than or equal to the pivot are sorted. When this result is known, the numbers larger than the pivot are sorted. When this second intermediate result is known, a sorted list built using `append` is given as input to the given continuation to finish the computation.

In this new version of `quick-sorting`, all delayed operations have been eliminated. This means that only two values, `a-lon` and `k`, are needed from one call to the next and there is no need for ISL+ to return to finish a delayed operation. It is, of course, natural to ask if transforming the function to continuation-passing style has a positive impact on running time. To explore this, the following experiments were executed five times:

```
(define L (build-list 100000 (λ (i) (random 1000000))))

(time (quick-sorting L))
(time (quick-sorting/k L endk))
```

The following table displays in milliseconds the CPU times obtained (after subtracting, if any, garbage collection time):

Fig. 52 The CPS design recipe

1. Add a continuation parameter to each programmer-written function.
2. If the value returned is the result of a programmer-written function call in tail-position add the given continuation as an argument.
3. If the value returned is computed without calling a programmer-written function then apply the given continuation to it.
4. Whenever a function call occurs in an expression, e, in an argument position evaluate the function call using a new one-input continuation whose body is obtained by substituting e with the continuation's parameter.

	quick-sorting	quick-sorting/k
Run 1	1344	1328
Run 2	1328	1312
Run 3	1297	1157
Run 4	1281	1140
Run 5	1250	1093
Average	1300	1206

The obtained data suggests that the continuation-passing style version is faster. For every experiment `quick-sorting/k` is faster. The average's relative difference suggests that `quick-sorting/k` is about 8% faster. Clearly, there is a gain in performance for quick sorting.

69 The CPS Design Recipe

We can now generalize the steps to convert a program to continuation-passing style. For our purposes, we assume that all ISL+ functions do not grow the control context when used in an argument position. If this assumption does not hold for an ISL+ function, `f`, then the program must be redesigned and not use `f` in an argument position. This may require writing a version of `f` and not use ISL+'s `f`. Fig. 52 displays the CPS design recipe. The first step has you add a continuation parameter to every defined function. This includes all locally defined functions and all λ-expressions.

Step 2 has you use the given continuation to call any function that appears in tail-position. That is, a function call that is not in an argument position. Step 3 asks you to apply the given continuation to any value returned that does involve using a defined function.

Step 4 is used to transform expressions in an argument position that have calls to defined functions. In this step you "pull out" a function call that is

n	pairs
0	1
1	1
2	2
3	3
4	5
5	8
⋮	⋮

Table 7: A partial table of Fibonacci numbers

in an argument position and evaluate it using a new continuation. The new continuation has a single parameter for the value of the pulled out function call. The body of the continuation is obtained by substituting the pulled out function call with the new continuation's parameter. Steps 3 and 4 need to repeated for the body of any new continuation.

70 Computing Fibonacci Numbers

In 1202, the Italian mathematician Leonardo Bonacci (better known today as Fibonacci[13]) wrote a book entitled *Liber Abaci* (i.e., *The Book of Calculation*). In this book Fibonacci calculates the growth of an idealized rabbit population. A pair of mating rabbits produces their first new pair of mating rabbits after 2 months and every month after that. At the beginning (after 0 months), there is only one pair of rabbits. After 1 month, there is still just one pair of rabbits. After 2 months, there are two pairs of rabbits (the original pair and the first new pair). At the end of 3 months, there are three pairs of rabbits (the original pair produces their second new pair). At the end of the fourth month, there are five pairs: the original pair, three pairs produced by the original pair, and a new pair produced by the first pair produced by the original pair. At the end of the fifth month, there are eight pairs of rabbits: the original pair, four pairs produced by the original pair, two pairs produced by the first pair descending from the original pair, and the first pair produced by the second pair descending from the original pair. The number of pairs after n months is visualized in Table 7. The numbers in the `pairs` column are known as the *Fibonacci numbers*. There is a definite (recursive) pattern for the number of pairs. If n is less than 2, the number of pairs is 1. If n is greater than or equal to 2, then the number of pairs is equal to the number

---

[13] Some consider the appellative *Fibonacci* a short form of *filius Bonacci* which means son of Bonacci.

Fig. 53 The Function to compute the nth Fibonacci number

```
;; natnum → natnum
;; Purpose: Compute the nth Fibonacci number
(define (fib n)
  (if (< n 2)
      1
      (+ (fib (sub1 n)) (fib (- n 2)))))

;; Sample expressions for fib
(define FIB0 1)
(define FIB1 1)
(define FIB5 (+ (fib 4) (fib 3)))
(define FIB9 (+ (fib 8) (fib 7)))

;; Tests using sample computations for fib
(check-expect (fib 0) FIB0)
(check-expect (fib 1) FIB1)
(check-expect (fib 5) FIB5)
(check-expect (fib 9) FIB9)

;; Tests using sample values for fib
(check-expect (fib 4)  5)
(check-expect (fib 6) 13)
```

of pairs after n - 1 months plus the number of pairs after n - 2 months.
For example, for the number of pairs after 5 months, we have:

```
pairs after 5 months = pairs after 4 months +
                       pairs after 3 months
                     = 5 + 3
                     = 8
```

These observations lead to mathematical definition for the nth Fibonacci number:

$$fibonacci(n) = \begin{cases} 1 & \text{if } n < 2 \\ fibonacci(n-1) + fibonacci(n-2) & \text{if } n \geq 2 \end{cases}$$

The mathematical definition is used to design and implement the ISL+ program to compute the nth Fibonacci number displayed in Fig. 53.

70.1 Transforming to CPS

Observe that the function is not tail-recursive. That is, it contains calls to defined functions in an argument position making + a delayed operation. The goal now is to make the function tail-recursive by transforming it to CPS. The first step of the CPS design recipe adds a continuation parameter to every function. This step yields:

```
(define (fib n k)
  (if (< n 2)
      1
      (+ (fib (sub1 n)) (fib (- n 2)))))
```

The next step of the CPS design recipe adds the given continuation to any function call in tail-position. In the above function, there are no such calls. Therefore, nothing needs to be done for this step. The third step applies the given continuation to any value returned that does not involve a call to a programmer-defined function. This steps yields:

```
(define (fib/k n k)
  (if (< n 2)
      (k 1)
      (+ (fib/k (sub1 n)) (fib/k (- n 2)))))
```

The fourth step eliminates function calls in an argument position. In the above function, the else-expression has the first call to `fib` in an argument position. This means we must pull it out this function call and evaluate it using a new continuation. We call the result of `(fib/k (sub1 n))` `f1` and substitute the call with it to create the body of the new continuation. This yields:

```
(define (fib/k n k)
  (if (< n 2)
      (k 1)
      (fib/k (sub1 n)
             (λ (f1) (k (+ f1 (fib/k (- n 2))))))))
```

Observe that there is still a function call in an argument position. We use the fourth step again to pull out the call and create a new continuation. The result of `(fib/k (- n 2))` is named `f2`. This yields:

```
(define (fib/k n k)
  (if (< n 2)
      (k 1)
      (fib/k (sub1 n)
             (λ (f1)
               (fib/k (- n 2)
                      (λ (f2) (+ f1 f2)))))))
```

The body of the innermost continuation returns a value whose computation does not involve calling any programmer-defined functions. Step 3 of the CPS design recipe states that the given continuation must be applied to this value. This yields:

```
(define (fib/k n k)
  (if (< n 2)
      (k 1)
```

```
(fib/k (sub1 n)
       (λ (f1)
         (fib/k (- n 2)
                (λ (f2) (k (+ f1 f2)))))))))))
```

Observe that all function calls are in tail-position. This means that the function is in CPS. The tests for fib may be refactored as follows to test fib/k:

```
;; Tests using sample values for fib/k
(check-expect (fib/k 0 endk) FIB0)
(check-expect (fib/k 1 endk) FIB1)
(check-expect (fib/k 5 endk) FIB5)
(check-expect (fib/k 9 endk) FIB9)
(check-expect (fib/k 4 endk)  5)
(check-expect (fib/k 6 endk) 13)
```

Writing sample expressions for fib/k is possible, but they would be too long to add any clarity to how the returned value is computed. For this reason they are not developed. Therefore, fib's tests using sample computations are refactored into fib/k tests using sample values.

70.2 Performance

The performance of both versions is explored by running the following experiments 5 times:

```
(define N 35)

(time (fib N))
(time (fib/k N endk))
```

The obtained CPU times (after subtracting garbage collection time) are displayed in the following table:

	fib	fib/k
Run 1	1250	1437
Run 2	1282	1391
Run 3	1265	1437
Run 4	1219	1343
Run 5	1235	1375
Average	1250.2	1396.6

The data clearly suggests that fib is faster given that it is faster in each experiment. The relative difference for the average running time is about -0.1 suggesting that on average fib is 10% faster than fib/k. Alas, just like

Fig. 54 Computing Fibonacci numbers using two accumulators

```
;; natnum → natnum
;; Purpose: Compute the nth Fibonacci number
(define (fib-acc n)
  (local [;; [natnum natnum] natnum natnum → natnum
          ;; Purpose: Compute the nth Fibinacci number
          ;; Accumulator Invariants
          ;;   f1 = the (low-1)th Fibonacci number
          ;;   f2 = the (low-2)th Fibobacci number
          (define (fib-helper low high f1 f2)
            (if (< high low)
                f1
                (fib-helper (add1 low) high (+ f1 f2) f1)))]
    (if (< n 2)
        1
        (fib-helper 2 n 1 1))))

;; Tests using sample values for fib-acc
(check-expect (fib-acc 0) FIB0)
(check-expect (fib-acc 1) FIB1)
(check-expect (fib-acc 5) FIB5)
(check-expect (fib-acc 9) FIB9)
(check-expect (fib-acc 4)  5)
(check-expect (fib-acc 6) 13)
```

programs using accumulators to remember values, a program in CPS is not always faster.

70.3 Going Beyond the Design Recipe

Transforming `fib` to CPS resulted in a slower program. Does this mean that `fib` cannot be made faster? In general, it is very difficult to answer such a question. Further analysis is required to determine if a different design produces a faster program. Observe that in `fib/k` the two continuations receive as input the $(n - 1)$th and $(n - 2)$th Fibonacci numbers. Table 7 suggests that these numbers may be accumulated. That is, the continuations may be represented as two natural numbers instead of functions.

If the given natural number, n, is less than 2, then the function returns 1. What needs to happen if the given n is greater than or equal to 2? Table 7 suggests that the interval $[2..n]$ needs to be processed from left to right (i.e., from `low` to `high`). To process the interval, an auxiliary function is used. This function takes as input an interval and the two accumulators. The accumulators represent the two previous Fibonacci numbers. We may state their invariants as follows:

f1 = the $(low - 1)^{th}$ Fibonacci number
f2 = the $(low - 2)^{th}$ Fibonacci number

Initially, what are the values of the two accumulators? According to Table 7
f1 and f2, both start equaling 1. At each step, low is incremented by 1. What
should the new values of the accumulators be? When low is incremented by
1 f1 is the new value for f2 (i.e., f1 becomes the (low - 2)th Fibonacci
number). For f1 a new Fibonacci number is computed by adding f1 and f2
– the new (low - 1)th Fibonacci number. What value ought to be returned
when the interval is empty? When the interval is empty low is high + 1
= n + 1. According to the invariant, this means that f1 = nth Fibonacci
number. Therefore, f1 ought to be returned. This problem analysis leads to
the program in Fig. 54.

Observe that the program in Fig. 54 uses accumulative recursion. Is this
third implementation to compute the nth Fibonacci number an improvement
over fib/k and fib? To explore the answer to this question, the same experiment above is executed for fib-acc. The results obtained are displayed in
the following table:

	fib	fib/k	fib-acc
Run 1	1250	1437	0
Run 2	1282	1391	0
Run 3	1265	1437	0
Run 4	1219	1343	0
Run 5	1235	1375	0
Average	1250.2	1396.6	0

The obtained measurements clearly suggest that the version using two accumulators is significantly faster than both fib and fib/k. Why is fib-acc
significantly faster? Observe that when fib and fib/k are called with n ≥
2 two recursive calls are (eventually) generated. For example, when n = 10
fib and fib/k generate calls with n = 9 and n = 8. This is inefficient because work is being repeated. The call with n = 9 generates calls with n = 8
and n = 7. Observe that the Fibonacci number for n = 8 is computed twice.
Similarly, the call with n = 8 generates calls with n = 7 and n = 6. Once
again there is work done more than once (i.e., a call with n = 8 is evaluated
twice). To visualize the duplicated work, consider the calls made for (fib
4):

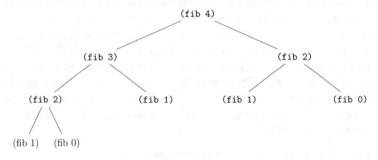

We can see that (fib 2) is computed twice, (fib 1) is computed 3 times, and (fib 0) is computed twice. In contrast, fib-acc only generates one call every time it is called with n ≥ 2. The calls for (fib-acc 4 1 1) may be visualized as follows:

```
(fib-acc 4) = (fib-helper 2 4 1 1)
            = (fib-helper 3 4 2 1)
            = (fib-helper 4 4 3 2)
            = (fib-helper 5 4 5 3)
```

There are no calls to fib-helper with the same n value and, therefore, no repeated work done. This is why fib-acc is significantly faster.

The lesson to derive is that writing programs in continuation-passing style is another tool in the problem-solver's toolbox. It joins other tools like structural recursion, generative recursion, accumulative recursion, the use of a heuristic, the use of a local-expression, and code refactoring. Like any other tool, continuation-passing style will not always be the best tool to use. Always keep in mind that when problem-solving using a given tool, other tools may be a better fit and produce faster more elegant solutions.

71 Revisiting List Reversal

Consider the function to reverse a list using structural recursion in Fig. 41. In it append is a delayed operation. To eliminate the delayed operation, an accumulator is introduced which results in the program displayed in Fig. 42. Experimentation in Sect. 53.2.6 reveals that the version using an accumulator is significantly faster. Complexity analysis revealed that the use of an accumulator significantly changed the abstract running time, thus, explaining the significant improvement in execution time.

Can transforming to CPS achieve or surpass the improvement obtained using an accumulator to store the reversed list so far? Let us transform rev-lox from Fig. 41:

```
;; (listof X) → (listof X)
;; Purpose: Reverse the given list
(define (rev-lox a-lox)
  (if (empty? a-lox)
      '()
      (append (rev-lox (rest a-lox)) (list (first a-lox))))))
```

The first CPS-design-recipe step adds a continuation parameter to all functions:

```
;; (listof X) ((listof X) → (listof X)) → (listof X)
;; Purpose: Reverse the given list
```

Fig. 55 Reversing a (listof X) in CPS

```
;; X → X
;; Purpose: Return the given value
(define (endk v) v)

;; (listof X) ((listof X) → (listof X)) → (listof X)
;; Purpose: Reverse the given list
(define (rev-lox/k a-lox k)
  (if (empty? a-lox)
      (k '())
      (rev-lox/k
        (rest a-lox)
        (λ (revr)
          (k (append revr (list (first a-lox))))))))

;; Sample expressions for rev-lox/k
(define REV-ELOXK '())
(define REV-LOXK1 (rev-lox/k
                    (rest LOX1)
                    (λ (revr)
                      (endk (append revr
                                    (list (first LOX1)))))))
(define REV-LOXK2 (rev-lox/k
                    (rest LOX2)
                    (λ (revr)
                      (endk (append revr
                                    (list (first LOX2)))))))

;; Tests using sample computations for rev-lox/k
(check-expect (rev-lox/k ELOX endk) REV-ELOXK)
(check-expect (rev-lox/k LOX1 endk) REV-LOXK1)
(check-expect (rev-lox/k LOX2 endl) REV-LOXK2)

;; Tests using sample values for rev-lox/k
(check-expect (rev-lox/k '(1 2 3 4 5) endk)
              '(5 4 3 2 1))
(check-expect (rev-lox/k '(red white blue) endk)
              '(blue white red))
```

```
(define (rev-lox/k a-lox k)
  (if (empty? a-lox)
      '()
      (append (rev-lox/k (rest a-lox)) (list (first a-lox)))))
```

The name of the function is changed so that it better reflects its design and to allow it to exist in the same file as `rev-lox`. Observe that the continuation takes as input a (listof X). This is because the expression containing the function call in an argument position, (rev-lox/k (rest a-lox)), evaluates to a (listof X). The continuation returns a (listof X) because this is the type of value that is returned by `rev-lox`.

There are no programmer-written function calls in tail-position. Therefore, step 2 of the CPS design recipe yields no changes. For step 3, the continuation is applied to returned values that do not involve a call to a programmer written function. This step yields:

```
;; (listof X) ((listof X) → (listof X)) → (listof X)
;; Purpose: Reverse the given list
(define (rev-lox/k a-lox k)
  (if (empty? a-lox)
      (k '())
      (append (rev-lox/k (rest a-lox)) (list (first a-lox)))))
```

The fourth step of the CPS design recipe pulls out the function call in an argument position and evaluates it using a new continuation:

```
;; (listof X) ((listof X) → (listof X)) → (listof X)
;; Purpose: Reverse the given list
(define (rev-lox/k L k)
  (if (empty? L)
      (k '())
      (rev-lox/k (rest L)
                 (λ (revr)
                   (k (append revr (list (first L))))))))
```

In the body of the new continuation, the given continuation is applied to the returned value because it does not involve calling any programmer-defined function.

The complete program is displayed in Fig. 55. The end-continuation, endk, is defined because it is needed to call rev-lox/k. The sample expressions and tests from Fig. 41 are refactored for rev-lox/k. The sample expression for when the given list is not empty are written using endk in the body of the new continuation. Observe that endk is also used in the tests to call rev-lox/k.

To test the performance of this new solution for reversing a list, the same list as in Sect. 53.2.6 is used:

```
(define L (build-list 50000 (λ (i) (random 100000))))
```

The following experiment is executed five times:

```
(time (rev/k L endk)))
```

The results are added to the table with CPU times from Sect. 53.2.6:

	Run 1	Run 2	Run 3	Run 4	Run 5	Average
rev-lox	12172	12313	12187	12562	11829	12212.6
rev-lox2	15	15	15	0	0	9
rev-lox/k	12485	12640	12875	13032	10313	12269

First, we observe that rev-lox/k's performance is about the same as the performance as rev-lox. The data suggests that rev-lox may be slightly faster but for `Run 5 rev-lox/k` performed better. There is not a clear winner. Second, we observe that `rev-lox2` is significantly faster than `rev-lox/k`. How are these empirical observations explained? In essence, the transformation to CPS does not change the algorithm. Both `rev-lox` and `rev-lox/k` use `append` making the abstract running time $O(n^2)$. In contrast, `rev-lox2` uses `cons` to accumulate the reversed list, thus, making its complexity $O(n)$.

In general, use an accumulator to eliminate delayed operations, and build the result one step at a time. If it is not clear how to use an accumulator to eliminate a delayed operation, like with quick sorting, then try transforming the program to CPS. Always keep in mind that empirical experimentation is necessary to determine if rewriting using an accumulator or CPS yields any gains in performance.

1 Transform `lon-double` from Sect. 5 into CPS.

2 Transform `nested-squares` from Sect. 20 into CPS.

3 Transform `all-primes<=n` from Sect. 22 into CPS. HINT: Do not pull an expression outside of its stanza in the `cond`-expression.

4 Transform the program for merge sorting from Sect. 26 into CPS.

5 Transform `linear-search` from Sect. 28 into CPS.

6 Is it a good idea to transform the program for binary search from Sect. 29 into CPS? Why or why not?

7 Convert the following (partial) program to CPS:

```
;; natnum → natnum
;; Purpose: Compute the nth triangular number
;;          given natnum
(define (nth-tri a-natnum)
  (if (= a-natnum 0)
      0
      (+ a-natnum (nth-tri (sub1 a-natnum)))))

;; natnum → natnum
;; Purpose: Compute the nth tetrahedral number
(define (nth-tetra a-natnum)
  (if (= a-natnum 0)
      0
      (+ (nth-tri a-natnum) (nth-tetra (sub1 a-natnum)))))
```

8 Convert the following partial function to CPS:

```
;; [int..int] → int
;; Purpose: Compute the product of the ints in the given
;;          interval
(define (interval-product low high)
  (if (> low high)
      1
      (* high (interval-product low (sub1 high)))))
```

9 In computability theory, a total computable function is one that given an element of the domain can always compute its result. It corresponds to the notion of an algorithm. A primitive recursive function is one for which the number of steps needed to compute its value may be computed in advance (like those to process a list, a natural number, or an interval using structural recursion). All primitive recursive functions are total functions. The Ackermann function is one of the earliest examples of a total computable function that is not primitive recursive. The Ackermann function is:

```
(define (ackermann m n)
  (cond [(zero? m) (add1 n)]
        [(zero? n) (ackermann (sub1 m) 1)]
        [else (ackermann (sub1 m) (ackermann m (sub1 n)))]))
```

Transform the ackermann function to CPS. Is the CPS version faster? Justify your answer. Be careful in using this function because the number of steps needed to compute its value grows very fast. You may use, for example, (ackermann 3 10) as a benchmark to justify your answer.

10 Another total computable function that is not primitive recursive is the Sudan function:

```
(define (sudan n x y)
  (cond [(= n 0) (+ x y)]
        [(= y 0) x]
        [else (sudan (sub1 n)
                     (sudan n x (sub1 y))
                     (+ (sudan n x (sub1 y)) y))]))
```

Transform the sudan function to CPS. Is the CPS version faster? Use (sudan 1 30 25) as a benchmark to justify your answer.

72 What Have We Learned in This Chapter?

The important lessons of this chapter are summarized as follows:

- A program with function calls in an argument position must remember control information to finish delayed operations.
- An accumulator may be used to make programs tail-recursive and eliminate the need to remember control information.
- When it is difficult to see how an accumulator may be used to eliminate delayed operations, a program may be rewritten in continuation-passing style.
- A computation may be divided into two parts: the evaluation of an argument and the rest of the computation.
- The rest of the computation may be represented as a function, called a continuation, that accumulates control information and that takes as input an intermediate result to complete the computation.
- The CPS design recipe outlines the steps to convert an arbitrary function to continuation-passing style.
- A computation using continuations always starts with a continuation that returns its input.
- In a program written in CPS all calls to programmer-defined functions are in tail position.
- Transforming into CPS linearizes a computation.
- Transforming a program into CPS does not always yield a faster program.
- Insight into a problem may allow for continuations to be represented as value-accumulators yielding a function that uses accumulative recursion.
- Writing programs in continuation-passing style is another tool in the problem-solver's toolbox.

Part IV
Mutation

Chapter 14
Sharing Values

Congratulations! You have reached the next level in your journey exploring program design. From now on, use the Advanced Student Language (ASL). Go to the language menu in DrRacket to change the programming language you use. All the programs that you have written using ISL+, ISL, and BSL will still work using ASL. They work because ISL+, ISL, and BSL are each a proper subset of ASL. That is, everything in these languages is in ASL but not everything in ASL is in these other student languages. This means that you will need to learn new syntax to use new programming constructs.

It is not uncommon for functions that do not call each other to have to share values. That is, they need to operate on the same data. To make this concrete, consider keeping track of your quiz grades in a given course this semester. Assuming that quizzes are graded on a scale of 100 points, we may define a quiz grade as follows:

```
;; A quiz grade (quiz) is a number in [0..100]

;; Sample quiz grade
(define Q1 85)
(define Q2 100)
```

The number of quizzes is arbitrary, and, therefore, we may represent the quizzes using a list. Let us assume that there is at least one quiz in a class. We may define a list of quiz grades as follows:

```
;; A list of quizzes (loq) is either:
;;   (list quiz)
;;   (cons quiz loq)

;; Sample loq
(define ALOQ1 (list Q1))
(define MYQZS (list Q2 90 Q2))
```

© The Author(s), under exclusive license to Springer Nature Switzerland AG 2022   341
M. T. Morazán, *Animated Program Design*, Texts in Computer Science,
https://doi.org/10.1007/978-3-031-04317-8_14

Fig. 56 Program to compute a quiz average

```
;; A quiz grade (quiz) is a number in [0..100]

;; Sample quiz grade
(define Q1 85)
(define Q2 100)

;; A list of quizzes (loq) is either:
;;   (list quiz)
;;   (cons quiz loq)

;; Sample loq
(define ALOQ1 (list Q1))
(define MYQZS (list Q2 90 Q2))

;; loq → number
;; Purpose: Compute the quiz average
(define (quiz-avg a-loq)
   (/ (foldl (λ (q r) (+ q r)) 0 a-loq)
      (length a-loq)))

;; Sample Expressions for quiz-avg
(define ALOQ1-VAL (/ (foldl (λ (q r) (+ q r)) 0 ALOQ1)
                     (length ALOQ1)))

(define AMYQZS-VAL (/ (foldl (λ (q r) (+ q r)) 0 MYQZS)
                      (length MYQZS)))

;; Tests using sample computations for quiz-avg
(check-within (quiz-avg ALOQ1) ALOQ1-VAL 0.01)
(check-within (quiz-avg MYQZS) MYQZS-VAL 0.01)

;; Tests using sample values for quiz-avg
(check-within (quiz-avg '(80 80 70 75 70)) 75 0.01)
```

1 Develop a template for functions on a `loq`.

A value you are likely to compute from a `loq` is the quiz average. The program in Fig. 56 computes a quiz average. This program suffices if all quiz grades are known. However, what needs to happen in the middle of the semester when a new quiz grade is earned? The new quiz grade needs to be added to, `MYQZS`, the list of quiz grades. Naturally, you need a function to add a quiz grade as follows:

```
(add-quiz! 90)
```

What is `add-quiz!` supposed to do? It needs to change `MYQZS`'s value to:

```
(list 90 100 90 100)
```

This is something we have not done before. In fact, how is this even possible? In all your Mathematics courses, for example, you never changed the value of a variable. It turns out that in most programming languages (including ASL), a variable is not the same as a variable in Mathematics. In most programming, a variable is a memory location that has been given a name. For example, (define X 10) places 10 in an unused memory location and associates that location with X. Therefore, a variable in an ASL program is a memory location (or what is called a pointer or reference). When X is evaluated in an ASL program, the content of the memory location associated with X is returned. This is why when X is typed at DrRacket's prompt, it evaluates to 10.

Why would it be necessary to mutate (i.e., change) the value of a variable (i.e., the content of a memory location)? The answer becomes clear when you think about adding a new quiz to MYQZS. A new quiz is added so that a new quiz average may be computed. That is, quiz-avg needs to know about all the new quiz grades obtained. We have a situation in which both quiz-avg and add-quiz! need MYQZS's value but neither call each other. How can these functions communicate to each other the value of MYQZS without calling each other? These functions communicate by sharing MYQZS instead of calling each other. One of the primary goals of mutation is to share variables among functions that do not call each other. By mutating a variable (i.e., changing the value), functions communicate new values.

73 set! and begin Expressions

The need to share variables among functions that do not call each other raises the need to mutate variables. Variables that are mutated are called *state variables*. How is a variable mutated? ASL provides a set!-expression to do so. The syntax for a set!-expression is:

    expr ::= (set! variable expr)

We say that the variable is the left-hand side of the mutation. It must be a defined variable (i.e., declared using define). A consequence of this is that a function parameter may not be mutated. The variable is never evaluated. In other words, it is not a subexpression in a set!-expression. Instead, it represents a memory location. The expr is called the right-hand side of the mutation. This subexpression is always evaluated when a set!-expression is evaluated. The value of the subexpression is used to change the value stored in the memory location associated with the variable. This means that the value of the variable is clobbered and gone forever after the set!-expression is evaluated. This is why there is a ! in set!. It signals a dangerous operation. Once a variable is mutated, it is impossible to recover its old value. The programmer is responsible for only mutating a variable only when its current value is no longer needed. The value returned by a set!-expression is always the value of (void). You may think of this value as the no-value value or an invisible value.

The syntax for a set!-expression may be deceptive. It may suggest that set! is a function but it is not. It cannot be passed as a value to another function nor can it be returned as the value of a function. It is just part of the syntax to mutate a state variable. If you think about it, this is made clear by the fact that the variable in a set!-expression is not evaluated. As you know, in ASL and the other student languages, all arguments to a function must be evaluated before a function is called. Given that the variable in a set!-expression is not evaluated, we can conclude that there is no function call in this expression. That is, a set!-expression is not a function application.

Let us now return to our quizzes problem. We can now write add-quiz!. Observe the use of ! in the function name. Our convention shall be to use ! whenever a *mutator* is written. A mutator is a function that has an effect. An effect is the mutation of one or more variables. The add-quiz! function may be written as follows:

```
;; quiz → (void)
;; Purpose: Add the given quiz grade to MYQZS
;; Effect: Add the given quiz grade to the front of MYQZS
(define (add-quiz! q)
  (set! MYQZS (cons q MYQZS)))
```

This function takes as input a quiz and returns (void) because it does not compute a value. The sole purpose for calling this function is for its effect: adding the given quiz grade to the front of MYQZS. Whenever a mutator is written, a new step is required. An effect statement must be written much like a purpose statement is written. An effect statement is written to clearly explain to any reader of the code (including ourselves) how variables are mutated. This enables any reader to responsibly use the mutator. The body of the mutator contains a set!-expression that mutates MYQZS. MYQZS is mutated to be a new list that has the given quiz (as its first element) and the previous quizzes (as the rest of the list). Recall that a set!-expression returns (void), thus satisfying the mutator's signature.

Notice that sample expressions are not written for a mutator. Sample expressions are not written because mutations are permanent. Evaluating a sample expression mutates a variable, and then running the corresponding test using a sample computation mutates the variable again. This may be very confusing. Consider, for example, writing the following sample expression:

```
(define ADD97 (set! MYQZS (cons 97 MYQZS)))
```

Evaluating this sample expression permanently adds 97 to the front of MYQZS. Now consider the following test:

```
(check-expect (add-quiz! 97) (cons 97 MYQZS))
```

Does this test make sense? This test does not make sense because add-quiz! returns (void). It does not return a loq as the expected value suggests. Instead, MYQZS's new value may be tested as follows:

```
(check-expect MYQZS (list 97 100 90 100))
```

This test does pass but it fails to test **add-quiz!**. This test does not illustrate how the mutator works.

Tests for a mutator must illustrate the effect. That is, it must illustrate that the desired effect is achieved. This means that the tested expression must call the mutator and return a value to test. The natural question that arises is how do we call a mutator and return a value to be tested? One possible strategy is to define a local variable to call the mutator and then return a value to be tested as follows:[14]

```
(check-expect (local [(define dummyvar (add-quiz! 90))]
              MYQZS)
  (list 90 100 90 100))
```

The local variable is not used in the **local**-expression's body. The sole purpose for its definition is to provide a mechanism to call the mutator. Such variables are commonly called *dummy variables*. Observe that the local expression returns **MYQZS** after it has been mutated. The expected value reflects **MYQZS**'s expected value after the mutation. In this manner, the effect is illustrated. It is, of course, highly advisable to write more than one test. Further tests must work with the new value, not the original value, of **MYQZS** because mutations are permanent. There is no way to recover the original value of **MYQZS**. A second test may be written as follows:

```
(check-expect (local [(define dummyvar (add-quiz! 92))]
              MYQZS)
  (list 92 90 100 90 100))
```

Observe that the expected value contains the 90 added by the first test. This may be a bit confusing to a reader because it is unclear where the first 90 came from. The tests may be combined into a single test to more clearly communicate how the function works as follows:

```
(check-expect (local [(define dummyvar1 (add-quiz! 90))
                      (define dummyvar2 (add-quiz! 92))]
              MYQZS)
  (list 92 90 100 90 100))
```

In this manner, it is clear how and when the two new values were added to **MYQZS**. Observe that 90 is added first and 92 second. The additions are sequenced based on the order that local definitions are evaluated.

Defining local variables to sequence mutations is rather cumbersome. ASL provides the programmer with more concise syntax for this in the form of a **begin**-expression. A **begin**-expression is used to sequence mutations without having to use a **local**-expression. The syntax for a **begin**-expression is:

> **expr** ::= (begin <expression>⁺)

Inside parentheses, you type the keyword **begin** followed by one or more expressions. Just as with **set!**, **begin** is not a function. Usually each of the

---

[14] Remove the definition for **ADD97** and the test using **MYQZS** from your program.

expressions inside a `begin`-expression is either a `set`-expression or a call to a mutator. The value of a `begin`-expression is the value of its last subexpression. Consider the following program:

```
(define x 10)

(begin
  (set! x 2))
```

The `begin`-expression mutates x to 2 and returns (void). The value returned is (void) because the last expression in the `begin` is a `set`-expression (which returns (void)). In contrast, consider this program:

```
(define y -4)

(begin
  (set! y (add1 y))
  y)
```

The `begin`-expression mutates y to be -3 and returns -3. The value -3 is returned because y is the last expression in the `begin`-expression.

A `begin`-expression may be used to simplify the writing of tests for a mutator. The last test for add-quiz! above may be rewritten as follows:

```
(check-expect (begin
                (add-quiz! 90)
                (add-quiz! 92)
                MYQZS)
              (list 92 90 100 90 100))
```

Observe that the addition of quizzes is serialized in the same order as using a `local`-expression defining dummy variables. You can appreciate how much simpler and elegant it is to use a `begin`-expression. A natural question that arises is whether or not more than one test ought to be written for a mutator. The answer is an unequivocal yes. To simplify this task for each state variable, a mutator to initialize the variable is written. For add-quiz!, we may write:

```
;; loq
;; Purpose: Store the quizzes for this semester
(define MYQZS 'uninitialized)

;;  → (void)
;; Purpose: Initialize MYQZS
;; Effect:  MYQZS is initialized to '(100 90 100)
(define (initialize-myqzs)
  (set! MYQZS '(100 90 100)))
```

```
;; quiz → (void)
;; Purpose: Add the given quiz grade to MYQZS
;; Effect: Add the given quiz grade to the front of MYQZS
(define (add-quiz! q)
  (set! MYQZS (cons q MYQZS)))
```

There are several new elements in this code. First, every state variable needs a type specification and a purpose statement. The type defines the kind of data stored in the state variable. The purpose statement explains the purpose of the state variable once it is initialized. Second, the symbol 'uninitialized is used as the initial value for an uninitialized state variable. That is, the value of a state variable is undefined until it is initialized. Third, the initializer for MYQZS, initialize-myqzs, takes no inputs. This is reflected in the signature with not types before the arrow. In ASL it is possible to write a function or a mutator that does not take any input. In the code above, initialize-myqzs assigns MYQZS its default value. Having an initializer for a state variable allows us to easily write multiple tests:

```
(check-expect (begin
              (initialize-myqzs)
              (add-quiz! 90)
              (add-quiz! 92)
              MYQZS)
             (list 92 90 100 90 100))

(check-expect (begin
              (initialize-myqzs)
              (add-quiz! 88)
              MYQZS)
             (list 88 100 90 100))
```

Observe that the first step for any test is to initialize the state variable (or variables if appropriate). In this manner, all tests may be written assuming the state variable contains its default value. The only thing you must keep in mind is that before the program is used, the state variables must be reinitialized. Otherwise, each will have the value assigned by the last mutation in the tests.

Although mutation may prove useful for some applications as problem-solvers, it is important to realize that its use comes at a cost. Consider, for example, the following test:

```
(check-expect (begin
              (add-quiz! 88)
              MYQZS)
             (begin
              (add-quiz! 88)
              MYQZS))
```

This test fails. Alas, the value of two identical expressions is not the same. We faced such a scenario earlier in Sect. 15. Just like programs using `random`, programs that use mutation lose referential transparency. We can no longer assume that the same expression always evaluates to the same value. We shall see as we progress that the loss of referential transparency makes mutation-based computation significantly more difficult and requires much care by a problem-solver to use it responsibly.

---

2 Consider the following definitions:

```
;; A
;; Purpose: To store any type of value
(define X 89)

;; B
;; Purpose: To store any type of value
(define Y 'CSAS1115)
```

Write an expression to mutate X and Y by swapping their values. HINT: Using a `local`-expression may be useful.

---

3 Consider the following definitions:

```
;; number
;; Purpose: To store a number
(define X 78)

;; number
;; Purpose: To store a number
(define Y 44)
```

Write an expression to mutate X and Y by swapping their values. Do not use a `local`-expression.

---

74 Design Recipe for Mutators

We are now ready to develop a design recipe for mutators. The design recipe for mutators is displayed in Fig. 57. The first step asks you to outline how the problem is solved and identify the need for one or more state variables. In this step, choose a representation for the data to be manipulated by the program. The second step has you define each state variable as uninitialized. Each definition must include the type of a variable and its purpose. This is an

Fig. 57 The design recipe for mutators

1. Problem and Data Analysis
2. Define the State Variables to be Uninitialized
3. Design and Define Initializers for Each State Variable
4. Perform Problem Analysis for a Mutator
5. Write the Mutator's Signature, Purpose Statement, Effect Statement, and Function Header
6. Write Tests that Illustrate the Effects of the Mutator
7. Write the Body of the Mutator
8. Run the Tests

important step to clearly communicate the role and the type of data that is mutated. The uninitialized value used should be a value that does not satisfy the state variable's type nor purpose. That is, the state variable ought to be useless to the program until it is initialized.

The third step asks you to design and define an initializing mutator for each state variable. This mutator initializes a state variable to a default value if it takes no input or to a given value if it requires an input. This is the mutator that must be called to initially make the state variable useful for the program. The initial value of a state variable must satisfy the state variable's type and purpose. The body of an initializer is a set-expression.

Steps 4–7 are repeated for each needed mutator. Step 4 requires that you perform problem analysis for the mutator. This is akin to what you do for a function that is not a mutator. This step outlines the values used to mutate any state variables changed. Step 5 has you write a signature, a purpose statement, an effect statement, and a function header for the mutator. The new element in this step is the development of an effect statement to describe mutations to any reader of the code. Step 6 has you develop tests that illustrate the effects outlined in the effect statement. Each test ought to first call the initializers for every state variable used or mutated by the function. Step 7 has you write the body of the mutator. If more than one mutation needs to be performed or more than one mutator needs to be called, use a begin-expression.

Finally, Step 8 asks you to run the tests. If any tests fail, redesign by checking the results for each step of the design recipe in Fig. 57.

75 A Bank Account

To illustrate the steps of the design recipe, we shall design a program for a bank account. The program will offer three common services associated with a bank account: deposit, withdrawal, and balance inquiry.

75.1 Problem and Data Analysis

A bank account has a balance. This balance is needed to make deposits, to make withdrawals, and to respond to balance inquiries. The functions to deposit, withdraw, and get the account's balance have no need to call each other. This means that the balance must be represented using a state variable that is shared by these functions.

The state variable for the balance must be a nonnegative number. In other words, overdrafts are allowed for this account. A balance mutator must make sure that balance always satisfies this invariant property.

75.2 State Variable Definitions

There is only one state variable needed, and it may be defined as follows:

```
;; number≥ 0
;; Purpose: Store the balance of the account
(define mybalance 'uninitialized)
```

The type and the purpose make it clear the role the state variable plays in the program. Observe that it is defined to a value, 'uninitialized, that does not satisfy the type nor purpose. This guarantees that the state variable is not useful until it is properly initialized.

75.3 State Variable Initializers

There is only one state variable, and, therefore, only one initializing function is needed. The initializer takes as input the initial balance for the account. The effect of the initializer is to mutate balance to become the given initial balance. The initializer does not return a value, and, therefore, its return type is (void).

To guarantee that a (malicious) user is unable to initialize mybalance to a value that violates its type or design, the initializer is a *guarded initializer*. A guarded initializer receives a value and makes sure that the given value is of the right type and satisfies the purpose before mutating the state variable. If either condition is not met, the guarded initializer throws an error.

The initializer for mybalance is defined as follows:

```
;; number → (void) throws error
;; Purpose: Initialize mybalance
;; Effect: mybalance is mutated to be the given number
```

```
(define (initialize-mybalance! init-balance)
  (if (or (not (number? init-balance)) (< init-balance 0))
      (error
        'initialize-mybalance!
        "Balance cannot be initialized to the given value")
      (set! mybalance init-balance)))
```

Observe that the mutator first checks that the given value is of the right type and that the given value satisfies mybalance's purpose. If either fails, an error is thrown with an informative message. If both conditions pass, then mybalance is mutated to the given initial balance.

The initializer is tested by checking that it correctly throws an error and that it correctly mutates the mybalance. An error is thrown by passing the wrong type of value to the initializer or by passing a negative number. Therefore, two tests are needed:[15]

```
;; Tests for initialize-mybalance!
(check-error
  (initialize-mybalance! "-200")
  "initialize-mybalance!:
  Balance cannot be initialized to the given value")

(check-error
  (initialize-mybalance! -10)
  "initialize-mybalance!:
  Balance cannot be initialized to the given value")
```

To test the initializer when a valid initial balance is given as input, a begin-expression is used. The initializer is called first, and then the value of the state variable is returned. Sample tests are:

```
(check-expect (begin
                (initialize-mybalance! 75)
                mybalance)
              75)
(check-within (begin
                (initialize-mybalance! 43.54)
                mybalance)
              43.54
              0.01)
```

---

[15] In DrRacket, the expected string ought to be written on one line, not two.

75.4 The Mutator for Deposits

75.4.1 Problem Analysis

The mutator to process a deposit expects a number representing the amount of the deposit as input. Given that this is a mutator that is to be used directly by the program's user, it shall be a guarded mutator. If the given value is not a number or is a number less than or equal to 0, then an error is thrown. Otherwise, `mybalance` is mutated to be the sum of `mybalance` and the given amount.

75.4.2 Signature, Statements, and Function Header

This function is solely called to mutate `mybalance`. Therefore, given a number, it returns `(void)` or throws an error. The purpose is to make a deposit, and the effect is that the given amount is added to `mybalance`. Based on these observations, the next step of the design recipe yields:

```
;; number → (void) throws error
;; Purpose: To make a deposit
;; Effect: The given amount is added to mybalance
(define (deposit! amt)
```

75.4.3 Tests

The tests need to illustrate the behavior of the mutator when an error is thrown and when a valid amount to deposit is received. An error is thrown when the received is not a number or when it is not a positive number. For each, there is a different error message. Respectively, the chosen messages are "deposit!: A deposit must be a positive number" and "deposit!: A deposit cannot be <= 0". Sample tests for when an error is thrown are written as follows:

```
;; Tests for deposit!
(check-error (begin
             (initialize-mybalance! 100)
             (deposit! #t))
            "deposit!: A deposit must be a positive number")

(check-error (begin
             (initialize-mybalance! 100)
             (deposit! -100))
            "deposit!: A deposit cannot be <= 0")
```

Testing that the mutation is performed correctly is done by making one or more deposits. The tests initialize `mybalance`, make one or more deposits, and return the value of `mybalance`. The tests are:

```
(check-expect (begin
                (initialize-mybalance! 100)
                (deposit! 100)
                mybalance)
              200)
(check-expect (begin
                (initialize-mybalance! 5000)
                (deposit! 700)
                (deposit! 1300)
                mybalance)
              7000)
```

75.4.4 Function Body

The function body needs to distinguish three conditions: the given input is not a number, the given input is not a positive number, and the given input is a positive number. To decide which of the three is faced, a cond-expression is used. The body of the function is:

```
(cond
  [(not (number? amt))
   (error 'deposit! "A deposit must be a positive number")]
  [(<= amt 0)
   (error 'deposit! "A deposit cannot be <= 0")]
  [else (set! mybalance (+ mybalance amt))]))
```

75.5 The Mutator for Withdrawals

75.5.1 Problem Analysis

To withdraw a given amount, several conditions need to be met:

1. The given input must be a number greater than 0.
2. The given amount must be less than or equal to `mybalance`.

The mutator, `withdraw!`, shall be a guarded mutator that throws an error when either of the two conditions above are not met. If the given input is an amount that may be withdrawn, then `mybalance` is mutated to be the difference of `mybalance` and the given amount.

75.5.2 Signature, Statements, and Function Header

The input is a number. The returned value is (void) because this function
is solely called to mutate mybalance. If the given input is not a value that
may be withdrawn, an error is thrown. The purpose is to withdraw the given
amount. Finally, the effect is to subtract the given amount from mybalance.
The signature, purpose and effect statements, and function header are:

```
;; number → (void) throws error
;; Purpose: To make a withdrawal
;; Effect: The given amount is subtracted from mybalance
(define (withdraw! amt)
```

75.5.3 Tests

The tests for withdraw! must illustrate that the appropriate error message
is thrown or that the effect is properly done. To test the error returned if
the first condition in our problem analysis is not met, the tests attempt to
withdraw a value that is not a number and a value that is negative. The
error message informs the user that the amount must be a positive number.
Sample tests are:

```
;; Tests for withdraw!
(check-error
  (begin
    (initialize-mybalance! 22)
    (withdraw! (make-posn 0 0)))
  "withdraw!: The amount must be a positive number.")
(check-error
  (begin
    (initialize-mybalance! 50)
    (withdraw! -30))
  "withdraw!: The amount must be a positive number.")
```

To test the error returned if the second condition in our problem analysis
is not met, the tests attempt to withdraw an amount that is greater than
mybalance. The returned error message informs the user that there are insufficient funds. Observe that a different error message is generated for the
different conditions in our problem analysis. Sample tests are:

```
(check-error (begin
              (initialize-mybalance! 160)
              (withdraw! 200))
            "withdraw!: Insufficient funds")

(check-error (begin
              (initialize-mybalance! 750)
              (withdraw! 900))
            "withdraw!: Insufficient funds")
```

The tests to illustrate that the effect is properly carried out withdraw one or more amounts. Withdrawing multiple amounts illustrates that the effect persists beyond a single withdrawal. Sample tests are:

```
(check-expect (begin
                (initialize-mybalance! 667)
                (withdraw! 500)
                mybalance)
              167)

(check-expect (begin
                (initialize-mybalance! 1500)
                (withdraw! 800)
                (withdraw! 200)
                mybalance)
              500)
```

75.5.4 Function Body

The function body uses a cond-expression with three stanzas. The first two are to detect the different types of errors identified in problem analysis. The third stanza mutates mybalance. The body of the mutator is:

```
(cond
  [(or (not (number? amt)) (<= amt 0))
   (error 'withdraw! "The amount must be a positive number.")]
  [(< mybalance amt)
   (error 'withdraw! "Insufficient funds")]
  [else (set! mybalance (- mybalance amt))]))
```

75.6 The Observer for Getting the Balance

A function that accesses but does not mutate a state variable to compute or retrieve a value is called an observer. Such functions are designed using any appropriate design recipe you have studied. The only observer for the bank account according to our problem analysis is the function to retrieve the balance. This function does not take any input and returns the value of mybalance. The function is written a follows:

```
;;   → number
;; Purpose: Return the current balance
(define (get-balance) mybalance)
```

Observers are tested by initializing the state variables and then calling the observer. For our bank account program, this means initializing `balance` and then calling `get-balance`. Tests for `get-balance` may be written as follows:

```
;; Tests for get-balance
(check-expect (begin
                (initialize-mybalance! 250)
                (get-balance))
              250)


(check-expect (begin
                (initialize-mybalance! 335)
                (deposit! 665)
                (withdraw! 200)
                (get-balance))
              800)
```

Observe that the second test illustrates that effects are properly achieved when withdrawals and deposits are intermingled. This concludes the design and implementation of our bank account program. Run all the tests and make sure they pass.

4 Add functionality to the bank account program by allowing an overdraft limit. Redesign introducing a state variable for the overdraft limit. To initialize the bank account, the state variables for the balance and the overdraft limit must be initialized. Add a mutator to initialize the overdraft limit state variable, update the mutator for withdrawals, and update the tests to initialize both state variables.

5 A `contact` is a structure:

> `(make-contact string number)`

The string represents a name and the number represents a telephone number. A contact list is defined as:

> `(listof contact)`

The following services are provided by a contact list: look up a number given a name, look up a name given a number, change the number associated with a given name, add a contact, and delete a contact. Design and implement a program to create and manage contact lists.

6 Consider the following definitions:

```
(define LON (build-list 10000 (λ (i) (random 10000000))))

;; number
;; Purpose: To store the number of even numbers in LON
(define NUMEVENS 0)
```

Design and write a program that sets NUMEVENS to the number of even numbers in LON.

7 Consider the following definitions:

```
(define L (build-list 1000 (λ (i) (random 1000000))))

;; number
;; Purpose: To store the maximum value in L
(define LMAX -infty.0)
```

Design and write a program that sets LMAX to the maximum number in L. In ASL, -infty.0 represents negative infinity.

76 Abstraction Over State Variables

A bank account program with a single bank account is hardly interesting or useful. A bank, for example, needs to manage thousands of accounts. How is this achieved? Do we define thousands of state variables and thousands of mutators? To start, consider extending our bank account program with a second bank account. A second state variable is needed for its balance along with mutators to initialize the new state variable, to make deposits, and to make withdrawals and an observer to get the balance. These are needed for every subsequent bank account that was created. All of the new code would be very similar to the code developed for the bank account program above. The only difference would be the state variable manipulated. Figure 58 displays the definitions needed for a second bank account. It is now clear that an abstraction is needed to avoid all the code repetition.

The functions that access or mutate a given state variable, like mybalance or mybalance2, must still share it. The functions for a given set of state variables should not be able to access or mutate a different set of state variables. For example, the functions for mybalance should not be able to access or mutate mybalance2 and vice versa. How do we hide state variables from the mutators for other state variables? To abstract over state variables, encapsulation is used. That is, we write a function that encapsulates all the

Fig. 58 Function definitions for a second bank account

```
(define mybalance2 'uninitialized)

(define (initialize-mybalance2! init-balance)
  (if (or (not (number? init-balance))
          (< init-balance 0))
      (error 'initialize-mybalance2! "Balance cannot be initialized to the given value")
      (set! mybalance2 init-balance)))

(define (deposit2! amt)
  (cond [(not (number? amt))
         (error 'deposit2! "A deposit must be a positive number")]
        [(<= amt 0)
         (error 'deposit2! "A deposit cannot be <= 0")]
        [else (set! mybalance2 (+ mybalance2 amt))]))

(define (withdraw2! amt)
  (cond [(or (not (number? amt)) (<= amt 0))
         (error 'withdraw! "The amount must be a positive number.")]
        [(< mybalance2 amt)
         (error 'withdraw! "Insufficient funds")]
        [else (set! mybalance2 (- mybalance2 amt))]))

(define (get-balance2) mybalance2)
```

definitions needed including the state variables to hide them from mutators for other state variables. Such a function is called a *class*, and we say it implements an *interface*. An interface defines the services or behavior expected from a data type. The class is used to construct instances of the data type, and these instances are called *objects*. An object knows how to perform all the services in the interface using the data the object stores. For instance, a bank account interface offers four services: initialization, getting the balance, making a deposit, and making a withdrawal. Every bank account object needs a mechanism to determine what service is requested from it. This is achieved using *message-passing*. A message-passing function is at the heart of every object. It takes as input a message that identifies the service requested, and it provides the service. If a service may be performed without any further input, it is performed using the data in the object. If further input is required, the message-passing function returns a function that consumes the extra input. An object, therefore, is a curried function—a function that consumes its input in stages.

76.1 Bank Account State Variables and Interface

We shall use our original bank account program and the program in Figure 58 to illustrate the abstraction process. There is a single difference among these programs: the state variable that is manipulated. A bank account is an interface, `ba`, that has a single state variable and offers the following services:

```
'get-balance:  number
'init:   number →(void)
'deposit:  number →(void)
'withdraw:  number →(void)
```

Simultaneously, the bank account interface and the message data definition are defined. A message is an enumeration type containing `'get-balance`, `'init`, `'deposit`, and `'withdraw`. For `'get-balance`, the interface returns a number because no further input is needed. For the other three messages, the interface returns a function, respectively, to initialize the balance, to make a deposit, and to make a withdrawal because further input is required.

76.2 Bank Account Class Template

Based on the interface and message definitions, we develop a template for the `ba` class displayed in Fig. 59. The template suggests locally defining a state variable for the balance and an observer or a mutator for each service. The message-passing function, `bank-account-object`, uses a conditional to process a message. The body of the `local`-expression returns the message-passing function (i.e., the object) that is capable of providing all the expected services in the interface.

76.3 Bank Account Message-Passing Function Design

The next step is to specialize the message-passing function in the template. Based on the interface definition, getting the balance only requires returning, `mybalance`, a number. Initializing the balance requires extra input and returns the mutator `initialize-mybalance!` to consume the extra input and provide the service. Similarly, making a deposit and a withdrawal require extra input and, respectively, return deposit! and withdraw! to consume the

Fig. 59 The template for the ba class

```
#|    ;;  --> ba
    ;; Purpose: To construct a bank account
    (define (make-bankaccount)
      (local [;; number ≥ 0
              ;; Purpose: Store the balance of the bank account
              (define mybalance 'uninitialized)

              ;; number → (void) throws error
              ;; Purpose: Initialize mybalance
              ;; Effect: mybalance is mutated to the given number
              (define (initialize-mybalance! init-balance) ...)

              ;; number → (void) throws error
              ;; Purpose: To make a deposit
              ;; Effect: The given amount is added to mybalance
              (define (deposit! amt) ...)

              ;; number → (void) throws error
              ;; Purpose: To make a withdrawal
              ;; Effect: The given amount is subtracted from mybalance
              (define (withdraw! amt) ...)

              ;;  → number
              ;; Purpose: Return the current balance
              (define (get-balance) ...)

              ;; message → ba
              ;; Purpose: To manage bank account services
              (define (bank-account-object a-message)
                (cond [(eq? a-message 'get-balance) ...]
                      [(eq? a-message 'init) ...]
                      [(eq? a-message 'deposit) ...]
                      [(eq? a-message 'withdraw) ...]
                      [else
                       (error 'bank-account-object
                              (format "Unknown message received: ~s"
                                      a-message))]))]
        bank-account-object))                                        |#
```

extra input and provide the required service. The message-passing function
is written as follows:

```
    ;; message → bank account service throws error
    ;; Purpose: To manage bank account services
    (define (bank-account-object a-message)
      (cond [(eq? a-message 'get-balance) mybalance]
            [(eq? a-message 'init) initialize-mybalance!]
            [(eq? a-message 'deposit) deposit!]
            [(eq? a-message 'withdraw) withdraw!]
```

```
      [else
       (error 'bank-account-object
              (format "Unknown message received: ~s"
                      a-message))])))
```

The `format` function allows you format a string by embedding values into it. Read about `format` in the Help Desk.

76.4 Bank Account Auxiliary Function Design

The next step is to specialize the auxiliary functions needed by the message-passing function. We can do so by abstracting over the two bank account implementations we have already developed. In essence, for this bank account problem, we can simply copy one of the implementations. Without loss of generality, we use the functions developed for the original bank account program:

```
;; number → (void) throws error
;; Purpose: Initialize mybalance
;; Effect: mybalance is mutated to the given number
(define (initialize-mybalance! init-balance)
  (if (or (not (number? init-balance))
          (< init-balance 0))
      (error 'initialize-mybalance! "Balance cannot be initialized to the given value")
      (set! mybalance init-balance)))

;; number → (void) throws error
;; Purpose: To make a deposit
;; Effect: The given amount is added to mybalance
(define (deposit! amt)
  (cond [(not (number? amt))
         (error 'deposit! "A deposit must be a positive number")]
        [(<= amt 0)
         (error 'deposit! "A deposit cannot be <= 0")]
        [else (set! mybalance (+ mybalance amt))]))

;; number → (void) throws error
;; Purpose: To make a withdrawal
;; Effect: The given amount is subtracted from mybalance
(define (withdraw! amt)
  (cond [(or (not (number? amt)) (<= amt 0))
         (error 'withdraw! "The amount must be a positive number.")]
        [(< mybalance amt)
         (error 'withdraw! "Insufficient funds")]
        [else (set! mybalance (- mybalance amt))]))
```

8 Improve the error messages for the auxiliary functions using `format`.

With the code implemented so far, we are able to create bank account objects. For example, we may create the following two bank accounts:

```
;; Sample ba
(define acct1 (make-bankaccount))
(define acct2 (make-bankaccount))
```

The bank accounts may be initialized and used by passing messages to them. For example, we may initialize the bank accounts as follows:

```
((acct1 'init) 500)
((acct2 'init) 200)
```

Let us make sure we understand these expressions. Recall that acct1 and acct2 are objects. That is, they are each a message-passing function that is capable of performing all the services in the bank account interface. The subexpression (acct1 'init) applies acct1 to 'init (i.e., it sends the message 'init to acct1). This subexpression evaluates to the initialize-mybalance! mutator. This mutator is then applied to 500, and acct1's mybalance is mutated to be 500. Similarly, ((acct2 'init) 200) mutates acct2's mybalance to be 200. Once initialized, the bank accounts may be used to make balance inquiries, deposits, and withdrawals. For instance, balance inquiries may be done as follows:

```
(acct1 'get-balance)
(acct2 'get-balance)
```

Each object is sent the message 'get-balance, and each object returns the value of its mybalance.

76.5 Bank Account Wrapper Functions and Tests

Any user of our bank account interface is likely to find the use of message-passing cumbersome. Correctly, they would complain about having to know the messages when they only want to use bank account objects. This occurs because the program exposes the implementation. The typical user does not need to know that message-passing is used to implement a bank account. To hide these implementation details, a *wrapper function* for each service may be written. A wrapper function hides the implementation details and presents a user-friendly interface. The idea is that a user provides the object to manipulate and extra inputs, if any, to the wrapper function for a given service. The wrapper function sends the message for the proper service and, if necessary, provides the extra inputs to the returned function. An interface's implementation is tested by writing tests for the wrapper functions.

The wrapper function for a balance inquiry takes as input a ba and returns a number. The purpose is to get the balance of the given ba. The function's body sends the given ba the 'get-balance message. The wrapper function for balance inquiries is written as follows:

```
;; ba → number
;; Purpose: To get the balance of the given bank account
(define (get-balance ba) (ba 'get-balance))
```

To test any service, a bank account must first be initialized, and then a service may be performed. To test balance inquiries, the sample accounts are initialized, and then their balance is requested as follows:

```
;; Tests using sample computations for get-balance
(check-expect (begin
                (initialize! acct1 500)
                (get-balance acct1))
             500)

(check-expect (begin
                (initialize! acct2 200)
                (get-balance acct2))
             200)
```

Observe that the wrapper function to initialize a bank account, still unwritten, is used in these tests.

The wrapper function to initialize a bank account takes as input a bank account object and the initial balance. Its body applies the given ba to the 'init message and applies the returned function to the given initial amount. The effect is to mutate the given bank account's balance to the given amount. The wrapper function is written as follows:

```
;; ba number → (void)
;; Purpose: To initialize the given bank account with the
;;          given balance
;; Effect: Change the given ba's balance to the given number
(define (initialize! ba amt) ((ba 'init) amt))
```

The tests to initialize an account must test the errors thrown and the successful effect of initializing a bank account. Not surprisingly, testing the effect is remarkably similar to the tests for balance inquiries. This is because the only way to know if a bank account has been properly initialized is by obtaining its balance. The tests are:

```
;; Tests using sample computations for initialize
(check-error
  (initialize! acct1 -78)
    "initialize-mybalance!: Balance cannot be initialized to the given value")

(check-error
  (initialize! acct1 #t)
    "initialize-mybalance!: Balance cannot be initialized to the given value")
```

```
(check-expect (begin
                (initialize! acct1 3400)
                (get-balance acct1))
              3400)

(check-expect (begin
                (initialize! acct2 788)
                (get-balance acct2))
              788)
```

The wrapper function for deposits takes as input a bank account object and an amount to deposit. It applies the object to the 'deposit message and then provides the given amount to the returned function. The effect is to add the given amount to the given ba's balance. The wrapper function is implemented as follows:

```
;; ba number → (void)
;; Purpose: To deposit the given amount in the given
;;          bank account
;; Effect: Increase the balance of the given ba by the
;;         given amount
(define (make-deposit! ba amt) ((ba 'deposit) amt))
```

The tests illustrate that the proper errors are thrown and that the effect is achieved. An error is thrown when the given amount is not a number or when the given amount is negative. The effect is illustrated by showing that the given account's balance is properly mutated. We take the opportunity to also illustrate that the effect of more than one deposit is properly achieved. The tests are:

```
;; Tests using sample computations for make-deposit
(check-error
  (begin
    (initialize! acct1 500)
    (make-deposit! acct1 'a))
  "deposit!: A deposit must be a positive number")

(check-error (begin
               (initialize! acct1 500)
               (make-deposit! acct1 -300))
             "deposit!: A deposit cannot be <= 0")

(check-expect (begin
                (initialize! acct1 500)
                (make-deposit! acct1 300)
                (get-balance acct1))
              800)
```

```
(check-expect (begin
                (initialize! acct2 200)
                (make-deposit! acct2 550)
                (make-deposit! acct2 250)
                (get-balance acct2))
              1000)
```

The wrapper function for withdrawals takes as input a bank account object and an amount to withdraw. It applies the object to the 'withdraw message and then provides the given amount to the returned function. The effect is to subtract the given amount from the given ba's balance. The wrapper function is implemented as follows:

```
;; bankaccount number → (void)
;; Purpose: To withdraw the given amount from the given
;           bank account
;; Effect: Decrease the balance of the given ba by the
;;          given amount
(define (make-withdrawal! ba amt) ((ba 'withdraw) amt))
```

The tests illustrate that the proper errors are thrown and that the effect is achieved. An error is thrown when the given amount is not a number, when the given amount is negative, or when there are insufficient funds. The effect is illustrated by showing that the given account's balance is properly mutated. We take the opportunity to also illustrate that the effect of intermingling deposits and withdrawals is properly achieved. The tests are:

```
;; Tests using sample computations for make-withdrawal
(check-error
  (begin
    (initialize! acct1 10)
    (make-withdrawal! acct1 'a))
  "withdraw!: The amount must be a positive number.")

(check-error
  (begin
    (initialize! acct1 45)
    (make-withdrawal! acct1 -10))
  "withdraw!: The amount must be a positive number.")

(check-error (begin
                (initialize! acct1 750)
                (make-withdrawal! acct1 800))
              "withdraw!: Insufficient funds")
```

Fig. 60 The design recipe for interfaces

1. Identify the values that must be stored and the services that must be provided.
2. Develop an interface data definition and a data definition for messages.
3. Develop a function template for the class that consumes the values that must be stored and whose body is a `local`-expression returning the message-processing function.
4. Specialize the signature, purpose, class header, and message-processing function.
5. Write and make local the auxiliary functions needed by the message-passing function.
6. Write and test a wrapper function for each service.

```
(check-expect (begin
                (initialize! acct1  500)
                (make-withdrawal! acct1 250)
                (get-balance acct1))
              250)
```

```
(check-expect (begin
                (initialize! acct2 200)
                (make-withdrawal! acct2 200)
                (make-deposit! acct2 400)
                (get-balance acct2))
              400)
```

This completes the abstraction for bank accounts. Run the tests and make sure they pass.

9 Add the functionality for overdrafts to bank accounts. Extend the bank account definition with an overdraft state variable, and redesign the class implementation. In such an account, the balance may become negative after a withdrawal as long as it does not exceed the limit established by the overdraft state variable.

77 A Design Recipe for Interfaces

Based on the design and implementation of the bank account interface, Fig. 60 displays the design recipe for interfaces. The first step is problem analysis. It asks you to identify the information that specializes each object (i.e., the required variables) and the services that an object must provide. Identify the values, if any, that must be provided when an object is created. The class must have a parameter for each of these values. The services must include a selector for each piece of information that specializes an object. The second

Fig. 61 Growing disk simulation part I

```
(define H 650)
(define W 600)
(define E-SCENE (empty-scene W H))

;; A world is a structure, (make-world posn number color), with
;; a posn, a radius, and a color representing a circle.
(define-struct world (p radius color))

;; Sample worlds
(define INIT-WORLD (make-world (make-posn (/ W 2) (/ H 2)) 5 'green))
(define WORLD2 (make-world (make-posn 20 20) 10 'blue))
(define WORLD3 (make-world (make-posn 400 300) 40 'yellow))
(define WORLD4 (make-world (make-posn 200 400) 60 'red))
(define WORLD5 (make-world (make-posn 1 1) 400 'red))
```

step asks you to develop an interface definition and a message data definition. There must be a message for each service identified in Step 1.

The third step asks for the development of a function template for the class. Its parameters correspond to the values identified in Step 1 needed to create an object. The function's body is a `local`-expression to encapsulate all needed functions and state variables and returns the message-processing function. The fourth step has you specialize the class header and the template for local message-passing function. The message-passing function must contain a conditional that processes a **message** as defined in Step 2. The fifth step asks you to develop all the auxiliary observers/mutators needed by the message-processing function. Each auxiliary function is developed using the design recipe.

The sixth step has you write a wrapper function for each service in the interface developed in Step 2. These functions take as input the object that is providing the service and the extra input, if any, required. The body of each wrapper function applies the object providing the service to the appropriate message. If extra input is needed, the function returned by the object is applied to the extra input.

10 Design and implement an interface for a contact book. Every contact has a name and a telephone number. Every contact must have a unique name and a unique telephone number. A contact book offers the following services: add a contact, delete a contact, update the name of a contact, update the telephone number of a contact, look up the number of a contact given a name, look up the name of a contact given a telephone number, and inquire how many contacts there is in the contact book.

Fig. 62 Growing disk simulation part II

```
;; world arrow image       Purpose: Draw the circle for the given world
(define (draw-world w)
  (place-image (circle (world-radius w) 'solid (world-color w))
               (posn-x (world-p w))
               (posn-y (world-p w))
               E-SCENE))
;; Sample expressions for draw world
(define WIMG1 (place-image (circle (world-radius INIT-WORLD)
                                   'solid (world-color
                                           INIT-WORLD))
                           (posn-x (world-p INIT-WORLD))
                           (posn-y (world-p INIT-WORLD))
                           E-SCENE))
(define WIMG2 (place-image (circle (world-radius WORLD2)
                                   'solid
                                   (world-color WORLD2))
                           (posn-x (world-p WORLD2))
                           (posn-y (world-p WORLD2))
                           E-SCENE))
;; Tests using sample computations for draw-world
(check-expect (draw-world INIT-WORLD) WIMG1)
(check-expect (draw-world WORLD2) WIMG2)

;; Tests using sample values for draw-world
(check-expect (draw-world (make-world (make-posn 60 60) 30 'yellow))
```

```
                                                             )
(check-expect (draw-world (make-world (make-posn 300 350) 50 'blue))
```

```
                                                             )
```

11 Design and implement an interface for a **student**. Every **student** has a name, a **student** number, and a list of courses taken. A course consists of a unique course number, a number of credits, and an integer grade in [0..4] (for F, D, C, B, and A). A student interface provides the following services: get student name, get student number, get courses taken, compute grade point average, add a course, and change the grade of a course.

Fig. 63 Growing disk simulation part III

```
;; world → world
;; Purpose: To process a clock tick.
;; Effect: The given world's radius is incremented by 1
(define (process-tick w)
  (begin
    (set-world-radius! w (add1 (world-radius w)))
    w))


;; Sample expressions for process-tick
(define PT1 (begin
            (set-world-radius! WORLD3 (add1 (world-radius WORLD3)))
            WORLD3))

(define PT2 (begin
            (set-world-radius! WORLD4 (add1 (world-radius WORLD4)))
            WORLD4))

;; Tests using sample computations for process-tick
(check-expect (process-tick WORLD3) PT1)
(check-expect (process-tick WORLD4) PT2)

;; Tests using sample values for process-tick
(check-expect (process-tick (make-world (make-posn 10 40) 5 'yellow))
            (make-world (make-posn 10 40) 6 'yellow))

(check-expect (process-tick (make-world (make-posn 7 7) 19 'red))
            (make-world (make-posn 7 7) 20 'red))
```

78 Mutation and Structures

ASL structures are mutable. When you define a structure a constructor, an observer for each field, and a mutator for each field are created. For example, consider the following structure definition:

```
(define-struct student (name gpa credits))
```

ASL creates the constructor and observers that you are accustomed to:

```
make-student
student-name
student-gpa
student-credits
```

In addition, ASL also creates a mutator for each field:

```
set-student-name!
set-student-gpa!
set-student-credits!
```

Fig. 64 Growing disk simulation part IV

```
;; world arrow Boolean
;; Purpose: To determine if the simulation is over
(define (done? w) (>= (world-radius w) (/ W 2)))

;; Sample expressions for done?
(define DONE1 (>= (world-radius INIT-WORLD) (/ W 2)))
(define DONE2 (>= (world-radius WORLD5)
                  (/ W 2)))

;; Tests using sample computations for done?
(check-expect (done? INIT-WORLD) #false)
(check-expect (done? WORLD5) #true)

;; Tests using sample values for done?
(check-expect (done? (make-world (make-posn 0 0) 5    'green)) #false)
(check-expect (done? (make-world (make-posn 6 2) 350 'pink))  #true)

;;  arrow world
;; Purpose: To run the simulation
(define (run)
  (big-bang
     INIT-WORLD
    (on-draw draw-world)
    (on-tick process-tick)
    (stop-when done?)))
```

These mutators take as input a **student** and the new field value. It is important to understand that the mutators do not create a new **student** like the constructor **make-student**. Instead, they mutate a field inside a **student** structure instance. That is, they clobber the value of a field and substitute it with a new value. The old value of the field is gone forever, and there is no way to retrieve it. Consider the following **students**:

```
(define S1 (make-student "Dr. Strange" 4.0 120))
(define S2 (make-student "Tony Stark"  4.0 160))
```

We can use, for example, **set-student-credits!** to change the number of credits for either of them. After performing the following mutation, the tests pass:

```
(set-student-credits! S1 150)

(check-expect (student-credits S1) 150)
(check-expect (student-credits S2) 160)
```

Observe that using the mutator only changes the credits for, S1, the given student. S2's credits remain unchanged.

A natural question that arises is why is this important or useful. After all, we can always create a new **student** instead of mutating a value. To understand why this is important, we must understand what happens when a constructor is used. A new structure is created as you know. This means that memory is allocated to store the fields of the new structure instance. A program that allocates too much memory may be inefficient or the computer may run out of allocatable memory. This may occur on systems that have a limited amount of memory. In such cases, it is desirable to minimize memory allocation.

A **universe** program, for instance, may allocate a lot of memory. This may occur if a new world is created after each clock tick. To avoid such allocations, the given world may be mutated and returned instead of creating and returning a new world. Figures 61, 62, 63, and 64 displays the code for a simulation of a growing disk rendered in the center of the scene. The disk starts small, and at each clock tick, its radius is increased by 1. The simulation stops when the disk's radius exceeds half the scene's width.

Observe that in Fig. 63 `process-tick` mutates the given `world` instead of creating a new `world`. This means that only one `world`, `INIT-WORLD`, is allocated to run the simulation. You may contrast this with an implementation that allocates memory to create a new `world` every time `process-tick` is called. In addition to sharing values, mutation may be useful in reducing memory allocation by reusing/mutating memory that has already been allocated.

12 Write an imperative interactive simulation of a rocket landing. The user may move the rocket left or right. Use the following definitions:

```
;; A world is a posn such that 0≤x≤WIDTH and 0≤y≤HEIGHT

(define INIT-WORLD (make-posn (/ WIDTH 2) 0))
```

The dimensions of the scene are `WIDTH` and `HEIGHT`. Your program should not use `make-posn` other than to create the initial `world` above.

13 Redesign the growing disk simulation to have the color change every 30 clock ticks.

79 The Concept of Equality

The introduction of mutation in a programming language forces us to ask what does it mean to be equal. Instinctively, we are tempted to say that two values are equal if they are the same. That is, 3 is equal to 3, and (`make-posn` 0 0) and (`make-posn` 0 0) are equal because they are the same value. This is called *extensional equality*. There is extensional equality when the values are the same. This, however, is not the only definition of equality that exists in the presence of mutation. Consider the following definitions:

```
(define P1 (make-posn 10 15))
(define P2 (make-posn 10 15))
(define P3 P1)
```

Are these three posns equal? Clearly, there is extensional equality. All three posns have the same x value and the same y value. Does this mean they are the same? Run the following code:

```
(set-posn-x! P1 0)

(check-expect P1 P2)
(check-expect P1 P3)
(check-expect P3 P2)
```

Alas, the first and third tests fail! Therefore, in some sense, our three posns are not equal or the same. To understand what is occurring, it is useful to visualize the variables and the memory that they refer to. When the P1 definition is evaluated, two memory locations, for 10 and 15, are allocated. When the P2 definition is evaluated, two more memory locations, for 10 and 15, are allocated. When the P3 definition is evaluated, no memory is allocated because nothing is constructed. Instead, P3 is defined to be whatever P1 is. We may visualize the state of the variables as follows:

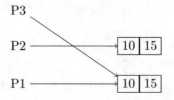

P1 and P3 refer to the same memory location, while P2 refers to a different memory location. When (set-posn-x! P1 0) is evaluated, the picture changes to:

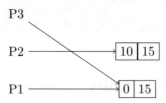

Now it becomes clear why the first and third tests above fail. P2's x-coordinate is different from P1's and P3's x-coordinate. The second test does not fail because both coordinates for P1 and P3 are the same. They are the same because they refer to the same data in memory. This is called *intensional equality*. Two values have intensional equality when they refer to the same values in memory. We say that intensional equality is sufficient for extensional equality. That is, intentional equality means that two values are the same (because they are the same value in the same memory location like P1 and P3). Extensional equality is necessary but not sufficient for intensional equality. That is, if two values have extensional equality, they may also have intensional equality. If two values do not have extensional equality, then they also do not have intensional equality.

ASL offers two predicates to test for equality. To test for extensional equality, use `equal?`. To test for intensional equality, use `eq?`.

This leads to a necessary word of caution about using mutation in programs. Observe that only P1 is mutated above but the value of P3 is also mutated. This occurs because P1 and P3 are the same value in memory. Mutating one of them means that both are mutated. This is a common source of bugs in modern software. Consider X and Y are shared variables that have intensional equality in a program that is divided into two pieces, A that manipulates X and B that manipulates Y, developed by different programming teams. Each team successfully tests their part of the program. When the two parts are brought together, however, the tests fail. This may occur because mutations to X in part A cause errors with Y in part B or mutations to Y in part B cause errors with X in part A. This is one of the major pitfalls of *imperative programming* (programming using mutation) and is why mutation must be used with extreme caution. Be aware that such bugs may exist and do not always manifest themselves. As problem-solvers and programmers, it is our responsibility to mitigate mutation-based bugs. How can we be more confident that we are correctly using assignment? The answer is logic, specifically, Hoare logic that we shall study Chapter 15.

14 Consider:

```
(define X 3)
(define Y 3)
```

Typing `(eq? X Y)` at the prompt returns `#true`. Observe that when X is mutated to be 4, `(eq? X Y)` returns `#false`:

```
> (set! X 4)
(void)
> (eq? X Y)
#false
```

What happens when Y is set to 4? What does this tell you about small integers?

15 Use `fact2` from Figure 38 to define the following variables:

```
(define F30  (fact2 30))
(define FT30 (fact2 30))
```

Consider the following interactions:

```
> F30
265252859812191058636308480000000
> FT30
265252859812191058636308480000000
> (eq? F30 FT30)
#false
> (equal? F30 FT30)
#true
```

What does this tell you about large integers?

80 What Have We Learned in This Chapter?

The important lessons of this chapter are summarized as follows:

- It is not uncommon for functions that do not call each other to communicate values through shared variables.
- In most programming languages, a variable is a memory location that has been given a name, and the value stored in that memory location may be mutated.
- One of the primary goals of mutation is to share variables among functions that do not call each other.
- In ASL, set-expression is used to mutate defined variables and has the following syntax:
  expr ::= (set! variable expr)
- set! is not a function.
- In ASL, a begin-expression is used to sequence mutations.
- The syntax for a begin-expression is:
  expr ::= (begin <expression>⁺)
- A mutator is a function that has an effect.

- An observer is a function that accesses but does not mutate a state variable.
- The mutator design recipe is:
  1. Problem and Data Analysis
  2. Define the State Variables to Be Uninitialized
  3. Design and Define Initializers for Each State Variable
  4. Perform Problem Analysis for a Mutator
  5. Write the Mutator's Signature, Purpose Statement, Effect Statement, and Function Header
  6. Write Tests That Illustrate the Effects of the Mutator
  7. Write the Body of the Mutator
  8. Run the Tests

- To abstract over state variables, encapsulation is used.
- An interface defines the services or behavior expected from a data type.
- If no further input is needed for a service, the interface defines the type of value returned.
- If further input is needed for a service, the interface defines the function type returned to consume the extra input.
- A class implements an interface using message-passing.
- Instances of a class are objects that are able to perform all the services in the interface.
- An object is a curried function.
- A wrapper function hides the implementation details and presents a user-friendly interface.
- An interface's implementation is tested by writing tests for the wrapper functions.
- Structures are mutable.
- A structure definition creates a mutator for each field.
- Mutation may be useful in reducing memory allocation.
- Extensional equality means the values compared are the same value.
- Intensional equality means the values compared are the same value in memory.
- Imperative programming is programming using mutation.

Chapter 15
Mutation Sequencing

In Chap. 11, we studied the design of tail-recursive functions. These functions are interesting because they do not have delayed operations. This means that variable values in one recursive call are not needed in the future of the computation after a recursive call is made. That is, every recursive call only needs its input to proceed with the computation, and the function never needs to return to finish a delayed operation.

One of the tail-recursive functions designed computes $n!$ (see Fig. 38). This function is partially reproduced in Fig. 65.[16] This function may be evaluated without having to remember values from one recursive call to the next. We can visualize the computation of $6!$ using fact2 as follows:

```
(fact2 6) = (fact-accum 6    1)
          = (fact-accum 5    6)
          = (fact-accum 4   30)
          = (fact-accum 3  120)
          = (fact-accum 2  360)
          = (fact-accum 1  720)
          = (fact-accum 0  720)
          = 720
```

Observe that the values of k and accum for one call are not needed in future calls. This suggests that state variables may be used to represent k and accum. At each step, k is mutated to be decremented by 1, and accum is mutated to be the product of itself and the value of k. We may visualize the mutations as follows:

$$
\begin{aligned}
k &= \cancel{6}\ \cancel{5}\ \cancel{4}\ \cancel{3}\ \cancel{2}\ \cancel{1}\ 0 \\
accum &= \cancel{1}\ \cancel{6}\ \cancel{30}\ \cancel{120}\ \cancel{360}\ \cancel{720}\ 720
\end{aligned}
$$

The values of k and accum are mutated, while k is not equal to 0. When k becomes 0, the mutations stop (given that the recursion stops), and accum is returned as the value of $6!$.

---

[16] For clarity, the first parameter of fact-accum has been renamed k.

© The Author(s), under exclusive license to Springer Nature Switzerland AG 2022   377
M. T. Morazán, *Animated Program Design*, Texts in Computer Science,
https://doi.org/10.1007/978-3-031-04317-8_15

Fig. 65 The program to compute n! based on accumulative recursion

```
;; natnum → natnum
;; Purpose: Compute the factorial of the given natural number
(define (fact2 n)
  (local [;; natnum natnum → natnum
          ;; Purpose: Compute the factorial of the first
          ;;               given natural number
          ;; Accumulator invariant
          ;;    accum = the product of the natural numbers in [k+1..n]
          (define (fact-accum k accum)
            (if (= k 0)
                accum
                (fact-accum (sub1 k) (* k accum))))]
    (fact-accum n 1)))

;; Tests using sample values for fact2
(check-expect (fact2 0)  1)
(check-expect (fact2 5)  120)
(check-expect (fact2 10) 3628800)
(check-expect (fact2 2)  2)
(check-expect (fact2 6)  720)
```

We may define k and accum as local state variables. Initially, these state variables are defined to be (void). Their purpose is the same as for the tail-recursive version of fact2 displayed in Fig. 65. They may be locally defined as follows:

```
;; natnum
;; Purpose: The next possible accum factor
(define k (void))

;; natnum
;; Purpose: The current approximation of n!
(define accum (void))
```

The body of the local-expression must initialize n and accum. What should their initial values be? The answer is given to us by the tail-recursive function in Fig. 65. The initial call to fact-accum provides n as the value for k and 1 as the value for accum. Therefore, it is reasonable to initialize the state variables to the same values before calling, fact-state!, the imperative version of fact-accum as follows:

```
(begin
  (set! k n)
  (set! accum 1)
  (fact-state!))
```

Fig. 66 Two plausible implementations of mutation-based factorial

```
;; natnum → natnum                          ;; natnum → natnum
;; Purpose: To compute n!                   ;; Purpose: To compute n!
(define (fact2-v1 n)                        (define (fact2-v2 n)
 (local                                      (local
  [;; natnum                                  [;; natnum
   ;; Purpose: Next accum factor               ;; Purpose: Next accum factor
   (define k (void))                           (define k (void))

   ;; natnum                                   ;; natnum
   ;; Purpose: The product so far              ;; Purpose: The product so far
   ;; Invariant: accum=Π_{i=k+1}^{n} i         ;; Invariant: accum=Π_{i=k+1}^{n} i
   (define accum (void))                       (define accum (void))

   ;; → natnum                                 ;; → natnum
   ;; Purpose: Compute n!                      ;; Purpose: Compute n!
   ;; Effect: k is decremented and             ;; Effect: k is decremented and
   ;;   accum is multiplied by k               ;;   accum is multiplied by k
   (define (fact-state!)                       (define (fact-state!)
    (if (= k 0)                                 (if (= k 0)
        accum                                       accum
        (begin                                      (begin
          (set! k (sub1 k))                           (set! accum (* k accum))
          (set! accum (* k accum))                    (set! k (sub1 k))
          (fact-state))]))]                           (fact-state))]))]
  (begin                                      (begin
    (set! k n)                                  (set! k n)
    (set! accum 1)                              (set! accum 1)
    (fact-state!))))                            (fact-state!))))

(check-expect (fact2-v1 0)  1)              (check-expect (fact2-v2 0)  1)
(check-expect (fact2-v1 5)  120)            (check-expect (fact2-v2 5)  120)
(check-expect (fact2-v1 10) 3628800)        (check-expect (fact2-v2 10) 3628800)
(check-expect (fact2-v1 2)  2)              (check-expect (fact2-v2 2)  2)
(check-expect (fact2-v1 6)  720)            (check-expect (fact2-v2 6)  720)
```

The mutator `fact-state` must do the job of `fact-accum` by mutating the state variables. If `k` is 0, then `accum` is returned. How do we know `accum` is equal to `n!`? Consider the assertions that must hold:[17]

$$\text{accum} = \Pi_{i=k+1}^{n} i \;\land\; k = 0$$

The first is the accumulator invariant, and the second is the condition that stops the recursion. Let us explore what they imply:

$$\text{accum} = \Pi_{i=k+1}^{n} i \;\land\; k = 0 \Rightarrow \text{accum} = \Pi_{i=0+1}^{n} i$$
$$\Rightarrow \text{accum} = \Pi_{i=1}^{n} i$$
$$\Rightarrow \text{accum} = n!$$

---

[17] $\Pi_{i=k+1}^{n} i$ denotes the product of all the integers in $[k+1..n]$.

Given that k is 0, we can plug it into the equality for accum. Observe that 0
+ 1 is 1. Therefore, accum is the product of all the natural numbers in [1..n].
This is exactly the definition of n!. Therefore, it is correct to return accum.

All that is required is that the state variables be correctly mutated when
k is not 0. How should these variables be mutated? Once again, we look
at the code in Fig. 65. For each recursive call, k is decremented, and accum
is multiplied by k. This suggests that two mutations are needed: one for
each state variable. This presents a problem that we must solve. How should
the mutation be sequenced? Should k be mutated first, or should accum be
mutated first? These two plausible options for our program are displayed in
Fig. 66. The program on the left, fact2-v1, decrements k first, while the
program on the right, fact2-v2, decrements k second. This is the only real
difference between the two programs. How do we decide which to choose?
Are the two programs equivalent? Go ahead and run the programs.

Alas, the programs are not equivalent. After running the tests, you have
discovered that three tests for fact2-v1 fail, while no tests for fact2-v2 fail.
Therefore, you are sure to argue that the correct imperative program to compute factorial is fact2-v2. This exercise reveals two important observations.
The first is that using mutation adds a great deal to the responsibilities of
a programmer. A programmer must solve a problem (as before) and must
determine the correct sequencing of the mutations. This latter part is something that we do not need to worry about when mutation is not used (as
the code in Fig. 65). The second important observation is that the approach
used to determine which program we believe is correct is not scalable. In
other words, the approach is unfeasible for larger programs. When only two
mutations are needed, there are only two ways to sequence the mutations.
Therefore, it is easy to write both versions of the program, run the tests,
and determine for which the tests pass. Imagine, however, that an imperative function requires ten state variables and ten mutations. There are 10!
= 3628800 different ways the mutations can be sequenced. Are we to write
over 3.5 million programs to determine which we believe is correct? Clearly,
we need a better approach to decide the correct sequencing of the mutations.

81 Hoare Logic

A useful tool to properly sequence assignment statements and to establish
the correctness of imperative programs is *Hoare logic*.[18] Hoare logic is a formal system to rigorously reason about and develop imperative programs. At
the heart of Hoare logic is the *Hoare triple*. A Hoare triple consists of two
assertions and a mutation or a call to a mutator. They are written as follows:

---

[18] Named after its developer, Tony Hoare, whose quick sorting algorithm we studied in
Sect. 25.

```
;; P
M
;; Q
```

P is an assertion that describes the value of one or more state variables
before the mutation(s) performed by M. P is called the *precondition*. Q is
an assertion that describes the value of one or more state variables after
the mutation(s) performed by M. Q is called the *postcondition*. For instance,
consider the following Hoare triple:

```
;; X = 2
(set! X (add1 X))
;; X = 3
```

In this triple, P is X = 2, M is (set! X (add1 X)), and Q is X = 3. It states
that if X is 2 before its mutation, then after its mutation, X is 3.

Hoare triples may be written around any valid syntax in which there is
one or more mutations. The following is a valid Hoare triple involving a
conditional:

```
;; X is a number
(if (< X 0)
    (set! Y (abs X))
    (set! Y X)
;; X is a number ∧ Y = |X|
```

This triple states that if X is a number before the if-expression then after
the if-expression X is number and Y is the absolute value of X. The symbol
∧ means *and*. How do we demonstrate that this is true? We can *drag* P, the
first assertion stating that X is a number, through the if-expression. Note
that comparing X to 0 does not change the value of X. Therefore, before the
assignment in both branches of the if-expression P is true. We can now start
writing a Hoare triple for each branch of the if-expression as follows:

```
;; X is a number
(if (< X 0)
    ;; X < 0
    (set! Y (abs X))
    ;; Q for then branch

    ;; X ≥ 0
    (set! Y X)
    ;; Q for else branch
;; X is a number ∧ Y = |X|
```

We are stating that if X is a number before the if-expression then we know
X is a number less than 0 before the mutation in the then branch and we
know X is a number greater than or equal to 0 before the mutation in the else

branch. Observe that for both branches, Y equals |X| after the corresponding mutation. Therefore, we may complete both triples as follows:

```
;; X is a number
(if (< X 0)
    ;; X < 0
    (set! Y (abs X))
    ;; X is a number ∧ Y = |X|

    ;; X ≥ 0
    (set! Y X)
    ;; X is a number ∧ Y = |X|
;; X is a number ∧ Y = |X|
```

Regardless of the branch that is evaluated, we have that the postcondition of the if-expression, X is a number ∧ Y = |X|, holds. This is how we know that original triple is valid.

The use of Hoare logic frequently involves logical implication:

$$A \Rightarrow B$$

The above states that A implies B. A is called the *antecedent*, and B is called the *consequent*. An implication is an assertion that means that if A is true, then B is true. The truth table for an implication is the following:

A	B	$A \Rightarrow B$
false	false	true
false	true	true
true	false	false
true	true	true

Observe that an implication is always true except when the antecedent is true and the consequent is false. Therefore, to prove that an implication is true, we only need to prove that the consequent is true when the antecedent is true. For instance, consider proving:

$$x = 3 \Rightarrow x^2 = 9$$

Assume that x is 3. We must show that x^2 is 9. This is achieved as follows:

```
x² = 9
3² = 9  by plugging in the value of x
 9 = 9  by definition of squaring
true
```

The above demonstrates that if x is 3, then x^2 is 9. Therefore, when the antecedent is true, the consequent is true, and we may conclude the implication is true. Why? This follows from observing that if the antecedent is false, then the implication is true and from observing that the third line of the truth table above can never be the case given that we have proven that when the antecedent is true, the consequent is also true. In summary, proving an implication requires assuming the antecedent is true and proving the consequent is true.

81.1 Using Hoare Triples

Hoare logic may be used to guide imperative code development instead of guessing the correct sequence of mutations. An important step is to know the postcondition: the assertion that needs to be true after the mutations. For instance, assume that A = n and that B = j, where n and j are numbers. We wish to write a program that doubles A and triples B. To start, we may write the precondition and postcondition as follows:

```
;; A = n ∧ B = j
```

```
;; A = 2n ∧ B = 3j
```

Our goal, therefore, is to write a sequence of mutations that take the state variables from the precondition to the postcondition. Observe that there is no dependency between the variables. That is, their values do not affect each other. In such a case, we may choose to mutate either variable first. Without loss of generality, let us mutate A first. To mutate A, we must multiply it by 2. The result of this first step is:

```
;; A = n ∧ B = j
(set! A (* 2 A))
;; A = 2n ∧ B = j
```

```
;; A = 2n ∧ B = 3j
```

The new assertion after the mutation states A is 2n and B remains unchanged. How do we know A is 2n? The precondition tells us that before the mutation, A = n. The right-hand side of the mutation is (* 2 A). Therefore, we can plug in the value of A into the right-hand side. This yields that the right-hand side is (* 2 n). So, indeed, A is 2n after the mutation. Mutating A, of course, does not change the value of B.[19] Observe that we have achieved part of the postcondition. We now have to achieve the remaining part of the postcondition without affecting the first part. To do so, we mutate B to be its triple. This mutation yields:

```
;; A = n ∧ B = j
(set! A (* 2 A))
;; A = 2n ∧ B = j
(set! B (* 3 B))
;; A = 2n ∧ B = 3j
```

---

[19] We are assuming that intensional equality does not hold between A and B.

Observe that after the second mutation, the postcondition is true. Therefore, our job is done, and we have successfully developed the needed program.

There might, however, be dependencies between the variables mutated. Consider writing an imperative program to achieve the postcondition in the following partial Hoare triple:

```
;; A = n

;; A = n + 1 ∧ B = 2n
```

For this problem, we must be more careful because the value of B in the postcondition depends on the value of A before A is mutated. A program development strategy is to first mutate the variables that are not dependent on other variables. In this case, B may be mutated first because its value is not needed to correctly mutate A. Following this approach yields:

```
;; A = n
(set! B (* 2 A))
;; A = n ∧ B = 2n

;; A = n + 1 ∧ B = 2n
```

Observe that part of the postcondition has been achieved. Now that B has been mutated, there is nothing that depends on A. Therefore, we are free to mutate A. This yields:

```
;; A = n
(set! B (* 2 A))
;; A = n ∧ B = 2n
(set! A (add1 A))
;; A = n + 1 ∧ B = 2n
```

Observe that the postcondition has been achieved and, therefore, we have successfully developed the needed program.

The dependencies between variables may be circular. For instance, consider writing an imperative program for the following pre- and postcondition:

```
;; A = n ∧ B = m

;; A = m ∧ B = n
```

There is a circular dependency between the state variables. The value of A in the postcondition depends on the value of B in the precondition. Similarly, the value of B in the postcondition depends on the value of A in the precondition. In such a case, the circularity must be broken. This may be achieved using local variables. We can define a local variable to store the value of one of the variables to break the circularity as follows:

```
;; A = n ∧ B = m
(local [(define temp A)]
```

```
    ...)
;; A = m ∧ B = n
```

We can now say that in the postcondition, A depends on the value of B and B depends on the value of temp. Given that nothing depends on the value of A, we are free to mutate it and make progress toward achieving the postcondition as follows:

```
;; A = n ∧ B = m
(local [(define temp A)]
  (begin
    ;; A = n ∧ B = m ∧ temp = n
    (set! A B)
    ;; A = m ∧ B = m ∧ temp = n
    ...))
;; A = m ∧ B = n
```

We add what we know about temp to the assertion before the mutation because it is needed to eventually establish that B is correctly mutated. The assertion after the mutation captures the change made to A. Observe that part of the postcondition has been achieved. To finish achieving the postcondition, B is mutated as follows:

```
;; A = n ∧ B = m
(local [(define temp A)]
  (begin
    ;; A = n ∧ B = m ∧ temp = n
    (set! A B)
    ;; A = m ∧ B = m ∧ temp = n
    (set! B temp)
    ;; A = m ∧ B = n))
;; A = m ∧ B = n
```

The assertion after the second mutation captures the change made to B. This assertion is the same as the postcondition. Given that finishing the evaluation of the local-expression does not mutate any variables, we may conclude that the postcondition has been achieved, and we have successfully written the needed program.

81.1.1 Developing fact-state!

We can now tackle developing fact-state! for the mutation-based factorial program. We need to establish that the accumulator invariant for accum is true every time fact-state! is called. Thus, we have the following framework to get us started:

```
;; accum = Π_{i=k+1}^{n} i
<body for fact-state!>
```

The first step is to make sure the state variables are initialized in a manner that makes the invariant holds. In both versions of the program in Fig. 66, k is initialized to n, and accum is initialized to 1. Let us plug in these values into the invariant to determine if it holds:

```
;; accum = Π_{i=k+1}^{n} i
;;   1   = Π_{i=n+1}^{n} i
;;   1   = 1
```

We start with the invariant as our assertion. The first step is to plug in the values of the state variables. This yields the second assertion. By definition, Π_a^b is 1 when $a > b$. This allows to substitute the product in the second assertion for 1 to obtain the third assertion. Clearly, $1 = 1$, and, therefore, we know the invariant holds the first time fact-state! is called.

We now need to develop the code that guarantees the accumulator invariant holds for every subsequent call to fact-state!. Based on the programs in Fig. 66, our job is a bit simplified because we already know that an if-expression is needed and that accum is returned in the then branch. Let us drag the invariant through the then branch:

```
;; accum = Π_{i=k+1}^{n} i
(if (= k 0)
    ;; accum = Π_{i=k+1}^{n} i ∧ k = 0
    ;; ⇒ accum = Π_{i=1}^{n} i
    ;; ⇒ accum = n!
    accum
    ;; else branch
    <code for else branch>)
```

The comparison of k with 0 does not mutate any variables, and, therefore, the accumulator invariant holds in the then branch. In addition, we know that the comparison returned #true meaning that k is 0. Knowing that k is 0 implies that accum is n!. Thus, we may conclude that the function returns the correct value as long as the invariant holds every time fact-state! is called.

The else branch must perform mutations such that the invariant holds for the next call to fact-state!. Let us write the assertions that hold before the program evaluates the else branch:

```
;; accum = Π_{i=k+1}^{n} i
(if (= k 0)
    ;; accum = Π_{i=k+1}^{n} i ∧ k = 0
    ;; ⇒ accum = Π_{i=1}^{n} i
    ;; ⇒ accum = n!
    accum
    ;; else branch
    ;; accum = Π_{i=k+1}^{n} i ∧ k ≠ 0
    <code for else branch>)
```

Based on the programs in Fig. 66, the else branch must perform two mutations: k must be decremented, and accum must be multiplied by k. Observe that there is only one dependency: accum's new value depends on k's value. This suggests that accum ought to be mutated first. Let us make this mutation first and drag the assertion down through the mutation:

```
;; accum = Π_{i=k+1}^{n} i
(if (= k 0)
    ;; accum = Π_{i=k+1}^{n} i ∧ k = 0
    ;; ⇒ accum = Π_{i=1}^{n} i
    ;; ⇒ accum = n!
    accum
    ;; else branch
    (begin
        ;; accum = Π_{i=k+1}^{n} i ∧ k ≠ 0
        (set! accum (* k accum))
        ;; accum = Π_{i=k}^{n} i
        ⋮
    ))
```

Mutating accum to be (* k accum) makes k a factor in the product stored in accum. Thus, the product starts at k, not at k+1, after the mutation. Observe that the assertion after the mutation is not the same as the invariant. This means that more mutations are needed to reestablish the invariant. Let us perform the mutation on k and drag the assertion beyond this mutation:

```
;; accum = Π_{i=k+1}^{n} i
(if (= k 0)
    ;; accum = Π_{i=k+1}^{n} i ∧ k = 0
    ;; ⇒ accum = Π_{i=1}^{n} i
    ;; ⇒ accum = n!
    accum
    ;; else branch
    (begin
        ;; accum = Π_{i=k+1}^{n} i ∧ k ≠ 0
        (set! accum (* k accum))
        ;; accum = Π_{i=k}^{n} i
        (set! k (sub1 k))
        ;; accum = Π_{i=k+1}^{n} i
        ⋮
    ))
```

The new value of k is not a factor of the product stored in accum. Relative to the new value of k, the factors of this product start at k+1, not k. This is reflected in the assertion after the second mutation. Observe that we have reestablished the invariant and now can safely make the recursive call:

```
;; accum = Π_{i=k+1}^{n} i
(if (= k 0)
    ;; accum = Π_{i=k+1}^{n} i ∧ k = 0
    ;; ⇒ accum = Π_{i=1}^{n} i
    ;; ⇒ accum = n!
    accum
    ;; else branch
    (begin
        ;; accum = Π_{i=k+1}^{n} i ∧ k ≠ 0
        (set! accum (* k accum))
        ;; accum = Π_{i=k}^{n} i
        (set! k (sub1 k))
        ;; accum = Π_{i=k+1}^{n} i
        (fact-state!)))
```

This means that in Fig. 66, `fact2-v2` is the correct implementation of an imperative program to compute `n!`. Proving that an invariant always holds and the correct value is returned is called *partial correctness*. Proving partial correctness, in general, is difficult but more powerful than testing because it establishes that the program works for all valid inputs. Testing, nonetheless, is always required because even the most experienced software developers may have bugs in their proofs.

Finally, we need a termination argument for `fact2-v2`. Observe that `k` is a natural number that is decremented with each recursive call. Eventually, `k` becomes 0, and the recursion stops. A proof of partial correctness and a termination argument is called *total correctness*. It establishes that for all valid inputs, the program terminates and returns the correct value. The complete program for fact-v3 is displayed in Fig. 67.

81.2 Imperative Code Debugging

Hoare logic may also be used to debug imperative code. To illustrate this process, let us debug `fact2-v1` from Fig. 66. We shall debug it from the point of view of someone that did not develop the code but needs to maintain it. In other words, this person is not aware of the accumulator-based tail-recursive program displayed in Fig. 65. The code is the same as `fact2-v2` except for the else branch of the conditional in `fact-state!`. We can, therefore, start with the following code and assertions:

```
;; accum = Π_{i=k+1}^{n} i
(if (= k 0)
    ;; accum = Π_{i=k+1}^{n} i ∧ k = 0
    ;; ⇒ accum = Π_{i=1}^{n} i
    ;; ⇒ accum = n!
    accum
```

Fig. 67 An imperative recursive function for n!

```
;; natnum → natnum
;; Purpose: Compute the factorial of the given natural number
(define (fact2-v3 n)
  (local [;; natnum
          ;; Purpose: The next possible accum factor
          (define k (void))

          ;; natnum
          ;; Purpose: The current approximation of n!
          (define accum (void))

          ;; natnum natnum → natnum
          ;; Purpose: Compute the factorial of the first
          ;;              given natural number
          ;; Effect: k is decremented and
          ;;              accum is multiplied by k
          ;; Accumulator invariant: accum = Π_{i=k+1}^{n} i
          (define (fact-state!)
            ;; accum = Π_{i=k+1}^{n} i
            (if (= k 0)
                ;; accum = Π_{i=k+1}^{n} i ∧ k = 0
                ;; ⇒ accum = Π_{i=1}^{n} i
                ;; ⇒ accum = n!
                accum
                ;; else branch
                (begin
                  ;; accum = Π_{i=k+1}^{n} i ∧ k ≠ 0
                  (set! accum (* k accum))
                  ;; accum = Π_{i=k}^{n} i
                  (set! k (sub1 k))
                  ;; accum = Π_{i=k+1}^{n} i
                  (fact-state!))))
          ;; Termination argument:
          ;; k is a natural number that is decremented with each
          ;; recursive call.Eventually, k becomes 0 and the
          ;; recursion stops.
          ]
    (begin
      (set! k n)
      (set! accum 1)
      (fact-state!))))

;; Tests using sample values for fact2-v3
(check-expect (fact2-v3 0)  1)
(check-expect (fact2-v3 5)  120)
(check-expect (fact2-v3 10) 3628800)
(check-expect (fact2-v3 2)  2)
(check-expect (fact2-v3 6)  720)
```

```
;; else branch
(begin
  ;; accum = $\Pi_{i=k+1}^{n}$ i $\wedge$ k $\neq$ 0
     ⋮
))
```

The first mutation made is to decrement k. Let us code such mutation and write the assertion that holds after it:

```
;; accum = $\Pi_{i=k+1}^{n}$ i
(if (= k 0)
    ;; accum = $\Pi_{i=k+1}^{n}$ i $\wedge$ k = 0
    ;; $\Rightarrow$ accum = $\Pi_{i=1}^{n}$ i
    ;; $\Rightarrow$ accum = n!
    accum
    ;; else branch
    (begin
      ;; accum = $\Pi_{i=k+1}^{n}$ i $\wedge$ k $\neq$ 0
      (set! k (sub1 k))
      ;; accum = $\Pi_{i=k+2}^{n}$ i

         ⋮
    ))
```

Observe that before the mutation, the smallest factor of the product stored in accum is k+1. Given the new value of k, the lowest factor is k+2, not k+1, after the mutation. Also note that after the mutation, k may or may not be 0.

Think about what is needed to restore the invariant. The smallest factor must be k+1. We can restore the invariant by multiplying accum by k+1. This approach yields the following code:

```
;; accum = $\Pi_{i=k+1}^{n}$ i
(if (= k 0)
    ;; accum = $\Pi_{i=k+1}^{n}$ i $\wedge$ k = 0
    ;; $\Rightarrow$ accum = $\Pi_{i=1}^{n}$ i
    ;; $\Rightarrow$ accum = n!
    accum
    ;; else branch
    (begin
      ;; accum = $\Pi_{i=k+1}^{n}$ i $\wedge$ k $\neq$ 0
      (set! k (sub1 k))
      ;; accum = $\Pi_{i=k+2}^{n}$ i
      (set! accum (* (add1 k) accum))
      ;; accum = $\Pi_{i=k+1}^{n}$ i
      (fact-state!)
    ))
```

Observe that the invariant is restored and it is safe to make the recursive call. We can now see that the bug was in the mutation of accum. The resulting program is interesting because it does not directly correspond to the program in Fig. 65. It contains (* (add1 k) accum) as an expression. This expression does not appear in the program displayed in Fig. 65. Does this mean that this new code is incorrect? The answer is an unequivocal no. We have established partial correctness, and the same termination argument developed for fact2-v3 in Fig. 67 establishes total correctness. The debugging process has led us to develop a slightly different way of computing n!.

You now have two powerful reasons to become proficient in using Hoare logic: imperative program development and imperative code debugging. These two tasks are likely to play an important role as you progress as a student and when you start your professional career. Studies have shown that programmers that take time to develop invariants tend to write better and bug-free code. In short, spend more time designing and less time coding and debugging.

1 Design and implement an imperative program to sum the elements of a list of numbers based on the tail-recursive code developed for sum-lon-accum in Sect. 53.1.2. Prove total correctness.

2 Design and implement an imperative program to reverse a (listof X) based on the tail-recursive code developed for rev-lox-accum in Sect. 53.2. Prove total correctness.

3 Design and implement an imperative program to compute the lengths of the strings in a (listof String) based on the tail-recursive code developed for lengths-lostr-accum in Sect. 54.1.3. Prove total correctness.

4 Design and implement an imperative program to fold a list from right to left based on the tail-recursive code developed for fold-from-right in Fig. 50. Prove total correctness.

5 Design and implement an imperative program to add all the integer elements in, [low..high], a given interval. Prove total correctness.

82 New Syntax: `while` Loops

In many programming languages, it is common practice to package the repeated mutations of state variables using syntax in which the recursive call is
not explicit. Such syntactic constructs are called *loops*, and they come in several variations. For example, there are `for`, `while`, and `repeat-until` loops.
These different loop varieties are all very similar, and their differences are
mostly small variations in syntax.

We shall focus on `while` loops. To use a `while` loop in ASL you must
install a teachpack that extends the language with the proper syntax. The
needed files may be found at:

> https://github.com/morazanm/while-loops-for-Animated-Programming

To install the package, go to the `File` menu in `DrRacket` and click on `Package`
`Manager....` For `Package Source`, type the above url followed by `.git` as
follows:

> https://github.com/morazanm/while-loops-for-Animated-Programming.git

Click on `Install`. When the package finishes installing, you may close the
package manager window. To write programs using `while` loops in ASL the
first line in your program must require the `while` teachpack as follows:

> `(require while)`

82.1 Syntax and Semantics

The syntax for a `while`-loop is:

> `(while expr`
>   `expr⁺)`

In parenthesis, we have the keyword `while` followed by an expression followed
by one or more expressions. The first expression is called the *loop driver* (or
simply the driver), and the set of expressions after it are called the *loop body*
(or simply the body).

The semantics of a `while` loop are fairly straightforward. The driver is
evaluated. If it evaluates to `#false`, the loop ends and returns `(void)`. If
the driver evaluates to `#true`, then the body is evaluated, and the process
is repeated. Presumably, the body of the loop mutates variables to make
progress toward termination. That is, the state variables are mutated to have
values that bring the computation closer to having the driver evaluate to
`#false`. If the body of the loop fails to make progress toward termination,
then you have an *infinite loop*. This is akin to an infinite recursion, and it
means that the `while` loop runs forever. An infinite loop is a common bug,
and it is the programmer's responsibility to make sure that any loop they
write terminates.

82.2 Transformation from an Imperative Recursive Function to a while Loop

If a tail-recursive function has been transformed into a recursive imperative function, like done for fact2-v2 in Fig. 66, then the transformation into a while loop is mostly a matter of rearranging expressions. The following steps are needed:

1. Initialize the state variables to achieve the invariant.
2. The conjunction (i.e., and-ing) of the negation of the conditions for non-recursive cases is the loop's driver.
3. The body of the loop is composed of the code in the recursive cases of the conditional.

To illustrate the process, let us refactor fact2-v3 from Fig. 67. The goal is to rewrite fact-state! to perform all the mutations. This gives us a starting point for the new program:

```
;; natnum → natnum
;; Purpose: Compute the factorial of the given natural number
(define (fact2-v4 n)
  (local [;; natnum
          ;; Purpose: The next possible accum factor
          (define k (void))

          ;; natnum
          ;; Purpose: The current approximation of n!
          (define accum (void))

          ;; natnum natnum → natnum
          ;; Purpose: Compute the factorial of the first
          ;;           given natural number
          ;; Effect: k is decremented and
          ;;           accum is multiplied by k
          (define (fact-state!)
            ...)
          ]
    (fact-state!)))

;; Tests using sample values for fact2-v4
(check-expect (fact2-v4 0)  1)
(check-expect (fact2-v4 5)  120)
(check-expect (fact2-v4 10) 3628800)
(check-expect (fact2-v4 2)  2)
(check-expect (fact2-v4 6)  720)
```

Observe that the body of the local-expression only contains a call to
fact-state!. This is consistent with the goal of having all mutations inside fact-state!. We proceed to develop the body of fact-state!.

In the program displayed in Fig. 67, the first action is to initialize the
state variables. Given that k and accum are in scope, this can be done in
fact-state!. This yields:

```
;; natnum natnum → natnum
;; Purpose: Compute the factorial of the first
;;              given natural number
;; Effect: k is decremented and
;;              accum is multiplied by k
(define (fact-state!)
  (begin
    (set! k n)
    (set! accum 1)
    ;; INV: accum = $\Pi_{i=k+1}^{n}$ i
  ...)
)
```

Just as with the code in Fig. 67, the invariant is achieved. This is important
because the while loop is expected to do the same work as the recursive
function. This means that if the invariant holds every time the recursive
function is called, then the invariant must hold every time the top of the
loop is reached. We have already demonstrated that with the initializations
above, the invariant holds.

The next step is to determine the loop's driver. The loop ought to execute
the same code as the recursive cases in Fig. 67. This means that taking the
negation of the conditions for the nonrecursive cases yields the loop's driver.
In this example, there is only one nonrecursive condition, and all that is
needed is to negate it:

```
;; natnum natnum → natnum
;; Purpose: Compute the factorial of the first
;;              given natural number
;; Effect: k is decremented and
;;              accum is multiplied by k
(define (fact-state!)
  (begin
    (set! k n)
    (set! accum 1)
    ;; INV: accum = $\Pi_{i=k+1}^{n}$ i
    (while (not (= k 0))
      ;; accum = $\Pi_{i=k+1}^{n}$ i $\wedge$ k $\neq$ 0
      ...))
  ...
)
```

If the invariant holds before evaluating the driver, then the invariant and the driver hold inside the loop. The next step is to perform the mutations in the else branch of `fact-state!` in Fig. 67. Given that the same mutations are performed, the invariant may be dragged through the mutations in the body of the `while` loop:

```
;; natnum natnum → natnum
;; Purpose: Compute the factorial of the first
;;              given natural number
;; Effect: k is decremented and
;;              accum is multiplied by k
(define (fact-state!)
  (begin
    (set! k n)
    (set! accum 1)
    ;; INV: accum = Π_{i=k+1}^{n} i
    (while (not (= k 0))
      ;; accum = Π_{i=k+1}^{n} i ∧ k ≠ 0
      (set! accum (* k accum))
      ;; accum = Π_{i=k}^{n} i ∧ k ≠ 0
      (set! k (sub1 k))
      ;; accum = Π_{i=k+1}^{n} i))
    ...
  )
```

Observe that the invariant temporarily does not hold in the middle of the loop but at the end the mutations restore the invariant and make progress toward termination.

The final step is to determine the needed code after the loop. This code corresponds to the code for the nonrecursive cases in Fig. 67. There is only one such case, and it returns `accum`. The same is done after the loop:

```
;; natnum natnum → natnum
;; Purpose: Compute the factorial of the first
;;              given natural number
;; Effect: k is decremented and
;;              accum is multiplied by k
(define (fact-state!)
  (begin
    (set! k n)
    (set! accum 1)
    ;; INV: accum = Π_{i=k+1}^{n} i
    (while (not (= k 0))
      ;; accum = Π_{i=k+1}^{n} i ∧ k ≠ 0
      (set! accum (* k accum))
      ;; accum = Π_{i=k}^{n} i ∧ k ≠ 0
      (set! k (sub1 k))
      ;; accum = Π_{i=k+1}^{n} i)
```

```
;; accum = $\Pi_{i=k+1}^{n}$ i $\wedge$ k = 0
;; $\Rightarrow$ accum = $\Pi_{i=1}^{n}$ i
;; $\Rightarrow$ accum = n!
accum))
;; Termination argument:
;; k is a natural number that is decremented with each
;; time through the loop. Eventually, k becomes 0 and
;; the loop stops.
```

Observe that the same proof is used to document what accum's value is after the loop. The termination argument is included at the end of the mutator to establish total correctness and to keep all of the function's documentation together. It should now be clear that writing a while loop requires the same expressions as writing a recursive imperative function. The difference is that with a while loop the programmer is also responsible for correctly sequencing the mutations.

Observe that fact2-v4 does not call itself. Instead, the while loop implements the recursion. This means that we may inline fact2-v4's body into the local-expression's body and eliminate its definition. The result is displayed Fig. 68. Many professionals in Computer Science may try to tell you that fact2-v4 in Fig. 68 is not recursive but now you know better. A while loop is recursion in disguise.

6 Design and implement an imperative program using a while-loop to sum the elements of a list of numbers. Prove total correctness.

7 Design and implement an imperative program using a while-loop to reverse a (listof X). Prove total correctness.

8 Design and implement an imperative program using a while-loop to compute the lengths of the strings in a (listof String). Prove total correctness.

9 Design and implement an imperative program using a while-loop to fold a list from right to left. Prove total correctness.

10 Design and implement an imperative program using a while-loop to add all the integer elements in, [low..high], a given interval. Prove total correctness.

Fig. 68 An imperative recursive function using a while loop for n!

```
(require while)

;; natnum → natnum
;; Purpose: Compute the factorial of the given natural number
(define (fact2-v4 n)
  (local [;; natnum
          ;; Purpose: The next possible accum factor
          (define k (void))

          ;; natnum
          ;; Purpose: The current approximation of n!
          (define accum (void))]
    (begin
      (set! k n)
      (set! accum 1)
      ;; INV: accum = $\Pi_{i=k+1}^{n}$ i
      (while (not (= k 0))
        ;; accum = $\Pi_{i=k+1}^{n}$ i $\land$ k $\neq$ 0
        (set! accum (* k accum))
        ;; accum = $\Pi_{i=k}^{n}$ i $\land$ k $\neq$ 0
        (set! k (sub1 k))
        ;; accum = $\Pi_{i=k+1}^{n}$ i
      )
      ;; accum = $\Pi_{i=k+1}^{n}$ i $\land$ k = 0
      ;; $\Rightarrow$ accum = $\Pi_{i=1}^{n}$ i
      ;; $\Rightarrow$ accum = n!
      accum)
    ;; Termination argument:
    ;; k is a natural number that is decremented with each loop
    ;; iteration. Eventually, k becomes 0 and the loop stops.
    ))

;; Tests using sample values for fact2-v4
(check-expect (fact2-v4 0)  1)
(check-expect (fact2-v4 5)  120)
(check-expect (fact2-v4 10) 3628800)
(check-expect (fact2-v4 2)  2)
(check-expect (fact2-v4 6)  720)
```

83 A Design Recipe for while loops

Although while loops are recursion in disguise, it is likely that you will be
required to program and maintain code involving while loops. This is not
completely senseless – yet – given that many programming languages do not
optimize tail calls. That is, they allocate new memory for each recursive call
instead of mutating variables as suggested at the beginning of this chapter.
This may make programs slower. When the implementation of a programming

Fig. 69 The design recipe for `while`-loop-based functions

1. Problem Analysis

    a. Outline how the problem is solved
    b. Pick a mutable data representation

2. Write the signature, the purpose, effect, and how statements, and the function header
3. Write Tests
4. Develop the Loop Invariant
5. Begin writing the function's body. It must contains a `local`-expression that:

    a. Locally declares the state variables as (`void`)
    b. Defines the type and purpose for each state variable
    c. Defines headers for helper functions

6. Write the `local`-expression's body using a `begin`-expression that:

    a. Initializes the state variables to achieve the invariant
    b. Defines the while loop
        i. Define the driver and write the loop header
        ii. Use the invariant to correctly sequence mutations
        iii. Make progress towards termination

7. Design the Post-Loop Code

    a. Use the negation of the driver and the invariant to determine the value, if any, to return

8. Design the Auxiliary Functions
9. Develop a Termination Argument
10. Run Tests

---

language does not optimize tail calls, it may make sense to program using `while loops`.

To help with the development of `while loops` the design recipe displayed in Fig. 69 has been developed. This design recipe aims to help you to directly develop `while`-loop-based functions without going through the transformations discussed in the previous sections.[20] Every step in the `while loop` design recipe has a specific result that helps in program development.

The first step asks you to perform problem analysis to decide on the data representation to use and on how to solve the problem. If you can outline how the problem may be solved by repeatedly mutating a finite number of variables, then you may consider using a `while loop`. A useful way to determine this is to successfully trace an example using a table or picture containing the values of the state variables at each step. Some of these state variables will be accumulators, each requiring an accumulator invariant, and others may be the state variables around which the algorithm is designed (e.g., a natural number or a list) from which you can derive the halting condition.

---

[20] You always have the option to do so if you find it easier.

The second step asks you to write the signature, purpose and effect statements, and function header. In addition, if the solution is based on a generative recursion design, then include a how statement. The third step has you write tests to illustrate the behavior of the function. Remember that the tests must illustrate the effects, if any, of the function.

The fourth step asks you to develop the loop invariant. This is usually the hardest step. The invariant must establish the relationship between variables and the values each contains. If a state variable is an accumulator, then the accumulator invariant is part of the loop invariant. The invariant must include all the state variables mutated in the loop. To determine if you have a correct invariant, it helps to clearly state, P, the loop's postcondition and, S, the negation of the driver. If P and S are identified, then the following implication must hold:

$$\text{Loop Invariant} \wedge S \Rightarrow P$$

In other words, if the loop invariant and the negation of the driver are true, then you ought to be able to argue that the loop's postcondition is true. If you can do this, then you have, at the very least, a good approximation of the loop's invariant. Be patient with yourself when it comes to developing loop invariants. It requires the development of insights and a lot of practice.

The fifth step asks you start writing the function's body that contains a `local`-expression. The local declarations must capture the state variables. For each state variable, its type and purpose must be identified. In addition, write signatures, purpose/how/effect statements, and headers for helper functions. Each helper function is independently designed and implemented later. The design of the current function assumes that the local helper functions satisfy their signature and their purpose. Remember that a primary goal is to encapsulate everything that is needed.

For Step 6, finish writing the function's `local`-expression using a `begin`-expression in its body where mutations are performed and the `while`-loop is defined. The first steps in the `begin`-expression initialize the state variables to achieve the invariant. After initialization, a `while` loop is defined. This step is started by writing the loop header with its driver. The body of the loop is designed by dragging the invariant through the proposed mutations. This means that inside the loop's body, the invariant becomes temporarily false and must be restored before the body's end. In addition, make sure the mutations make progress toward termination. That is, one or more mutations must bring the computation one step closer to making the driver false.

Step 7 asks you to design and implement the code needed after the loop. This code must finish any necessary mutations and determine the correct value, if any, to return. Determine the value that must be returned, if any, using the invariant and the negation of the driver. Step 8 asks you to design and implement, if any, the auxiliary functions. These are designed using the appropriate design recipe.

Fig. 70 A template to design functions using `while` loops

```
; ... → ...
; Purpose:
; Effect:
(define (f-while ...)
  (local [; <type>
          ; Purpose:
          (define state-var1 (void))
            ...
          ; <type>
          ; Purpose:
          (define state-varN (void))
          <helper functions>]
    (begin
      (set! state-var1 ...)
      (set! state-varN ...)
      ; <Invariant>
      (while <driver>
        <while-body>)
      ; <Invariant> and (not <driver>)
      <return value code>))
    ; <Termination argument>
  )

(check-expect (f-while ...) ...)
  ...
(check-expect (f-while ...) ...)
```

Step 9 asks you to develop a termination argument and Step 10 asks you to run the tests. If any tests fail, then recheck your work. Tests can fail for two reasons. The first is that there is a bug in the design/code. To remedy this bug, check the results of each step of the design recipe, and make sure they have been correctly performed. The second is that a test has been incorrectly written. In this case, rewrite the test.

The steps of the design recipe suggest the function template displayed in Fig. 70. You may use this template as you develop answers for the steps of the design recipe. Specialize the template with the answer for each step as you advance. Always remember that following the steps of the design recipe communicates to others how the problem is solved.

84 Determining if an Interval Contains a Prime

Consider writing a predicate to determine if a given interval contains a prime number using a `while`-loop. We shall follow the steps of the design recipe to solve this problem.

84.1 Problem Analysis

To determine if an interval, `[low..high]`, contains a prime number, it may be traversed from `low` to `high`. As the interval is traversed, determine if the low element is a prime number. Determining if a given integer is a prime is a different problem and, therefore, delegated to an auxiliary predicate.

Two state variables may be used. The first, `l`, represents the next interval element for which it must be determined if it is a prime number. The second, `found`, is a Boolean accumulator that is true if there is a prime number in the traversed part of the given interval. The initial value of `l` is `low`, and the initial value of `found` is `#false` (given that a prime number has not been found). Each loop iteration mutates `found` to be the or-ing of testing if `l` is prime and `found` and mutates `l` to be `l+1`. The loop terminates when the interval `[l..high]` is empty.

84.2 Signature, Statements, and Function Header

The input is the interval to traverse and the output is a Boolean. The purpose is to determine if the given interval contains a prime. The predicate does not mutate any state variables defined outside of it, and, therefore, an effect statement is not needed. Finally, we assume that the given interval is not empty. This assumption removes the need to reason about every possible empty interval. The result of this step of the design recipe is:

```
;; [integer integer] → Boolean
;; Purpose: Determine if the given interval contains a prime
;; Assumption: The given interval is not empty
(define (contains-prime? low high)
```

84.3 Tests

The tests illustrate that the predicate works for intervals with different characteristics: empty, all positive numbers, all negative numbers, both positive and negative numbers, and varying lengths. In addition, tests are written for both possible outcomes. The result of this step of the design recipe is:

```
;; Tests for contains-prime?
(check-expect (contains-prime? 3 2)    #false)
(check-expect (contains-prime? 44 46) #false)
(check-expect (contains-prime? -9 -4) #false)
(check-expect (contains-prime? -5 5)   #true)
(check-expect (contains-prime? 19 19) #true)
```

84.4 Loop Invariant

To formulate the loop invariant, we start by writing the loop's postcondition. Based on the design so far, we need `found = #true` to mean that the given interval contains a prime and `found = #false` to mean that the given interval does contain a prime. We may write the postcondition as follows:

```
found ⇒ prime in [low..high] ∧
(not found) ⇒ no prime in [low..high]
```

Next we write the driver of the loop. The loop must iterate while [1..high] is not empty. This means the driver may be written as:

```
(>= high 1)
```

Recall that after the loop, the following implication must hold:

```
Loop Invariant ∧ (not driver) ⇒ Postcondition
```

Concretely, this means that we need a loop invariant that satisfies the following implication:

```
Loop Invariant ∧ (not (>= high 1))
⇒
found ⇒ prime in [low..high] ∧
(not found) ⇒ no prime in [low..high]
```

The loop's postcondition hints at some of the components the loop invariant needs. To start, two implications are needed. The implications in the postcondition refer to the entire interval (i.e., after it has been traversed). While the interval is being traversed, there is no way to know if the postcondition holds. We can, however, refer to the traversed part of the interval, instead of the entire interval, in the loop invariant. In this manner, components of the invariant are similar to the postcondition. The interval traversed each time the top of the loop is reached (i.e., before evaluating the driver) is [low..1-1]. This means that the loop invariant must contain:

```
found ⇒ prime in [low..1-1] ∧
(not found) ⇒ no prime in [low..1-1]
```

Ask yourself if the above is strong enough to be the loop invariant. By strong enough, we mean that the invariant and the negation of the driver imply the postcondition:

```
found ⇒ prime in [low..1-1] ∧
(not found) ⇒ no prime in [low..1-1] ∧ (1 > high)
⇒
found ⇒ prime in [low..high] ∧
(not found) ⇒ no prime in [low..high]
```

Observe that the antecedent does not contain enough information to conclude that 1-1 = high and, therefore, we cannot prove the consequent. This means that the invariant is not strong enough and must be improved. The negation of the driver informs us that (1 > high). What else do we need to conclude that 1-1 = high? The missing piece is 1 <= high+1. This must also be invariant as the loop executes. We may update the invariant to be:

```
1 ≤ high+1 ∧ found ⇒ prime in [low..1-1] ∧
(not found) ⇒ no prime in [low..1-1]
```

Observe that now the consequent can be proved:

```
INV ∧ (not driver) ⇒ postcondition

1 ≤ high+1 ∧ found ⇒ prime in [low..1-1] ∧
(not found) ⇒ no prime in [low..1-1] ∧ (1 > high)
⇒ 1 = high+1
⇒ found ⇒ prime in [low..high] ∧
    (not found) ⇒ no prime in [low..high]
```

In essence, the proof above is stating that we may conclude that 1 equals high+1, and by plugging in 1's value into the implications in the invariant, we obtain the postcondition.

84.5 Function Body

To start writing the function's body, a local-expression that declares the local state variables and contains the headers for auxiliary functions is needed. According to our problem analysis, two state variables are needed for the next integer to test if it is a prime and for a Boolean accumulator to indicate if a prime has been found. In addition, we write the header of the auxiliary predicate to determine if a given integer is a prime. This auxiliary predicate takes as input an integer and returns a Boolean. The result for this step of the design recipe is:

```
(local [;; integer
        ;; Purpose: Next integer to test
        (define 1 (void))

        ;; Boolean
        ;; Purpose: Indicate if a prime is found
        (define found (void))

        ;; integer → Boolean
        ;; Purpose: Determine if given integer is a prime
        (define (prime? n) ...)]
  ...)
```

84.6 The begin Expression

The body of the local-expression must be a begin-expression that first initializes the state variables. The values of the state variables are initialized to achieve the invariant. According to our problem analysis, the variables are initialized as follows:

```
(begin
(set! l low)
(set! found #false)
;; INV: l ≤ high+1 ∧ found ⇒ prime in [low..l-1] ∧
;;         (not found) ⇒ no prime in [low..l-1]
...)
```

Is the invariant achieved? Plug in the values of the state variables into the invariant to determine this:

```
;; INV: l ≤ high+1 ∧ found ⇒ prime in [low..l-1] ∧
;;         (not found) ⇒ no prime in [low..l-1]

;; INV: low ≤ high+1 ∧ #false ⇒ prime in [low..low-1] ∧
;;         (not #false) ⇒ no prime in [low..low-1]
```

Let us carefully outline why the invariant holds. Recall the assumption that the interval is not empty. This means that low ≤ high which implies l < high+1. The first implication is true because the antecedent is false. For the second implication, the antecedent is true. We must show that the consequent is true. Observe that the interval [low..low-1] is empty. There are no primes in the empty interval, and, therefore, the second implication is true. Given that all three parts of the conjunction are true, we have established that the invariant is achieved.

Given that the invariant is achieved, we may now begin to write the while-loop. We use the driver developed for the invariant definition step.

```
(begin
(set! l low)
(set! found #false)
;; INV: l ≤ high+1 ∧ found ⇒ prime in [low..l-1] ∧
;;         (not found) ⇒ no prime in [low..l-1]
(while (>= high l)
        ;; l <= high ∧ found ==> prime in [low..l-1] ∧
        ;; (not found) ==> no prime in [low..l-1]
        ...)
...)
```

Observe that if the driver is true, then l is strictly less than high+1. This is reflected in the first assertion written inside the while-loop. The next step is to perform the first mutation inside the loop. The new value of found depends on 1 (the program must determine if 1 is prime). The new value of 1 does not depend on anything but the value of 1. This suggests mutating found first. This yields:

```
(begin
 (set! l low)
 (set! found #false)
 ;; INV: l ≤ high+1 ∧ found ⇒ prime in [low..l-1] ∧
 ;;          (not found) ⇒ no prime in [low..l-1]
 (while (>= high l)
         ;; l <= high ∧ found ==> prime in [low..l-1] ∧
         ;; (not found) ==> no prime in [low..l-1]
         (set! found (or (prime? l) found))
         ;; l <= high ∧ found ==> prime in [low..l] ∧
         ;; (not found) ==> no prime in [low..l]
         ...)
 ...)
```

Before the mutation, the interval traversed and tested is [low..l-1]. By testing if 1 is prime, the traversed and tested interval is expanded to be [low..l]. Therefore, the assertion after the mutation is written in terms of 1 and not l-1. We must now establish that the assertion holds. The mutation does not change the value of 1 nor high, and, therefore, we have that 1 ≤ high holds. Before the mutation, we know that if found is true, then there is a prime in [low..l-1]. Otherwise, no such prime exists. After the mutation, found may be #true or #false. If found is #true, it means that either 1 is prime or there is a prime in [low.l-1]. Either way, the first implication in the assertion after the mutation holds, and the second implication also holds (given that the antecedent is false). If found is #false, it means that 1 is not prime and that there is no prime in [low.l-1]. This means that the first implication in the assertion after the mutation holds (because the antecedent is false) and the second implication holds because the consequent is true.

The remaining mutation is for 1. As per our problem analysis, 1 is mutated to be l+1. This means that after the mutation, 1 may be as large as high+1. Note that the new value of 1 has not been tested and, therefore, the traversed and tested interval is now [0..l-1]. The assertion after the mutation is written using these updated observations:

```
(begin
 (set! l low)
 (set! found #false)
 ;; INV: l ≤ high+1 ∧ found ⇒ prime in [low..l-1] ∧
 ;;          (not found) ⇒ no prime in [low..l-1]
 (while (>= high l)
         ;; l <= high ∧ found ==> prime in [low..l-1] ∧
         ;; (not found) ==> no prime in [low..l-1]
         (set! found (or (prime? l) found))
```

```
;; 1 <= high ∧ found ==> prime in [low..1] ∧
;; (not found) ==> no prime in [low..1]
(set! 1 (add1 1))
;; 1 <= high+1 ∧ found ==> prime in [low..1-1] ∧
;; (not found) ==> no prime in [low..1-1]
)
...)
```

The two implications hold because they refer to the same set of interval values referred to in the implications of the assertion before the second mutation. To visualize this, observe that before the second mutation, the implications hold for [low..1]. Let us assume that 1 = k. After mutating 1, we have no way of knowing if the implications hold for, k+1, the new value of 1. We can only guarantee that the implications hold for the interval [low..k] = [low..1-1].

84.7 Post-Loop Code

During invariant development, we proved that the loop's postcondition is achieved if the loop maintains the invariant. We have developed the code that does so. This means that if found is true, then there is a prime in the given interval. Otherwise, there is not. Either way, done is the value that informs us if there is a prime or not in the given interval. After the loop, this is the value that needs to be returned. The post-loop code is:

```
found
```

84.8 Auxiliary Functions

The next step is to design the auxiliary functions one at a time. For this problem, there is only one auxiliary predicate needed. In Sect. 22, a predicate, prime?, to determine if a given natural number is prime is developed and is displayed as part of the code in Fig. 28. Observe that prime? also works for an arbitrary integer. Therefore, we may use the same code with the signature and purpose written in Sect. 84.5.

84.9 Termination Argument

The state variable l starts at low. Each loop iteration increases l by 1. Eventually, [l..high] becomes empty when l = high + 1 and the loop terminates.

84.10 Run Tests

Run the tests and make sure they all pass. The complete program is displayed in Fig. 71.

> **11** The predicate contains-prime? always traverses the entire given interval. Refactor contains-prime? to stop the traversal when a prime is found.

85 Finding the Maximum in a List of Numbers

Consider writing a function to find the maximum in a lon using a while-loop. We shall follow the steps of the design recipe to solve this problem.

85.1 Problem Analysis

If the given list is empty, throw an error because an empty list does not have a maximum. Otherwise, traverse the given list, and use an accumulator to remember the maximum so far. Two state variables are used. The first represents the unprocessed part of the list, and the second is an accumulator to track the maximum so far (i.e., the maximum in the processed part of the given list). The unprocessed part of the list may be initialized to the given list, and the accumulator may be initialized to negative infinity. After traversing the list, the accumulator is returned.

To test the function, the following sample lons are defined:

```
(define L0 '())
(define L1 '(1 2 3 4 5 6))
(define L2 '(5 4 3 2 1 0 -1))
(define L3 '(9 0 -22 54 10 -89))
```

Fig. 71 The program to determine if a given interval contains a prime

```
;; [integer integer] → Boolean
;; Purpose: Determine if the given interval contains a prime
;; Assumption: The given interval is not empty
(define (contains-prime? low high)
  (local [;; integer      Purpose: Next integer to test
          (define l (void))
          ;; Boolean      Purpose: Indicate if a prime is found
          (define found (void))
          ;; integer → Boolean Purpose: Determine if given integer prime
          (define (prime? n)
            (local [;; [int int] → Boolean
                    ;; Purpose: Determine if n is divisible by any number
                    ;;          in the given interval
                    (define (any-divide? low high)
                      (if (< high low) #false
                          (or (= (remainder n high) 0)
                              (any-divide? low (sub1 high)))))]
              (if (< n 2) #false
                  (not (any-divide? 2 (quotient n 2))))))]
    (begin
      (set! l low)
      (set! found #false)
      ;; INV: l <= high+1 ∧ found ⇒ prime in [low..l-1] ∧
      ;;      (not found) ⇒ no prime in [low..l-1]
      (while (>= high l)
             ;; l <= high ∧ found ⇒ prime in [low..l-1] ∧
             ;; (not found) ⇒ no prime in [low..l-1]
             (set! found (or (prime? l) found))
             ;; l <= high ∧ found ⇒ prime in [low..l] ∧
             ;; (not found) ⇒ no prime in [low..l]
             (set! l (add1 l))
             ;; l <= high+1 ∧ found ⇒ prime in [low..l-1] ∧
             ;; (not found) ⇒ no prime in [low..l-1]
             )
      ;; l <= high+1 ∧ (l > high) ∧ found ⇒ prime in [low..l-1] ∧
      ;; (not found) ⇒ no prime in [low..l-1]
      ;; ⇒ l = high+1 ⇒ found ⇒ prime in [low..high] ∧
      ;;                  (not found) ⇒ no prime in [low..high]
      found)
   ;; Termination Argument: l starts at low. Each loop iteration increases
   ;; l by 1. Eventually, [l..high] becomes empty and the loop terminates
     ))
;; Tests for contains-prime?
(check-expect (contains-prime? 3 2)   #false)
(check-expect (contains-prime? 44 46) #false)
(check-expect (contains-prime? -9 -4) #false)
(check-expect (contains-prime? -5 5)  #true)
(check-expect (contains-prime? 19 19) #true)
```

85.2 Signature, Statements, and Function Header

The function takes an input a `lon` and returns a number or throws an error. Its purpose is to find the maximum number in the given `lon` and does not mutate any defined free variables outside of it. This yields the following answer for this step of the design recipe:

```
;; lon → number throws error
;; Purpose: Return the maximum of the given list
(define (max-lon L)
```

85.3 Tests

The tests illustrate that the correct error is thrown and that the correct value is returned using the sample `lon`s. The tests are written as follows:

```
;; Tests for max-lon
(check-error
  (max-lon L0)
    "The empty list does not have a maximum element.")
(check-expect (max-lon L1) 6)
(check-expect (max-lon L2) 5)
(check-expect (max-lon L3) 54)
```

85.4 Loop Invariant

Recall that to formulate the loop invariant, we start by writing the loop's postconditions and the negation of the driver to prove that:

```
loop invariant ∧ (not driver) ⇒ postcondition
```

According our problem analysis, the input, L, is a list of numbers, and two state variables are needed: one for the unprocessed part of the given list and one for the maximum value found so far. We shall call these state variables `ul` and `max`. The loop ought to stop when `ul` is empty. This suggests the following driver for the loop:

```
(not (empty? ul))
```

After the loop, `max` ought to equal the maximum of L. We may denote this postcondition as follows:

```
max = maximum(L)
```

Finally, we shall denote the processed part of the list as:

    (L - ul)

Let us trace an example to obtain insights into what needs to be true every time at the top of the loop (i.e., when the driver is evaluated). Consider finding the maximum in L = '(8 -5 47 8 -1). The following table traces the values of ul and max:

ul	max
'(8 -5 47 8 -1)	-inf.0
'(-5 47 8 -1)	8
'(47 8 -1)	8
'(8 -1)	47
'(-1)	47
'()	47

As per the problem analysis, ul and max are initialized, respectively, to L and negative infinity. At each step, ul is mutated to be the rest of ul, and max is mutated to be ul's first number if ul's first number is greater than max.

Ask yourself what is true about the relationship between the variables for every row in the table above to reveal the loop invariant. Use the implication above to assist you. We can observe that ul must always be the tail of L. We can capture this observation as follows:

    L = (append (L - ul) ul)

In English, this is stating that L is equal to appending the processed and unprocessed parts of L. According to our design idea, max is the maximum of the processed part of the list. We can capture this as follows:

    max = maximum(L-ul)

This suggest the following invariant:

    L = (append (L - ul) ul) ∧ max = maximum(L-ul)

Observe that the invariant specifies the relationship between the variables. Furthermore, the suggested invariant holds for every row of the trace table above.

The question is whether or not the invariant is strong enough to imply the postcondition. For this, we plug the invariant and the negation of the driver into the implication above:

    L = (append (L - ul) ul) ∧ max = maximum(L-ul) ∧ (empty? ul)
    ⇒
    max = maximum(L)

Given that ul is empty, we may simplify to:

    L = L ∧ max = maximum(L) ∧ (empty? ul) ⇒ max = maximum(L)

To prove that the implication holds, we assume that the antecedent is true and must show that the consequent is true. If we assume the antecedent, then we are assuming that `max = maximum(L)` which means, of course, that the consequence holds. This suggests that the proposed invariant is strong enough for us to conclude the postcondition holds. Our code, therefore, must achieve the invariant and maintain the invariant after an arbitrary number of loop iterations.

85.5 Function Body

The function body must first determine if the list is empty or not. If it is empty, an error is thrown with an informative message. Otherwise, a `local`-expression defines the state variables. For this problem, no auxiliary functions are needed. We, thus, start the function's body as follows:

```
(if (empty? L)
    (error "The empty list does not have a maximum element.")
    (local [;; lon
            ;; Purpose: Unprocessed part of L
            (define ul (void))

            ;; number
            ;; Purpose: The maximum in the processed part of L
            (define max (void))]
      ...))
```

Observe that the signature and the purpose for each state variable are clearly stated.

85.6 The `begin` Expression

The `begin`-expression in the body of the `local`-expression must first initialize the state variables to achieve the invariant. Based on the design so far, we can start the code as follows:

```
(begin
    (set! ul L)
    (set! max -inf.0)
    ;; INV: L = (append (L - ul) ul) ∧ max = maximum(L-ul)
    (while (not (empty? ul))
            ;; L = (append (L - ul) ul) ∧ max = maximum(L-ul)
            ...)
    ...)
```

Observe that the first part of the invariant holds. We can prove it by plugging in the ul's value:

```
L = (append (L - ul) ul)
L = (append (L - L) L)
L = (append '() L)
L = L
```

For the second part of the invariant, we need to define a value for the maximum of an empty lon. This must be a value that makes sense when none of the list has been processed. We may define such a value to be negative infinity because it is smaller than any list element. With this definition, the second part of the invariant holds:

```
    max = maximum(L-ul)
-infty.0 = maximum(L-L)
-infty.0 = maximum('())
-infty.0 = -infty.0
```

We have proven that the invariant holds with the initial values of the variables. We may now proceed to design the body of the while-loop. The body of the while-loop must decide if max is or is not updated. This is achieved by comparing ul's first element with max:

```
(if (> (first ul) max)
    ...
    ...)
```

Independently reason about each branch of the conditional. We start with the then branch. If the then branch is evaluated, it means that the condition and the invariant are both true and that both state variables must be mutated. For this, a begin-expression is needed, and we may write an assertion that holds before the mutations:

```
(if (> (first ul) max)
    (begin
       ;; L = (append (L - ul) ul) ∧ max = maximum(L - ul) ∧
       ;; (> (first ul) max)
       ...)
    ...)
```

A decision must be made on the order to perform the mutations. We can observe from the trace table developed for the loop invariant that the new value of max depends on ul and that the new value of ul does not depend on any other value. This suggests mutating max first:

```
(if (> (first ul) max)
    (begin
       ;; L = (append (L - ul) ul) ∧ max = maximum(L - ul) ∧
       ;; (> (first ul) max)
```

```
    (set! max (first ul))
    ;; L = (append (L - ul) ul) ∧
    ;; max = maximum(L - (rest ul))
    ...)
...)
```

After mutating `max`, the first element of `ul` has been processed. Neither the value of L nor `ul` is changed by the mutation. Therefore, the first part of the invariant still holds after the mutation. The other state variable, `max`, is more than just the maximum of processed part of the list. It is now the maximum of the processed part of the list and the first element of the unprocessed part of the list. This is reflected in the written assertion after the loop.

The next step is to mutate, `ul`, the remaining state variable:

```
(if (> (first ul) max)
    (begin
        ;; L = (append (L - ul) ul) ∧ max = maximum(L - ul) ∧
        ;; (> (first ul) max)
        (set! max (first ul))
        ;; L = (append (L - ul) ul) ∧
        ;; max = maximum(L-(rest ul))
        (set! ul (rest ul))
        ;; L = (append (L - ul) ul) ∧ max = maximum(L - ul)
    )
    ...)
```

The mutation removes `ul`'s first number from the unprocessed part of the given list and makes progress toward termination. Thus, we now have that `ul` is once again the maximum of the processed part of the given list. Further observe that the first part of the invariant also holds because the mutation makes the unprocessed tail of the given list shorter. Finally, observe that the invariant is restored and the loop may iterate again.

For the else branch, we know that `(<= (first ul) max)`. Therefore, `max` does not have to be mutated. We must still mutate `ul` to make progress toward termination. These observations lead to:

```
(if (> (first ul) max)
    (begin
        ;; L = (append (L - ul) ul) ∧ max = maximum(L-ul) ∧
        ;; (> (first ul) max)
        (set! max (first ul))
        ;; L = (append (L - ul) ul) ∧
        ;; max = maximum(L-(rest ul))
        (set! ul (rest ul))
        ;; L = (append (L - ul) ul) ∧ max = maximum(L-ul)
    )
    ;; else
```

```
;; L = (append (L - ul) ul) ∧ max = maximum(L-ul) ∧
;; (<= (first ul) max)
(set! ul (rest ul))
;; L = (append (L - ul) ul) ∧ max = maximum(L-ul)
)
```

Observe that the invariant holds after the mutation. We have that ul is still the unprocessed part of the given list and that max is the maximum of the processed part of the list including the number removed from the unprocessed part of the list by the mutation.

Regardless of the branch executed when the loop's body is evaluated, the invariant holds. Therefore, it is safe for the loop to iterate.

85.7 Post-Loop Code

As part of developing the invariant, we proved that loop's postcondition. That is, max = maximum(L). Thus, the only task that must be performed is to return max. The only expression after the loop (and the last expression of the begin-expression) is:

```
max
```

By returning max, the signature and purpose of the function are satisfied.

85.8 Termination Argument

Before the loop, ul is initialized to an nonempty lon. Each time the loop is executed, the length of ul is decreased by 1. Eventually, ul becomes empty and the loop terminates.

85.9 Run Tests

Run the tests. They should all pass. The complete program is displayed in Fig. 72.

> **12** Design and implement a function that uses a while-loop to find the minimum of a list of numbers.

> **13** Design and implement a function that uses a while-loop to find the length of a (listof X).

Fig. 72 An imperative program to find the maximum of a list of numbers

```
(require while)
(define L0 '())                    (define L1 '(1 2 3 4 5 6))
(define L2 '(5 4 3 2 1 0 -1)) (define L3 '(9 0 -22 54 10 -89))
;; lon → number throws error
;; Purpose: Return the maximum of the given list
(define (max-lon L)
  (if (empty? L)
      (error "The empty list does not have a maximum element.")
      (local
        [;; lon          Purpose: Unprocessed part of L
          (define ul (void))
          ;; number       Purpose: The maximum in the processed part of L
          (define max (void))]
        (begin
          (set! ul L)
          (set! max -inf.0)
          ;; INV: L = (append (L - ul) ul) ∧ max = maximum(L-ul)
          (while (not (empty? ul))
                 ;; L = (append (L - ul) ul) ∧ max = maximum(L-ul)
                 (if (> (first ul) max)
                     (begin
                       ;; L = (append (L - ul) ul) ∧ max = maximum(L-ul) ∧
                       ;; (> (first ul) max)
                       (set! max (first ul))
                       ;; L = (append (L - ul) ul) ∧
                       ;; max = maximum(L-(rest ul))
                       (set! ul (rest ul))
                       ;; L = (append (L - ul) ul) ∧ max = maximum(L-ul)
                       )
                     ;; else
                     ;; L = (append (L - ul) ul) ∧ max = maximum(L-ul) ∧
                     ;; (<= (first ul) max)
                     (set! ul (rest ul))
                     ;; L = (append (L - ul) ul) ∧ max = maximum(L-ul)
                 ))
          ;; L = (append (L - ul) ul) ∧ max = maximum(L-ul) ∧ (empty? ul)
          ;; ⇒ max = maximum(L)
          max
          ;; Termination Argument
          ;; ul starts as a nonempty lon. Each loop iteration decrements
          ;; ul's length by 1. Eventually, ul becomes empty and
          ;; the loop terminates.
          ))))
;; Tests for max-lon
(check-error   (max-lon L0)
               "The empty list does not have a maximum element.")
(check-expect (max-lon L1) 6)
(check-expect (max-lon L2) 5)
(check-expect (max-lon L3) 54)
```

14 Design and implement a function that uses a `while`-loop to return all the prime numbers less than or equal to a given natural number.

15 Design and implement a function that uses a `while`-loop to compute n^2 by adding the first n odd numbers.

16 Design and implement a function that uses a `while`-loop to add two natural numbers using repetitive addition. Repetitive addition is mathematically defined as follows:

$$\text{plus}(a,b) = \begin{cases} b & \text{if } a = 0 \\ \text{plus}(a-1, \ b+1) & \text{otherwise} \end{cases}$$

86 What Have We Learned in This Chapter?

The important lessons of this chapter are summarized as follows:

- The parameters of tail-recursive functions may be substituted with state variables.
- A programmer must determine the correct sequencing of mutations.
- Exhaustively writing all possible mutation orderings to determine the correct mutation sequence is unfeasible for even modestly sized programs.
- Hoare logic is a formal system to rigorously reason about and develop imperative programs.
- A Hoare triple consists of two assertions, a precondition and a postcondition, and a mutation or a call to a mutator.
- In a Hoare triple, the precondition states what is true about the state variables before the mutation(s), and the postcondition states what is true about the state variables after the mutation(s).
- Logical implication, $A \Rightarrow B$, states that if the antecedent, A, is true, then the consequent, B, is also true.
- Hoare logic may be used to correctly develop or to debug imperative programs.
- A `while`-loop is syntax to make recursive calls implicit.
- The syntax for a `while`-loop is:

```
(while expr
       expr⁺)
```

- A while-loop iterates until the driver is false.
- A loop invariant is an assertion that captures the relationship between variables every time the top of the loop is reached.
- Proving that an invariant always holds and the correct value is returned is called partial correctness.
- Proving partial correctness is difficult but more powerful than testing.
- A proof of total correctness establishes that the program terminates and returns the correct value.
- The following implication is useful in establishing partial/total correctness and in determining if the loop invariant is strong enough:

$$\texttt{loop invariant} \land \texttt{(not driver)} \Rightarrow \texttt{postcondition}$$

- Every while-loop requires a termination argument.

Chapter 16
Vectors

Accessing the nth element of a list takes time proportional to $O(n)$. This is the case because the first $n-1$ elements must be traversed to access the nth element. For instance, consider the expression used to access a fortune in Fig. 22:

```
(list-ref FORTUNES (random (length FORTUNES)))
```

Accessing a random fortune is an $O(n)$, where n is the length of FORTUNES, because in the worst case list-ref may have to traverse the entire list to access the last fortune. This is inefficient because once the server for the distributed fortune telling game from Sect. 18 is running, the number of fortunes is fixed. That is, the list FORTUNES does not grow or shrink. In essence, it is compound data of fixed, not arbitrary, size akin to a structure.

If this is the case, why not use a structure? Structures can be cumbersome. For instance, in the distributed fortune telling game developed in Sect. 18, FORTUNES has 23 fortunes. Do programmers want to write a structure with 23 fields and use 23 different observers (1 for each field) and 23 different mutators (again, 1 for each field)? It is more than likely that programmers would prefer not to have 23 different observers and 23 different mutators.

Most programming languages, including ASL, offer a built-in solution: *vectors* (a.k.a. arrays). A vector is compound data of fixed size that is allocated in consecutive memory locations. Given that a vector is allocated in consecutive memory locations, any element in the vector may be accessed in, $O(k)$, constant time. That is, vectors permit random access to any element. You may visualize a (vectorof X) of length 8 as follows:

X_0	X_1	X_2	X_3	X_4	X_5	X_6	X_7

The vector is allocated using eight consecutive memory positions. Each position stores an X instance. The positions are numbered [0..7] as indicated by the subscripts of the Xs. The valid indices into the vector are 0, 1, 2, 3,

© The Author(s), under exclusive license to Springer Nature Switzerland AG 2022   419
M. T. Morazán, *Animated Program Design*, Texts in Computer Science,
https://doi.org/10.1007/978-3-031-04317-8_16

4, 5 , 6, and 7. If an attempt is made to access the vector with an index
less than 0 or an index greater than 7, an error is thrown. Constant access
time is possible because all the values in the vector are accessible by adding
a constant to the address of the 0th vector position.

87 Vector Basics

The interface for vectors is:

(vector $X_0...X_{n-1}$):   Builds a size n vector with X_i in the ith position.

(build-vector n f):   Builds a size n vector by applying f to the natural numbers in [0..n-1] and placing (f i) in the ith vector position.
The signature for f is natnum $\rightarrow$ X.

(vector-length (vectorof X)):   Returns the given vector's length.

(vector-ref (vectorof X) natnum):   Returns the given vector's value
indicated by the given index. The given index must be a natural number
in [0..vl-1], where vl is the given vector's length. If the given index is
not in [0..vl-1], then an error is thrown. The ith element of a vector is
denoted V[i].

(vector? X):   A predicate to determine if the given X is a vector.

(vector-set! (vectorof X) natnum X):   Mutates the vector position
indicated by the given index to be the given X. The given index must be
in a natural number in [0..vl-1], where vl is the given vector's length.
If the given index is not in [0..vl-1], then an error is thrown.

Even though vectors may be accessed in any manner (even randomly),
they are usually processed using an interval of valid indices into the vector.
For a given vector V, an interval of valid indices is not arbitrary. All indices
into the vector must be in [0..(sub1 (vector-length V))]. That is, the
vector interval depends on the vector. This means that a *dependent type* is
needed to define a vector interval. A dependent type is a type whose definition
depends on a value. The definition of a vector interval for V, therefore, must
be a dependent type using V. We define a vector interval as follows:

> For a vector, V, of size N, a vector interval, VINTV1, is
> two integers, low $\geq$ 0 and -1 $\leq$ high $\leq$ N-1, such that it
> is either:
>   1. empty (i.e., low > high)
>   2. [[low..(sub1 high)]..high],
>   where   [low..(sub1 high)] is a VINTV1
> $\wedge$ low $\leq$ high

Fig. 73 The template for functions on a vector

```
;; Sample (vectorof X)
(define VECTOR0 ...)
         .
         .
         .
(define VECTORK ...)

;; f-on-vector: (vector X) ... → ...
;; Purpose:
(define (f-on-vector V ...)
  (local
    [;; f-on-VINTV1: [int int] ... → ...
     ;; Purpose: ...
     (define (f-on-VINTV1 low high ...)
       (if (> low high)
           ...
           ...(vector-ref V high)...(f-on-VINTV1 low (sub1 high))))

     ;; f-on-VINTV2: [int int] ... → ...
     ;; Purpose:
     (define (f-on-VINTV2 low high ...)
       (if (> low high)
           ...
           ...(vector-ref V low)...(f-on-VINTV2 (add1 low) high)))
     ...))

;; Tests using for f-on-vector
(check-expect (f-on-vector ... ...) ...)
         .
         .
         .
```

Observe that this data definition restricts a VINTV to only contain valid indices into the vector when it is not empty. That is, it depends on, N, the size of V. Further observe that the structure of a vector interval is exactly the same as the structure of an interval. There is, however, a difference when processing a VINTV. We are interested in processing vector elements instead of interval elements. This means that in the body of a function to process a VINTV, a vector must be referenced. The above data definition suggests processing a vector interval from high to low: process (vector-ref V high) and recursively process [low..(sub1 high)]. Like an interval, a vector interval may also be processed from low to high. This suggest that an alternative data definition for a vector interval is:

```
For a vector, V, of size N, a vector interval, VINTV2,
is two integers, high ≥ 0 and 0 ≤ low ≤ N+1,
such that it is either:
  1. empty  (i.e., low > high)
  2. [low..[(add1 low)..high]],
     where    [(add1 low)..high] is a VINTV2
              ∧ low ≤ high
```

This data definition suggests processing a vector interval from `low` to `high`: process (`vector-ref` V `low`) and recursively process [(`add1 low`)`..high`].

Put together, the two vector interval data definitions suggest the function template displayed in Fig. 73. The contract states that any function that processes a vector must at least take as input a vector with elements of any type (i.e., (`vectorof X`)). The body of the function is a `local`-expression. The template suggests that one or more local functions process a vector interval. The `local`-expression's body is an expression that depends on the problem being solved. It may be, for example, an expression that returns the value of processing a vector interval or an expression that combines several values obtained from processing one or more vectors.

1 The two vector interval definitions suggest always processing a vector element from the same end. The vector element processed is always indexed either by `low` vector or by `high`. Given that vectors are random access, there is no restriction that forces a programmer to always process the `low` vector element or the `high` vector element. Another possibility is to sometimes process the `high` vector element and sometimes process the `low` vector element. Write a dependent type data definition for a vector interval that takes this observation into account. Add an appropriate local definition template to the template for functions on a vector displayed in Fig. 73.

2 The two vector interval definitions developed include both `low` and `high`. Write vector interval definitions for (`low..high`], [`low..high`), and (`low..high`). For each, add an appropriate local definition template to the template for functions on a vector displayed in Fig. 73.

88 Vector Processing Using Structural Recursion

To explore how to process vectors, we start with problems solved using a design based on the structure of the data. First, the dot product of two vectors of numbers is presented. Second, merging two sorted vectors using a `while`-loop is presented.

88.1 The Dot Product of Two Vectors of Numbers

88.1.1 Problem Analysis

Given two vectors of numbers, V1 and V2, the dot product is defined as:

$$V1 \cdot V2 = \Sigma_{i=0}^{n-1} \, V1[i]*V2[i],$$

where n is the length of the vectors.

The two vectors must have the same length. The products of corresponding elements are summed. Given that corresponding elements must be multiplied, both vectors must be simultaneously processed, and the function is designed around processing one vector interval, [low..high], to reference both vectors. The vector interval may be processed from high to low or from low to high given that addition is commutative. Without loss of generality, the vector interval is processed from low to high. As an exercise, you may design a function that processes the vector interval from high to low.

For both V1 and V2, the entire vector must be processed. This means that initially the vector interval to process is [0..(sub1 (vector-length V1))]. Observe that the proposed initial vector interval contains all the valid indices into V1 and V2. This vector interval is processed by calling an auxiliary function as suggested by the function template displayed in Fig. 73. Template specialization begins as follows:

```
;; Sample (vectorof X)
(define VECTOR0 (vector))
(define VECTOR1 (vector 1 2 3))
(define VECTOR2 (vector -1 -2 8))
(define VECTOR3 (vector 5 10 20 40))


;; (vector number) (vector number) → number.
;; Purpose: To compute the dot product of the given vectors
;; Assumption: Given vectors have the same length
(define (dot-product V1 V2)
  (local
    [;; [int int] ... → ...
     ;; Purpose: ...
     (define (sum-products low high sum)
       (if (> low high)
           ...
           ...(vector-ref V low)...(f-on-VINTV2 (add1 low) high)))]
    (sum-products 0 (sub1 (vector-length V1)) 0)))


;; Tests using sample values for dot-product
(check-expect (dot-product VECTOR0 VECTOR0) 0)
(check-expect (dot-product VECTOR1 VECTOR2) 19)
(check-expect (dot-product VECTOR3 VECTOR3) 2125)
```

Several vectors of varying lengths are defined including, VECTOR0, a vector of length 0. The inputs are two vectors of numbers, and the purpose is to compute the dot product of the given vectors. The assumption that the vectors are of the same length is made explicit so that any reader of the code understands how to properly use the function. The function header contains a descriptive function name and two parameters as per the signature. The body of the local-expression calls a function, sum-products, that processes a vector interval with the entire interval of valid indices into the given vectors and an initial accumulator value of 0 for the sum of products. Finally, the tests illustrate how the function works. Observe that for each test, two vectors of the same size are given as input to dot-product. All that is left is to design sum-products and run the tests.

88.1.2 Problem Analysis for sum-products

If the given vector interval, [low..high], is empty, then the accumulator is returned. Otherwise, a recursive call is made with a new interval obtained by incrementing low and by adding to the accumulator the product of V1[low] and V2[low].

The given vector interval contains the unprocessed indices into V1 and V2. The processed indices, therefore, are [0..low-1]. This means that the accumulator invariant that must hold every time sum-products is called is:

$$\text{sum} = \sum_{i=0}^{\text{low}-1} \text{V1[i]} * \text{V2[i]}$$

It is always a good idea to trace an example to validate the invariant. Consider computing VECTOR1·VECTOR2. The following table displays the values for each call to sum-products:

low	high	sum
0	2	0
1	2	-1
2	2	-5
3	2	19

Observe that the proposed accumulator invariant holds for each row of the table. For example, the invariant is achieved with the values in the first row:

$$\text{sum} = \sum_{i=0}^{\text{low}-1} \text{V1[i]} * \text{V2[i]}$$

$$0 = \sum_{i=0}^{0-1} \text{V1[i]} * \text{V2[i]}$$

$$0 = \sum_{i=0}^{-1} \text{V1[i]} * \text{V2[i]}$$

$$0 = 0$$

Recall that the sum is 0 when the sum's upper bound is less than the sum's lower bound. Similarly, we may verify that the invariant holds for the other rows of the table. For the third row, we have:

sum = $\Sigma_{i=0}^{\text{low}-1}$ V1[i]*V2[i]

-5 = $\Sigma_{i=0}^{2-1}$ V1[i]*V2[i]

-5 = $\Sigma_{i=0}^{1}$ V1[i]*V2[i]

-5 = (1 * -1) + (2 * -2)

-5 = -5

Finally, we can verify that the right value is returned when the recursion stops (the fourth line in the table):

sum = $\Sigma_{i=0}^{\text{low}-1}$ V1[i]*V2[i]

19 = $\Sigma_{i=0}^{3-1}$ V1[i]*V2[i]

19 = $\Sigma_{i=0}^{2}$ V1[i]*V2[i]

19 = (1 * -1) + (2 * -2) + (3 * 8)

19 = 19

3 Verify that the invariant holds for row 2 of the table.

When programming with vectors, however, it is not enough for the invariant to help you prove that the right value is returned. Recall that the programmer is also responsible for making sure that vectors are only accessed with valid indices to prevent the program from throwing an error. Therefore, the invariant must also help the programmer establish that only valid indices are used to reference any vector. For our problem, we must be able to establish that low is a valid index whenever V1 and V2 are referenced. This means that whenever either vector is indexed, we must show that $0 \leq$ low $\leq$ (vector-length V1). According to our design idea, this only occurs when the vector interval is not empty, that is, when low $\leq$ high. This is not enough to prove that low is a valid index into V1 and V2 because, for example, the inequality holds when low is negative. To determine what is needed to be invariant, it is useful to think about how to satisfy the following implication:

Invariant $\wedge$ low $\leq$ high $\Rightarrow$ $0 \leq$ low $\leq$ (sub1 (vector-length V1))

Ask yourself what needs to be added to the invariant to make the implication hold. A first attempt may be to add the following to the invariant:

```
low ≤ high
```

If you think about it carefully, this assertion cannot be invariant. Why? If this assertion were invariant, then we would have an infinite recursion because it would never be the case that the given vector interval is empty. Think carefully about the values `low` takes on as the vector interval is traversed. We have already argued that `low` starts at 0, at every step it is incremented by 1, and the function ought to stop when the vector interval is empty. This means that the following assertion for `low` must hold:

```
0 ≤ low ≤ high+1
```

Observe that if the above is invariant, then the following implication holds:

```
0 ≤ low ≤ high+1 ∧ low ≤ high
⇒
0 ≤ low ≤ (sub1 (vector-length V1))
```

The above holds because `high = (sub1 (vector-length V1))`. Therefore, when the given vector interval is not empty, `low` is a valid index into the vector. The complete invariant is:

$$\text{sum} = \Sigma_{i=0}^{low-1} \text{V1[i]*V2[i]} \land 0 \leq low \leq high+1$$

88.1.3 Signature, Statements, and Function Header for sum-products

The input is a vector interval and the output is a number. The purpose is to sum the products of corresponding V1 and V2 elements for indices in the given vector interval. The function header is written using descriptive function and parameter names. The result for the next steps of the design recipe is:

```
;; [int int] number → number
;; Purpose: Sum the products of corresponding V1 & V2
;;          elements for indices in the given vector
;;          interval
;; ACCUM INV: sum = Σ_{i=0}^{low-1} V1[i]*V2[i] ∧ 0 ≤ low ≤ high+1
(define (sum-products low high sum)
```

88.1.4 Function Body for sum-products

The body of the function must decide if the given vector interval is or is not empty. An `if`-expression is used for this. If the given vector interval is empty, according to our problem analysis, `sum` is returned. Otherwise, the value of

a recursive call is returned. The recursive call is made by incrementing `low`
and by adding the product of the two `low` vector elements to `sum`. The body
of the function is:

```
(if (> low high)
    sum
    (sum-products (add1 low)
                  high
                  (+ (* (vector-ref V1 low)
                        (vector-ref V2 low))
                     sum)))
```

Given that we have already established that in the else branch `low` is a
valid index into the vectors, no indexing errors are possible. Also note that
we have already argued that the correct value is returned. This completes
`dot-product`'s design and implementation. Make sure all the tests pass.

88.2 Merging Two Sorted Vectors

The next illustrative vector-processing example is the merging of two
(`vectorof number`)s that are sorted in nondecreasing order. The design is
based on structural recursion, but to sharpen our skills, the implementation
uses a `while`-loop. The steps for the design recipe displayed in Fig. 69 are
outlined to specialize the function template displayed in Fig. 70.

88.2.1 Problem Analysis

The merging of two vectors, `V1` and `V2`, sorted in nondecreasing order returns
a vector sorted in nondecreasing order that contains all the elements of `V1`
and of `V2`. For example, consider the following two vectors for `V1` and `V2`:

0	1	4	6

-5	1	3	8

The result of merging of this two vectors, `res`, is:

-5	0	1	1	3	4	6	8

Observe that `res` is a new vector whose length is the sum of `V1`'s and `V2`'s
length.

To populate `res` with the proper values, `V1` and `V2` must be traversed.
That is, the vector intervals:

```
[0..(sub1 (vector-length res))]
[0..(sub1 (vector-length V1))
[0..(sub1 (vector-length V2))]
```

must be traversed, respectively, for `res`, `V1`, and `V2`. Without loss of generality, we choose to traverse the vector intervals from the low end to the high end. This means that three state variables are needed to represent the low end of the vector intervals as they are processed: `lowres`, `lowV1`, and `lowV2`.

Think of each vector interval as divided into two parts: the processed part and the unprocessed part. The following table outlines the two parts for each vector:

	Processed	Unprocessed
V1	[0..lowV1-1]	[lowV1..(sub1 (vector-length V1))]
V2	[0..lowV2-1]	[lowV2..(sub1 (vector-length V2))]
V3	[0..lowres-1]	[lowres..(sub1 (vector-length res))]

If the vector interval for the unprocessed part of `res` is empty, the `while`-loop stops, and `res` is returned. Otherwise, the smallest element in the unprocessed parts of `V1` and `V2` is added to `res`, and the vector intervals for the unprocessed part of `res` and the vector containing the smallest element are reduced by 1.

To select the smallest element in the unprocessed parts of `V1` and `V2`, there are three conditions that must be distinguished: both unprocessed vector intervals for `V1` and `V2` are not empty, only the unprocessed vector interval for `V1` is not empty, and only the unprocessed vector interval for `V2` is not empty. In the first case, the smallest element between `V1[lowV1]` and `V2[lowV2]` is placed in `res[lowres]`. In the second case, `V1[lowV1]` is placed in `res[lowres]`. In the third case, `V2[lowV2]` is placed in `res[lowres]`.

To test the merging function, the following vectors are defined:

```
;; Sample (vectorof number)
(define V0 (vector))
(define V1 (vector 1 2 3))
(define V2 (vector -8 -4 -2 10))
(define V3 (vector 4 5 6))
```

88.2.2 Signature, Statements, and Function Header

The inputs are two vectors of numbers, and the output is a vector of numbers. The purpose is to merge the two given vectors into a single vector that is in nondecreasing order. We assume that the two given vectors are in nondecreasing order.

A descriptive function name is `merge-vectors`, and the names for the given vectors are `V1` and `V2`. The next step of the design recipe yields:

```
;; (vectorof number) (vectorof number) → (vectorof number)
;; Purpose: To merge the two given vectors
;; Assumption: The given vectors are sorted in
;;                nondecreasing order
(define (merge-vectors V1 V2)
```

88.2.3 Tests

The tests are written using the sample (`vectorof number`)s defined. They illustrate that the function works when either or both of the vectors are empty and when neither vector is empty. In addition, they illustrate that the function works when the processing of the first given vector ends first (the last test) and when the processing of the second given vector ends first (the next to last test). The tests are:

```
;; Tests for merge-vectors
(check-expect (merge-vectors V0 V0) V0)
(check-expect (merge-vectors V0 V1) V1)
(check-expect (merge-vectors V2 V0) V2)
(check-expect (merge-vectors V2 V1) (vector -8 -4 -2 1 2 3 10))
(check-expect (merge-vectors V1 V3) (vector 1 2 3 4 5 6))
```

88.2.4 Loop Invariant

To formulate the loop invariant, start by formulating the postcondition. The goal is for the result vector, `res`, to contain all the elements of the given vectors, `V1` and `V2`, in nondecreasing order. We can formulate the postcondition as follows:

```
res[0..(vector-length res)-1] =
   (V1[0..(vector-length V1)-1] ∪ V2[0..(vector-length V2)-1])
   in nondecreasing order
```

The symbol ∪ denotes set union. Observe that the above equation refers to all elements of `res`, `V1`, and `V2`.

It is important to remember that the above assertion is only expected to hold after the `while`-loop is done. Before and during the execution of the `while`-loop, the above assertion may not hold. This means that the loop invariant must assert something about the contents of `res` in relation to the contents of `V1` and `V2`. Concretely, it needs to assert the `res`'s processed part contains `V1`'s and `V2`'s processed parts in nondecreasing order. This may be asserted as follows:

```
res[0..lowres-1] = (V1[0..lowV1-1] ∪ V2[0..lowV2-1])
                in nondecreasing order
```

In short, the above assertion states that `res` in `[0..lowres-1]` contains in nondecreasing order the union of `V1`-elements in `[0..lowV1-1]` and `V2`-elements in `[0..lowV2-1]`.

We need to determine if the above assertion is strong enough to be the loop invariant. According to the design idea, the loop halts when `res`'s entire vector interval has been processed. Therefore, we need to prove that:

```
loop invariant ∧ (not driver) ⇒ postcondition
```

```
   res[0..lowres-1] = (V1[0..lowV1-1] ∪ V2[0..lowV2-1])
                   in nondecreasing order
   ∧ lowres > (sub1 (vector-length res))
⇒
   res[0..(vector-length res)-1] =
   (V1[0..(vector-length V1)-1] ∪ V2[0..(vector-length V2)-1])
   in nondecreasing order
```

Clearly, the antecedent does not contain enough information to conclude what values are stored in `lowres`, `lowV1`, and `lowV2`. Without knowing these values, it is impossible to conclude that the consequent holds. It is necessary, therefore, to strengthen the proposed loop invariant.

We know something about the range of values that `res`, `V1`, and `V2` may take. Each must be greater than 0 and less than or equal to the length of the vector they index. Based on this, the loop invariant may be strengthened as follows:

```
     res[0..lowres-1] = (V1[0..lowV1-1] ∪
   ∧ 0 ≤ lowres ≤ (vector-length res)
   ∧ 0 ≤ lowV1  ≤ (vector-length V1)
   ∧ 0 ≤ lowV2  ≤ (vector-length V2)
```

Is the invariant now strong enough? Once again, ask yourself if the invariant and the negation of the driver imply the postcondition. That is, we now want to know if the following implication holds:

```
       res[0..lowres-1] = (V1[0..lowV1-1] ∪ V2[0..lowV2-1])
                       in nondecreasing order
   ∧ 0 ≤ lowres ≤ (vector-length res)
   ∧ 0 ≤ lowV1  ≤ (vector-length V1)
   ∧ 0 ≤ lowV2  ≤ (vector-length V2)
   ∧ lowres > (sub1 (vector-length res))
     ⇒
     res[0..(sub1 (vector-length res))]
       = (V1[0..(sub1 (vector-length V1))]
           ∪ V2[0..(sub1 (vector-length V2))])
         in nondecreasing order
```

There is a clear conclusion we may derive from the antecedent:

```
    0 ≤ lowres ≤ (vector-length res)
  ∧ lowres > (sub1 (vector-length res))
⇒
  lowres = (vector-length res)
```

Given that `lowres` is `(vector-length res)`, is it possible to conclude what values are stored in `lowV1` and `lowV2`? We know that the length of `res` is the sum `V1`'s and `V2`'s length. Observe that this allows us to conclude what values are stored in `V1` and `V2`:

```
    lowV1  ≤ (vector-length V1)
  ∧ lowV2  ≤ (vector-length V2)
  ∧ lowres = (vector-length V1) + (vector-length V2)
⇒
  lowV1 = (vector-length V1) ∧ lowV2 =(vector-length V2)
```

Recall that to prove an implication, we assume the antecedent is true. The consequent holds because any other values for `lowV1` and `lowV2` make the antecedent false and that contradicts our assumption. Therefore, the consequent must be true.

We must still determine if the proposed invariant permits us to conclude that vector indexing errors do not occur. The loop is only entered when the `res`'s vector interval is not empty. That is, the loop is entered when `lowres` ≤ `(sub1 (vector-length res))` and the loop invariant are true. This means that the following implication holds:

```
  res[0..lowres-1] = (V1[0..lowV1-1] ∪ V2[0..lowV2-1])
                    in nondecreasing order
  ∧ 0 ≤ lowres ≤ (vector-length res)
  ∧ 0 ≤ lowV1  ≤ (vector-length V1)
  ∧ 0 ≤ lowV2  ≤ (vector-length V2)
  ∧ lowres ≤ (sub1 (vector-length res))
⇒
  0 ≤ lowres ≤ (sub1 (vector-length res))
```

This informs us that `lowres` is a valid index into `res`. We cannot conclude, however, that `lowV1` and `lowV2` are, respectively, valid indices into `V1` and `V2`. This suggest that the invariant must still be strengthened.

Above we argued that after the loop executes, `lowres` is the sum of lengths of `V1` and `V2`. This suggests asking ourselves what value is stored in `lowres` inside the loop. Every time the loop's body is executed, a value is added to `res`, and `lowres` is incremented. In addition, either `lowV1` or `lowV2` is incremented depending on where the value added to `res` comes from. This suggests that `lowres` is equal to the sum of `lowV1` and `lowV2`. Let us add this to strengthen the invariant. The conjunction of the new proposed invariant and the driver now is:

```
res[0..lowres-1] = (V1[0..lowV1-1] ∪ V2[0..lowV2-1])
                     in nondecreasing order
∧ 0 ≤ lowres ≤ (vector-length res)
∧ 0 ≤ lowV1  ≤ (vector-length V1)
∧ 0 ≤ lowV2  ≤ (vector-length V2)
∧ lowres = lowV1 + lowV2
∧ lowres ≤ (sub1 (vector-length res))
```

As above observe that:

```
∧ 0 ≤ lowres ≤ (vector-length res)
∧ lowres ≤ (sub1 (vector-length res))
⇒
0 ≤ lowres ≤ (sub1 (vector-length res))
```

Adding the above consequent to the pool of knowledge of what is true when the loop is entered allows us to conclude that lowV1 and lowV2 are also, respectively, valid indices into V1 and V2:

```
∧ 0 ≤ lowres ≤ (sub1 (vector-length res))
∧ 0 ≤ lowV1  ≤ (vector-length V1)
∧ 0 ≤ lowV2  ≤ (vector-length V2)
∧ lowres = lowV1 + lowV2
⇒
    0 ≤ lowV1 < (vector-length V1)
  ∧ 0 ≤ lowV2 < (vector-length V2)
∨
    0 ≤ lowV1 < (vector-length V1)
  ∧ 0 ≤ lowV2 = (vector-length V2)
∨
    0 ≤ lowV1 = (vector-length V1)
  ∧ 0 ≤ lowV2 < (vector-length V2)
```

The symbol ∨ means or. In essence, the above implication is stating that when the loop is entered, either both vector intervals for V1 and V2 are not empty, the vector interval for V1 is not empty and the vector interval for V2 is empty, or the vector interval for V1 is empty and the vector interval for V2 is not empty. It is noteworthy that these observations are consistent with the design idea for selecting the smallest element of the unprocessed parts of V1 and V2.

In summary, the proposed invariant is:

```
res[0..lowres-1] = (V1[0..lowV1-1] ∪ (V2[0..lowV2-1])
                     in nondecreasing order
∧ 0 ≤ lowres ≤ (vector-length res)
∧ 0 ≤ lowV1  ≤ (vector-length V1)
∧ 0 ≤ lowV2  ≤ (vector-length V2)
∧ lowres = lowV1 + lowV2
```

This invariant is plausible because it allows us to conclude that the postcondition holds and that vector indexing errors do not occur. The job now is to sequence the mutations in a manner that makes progress toward termination and maintains the invariant every time the loop's body is evaluated. An important lesson to absorb is the process of iterative refinement applies loop invariant development as much as it applies to program development. A complex loop invariant is always developed using iterative refinement.

88.2.5 Function's Local Declarations

According to the design idea, four state variables are needed: one for the resulting (vectorof number) and three indexes for traversing each vector interval from the low end to the high end. The resulting vector, res, must have a length equal to the two given vectors' length. All res's elements are initialized to (void). The purpose for res is to store the elements of the given vectors, V1 and V2, in nondecreasing order. The three indexes are integers for the next vector position to process. They are initialized to (void). The result for this step of the design recipe is:

```
(local [;; (vectorof number)
        ;; Purpose: Stores V1 and V2 elements in
        ;;          nondecreasing order
        (define res (build-vector (+ (vector-length V1)
                                     (vector-length V2))
                                  (λ (i) (void))))

        ;; int
        ;; Purpose: The next V1 index to process
        (define lowV1 (void))

        ;; int
        ;; Purpose: The next V2 index to process
        (define lowV2 (void))

        ;; int
        ;; Purpose: The next res index to process
        (define lowres (void))]
  ...)
```

88.2.6 The local-expression's Body

The local-expression's body starts by setting the indexes to traverse the three vector intervals to 0:

```
(begin
  (set! lowV1  0)
  (set! lowV2  0)
  (set! lowres 0)
  #| INV:
          res[0..lowres-1] = (V1[0..lowV1-1] ∪ V2[0..lowV2-1])
                          in nondecreasing order
      ∧ 0 ≤ lowres ≤ (vector-length res)
      ∧ 0 ≤ lowV1 ≤ (vector-length V1)
      ∧ 0 ≤ lowV2 ≤ (vector-length V2)
      ∧ lowres = lowV1 + lowV2
  |#
```

Observe that initializing the indexes in this manner makes all three vector intervals in the loop invariant empty. Thus, the assertion about the contents of res holds. Further observe that the inequalities in the loop invariant also hold. Therefore, the invariant is achieved.

Upon entering the loop, the invariant and the driver are true. This means that lowres, lowV1, and lowV2 are valid indexes, respectively, into res, V1, and V2. Observe that the following implication holds:

```
lowres = lowV1 + lowV2 ∧ lowres < (vector-length res)
⇒
  lowV1 < (vector-length V1) ∨ lowV2 < (vector-length V2)
```

Thus, we have the following assertion upon entering the loop:

```
(while (<=  lowres (sub1 (vector-length res)))
  #|   res[0..lowres-1] = (V1[0..lowV1-1] ∪ V2[0..lowV2-1])
                        in nondecreasing order
    ∧ 0 ≤ lowres < (vector-length res)
    ∧ 0 ≤ lowV1  ≤ (vector-length V1)
    ∧ 0 ≤ lowV2  ≤ (vector-length V2)
    ∧ lowres = lowV1 + lowV2
  ⇒ lowV1 < (vector-length V1) ∨ lowV2 < (vector-length V2)
  |#
```

The assertion informs us that we need to determine if elements from both given vectors, only V1, or only V2 need to be processed. This means a cond-expression is needed to make this decision. We may begin to write the conditional as follows:

```
(cond [(and (< lowV1 (vector-length V1))
            (< lowV2 (vector-length V2)))
       ...]
      [(< lowV1 (vector-length V1)) ...]
      [else ...])
```

If the first condition holds, then there are elements in both V1 and V2 that
still need to be added to res. Observe that lowV1 is a valid index into V1
and that lowV2 is a valid index into V2. Adding a number to res requires
a conditional to determine the minimum of V1[lowV1] and V1[lowV2]. We
may outline the expression for the first condition as follows:

```
#|   res[0..lowres-1] = (V1[0..lowV1-1] ∪ V2[0..lowV2-1])
                        in nondecreasing order
 ∧ 0 ≤ lowres < (vector-length res)
 ∧ 0 ≤ lowV1  < (vector-length V1)
 ∧ 0 ≤ lowV2  < (vector-length V2)
 ∧ lowres = lowV1 + lowV2
|#
(if (≤  (vector-ref V1 lowV1) (vector-ref V2 lowV2))
    (begin
       ⋮
    )
    (begin
       ⋮
    ))
```

If V1[lowV1] is less than or equal to V2[lowV2], then the next element to
add to res is V1[lowV1]. We can mutate res to contain V1[lowV1]. Observe
that there is no need to reference V2. Given that lowV2 < (vector-length
V2) implies lowV2 ≤ (vector-length V2), we have that the Hoare triple
for this first assignment is:

```
#|   res[0..lowres-1] =   (V1[0..lowV1-1]
                        ∪ V2[0..lowV2-1])
                        in nondecreasing order
 ∧ 0 ≤ lowres < (vector-length res)
 ∧ 0 ≤ lowV1  < (vector-length V1)
 ∧ 0 ≤ lowV2  ≤ (vector-length V2)
 ∧ lowres = lowV1 + lowV2
 ∧ V1[lowV1] ≤ V2[lowV2]
|#
(vector-set! res lowres (vector-ref V1 lowV1))
#|   res[0..lowres] =   (V1[0..lowV1]
                      ∪ V2[0..lowV2-1])
                      in nondecreasing order
 ∧ 0 ≤ lowres < (vector-length res)
 ∧ 0 ≤ lowV1  < (vector-length V1)
 ∧ 0 ≤ lowV2  ≤ (vector-length V2)
 ∧ lowres = lowV1 + lowV2
|#
```

Observe that the assertion after the mutation captures the fact that `res` contains `V1[lowV1]`. The invariant must now be restored by mutating `lowV1` and `lowres`. Neither of these depend on each other, and we may arbitrarily choose to mutate `lowV1` first by incrementing it. Performing this mutation means that we can no longer state that `res` contains `V[lowV1]`. Furthermore, `lowV1` may be as large as `(vector-length V1)` and `lowres` is the sum of `lowV1-1` and `lowV2`. The mutation and post-mutation assertion are:

```
(set! lowV1 (add1 lowV1))
#|   res[0..lowres] =    (V1[0..lowV1-1]
                      ∪ V2[0..lowV2-1])
                         in nondecreasing order
∧ 0 ≤ lowres < (vector-length res)
∧ 0 ≤ lowV1  ≤ (vector-length V1)
∧ 0 ≤ lowV2  ≤ (vector-length V2)
∧ lowres = lowV1-1 + lowV2
|#
```

The remaining mutation increments `lowres`. This mutation means that `res`'s processed part contains the processed elements from `V1` and `V2`, that `lowres` may be as large as `(vector-length res)`, and that `lowres` is the sum of `lowV1` and `lowV2`. That is, the invariant is restored. We may write the mutation and post-mutation assertion as follows:

```
(set! lowres (add1 lowres))
;; INV
)
```

This completes the then branch of the if-expression. The code and logic for the else branch is essentially the same. The difference is that `lowV2`, not `lowV1`, is mutated. The Hoare logic triples are:

```
(begin
#|   res[0..lowres-1] =    (V1[0..lowV1-1]
                        ∪ (V2[0..lowV2-1])
                           in nondecreasing order
∧ 0 ≤ lowres < (vector-length res)
∧ 0 ≤ lowV1  ≤ (vector-length V1)
∧ 0 ≤ lowV2  < (vector-length V2)
∧ lowres = lowV1 + lowV2
∧ V1[lowV1] > V2[lowV2]
|#
(vector-set! res lowres (vector-ref V2 lowV2))
#|   res[0..lowres] =    (V1[0..lowV1-1]
                      ∪ (V2[0..lowV2])
                         in nondecreasing order
∧ 0 ≤ lowres < (vector-length res)
∧ 0 ≤ lowV1  ≤ (vector-length V1)
```

```
                ∧ 0 ≤ lowV2 < (vector-length V2)
                ∧ lowres = lowV1 + lowV2
                |#
                (set! lowV2 (add1 lowV2))
                #|   res[0..lowres] =   (V1[0..lowV1-1]
                                      ∪ (V2[0..lowV2-1])
                                      in nondecreasing order
                ∧ 0 ≤ lowres < (vector-length res)
                ∧ 0 ≤ lowV1  ≤ (vector-length V1)
                ∧ 0 ≤ lowV2  ≤ (vector-length V2)
                ∧ lowres = lowV1 + lowV2-1
                |#
                (set! lowres (add1 lowres))
                ;; INV
                ))]
```

Observe that regardless of the if-expression branch that is evaluated, the invariant is true, and the loop may safely iterate.

If both vector intervals for V1 and V2 are not empty, then the remaining vector interval that is not empty must be processed. The second branch of the cond-expression outlined above is used to process V1 elements when the vector interval for V2 is empty. Upon entering this branch of the cond-expression, the loop invariant and the following assertions hold:

```
(lowV1 ≥ (vector-length V1)) ⊕ (lowV2 ≥ (vector-length V2))

lowres < (vector-length res)

lowV1  < (vector-length V1)
```

The first assertion is the negation of the condition in the first branch of the cond-expression. The symbol ⊕ means *exclusive or*. The assertion A ⊕ B is true when only A or only B is true (i.e., when A ≠ B). Given that to enter the second branch of the conditional lowV1 < (vector-length V1) and the loop invariant hold, we have that the following implications hold:

```
    (lowV1 ≥ (vector-length V1)) ⊕ (lowV2 ≥ (vector-length V2))
  ∧ lowV1 < (vector-length V1)
⇒
  lowV2 ≥ (vector-length V2)


    lowV2  ≥ (vector-length V2)
  ∧ lowV2 ≤ (vector-length V2)
⇒
    lowV2 = (vector-length V2)
  ∧ [lowV2..(sub1 (vector-length V2))] is empty
```

This proves that only V1 has elements to place in res. Furthermore, lowV1 is a valid index into V1, and lowres is a valid index into res. Thus, rex[lowres] may be mutated to be V1[lowV1]. The Hoare triple for this first mutation is:

```
[(< lowV1 (vector-length V1))
 (begin
  #|   res[0..lowres-1] =   (V1[0..lowV1-1]
                          ∪ (V2[0..lowV2-1])
                           in nondecreasing order
   ∧ 0 ≤ lowres < (vector-length res)
   ∧ 0 ≤ lowV1  < (vector-length V1)
   ∧ 0 ≤ lowV2  ≤ (vector-length V2)
   ∧ lowres = lowV1 + lowV2
   ∧ [lowV2..(sub1 (vector-length V2))] is empty
  |#
  (vector-set! res lowres (vector-ref V1 lowV1))
  #|   res[0..lowres] =   (V1[0..lowV1]
                          ∪ (V2[0..lowV2-1])
                           in nondecreasing order
   ∧ 0 ≤ lowres < (vector-length res)
   ∧ 0 ≤ lowV1  < (vector-length V1)
   ∧ 0 ≤ lowV2  ≤ (vector-length V2)
   ∧ lowres = lowV1 + lowV2
  |#
```

After the mutation, res contains the value of V1[lowV1]. This is captured by the post-mutation assertion above. Given that it is no longer relevant that V2's vector interval is empty, it is omitted in the post-mutation assertion. Next, lowV1 and lowres need to be mutated to restore the invariant. The logic is similar to the logic for the first branch of the cond-expression. The mutations and assertions are:

```
(set! lowV1 (add1 lowV1))
#|   res[0..lowres] =   (V1[0..lowV1-1]
                        ∪ (V2[0..lowV2])
                         in nondecreasing order
 ∧ 0 ≤ lowres < (vector-length res)
 ∧ 0 ≤ lowV1  ≤ (vector-length V1)
 ∧ 0 ≤ lowV2  ≤ (vector-length V2)
 ∧ lowres = lowV1-1 + lowV2
|#
(set! lowres (add1 lowres))
;; INV
)]
```

Observe that after the second mutation, the loop invariant is restored. This informs us that it does not matter if the cond-expression's first or second branch is evaluated because after each the loop invariant holds and the while-loop may safely iterate.

The cond-expression's final branch is used to process V2 elements when V1's vector interval is empty. Upon entering this branch of the cond-expression, the loop invariant and the following assertions hold:

(lowV1 $\geq$ (vector-length V1)) $\oplus$ (lowV2 $\geq$ (vector-length V2))

lowres < (vector-length res)

lowV1 $\geq$ (vector-length V1)

The third assertion holds because it is the negation of the condition for the cond-expression's second branch. Based on the loop invariant and the above assertions, the following implications hold:

```
     (lowV1 ≥ (vector-length V1))
  ∧ lowV1  ≤ (vector-length V1)
⇒
  lowV1  = (vector-length V1)
⇒
  [lowV1..(sub1 (vector-length V1))] is empty
```

This proves that only V2 has elements that need to be placed in res. Furthermore, lowV2 is a valid index into V2, and lowres is a valid index into res. Thus, rex[lowres] may be mutated to be V2[lowV2]. The Hoare triple for this first mutation is:

```
            [else
             (begin
              #| res[0..lowres-1] =     (V1[0..lowV1-1]
                                     ∪ (V2[0..lowV2-1])
                                         in nondecreasing order
                  ∧ 0 ≤ lowres < (vector-length res)
                  ∧ 0 ≤ lowV1  ≤ (vector-length V1)
                  ∧ 0 ≤ lowV2  < (vector-length V2)
                  ∧ ∧ lowres = lowV1 + lowV2
                  ∧ [lowV1..(sub1 (vector-length V1))] is empty
              |#
              (vector-set! res lowres (vector-ref V2 lowV2))
              #| res[0..lowres] =     (V1[0..lowV1-1]
                                    ∪ (V2[0..lowV2])
                                        in nondecreasing order
                  ∧ 0 ≤ lowres < (vector-length res)
                  ∧ 0 ≤ lowV1  ≤ (vector-length V1)
                  ∧ 0 ≤ lowV2  < (vector-length V2)
                  ∧ lowres = lowV1 + lowV2
              |#
```

After the mutation, `res` contains the value of `V2[lowV2]`. This is captured by the post-mutation assertion above. Given that it is no longer relevant that V1's vector interval is empty, it is omitted in the post-mutation assertion. Next, `lowV2` and `lowres` need to be mutated to restore the invariant. The logic is similar to the logic for the first and second branches of the cond-expression. The mutations and assertions are:

```
(set! lowV2 (add1 lowV2))
#| res[0..lowres] =   (V1[0..lowV1-1]
                    ∪ (V2[0..lowV2-1])
                    in nondecreasing order
   ∧ 0 ≤ lowres < (vector-length res)
   ∧ 0 ≤ lowV1  ≤ (vector-length V1)
   ∧ 0 ≤ lowV2  ≤ (vector-length V2)
   ∧ lowres = lowV1 + lowV2-1
|#
(set! lowres (add1 lowres))
;; INV
)]))
        ⋮
)
```

Observe that after evaluating the cond-expression's third branch, the invariant holds. This proves that regardless of the branch evaluated every time the loop is entered, the invariant holds and the loop may safely iterate.

88.2.7 Post-Loop Code

After the loop, the invariant and the negation of the driver hold. As argued during invariant development, we may conclude that the postcondition holds. This means that after the loop, `res` is returned to fulfill the functions signature and purpose. The assertions and code are:

```
#| INV ∧ losres > (sub1 (vector-length res))
 ⇒  lowres = (vector-length res)
   ∧ lowV1  = (vector-length V1)
   ∧ lowV2  = (vector-length V2)
 ⇒
   res[0..(vector-length res)-1]
     =   (V1[0..(vector-length V1)-1]
       ∪ (V2[0..(vector-length V2)-1])
       in nondecreasing order
|#
res
```

88.2.8 Auxiliary Functions, Termination Argument, and Testing

No auxiliary functions are required. The termination argument is formulated as follows:

```
#| Termination argument
      The state variable lowres starts at 0. Every time
      through the loop it is incremented by 1. Eventually,
      lowres becomes greater than (sub1 (vector-length res))
      and the loop halts.
 |#
```

This completes `merge-vectors` design and implementation. Run the tests and make sure they all pass.

4 Design and implement a function to sum the elements of a (`vectorof number`) in a given vector interval using structural recursion.

5 Design and implement a function to sum the elements of a (`vectorof number`) in a given vector interval using a `while`-loop.

6 Design and implement a function to compute the average of a (`vectorof natnum`).

7 Design and implement a function to return the index of a (`vectorof string`)'s longest string using structural recursion.

8 Design and implement a function to return the index of a (`vectorof string`)'s longest string using a `while`-loop.

9 Design and implement a mutator to move the `posns` in a (`vectorof posn`) by some given amounts on the x and y axes. Do not create a new vector nor new `posns`.

10 Design and implement a function that takes as input two (vectorof number), V1 and V2, and returns a (vectorof posn). The returned vector pairs every element of V1 with every element of V2. For example, given

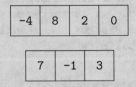

The function returns

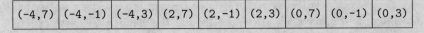

11 Design and implement a predicate that takes as input two (vectorof number), V1 and V2, of length n+1 to determine if for all i∈[0..n] V1[i] ≤ V2[i].

89 Vector Processing Using Generative Recursion: Revisiting the Sieve of Eratosthenes

Section 22 explored an algorithm, known as the Sieve of Eratosthenes, to compute all the prime numbers less than or equal to a given natural number. A list-based representation is used in Sect. 22 to represent the numbers that may still be prime. The idea is to start with a list of natural numbers from 2 (the smallest prime number) to, n, the given natural number. At each step, the first number in the list, i, is a prime that is added to the result, and the process is repeated with the members of the rest of the list that are not multiples of i. The process stops when i is larger than the given list of natural numbers.

We shall redesign the algorithm to use a vector-based representation for the numbers that may still be prime and a while-loop. Should we expect a faster execution time?

89.1 Problem Analysis

Given a natural number n, start by assuming that all natural numbers in [2..n] are prime. At each step, the multiples of the interval's first element are marked as nonprime. The process stops when the interval's first element doubled is larger than n.

To represent the numbers that are and are not prime so far as a (vectorof Boolean) of size n+1, is-prime is used as an accumulator. The vector interval of interest is [2..n]. Each element of the vector interval represents a number that may or may not be prime. The vector interval is processed from left to right (i.e., from the low end to the high end). If the first vector interval element, low, is prime (i.e., is-prime[low] is #true), then the multiples of low in the vector interval [2*low..n] are mutated to #false to indicate that they are not prime and low is incremented. If the first vector interval element is not prime (i.e., is-prime[low] is #false), then its multiples in the rest of the interval are already marked as not prime, and low is incremented. We know the multiples of low are marked as nonprime when low is marked as nonprime.[21]

Observe that [(quotient n 2)+1..n] contains no multiples of the natural numbers in this vector interval because any such multiples are all greater than n. This means that the while-loop only needs to traverse [2..(quotient n 2)]. To do so, a state variable, low, may be used. At each loop iteration, low is incremented as suggested above. The loop stops when low > (quotient n 2). The problem of marking the multiples of low as nonprime, when is-prime[low] is #true, is a subproblem that may be solved by an auxiliary function.

When the loop terminates, the list of prime numbers is created by traversing [2..n]. For any index, i∈[2..n] i is added to the list if is-prime[i] is #true. Constructing this list is a subproblem that is solved by an auxiliary function.

89.2 Signature, Statements, and Function Header

The input to the function is a natural number and the output is a (listof natnum). The purpose is to compute all the prime numbers less than or equal to n. The next steps of the design recipe yield:

```
;; natnum → (listof natmum)
;; Purpose: Return all the primes ≤ to the given natnum
(define (sieve-vector n)
```

---

[21] Any number that divides low also divides the multiples of low.

Observe that a descriptive name suggesting that this function implements the sieve of Eratosthenes is used. Also noteworthy is that this function does not require a how statement because it traverses [2..(quotient n 2)] by using the structure of the vector interval. In essence, the design of this function is based on structural recursion.

89.3 Tests

The input to sieve-vector is an unrestricted natural number. This means that the function must work for 0 and for any natural number greater than 0. For both 0 and 1, of course, the result is '(). The tests may be written as follows:

```
;; Tests for sieve-vector
(check-expect (sieve-vector 0)   '())
(check-expect (sieve-vector 1)   '())
(check-expect (sieve-vector 11) '(2 3 5 7 11))
(check-expect (sieve-vector 20) '(2 3 5 7 11 13 17 19))
```

89.4 Loop Invariant

According to the design idea, the loop is used to traverse [2..(quotient n 2)]. We shall refer to (quotient n 2) as high. In this manner, we may state the loop traverses the vector interval [2..high]. We also introduce the concept of a *proper divisor*. A proper divisor of a natural number, n, is any divisor of n not equal to n.

To formulate the loop invariant, first formulate the loop's postcondition. After the loop is evaluated, is-prime ought to tell us which numbers in [2..n] are prime. We can formulate the assertion as follows:

$$\forall \ j \in [2..n]$$
$$(\text{not is-prime}[j]) \Rightarrow j \text{ is not a prime}$$
$$\land \ \text{is-prime}[j] \Rightarrow j \text{ is prime}$$

The symbol $\forall$ means *for all*. The above assertion states that for all values j in the vector interval [2..n], two implications hold: if is-prime[j] is #false, then j is not prime, and if is-prime[j] is #true, then j is prime. If the above assertion is true, after the while-loop, then the list of prime numbers less than or equal to the given natural number is obtained by traversing the vector and creating a list containing all j such that is-prime[j] is #true.

The assertion above is intended to hold after the while-loop is evaluated and not during the its evaluation. Traversing [2..high] using the state variable low suggests that the loop invariant ought to include an assertion about the prime and nonprime numbers so far in relation to `low`. If `low` is the next vector interval index to process, then the assertion in the invariant ought to be written in terms of `[2..low-1]`. Given that only the multiples of the natural numbers in `[2..low-1]` are marked as nonprime, the following assertion is a plausible part of the loop invariant:

$\forall j \in [2..n]$
    (not is-prime[j]) $\Rightarrow$ $\exists$ a proper divisor of j in [2..low-1]
    $\wedge$ is-prime[j] $\Rightarrow$ $\nexists$ a proper divisor of j in [2..low-1]

The symbols $\exists$ and $\nexists$, respectively, mean *their exists* and *their does not exist*.

To be able to prove that the postcondition holds after the loop, it is necessary to determine the value of `low` after the loop. In addition, we must be able to establish that inside the loop, `low` is a valid index into `is-prime`. The above assertion does not suffice for either of these. We need an assertion that bounds `low`'s value. Given that the loop is used to traverse the vector interval `[2..high]`, we know that `low` must start at 2 and must stop when `low = high + 1`. We may add an assertion capturing this observation to the invariant:

$\forall j \in [2..n]$
    (not is-prime[j]) $\Rightarrow$ $\exists$ a proper divisor of j in [2..low-1]
    $\wedge$ is-prime[j] $\Rightarrow$ $\nexists$ a proper divisor of j in [2..low-1]
    $\wedge$ 2 $\leq$ low $\leq$ high + 1

Is the proposed invariant strong enough to prove the postcondition holds after the loop and that `low` is a valid index into `is-prime` when the loop is entered? The loop is entered when `[low..high]` is not empty, that is, when `low` $\leq$ `high`. Observe that:

    2 $\leq$ low $\leq$ high + 1 $\wedge$ low $\leq$ high
  $\Rightarrow$
    2 $\leq$ low $\leq$ high

The invariant and the driver prove that when the loop is entered, `low` is a valid index into `is-prime`.

To determine if the invariant is strong enough to establish the postcondition, we examine what the invariant and the negation of the driver imply:

$\forall j \in [2..n]$
    (not is-prime[j]) $\Rightarrow$ $\exists$ a proper divisor of j in [2..low-1]
    $\wedge$ is-prime[j] $\Rightarrow$ $\nexists$ a proper divisor of j in [2..low-1]
    $\wedge$ 2 $\leq$ low $\leq$ high + 1
    $\wedge$ low > high
  $\Rightarrow$
  low = high + 1

The value of `low` after the loop is known. This leads to the following implication:

```
    low = high + 1
⇒
∀j∈[2..n]
   (not is-prime[j]) ⇒ ∃ a proper divisor of j in [2..high]
∧ is-prime[j] ⇒ ∄ a proper divisor of j in [2..high]
=
∀j∈[2..n]
      (not is-prime[j]) ⇒ ∃ a proper divisor of j in
                              [2..(quotient n 2)]
∧ is-prime[j] ⇒ ∄ a proper divisor of j in
                              [2..(quotient n 2)]
```

We know that there are no divisors of any natural number in [2..n] in [(quotient n 2)+1..n]. Observe that this observation allows us to establish the postcondition:

```
∀j∈[2..n]
      (not is-prime[j]) ⇒ ∃ a proper divisor of j in
                              [2..(quotient n 2)]
∧ is-prime[j] ⇒ ∄ a proper divisor of j in
                              [2..(quotient n 2)]
∧ ∄ a proper divisor of j in [(quotient n 2)+1..n]
⇒
∀j∈[2..n]
      (not is-prime[j]) ⇒ ∃ a proper divisor of j in [2..n]
∧    is-prime[j] ⇒ ∄ a proper divisor of j in [2..n]
⇒
∀ j ∈ [2..n]    (not is-prime[j]) ⇒ j is not a prime
                ∧ is-prime[j] ⇒ j is prime
```

The proposed invariant is strong enough to establish the postcondition and to establish that low is a valid index into is-prime when the loop is entered. The problem-solver's task now is to sequence mutations inside the loop to maintain the invariant for every iteration.

89.5 Function's Local Definitions

The local declarations must include two state variables: is-prime and low. The first is a (vectorof Boolean) that accumulates the prime and nonprimes identified. The second is used to traverse the vector interval [2..(quotient n 2)]. In addition, a variable, high, is defined for the vector interval's high end.

In addition, two auxiliary functions are needed. The first is a mutator, mark-multiples!, that takes as input a natural number and a vector interval and that marks in is-prime the multiples of the given natural number in the given vector interval. It assumes that the given vector interval's low end is a multiple of the first given number. The second auxiliary function takes as input a vector interval into is-prime and returns a list containing the prime numbers found. That is, it returns a list of all the i such that is-prime[i] is #true.

At this stage of development, assume that the auxiliary functions work and will be written. The local declarations, for now, only contain the header of the auxiliary functions. The result for this step of the design recipe is:

```
(local [;; (vectorof Boolean)
        ;; Purpose: Track primes identified
        (define is-prime (build-vector (add1 n) (λ (i) #true)))

        ;; natnum
        ;; Purpose: Index of next potential prime
        (define low (void))

        (define high (quotient n 2))

        ;; [int int] → (void)
        ;; Purpose: Mark multiples of the given low as not
        ;;          prime
        ;; How: ...
        ;; Effect: In is-primes multiples of given i in
        ;;         [low..high] are set to #false
        ;; Assumption: low is a multiple of i
        (define (mark-multiples! i low high)
          ...)

        ;; [int int] → (listof natnum)
        ;; Purpose: Return the list of primes ≤ n
        (define (extract-primes low high)
          ...)
        ]
    ⋮
)
```

Observe that is-prime is constructed to contain only #true. This is done because the algorithm assumes at the beginning that all the numbers in [2..n] are prime.

89.6 The `local`-expression's Body

The `local`-expression's body starts by checking if the given number, n, is less than 2. If so, then there are no prime numbers less than or equal to n, and the empty list is returned. We may begin writing the needed `if`-expression as follows:

```
(if (< n 2)
    '()
    ...
)
```

If n is greater than or equal to 2, then the vector interval [2..(quotient n 2)] needs to be traversed. Mutating `low` to be 2 achieves the invariant:

```
(begin
 (set! low 2)
 ;; INV:
 ;; For j in [2..low-1]
 ;;    (not is-prime[j]) ⇒ ∃ a proper divisor of j ∈ [2..low-1]
 ;;    ∧ is-prime[j] ⇒ ∄ s proper divisor of j ∈ [2..low-1]
 ;; ∧ 2 ≤ low ≤ high + 1

   ⋮
)
```

Observe that the two implications hold because [2..low-1] = [2..1] is an empty vector interval and, therefore, the consequents are true. The inequality holds because `low` is 2 and `high + 1` is at least 2.

The loop iterates as long as [low..high] is not empty. Upon entering the loop, the loop invariant and the driver hold. The body of the loop must first determine if `low` is prime. We can outline the loop as follows:

```
(while (<= low high)
   ;; For j in [2..low-1]
   ;;    (not is-prime[j]) ⇒ ∃ a proper divisor of j∈[2..low-1]
   ;;    ∧ is-prime[j] ⇒ ∄ a proper divisor of j∈[2..low-1]
   ;; ∧ 2 ≤ low < high + 1
   (if (vector-ref is-prime low)
      ...
      ...
))
```

We know that `low < high + 1` holds because the loop's driver is true.

Focus first of the development of the then-expression when `is-prime[low]` is #true. This means that `low` is a prime number. Given that `low` is a prime number, its multiples in the rest of the vector interval [low+1..n] must be marked as nonprime. This needs to be done before the `low` is mutated.

As per the problem analysis, the marking is done by an auxiliary mutator. The vector interval that the mutator must traverse is [2*low..n] because the smallest multiple of low is 2*low. After the mutator is done marking the newly discovered nonprimes, is-prime[j] implies there is not a proper divisor of j in [2..low], and (not is-prime[j]) implies there is a proper divisor of j in [2..low]. Observe that the implications are no longer in terms of low - 1. To restore the invariant and to make progress toward termination, low is incremented. The mutations and the assertions that hold before and after the mutations are written as follows:

```
(begin
  ;; For j in [2..low-1]
  ;;   (not is-prime[j]) ⇒ ∃ a proper divisor of j∈[2..low-1]
  ;;   ∧ is-prime[j]  ⇒  ∄ a proper divisor of j∈[2..low-1]
  ;; ∧ 2 ≤ low < high + 1
  ;; ∧ low is a prime
  (mark-multiples! low (* 2 low) n)
  ;; For j in [2..low]
  ;;   (not is-prime[j]) ⇒ ∃ a proper divisor of j∈[2..low]
  ;;   ∧ is-prime[j] ⇒ ∄ a proper divisor of j∈[2..low]
  ;; ∧ 2 ≤ low < high + 1
  (set! low (add1 low))
  ;; INV
)
```

For the else branch, when is-prime[low] is #false, there is no need to mark the multiples of low as [low+1..n] because these were marked when low was marked. Thus, only progress toward termination must be made. That is, low must be incremented. This mutation guarantees that the invariant holds making it safe for the loop to iterate. The mutation and the assertions before and after the mutations are written as follows:

```
;; else branch
;; For j in [2..low-1]
;;   (not is-prime[j]) ⇒ ∃ a proper divisor of j∈[2..low-1]
;;   ∧ is-prime[j] ⇒ ∄ a proper divisor of j∈[2..low-1]
;; ∧ 2 ≤ low < high + 1
;; ∧ low is not prime
(set! low (add1 low))
;; INV
```

89.7 Post-Loop Code

In the loop invariant development step, it is established that the postcondition is achieved. This means that is-prime informs us which elements in

[2..n] are prime. To create the list of prime numbers less than or equal to n, this vector interval must be traversed. This traversal is done by an auxiliary function, and the value returned by the auxiliary function is the value returned by `sieve-vector`. The post-loop assertion and code is written as follows:

```
;; For j in [2..low-1]
;;    (not is-prime[j]) ⇒ ∃ a proper divisor of j∈[2..low-1]
;;    ∧ is-prime[j] ⇒ ∄ a proper divisor of j in [2..low-1]
;; ∧  2  ≤  low  ≤  high + 1
;; ∧  low > high
;; ⇒  low = high + 1
;; ⇒  For j in [2..high]
;;       (not is-prime[j]) ⇒ ∃ a proper divisor of j∈[2..high]
;;       ∧ is-prime[j] ⇒ ∄ a proper divisor of j∈[2..high]
;; ⇒  For j in [2..n]
;;       (not is-prime[j]) ⇒ j is not prime
;;       ∧ is-prime[j] ⇒ j is prime
(extract-primes 2 n)
```

89.8 Auxiliary Functions

89.8.1 The Design of `mark-multiples!`

This function takes as input a natural number, i, and an `is-prime` vector interval, [`low..high`], and marks as nonprime the multiples of the given natural number. The vector interval may be traversed using structural recursion, but this would be inefficient. Observe that if `low` is a multiple of i, then the next multiple of i is i + `low`. This means that there is no need to traverse the elements in [i..(i+low-1)]. Therefore, after marking `is-prime[low]` as nonprime, a new vector interval to traverse starting an (i+low) may be used to continue marking i's multiples. Observe that this suggest an algorithm based on generative recursion.

This function assumes that, `low`, the given vector interval's low end is the a multiple of i. Initially, this assumption is safe because the call in `sieve-vector` provides 2*low as the argument for `low`. If the given vector interval is empty, (void) is returned given that there are no multiples of i to mark in the given vector interval. Otherwise, `is-prime[low]` is mutated to be #false, and the vector interval [i+low..high] is recursively processed. The effect is that `is-primes`'s elements indexed by a multiple of i are mutated to be #false. Based on this design, the local generative recursive function developed following the steps of the design recipe is:

```
;; natnum [int int] → (void)
;; Purpose: Marks multiples of the given number as not
;;          prime in the given is-prime vector interval
;; How: Mutate is-prime[low] to be false and create a new
;;      vector interval to traverse starting with the next
;;      multiple of i by adding i to low
;; Effect: In is-primes multiples of given i in [low..high]
;;         are set to #false
;; Assumption: low is a multiple of i
(define (mark-multiples! i low high)
  (if (> low high)
      (void)
      (begin
        (vector-set! is-prime low #false)
        (mark-multiples! i (+ i low) high))))
;; Termination Argument
;; The given vector interval is [low..high]. Each recursive
;; call is made with a smaller interval: [i+low..high].
;; Eventually, the given vector interval becomes empty and
;; the function halts.
```

89.8.2 The Design of extract-primes

Creating the list of primes based on the Boolean values in is-prime is an exercise using structural recursion on, [low..high], the given vector interval. The given vector interval is traversed from low to high. Initially, the vector interval is [2..n] as evidenced by the call in sieve-vector, and every recursive call is made with the subinterval [low+1..high]. If the given vector interval is empty, the empty list is returned. If is-prime[low] is #true, then low is added to the resulting list. If is-prime[low] is #false, then low is not added to the resulting list.

Based on the problem analysis above, the template for functions on a vector interval is specialized. The resulting function is:

```
;; [int int] → (listof natnum)
;; Purpose: Return the list of primes ≤ n
(define (extract-primes low high)
  (cond [(> low high) '()]
        [(vector-ref is-prime low)
         (cons low (extract-primes (add1 low) high))]
        [else (extract-primes (add1 low) high)]))
```

89.9 Termination Argument and Running Tests

The loop traverses [2..(quotient n 2)] from the low end to the high end. The traversal starts with low equal to 2. Every time the body of the loop is evaluated, regardless of which path is taken in the if-expression, low is incremented reducing the size of the vector interval to traverse by 1. Eventually, the vector interval becomes empty when low = (quotient n 2) + 1 and the loop halts.

This completes the design and implementation of sieve-vector. Run the tests and make sure they all pass. It is noteworthy that the while-loop developed has a delayed operation. The call to mark-multiples! delays the mutation and subsequent iteration of the loop. The program must postpone the execution of the loop, make the call to mark-multiples!, and resume the execution of the loop upon completing the call to mark-multiples!. Be aware that a while-loop, just like recursive function, may have delayed operations and that following the steps of the design recipe for a while-loop may result in a loop with delayed operations.

89.10 Complexity and Performance

Define n to be the size of the interval processed by sieve-vector. The number of steps performed by the while-loop in sieve-vector is (quotient n 2)-2 = $O(n)$. The first time mark-multiples! is called, it performs $\frac{n}{2}$ steps in the worst case to mark the multiples of 2. The next time mark-multiples! is called, it performs $\frac{n}{3}$ steps in the worst case to mark the multiples of 3. The next time mark-multiples! is called, it performs $\frac{n}{5}$ steps in the worse case to mark the multiples of 5. As with the implementation of the sieve of Eratosthenes in Sect. 22, we have that the running time for sieve-vector is:

$$n*(\tfrac{1}{2} + \tfrac{1}{3} + \tfrac{1}{5} + \tfrac{1}{7} + \ldots)$$

Recall that the series above is equal to log (log (n)). This makes sieve-vector's complexity $O(n \log (\log(n)))$.

We see that the-primes<=n from Sect. 22 and sieve-vector have the same complexity. Which one should we use? Empirical experimentation is needed to make this decision. The experiments in Sect. 22 use 50,000 as input. The same input is used to run the following experiments five times:

```
(time (the-primes<=n 50000))
(time (sieve-vector  50000))
```

The CPU times obtained (after subtracting garbage collection time) are:

	Run 1	Run 2	Run 3	Run 4	Run 5	Average
the-primes<=n	375	375	406	407	401	392.8
sieve-vector	15	0	16	31	0	12.4

Observe that there are no outliers in the collected empirical data. For every run, `sieve-vector` is faster than `the-primes<=n`. On average, `the-primes<=n` takes about 393 milliseconds, while `sieve-vector` takes about 12 milliseconds. The conclusion is that `sieve-vector` is faster and ought to be used. Why is `sieve-vector` faster? Observe that `the-primes<=n` always traverses all the elements of an interval to determine if a number is prime. In contrast, for `sieve-vector`, `mark-multiples!` does not traverse through all the elements of an interval. Instead, it jumps over elements and only processes the multiples of a given number. This is why `sieve-vector` is faster.

12 Design and implement a function that takes as input a (vectorof number) and that returns the sum of the elements whose index is an even number.

13 Design and implement a function using generative recursion that takes as input a number and a (vectorof number) sorted in nondecreasing order and that uses binary search to return an index of a given number in the given vector. If the given number is not in the given vector, then the function returns −1.

14 Design and implement a function using a `while`-loop that takes as input a number and a (vectorof number) sorted in nondecreasing order and that uses binary search to return an index of a given number in the given vector. If the given number is not in the given vector, then the function returns −1.

90 What Have We Learned in This Chapter?

The important lessons of this chapter are summarized as follows:

- A vector is compound data of fixed size that is allocated in consecutive memory locations.
- Any vector element is accessed in constant time.
- An error is thrown when attempting to access or mutate a vector, V, with an index not in [0..(vector-length V)-1].

- There are two vector constructors: `vector` and `build-vector`.
- There are three vector observers: `vector-length`, `vector-ref`, and `vector?`.
- There is one vector mutator: `vector-set!`.
- Vectors are usually processed using a vector interval.
- A vector interval is a dependent type.
- A vector interval either is empty or only contains valid indices into a vector of length N.
- Vector intervals may be processed from their low end to their high end or vice versa using structural recursion.
- Vector intervals may be processed using generative recursion by constructing new vector intervals for a given vector.
- The process of iterative refinement applies to loop invariant development as much as it applies to program development.
- A `while`-loop may have delayed operations.
- Following the `while`-loop design recipe may result in a loop with delayed operations.

Chapter 17
In-Place Operations

In Chap. 5, different sorting algorithms are discussed to sort data represented using a list. As the computation advanced, new lists were created to finish the sorting process. For example, in Sect. 24, `insertion-sorting` creates a new list every time a number is inserted into a sorted list, and in Sect. 25, `quick-sorting` creates new lists for the numbers less than or equal to the pivot and for the numbers greater than the pivot. When the list being sorted is short, the allocation of new lists is unlikely to be of concern. When a list is large, on the other hand, the amount of memory allocated may become a concern. For example, devices with small amounts of memory may be unable to perform the needed sorted operation, or the allocation of memory may make a device run slower.

An alternative to allocating auxiliary data structures, like the intermediary lists allocated during list-sorting, is to use mutation to perform operations in place. Instead of allocating auxiliary data structures to store intermediate values during a computation, the data structure being manipulated is overwritten as the computation progresses. In this manner, memory allocation is lessened or eliminated. The danger, of course, is the loss of the original data structure and of referential transparency. Remember that once a data structure is mutated, its original value is lost.

91 Reversing a Vector

Consider the problem of reversing an arbitrary number of elements. A natural representation for the elements is a (`listof X`). This representation is attractive because we may use structural recursion to design a solution. Such a solution was discussed in Sect. 53.2 and is displayed in Fig. 41. Recall that if the given list is empty, then the reversed list is empty. If the given list is not empty, then the reversed list is obtained by appending the reverse of the

© The Author(s), under exclusive license to Springer Nature Switzerland AG 2022   455
M. T. Morazán, *Animated Program Design*, Texts in Computer Science,
https://doi.org/10.1007/978-3-031-04317-8_17

rest of the given list and a list that only contains the first element of the
given list.

Consider, however, `rev-lox`'s if-expression's else-branch:

```
(append (rev-lox (rest a-lox)) (list (first a-lox)))
```

Observe that for each call to `rev-lox`, except the last, three intermediate lists
are constructed: one containing only the first element of the given list, one
for the reverse of the rest of the given list, and one for the result of appending
these two lists. This may or may not be a problem depending on how much
memory is available for allocation. We do know, however, that `rev-lox` is
unnecessarily slow given that `append` is a delayed operation. To make the
implementation faster, Sect. 53.2 develops a design using an accumulator to
eliminate the delayed operation. The solution using an accumulator proved
significantly faster. In addition, it significantly reduces the amount of memory
allocated. Consider the else-branch in `rev-lox-accum`:

```
(rev-lox-accum (rest a-lox) (cons (first a-lox) accum)))
```

Observe that memory is only allocated for the result.

Although only allocating memory for the result is unlikely to have a significant impact on execution time, it may make it impossible for devices with
little memory to execute. To eliminate this memory allocation, the representation of elements to reverse may be changed to a `(vectorof X)`. If a vector
is used, then reversing in place is possible. This is safe to do as long as the
original ordering of the elements in the vector is not needed.

91.1 Problem Analysis

To reverse the elements in a vector, `V`, the first and last elements are
swapped, the second and the next to last elements are swapped, and so on.
This may be done by traversing the vector interval `[0..(sub1 (quotient
(vector-length V) 2))]`. Consider reversing the following vector of even
length:

X_0	X_1	X_2	X_3

The vector interval processed is `[0..1]`. `V[0]` is swapped with `V[3]`, and
`V[1]` is swapped with `V[2]`. Now consider reversing the following vector of
odd length:

X_0	X_1	X_2	X_3	X_4

The vector interval processed is [0..1]. V[0] is swapped with V[4], V[1] is swapped with V[3], and V[2] is not swapped. V[2] does not need to be swapped because it is the middle element and its value is the same in V and in V reversed.

The vector interval, [low..high], may be traversed from the low end to the high end. If the vector interval is empty, (void) is returned because there are no more elements to swap. If the vector interval is not empty, then V[low] is swapped with V[(sub1 (- (vector-length V) low))], and the rest of the vector interval is processed recursively.

91.2 The reverse-vector-in-place! Mutator

91.2.1 Problem Analysis

To process a given vector, this mutator needs to call a function to process a vector interval. The vector interval to process is [0..(sub1 (quotient (vector-length V) 2))].

To test the mutator, the following vectors are defined:

```
(define V0 (vector))
(define V1 (vector 1 2 3 4 5))
(define V2 (build-vector 5000 (λ (i) (make-posn i i))))
```

91.3 Signature and Statements

The input is a (vectorof X)s. Given that this mutator is only called for its effect, the output is (void). The purpose is to reverse the given vector's elements. The effect is the rearrangement of vector elements such that every element in the first half of the vector, V[i], is swapped with V[(vector-length V)-i-1]. The results for the next steps of the design recipe are:

```
;; (vectorof X) → (void)
;; Purpose: Reverse the elements in the given vector
;; Effect: Vector elements are rearranged such that
;;         ∀ i∈[0..(quotient n 2)] V[i] is
;;         swapped with V[(vector-length V)-i-1]
(define (reverse-vector-in-place! V)
```

91.3.1 Tests

The tests use the sample (vectorof X)s to show that the effect is properly
achieved. Observe that V2 is constructed using build-vector. To test the
reversal of V2, build-vector is also used. The tests are:

```
(check-expect (begin
                (reverse-vector-in-place! V0)
                V0)
              (vector))

(check-expect (begin
                (reverse-vector-in-place! V1)
                V1)
              (vector 5 4 3 2 1))

(check-expect
  (begin
    (reverse-vector-in-place! V2)
    V2)
  (build-vector 5000
                (λ (i)
                  (make-posn (- 5000 i 1) (- 5000 i 1)))))
```

91.3.2 Function Body

The body of the function calls an auxiliary function to process the entire
vector. It provides the vector interval for the first half of the vector. The
body of the function is:

```
(rev-vector! 0 (sub1 (quotient (vector-length V) 2)))))
```

91.4 The rev-vector! Mutator

91.4.1 Problem Analysis

This function must traverse the given vector interval, [low..high], to swap
vector elements. If the vector interval is empty, there are no more elements to
swap, and (void) is returned. Otherwise, V[low] is swapped with V[(sub1
(- (vector-length V) low))], and the rest of the vector interval is recursively processed.

91.4.2 Signature and Statements

The input is a vector interval into V and the returned value is (void). The purpose is to reverse V's elements. The effect is that for every index, i, in the given vector interval, V[i] is swapped with V[(vector-length V)-low-1].

To ensure that low and (vector-length V)-low-1 are valid indices into V, the function assumes that low is greater than or equal to 0 and that 2*high is a valid index into V. In this manner, when the vector interval is not empty, both low and (vector-length V)-low-1 are valid indices into V. This leads to the following results for the next steps of the design recipe:

```
;; [int int] → (void)
;; Purpose: Reverse V's elements
;; Effect: Vector elements in the given vector interval
;;         are rearranged such that  V[i] is swapped
;;         with V[(vector-length V)-i-1]
;; Assumption: low ≥ 0 ∧ 2*high is a valid index into V
(define (rev-vector! low high)
```

91.4.3 Testing

The design presented is for an encapsulated rev-vector!. This means that in the final code produced, we cannot write tests for rev-vector!. During development, however, this mutator is not encapsulated. Remember that encapsulation is done after testing.

During development, rev-vector! needs V as input because it is out of V's scope. It still takes as input a vector interval for V's first half. The following vectors, for example, may be defined to test rev-vector! during development:

```
(define VV0 (vector))
(define VV1 (vector 1 2 3 4))
(define VV2 (vector 1 2 3 4 5 6 7 8 9))
```

The tests based using the vectors above are:

```
(check-expect (begin
                (rev-vector! VV0 0 -1)
                VV0)
              (vector))
(check-expect (begin
                (rev-vector! VV1 0 1)
                VV1)
              (vector 4 3 2 1))
```

Fig. 74 The local mutator to swap V[i] and V[j]

```
;; natnum natnum → (void)
;; Purpose: Swap the elements at the given indices
;; Effect: V is mutated by swapping elements at given indices
(define (swap! i j)
  (local [(define temp (vector-ref V i))]
    (begin
      (vector-set! V i (vector-ref V j))
      (vector-set! V j temp))))
```

```
(check-expect (begin
                (rev-vector! VV2 0 3)
                VV2)
              (vector 9 8 7 6 5 4 3 2 1))
```

Observe that each test provides `rev-vector!` with a vector V and the vector interval [0..(sub1 (quotient (vector-length V) 2)].

Passing tests ought to give you some confidence that the function is properly implemented. It is at this point that the function may be encapsulated. Once encapsulated, V may be removed as an input to obtain the signature and function header from the previous step of the design recipe.

91.5 Function Body

The function body must determine if the given vector interval is empty or not. Therefore, an `if`-expression may be used. Following the problem analysis above, if the vector interval is empty, `(void)` is returned. Otherwise, `V[low]` is swapped with `V[(sub1 (- (vector-length V) low))]`, and the rest of the vector interval is processed recursively. The body of the function is:

```
(if (> low high)
    (void)
    (begin
      (swap! low (sub1 (- (vector-length V) low)))
      (rev-vector! (add1 low) high)))
```

91.6 The `swap!` Mutator and Running Tests

The `swap!` mutator takes as input two valid indices, i and j, into V and mutates V by swapping `V[i]` and `V[j]`. The local mutator obtained by encapsulating after following the steps of the design recipe is displayed in Fig. 74.

This completes `reverse-vector-in-place!`'s design and implementation. Run all the tests and make sure they pass.

91.7 Performance

Performance-wise, has anything been gained from in-place reversing? To answer this question, empirical data is collected from running the following experiments five times:

```
(define L4rev-lox  (build-list   50000 (λ (i) i)))
(define L4rev-lox2 (build-list   50000 (λ (i) i)))
(define V4rv-in-p  (build-vector 50000 (λ (i) i)))

(define T1 (time (rev-lox  L4rev-lox)))
(define T2 (time (rev-lox2 L4rev-lox2)))
(define T3 (time (reverse-vector-in-place! V4rv-in-p)))
```

The results are displayed in the following table:

	Run 1	Run 2	Run 3	Run 4	Run 5	Average
rev-lox	8984	9234	9141	12125	9188	9734.4
rev-lox2	15	15	15	15	15	15
reverse-vector-in-place!	0	0	0	0	0	0

The data clearly suggests that reversing a vector in place is much faster than reversing a list using structural recursion. The performance gap is much smaller when compared with reversing a list using accumulative recursion. On average reversing, a vector in place is 15 milliseconds faster. Such a small performance gap is not strong enough to conclude that reversing a vector in place is faster. Benchmarks using a larger list and a larger vector must be executed to confirm the conclusion suggested by the above data.

1 Run the experiments using a list and a vector of length 5,000,000. Do the results support the conclusion that reversing a vector in place is faster? What does the relative difference between the averages tell you?

2 Write a mutator, scale-in-place!, that takes as input a (vectorof number) and a number and that mutates every vector element, V[i], to be the product of V[i] and the given number.

3 Write a mutator, add-in-place!, that takes as input two (vectorof number), V1 and V2, and that mutates each vector element, V1[i], to be the sum of V1[i] and V2[i]. Assume that the two given vectors have the same length.

4 Write a mutator, `add-in-place!`, that takes as input two (`vectorof number`), V1 and V2, and that mutates each vector element, V1[i], to be the sum of V1[i] and V2[i]. Do not assume that the two given vectors have the same length.

5 Write a mutator, `swap-vectors!`, that takes as input two (`vectorof X`), V1 and V2, and that for all valid indices i swaps V1[i] with V2[i]. Assume that the two given vectors have the same length.

92 In-Place Quick Sorting

Section 25 discusses quick sorting a (`listof num`). If the list is empty, then the result is the empty list. If the list is not empty, then a pivot element is chosen, and two lists are created: one with the elements less than or equal to the pivot and one with the elements greater than the pivot. The solution is created by recursively sorting the two lists created and appending the sorted smaller elements and the list containing the pivot and the sorted greater elements. Observe that at each step, three lists are allocated.

To avoid the allocation of intermediate lists, the representation of the numbers to sort may be changed to be a (`vectorof number`) assuming that the original order is not needed in the future of the computation. The idea is to sort the numbers in place. Think about how this may be done. We need a pivot, and the vector must be partitioned into two pieces: the first contains the numbers less than or equal to the pivot, and the second contains the elements greater than pivot. The two pieces are then recursively sorted after placing the pivot in the position between the two pieces. We may summarize the design idea as follows using, [low..high], a vector interval:

```
If the vector interval is empty
  return (void)
else
  Pick a pivot (say, V[low])
  Partition the vector so that
     VINTV[low..i] contains the elements ≤ pivot
     VINTV[i+1..high] contains the elements > vector
  Swap V[low] and V[i]
  Recursively sort VINTV[low..i-1] and VINTV[i+1..high]
```

To test in-place quick sorting, the following sample vectors are defined:

```
(define V0 (vector))
(define V1 (vector 10 3 7 17 11))
(define V2 (vector 31 46 60 22 74 22 27 60 20 44
                   23 85 86 67 12 75 80 77 62 37))
(define V3 (build-vector 10 (λ (i) i)))
(define V4 (build-vector 10 (λ (i) (sub1 (- 10 i)))))
```

Observe that the sample vectors include a sorted vector and a vector in reversed order given that we already know that quick sorting exhibits its worse performance when the numbers are sorted or in reversed order.

92.1 The qs-in-place! Mutator

92.1.1 Problem Analysis

The given vector, V, must be sorted. This is done by processing the vector interval [0..(sub1 (vector-length V))]. To process this vector interval, an auxiliary function is used.

92.1.2 Signature, Statements, and Function Header

The input is a vector of numbers and the output is (void). The purpose is to sort the vector in nondecreasing order. The effect is that the vector elements are rearranged in place to satisfy the purpose. The results for the next steps of the design recipe are:

```
;; (vectorof number) → (void)
;; Purpose: Sort the given vector in nondecreasing order
;; Effect: Vector elements are rearranged in place in
;;         nondecreasing order
(define (qs-in-place! V)
```

92.1.3 Tests

The tests must illustrate that the effect is achieved. This is done by first sorting each sample (vectorof number) and then returning the vector. The expected value is a vector that contains the sorted elements of the vector used in the tested expression. The tests are written as follows:

```
(check-expect (begin
                (qs-in-place! V0)
                V0)
              (vector))

(check-expect (begin
                (qs-in-place! V1)
                V1)
              (vector 3 7 10 11 17))

(check-expect (begin
                (qs-in-place! V2)
                V2)
              (vector 12 20 22 22 23 27 31 37 44 46
                      60 60 62 67 74 75 77 80 85 86))
(check-expect (begin
                (qs-in-place! V3)
                V3)
              (vector 0 1 2 3 4 5 6 7 8 9))

(check-expect (begin
                (qs-in-place! V4)
                V4)
              (vector 0 1 2 3 4 5 6 7 8 9))
```

92.1.4 Function Body

The function body is a `local`-expression that defines the auxiliary functions.
Its body calls the mutator to process the vector interval for the valid indices
into the given vector. The function body is started as follows:

```
(local [...]
  (qs-aux! 0 (sub1 (vector-length V)))))
```

Before running the tests, the auxiliary functions must be designed and
written. Following a top-down approach, the first auxiliary function to design
and implement is the one called in the body of the function.

92.2 The qs-aux! Mutator

92.2.1 Problem Analysis

If the given vector interval is empty, then the function returns (void) because there are no vector elements to sort. To sort the elements in a given nonempty vector interval, [low..high], V[low] is chosen as the pivot. The elements in the given vector interval are partitioned putting the elements less than or equal to the pivot at the beginning of the interval and the elements greater than the pivot at the end of the vector interval. Let us refer to the largest index of the elements less than or equal to the pivot as pivot-pos. Observe that this is the position of the pivot in the sorted vector. Therefore, after partitioning the vector elements in the given vector interval, the pivot is swapped with V[pivot-pos]. At this point, V[pivot-pos] contains the value it must have in the sorted vector. This means that the elements before the pivot, in V[low..(sub1 pivot-pos)], and the elements after the pivot, in V[(add1 pivot-pos)..high], must be recursively sorted.

To illustrate the process, consider sorting the elements in the following vector interval [low..high]:

	low						high
V:	10	2	30	1	10	16	20

The pivot, V[low], is 10. After partitioning the vector, we have:

	low			pivot-pos		high	
V:	10	2	10	1	30	16	20

Observe that all the elements less than or equal to the pivot are at the beginning of the vector interval and that all the elements larger than the pivot are at the end of the vector interval. The pivot's position in the sorted vector is where the 1 is because 1 has the largest index among the elements less than or equal to the pivot. The pivot and 1 are swapped to obtain:

	low			pivot-pos		high	
V:	1	2	10	10	30	16	20

Observe that 10 is in the position it shall have when the vector is sorted. Now, both the smaller elements, before the pivot, and the larger elements, after the pivot, are recursively sorted.

92.2.2 Signature, Statements, and Function Header

The input is the vector interval to sort,[22] and the output is (void). The
purpose is to sort the elements in the given vector interval in nondecreasing
order. This is done by choosing V[low] as the pivot and partitioning the
elements in the given vector interval. The elements less than or equal to the
pivot are placed at the beginning of the vector interval and the other elements
at the end of the vector interval. Observe that partitioning a vector interval
is a different problem and, therefore, an auxiliary function is needed. This
auxiliary function processes the pivot and the vector interval [low..high]
and returns the position of the pivot in the sorted vector.

The pivot's position, pivot-pos, in the sorted vector may be locally defined. After partitioning, the pivot is swapped with the element V[pivot-pos],
and [low..(sub1 pivot-pos)] and [(add1 pivot-pos)..high] are recursively sorted. Observe that neither of the new vector intervals is used to construct the given vector interval. In other words, this is generative recursion,
and a termination argument is required as part of the design process.

The next steps of the design recipe yield:

```
;; [int int] → (void)
;; Purpose: Sort V's elements in the given vector interval
;;           in nondecreasing order
;; How: The vector is partitioned in two. The first element
;;      is placed in the vector position between the
;;      elements ≤ to it and the elements > than it. The
;;      The vector intervals for the two parts of the
;;      partition are recursively sorted
;; Effect: Vector elements in the given vector interval are
;;         rearranged in nondecreasing order.
(define (qs-aux! low high)
```

92.2.3 Function Body

The function's body must determine if the given vector interval is empty.
If so, the function returns (void) as per the problem analysis. Otherwise,
local variables are defined for the pivot and the pivot's position in the sorted
vector. The latter value is returned by an auxiliary mutator that partitions
the elements in the given vector interval. The index returned by the auxiliary
mutator is used to place the pivot in the correct position and to recursively
sort the vector interval for the smaller elements and the vector interval for
the larger elements. The body of the function is:

---

[22] V is not required as input when this function is encapsulated inside qs-in-place!.
During development and testing, before encapsulation, V is required as an input.

```
(if (> low high)
    (void)
    (local [(define pivot (vector-ref V low))
            (define pivot-pos (partition! pivot low high))]
      (begin
        (swap! low pivot-pos)
        (qs-aux! low (sub1 pivot-pos))
        (qs-aux! (add1 pivot-pos) high))))
```

92.2.4 Termination Argument

Every recursive call is made with an interval that does not include the pivot.
This means that every recursive call is made with a smaller vector interval.
Eventually, the given vector interval is empty, and the function halts. In the
program, the termination argument may be outlined as follows:

```
;; Termination Argument
;; A given nonempty vector interval is divided into two
;; smaller vector intervals and these are recursively
;; processed. Eventually, the given vector interval
;; becomes empty and the function halts.
```

92.3 The partition! Mutator

92.3.1 Problem Analysis

This mutator has to rearrange the vector elements in a given vector interval
such that all the numbers less than or equal to the pivot are before the
numbers greater than the pivot. That is, the numbers less than or equal to
the pivot must have indices smaller than the numbers greater than the pivot.
In addition, it must return the largest index of a number less than or equal to
the pivot after partitioning the elements. To achieve this, any two numbers
that are relatively out of order must be swapped. Ask yourself how can this
be done. Two numbers are relatively out of order if a vector element greater
than the pivot has an index that is smaller than another vector element that
is less than or equal to the pivot.

Assume that the given vector interval is [low..high]. To rearrange the
vector elements, the first index, searching from low to high, for a number
greater than the pivot and the first index, searching from high to low, for
a number less than or equal to the pivot are needed. Let us call these two
indices, respectively, i and j. Consider the vector interval [i..j]. If it is
empty, then V's elements in the given vector interval are partitioned, and j

is returned as it is the position of the pivot in the sorted vector. To illustrate
this, consider partitioning the following vector interval when the pivot is 7:

```
           low                                    high
    V:    | 4 | -3 | 87 | 10 | 31 | 24 | 78 |
```

The values for i and j, respectively, are low + 2 and low + 1. Observe that
[low+2..low+1] is empty, the elements are partitioned, and low + 1 (i.e.,
j) is the position of the pivot when V is sorted. What happens if the given
vector interval is empty? This may occur when V's length is 1. In such a
case, qs-aux! calls partition with [1..0]. The only position the pivot may
occupy in the sorted vector is 0 (i.e., j). In both cases, the value of j must
be returned.

If the vector interval [i..j] is not empty, then the two indexed elements
are swapped, and the partitioning process continues with [i..j]. To illustrate the process, consider partitioning the following vector interval when the
pivot is 10:

```
           low                                    high
    V:    | 9 | 11 | 87 | 0 | 4 | 15 | -3 |
```

Searching for the first number from the left that is greater than the pivot, 11,
and searching for the first number from the right that is less than or equal
to the pivot, −3, yield the following picture:

```
                                              j
           low    i                          high
    V:    | 9 | 11 | 87 | 0 | 4 | 15 | -3 |
```

Observe that V[i] and V[j] are relatively out of order and must be swapped
before continuing the partitioning process with [i..j]:

```
           low                                    high
    V:    | 9 | -3 | 87 | 0 | 4 | 15 | 11 |
```

Using the new vector interval, the next i and j values become:

```
           low    i            j         high
    V:    | 9 | -3 | 87 | 0 | 4 | 15 | 11 |
```

Once again, V[i] and V[j] are relatively out of order and must be swapped
before continuing the partitioning process with [i..j]:

```
                      low          high
         V:   9   -3   4    0   87   15   11
```

Searching for the indices i and j yields the following picture:

```
                              i
                      low   j   high
         V:   9   -3   4    0   87   15   11
```

Observe that the vector interval [i..j] is empty and that the vector elements are partitioned. The largest index to a number less than or equal to the pivot, 10, is j, and this index needs to be returned as it is the position of the pivot in the sorted vector.

In summary, if the given vector interval, [low..high], is empty, then no elements need to be rearranged, and the returned index for the pivot's position in the sorted vector is high. If the given vector interval is not empty, then the lowest index, first>pivot, of a number greater than the pivot and the highest index, first<=pivot, of a number less than or equal to the pivot are found. If [first>pivot..first<=pivot] is empty, then the index for the pivot's position in the sorted vector is first<=pivot. Otherwise, V[first>pivot] and V[first<=pivot] are swapped, and the partitioning recursively continues with [first>pivot..first<=pivot]. Observe that this is generative recursion given that the new vector interval is not part of [low..high]'s definition.

92.3.2 Signature, Statements, and Function Header

This mutator takes as input a number and a vector interval. It returns a natural number. The purpose is to return the position of the pivot in the sorted vector. This is done by finding the smallest index, i, for a number greater than the pivot; finding the largest index, j, for a number less than or equal to the pivot; swapping V[i] and V[j]; and recursively partitioning [i..j] until it is empty. The effect is to rearrange the vector elements in the given vector interval so that all the vector elements less than or equal to the pivot are at the beginning of the vector interval and all the vector elements greater than the pivot are at the end of the vector interval. The results for the next steps of the design recipe are:

```
;; number [int int] → natnum
;; Purpose: Return the position of the pivot in the
;;          sorted V
;; How: The smallest index of a vector element > pivot
;;      and the largest index of an element <= to the
```

```
;;        pivot are found. If they form an empty vector
;;        interval the largest index of an element <= to
;;        the pivot is returned. Otherwise, the two
;;        indexed values are swapped and the partitioning
;;        process continues with the vector interval
;;        formed by the two indices.
;; Effect: V's elements are rearranged so that all
;;             elements <= to the pivot are at the beginning
;;             of the vector interval and all elements > the
;;             pivot are at the end of the vector interval.
(define (partition! pivot low high)
```

92.3.3 Function Body

Problem analysis revealed three conditions that must be distinguished. If
the given vector interval is empty, then **high** is returned. Otherwise, the
lowest index of a number greater than the pivot and the largest index of a
number less than or equal to the pivot are found. These values are locally
defined and the searches are performed by auxiliary functions. If the interval
defined by these two indices is empty, then the largest index is returned. If
the interval defined is not empty, then the values at the lowest index and
at the largest index are swapped, and the partitioning recursively continues
with the interval defined by the lowest index and the largest index. The body
of the function is:

```
(local [(define first>pivot  (find> pivot low high))
        (define first<=pivot (find<= pivot low high))]
   (if (> first>pivot first<=pivot)
       first<=pivot
       (begin
         (swap! first>pivot first<=pivot)
         (partition! pivot
                     first>pivot
                     first<=pivot))))
```

Observe that both auxiliary functions are called with a nonempty vector
interval. This means that for both auxiliary functions, **low** and **high** are valid
indices into **V**. The auxiliary function **first<=pivot** must return a valid index
into **V** in order to return a valid index for the position of the pivot in the sorted
vector or to recursively process a valid vector interval into **V**. The auxiliary
function **find>pivot** must return a value greater than **high** or a valid index
into **V**.

92.3.4 Termination Argument

```
;; Termination Argument
;;    Every recursive call is made with a smaller vector
;;    interval that does not contain the beginning numbers
;;    <= to the pivot and the ending numbers > pivot.
;;    Eventually, the recursive call is made with an empty
;;    vector interval and the function halts.
```

92.4 The Design of first<=

92.4.1 Problem Analysis

This function searches the given vector interval for the largest index of a number less than or equal to the given pivot. This is accomplished by traversing the given vector interval from right to left. Problem analysis for partition! revealed that when the given vector interval, [low..high], is empty, high must be returned as the position of the pivot in the sorted vector. To guarantee that a valid index into V is returned, this function assumes that V[low] is the pivot. In this manner, the search is always successful. This assumption is safe because partition! calls this function with a vector interval that starts with the index for the pivot.

If the given vector interval is not empty, then there are two cases that must be distinguished. If V[high] is less than or equal to the given pivot, then high is returned as it is the largest index of a number less than or equal to the given pivot in the given vector interval. Otherwise, the search continues with the same pivot and the rest of the vector interval (i.e., [low..high-1]). Observe that the design is based on structural recursion and a termination argument is not required.

92.4.2 Signature, Statements, and Function Header

The function takes as input a number for the pivot's value and a vector interval, [low..high], into V and returns a natural number for the largest index for a number less than or equal to the pivot. It is assumed that V[low] is the pivot.

```
;; number [int int] → natnum
;; Purpose: Find the largest index, i, such that
;;              V[i] ≤ to the given pivot
;; Assumption: V[low] = pivot
(define (find<= pivot low high)
```

92.4.3 Function Body

Problem analysis revealed that `high` is returned when the given vector interval is empty or when the vector's high element is less than or equal to the
given pivot. Otherwise, the search continues using structural recursion. Given
that for the first two of the three conditions the same value is returned, the
function's body may be implemented using an `if`-expression as follows:

```
(if (or (> low high)
        (<= (vector-ref V high) pivot))
    high
    (find<= pivot low (sub1 high)))
```

92.5 The Design of `first>`

92.5.1 Problem Analysis

This function must find, if it exists, the smallest index, `i`, in the given vector
interval such that `V[i]` is greater than the given pivot. To do so, structural recursion is used to traverse the given interval from left to right. Consider what ought to be returned if the given vector interval is empty. This
means that `low` is greater than `high` and that there are no elements in `V`
for the given vector interval that are greater than the given pivot. Thus,
for the given vector interval, the elements are partitioned, and a value that
makes `[first>pivot..find<= pivot]` in `partition!` empty must be returned. Observe that such a value is `low`.

  If the given interval is not empty, then there are two cases. If `V[low]`
is greater than the given pivot, then `low` is the smallest index of a number greater than the given pivot, and it is returned. Otherwise, the search
continues with the same pivot and the rest of the vector interval (i.e.,
`[low+1..high]`). Observe that the design is based on structural recursion
and a termination argument is not required.

92.5.2 Signature, Statements, and Function Header

The function takes as input a number for the pivot and a vector interval into
`V` and returns a natural number. The purpose is to find the smallest index
in the given vector interval for a number greater than the given pivot. If no
such index exists, return a natural number greater than the high end of the
given vector interval. The next steps of the design recipe yield:

```
;; number [int int] → natnum
;; Purpose: If it exists, find smallest index ≥ low,
;;              i, such that V[i] > given pivot if it exists.
;;              Otherwise, return a value greater than high.
(define (find> pivot low high)
```

92.5.3 Function Body

Problem analysis revealed that `low` is returned when the given vector interval is empty or when `V[low]` is greater than the given pivot. Otherwise, the search continues using structural recursion. Given that for the first two of the three conditions the same value is returned, the function's body may be implemented using an `if`-expression as follows:

```
(if (or (> low high)
        (> (vector-ref V low) pivot))
    low
    (find> pivot (add1 low) high))
```

92.6 Completing the Design

The only function left to design and implement is `swap!`. This function takes as input two indices into `V` and swaps the two indexed elements. Such a function has been previously implemented and is displayed in Fig. 74.

This completes the design and implementation of in-place quick sorting. Run the tests and make sure they pass.

93 In-Place Heap Sorting

Section 25.8 discusses why, in the worst case, the complexity of quick sorting is $O(n^2)$. Recall that the problem is that if either the set of elements less than or equal to the pivot or the set of elements greater than the pivot is always empty, then a linear traversal of all of the unsorted elements is performed at each step. This takes the algorithm from $O(n * \lg(n))$ to $O(n^2)$. The same happens with in-place quick sorting when one of the intervals recursively processed is always empty.

At each sorting step, we would like to, at most, traverse half of the remaining elements to sort. If this is always the case, then sorting is made $O(n * \lg(n))$. This can only be guaranteed if the set of elements to sort are not randomly distributed. The elements must have a relative order to each other.

Fig. 75 Heap examples

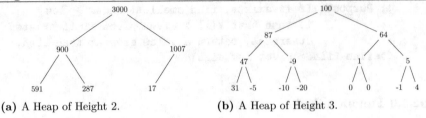

(a) A Heap of Height 2.   **(b)** A Heap of Height 3.

93.1 Heaps

The elements to sort may be represented as a *heap*. A heap is a binary tree in which only the last two levels may have empty subheaps and all nonempty subheaps are at a lesser level than any empty subheap or on the same level and to the left of any empty subheaps. In a heap, the elements are relatively ordered. If a heap is not empty, then the root value is larger than or equal to the root value of either subheap.[23] We may define the structure of a heap as follows:

```
A heap is either:
  1. empty
  2. (list number heap heap)
```

Figure 75 displays two sample heaps. A heap of height 2 is displayed in Fig. 75a.[24] Observe that at level 2, all the nonempty subheaps are to the left of all nonempty subheaps (the right subheap of 287 is the only empty subheap at level 2). The heap displayed in Fig. 75b is a heap of height 3 that has no empty subheaps at level 3.

93.2 Sorting

How can representing the elements as a heap assist in sorting? Observe that the maximum element is at the root of the heap. For example, the maximum element in Fig. 75a is 3000, and in Fig. 75b, it is 100. The root of the heap, therefore, may be removed and added as the next largest element to the result of sorting. The root is substituted with the rightmost leaf at the deepest level. Substituting the root means that the heap must be restored. This is accomplished by trickling the new root value down the binary tree until the heap is restored. A root value must be trickled down when it is not larger than the root of any subheaps below it. In such a case, the root is exchanged

---

[23] This is also known as a *max-heap*.

[24] Empty subheaps are not counted for height nor are they graphically displayed.

with its largest child, and the trickling down process is continued until it is larger than any roots below it or there are no nonempty subheaps below it.

To illustrate heap sorting, consider the heap displayed in Fig. 75a. At the beginning, the sorted result is empty. The root, 3000, is added to the result to make it (3000), and it is substituted with, 17, the value at the deepest rightmost leaf. The resulting binary tree is:

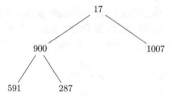

Observe that it is not a heap because 17 is relatively out of order with the roots of its two subtrees. Therefore, 17 must be trickled down to restore the heap. The largest subroot is swapped with 17 to obtain:

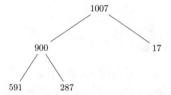

The resulting binary tree is a heap and the sorting process may continue. Removing the root makes the result so far (1007 3000), and after substituting the root with the deepest rightmost leaf, the binary tree is:

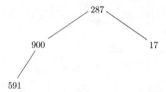

Observe that it is not a heap and the 287 must be trickled down to restore the heap. This leads to swapping the 287 with the largest subtree root value to obtain:

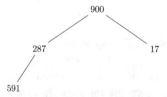

This tree is not a heap because 287 is still not larger than both of the subroots below it. Therefore, the trickling down process must continue. The 287 is swapped with the largest subroot to obtain:

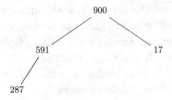

The binary tree is now a heap and the sorting process may continue. The root value is added to the result to make it (900 1007 3000). The rightmost value at the deepest level becomes to the root to make the resulting binary tree:

The new root is not larger than the two subroots and, therefore, it must be trickled down. The 287 is swapped with 591 to obtain:

287 now has no subroots and, therefore, the heap has been restored. The next sorting step may take place. The 591 is added to the result to make it (591 900 1007 3000). After replacing the root with the deepest rightmost leaf, we obtain:

The trickling down process yields:

The root value is added to the result to make it (287 591 900 1007 3000), and substituting the root with the deepest rightmost tree yields:

17

The binary tree is a leaf and that is clearly a heap. The root value is added to the result to make it (17 287 591 900 1007 3000). Once the root value is removed, the heap becomes empty. Observe that when the tree is empty, the result is sorted containing the numbers in nondecreasing order.

93.3 Mapping a Heap to a Vector

In order to sort a vector, V, in place using a heap, we need to map a heap onto a vector. That is, the elements of the vector need to represent a heap using the vector interval [0..(sub1 (vector-length V))]. How can this be done? Examining the sample heaps displayed in Fig. 75 reveals that from a parent element, the root of any existing subheap ought to be reachable and that from a child element, its parent ought to be reachable. This suggests that from the index of a parent, the index of any existing subheaps needs to be computable and that from the index of a child element, the index of its parent needs to be computable. How can the vector elements be organized to satisfy this property?

Observe that heap elements may be numbered level by level from top to bottom and within a level from left to right. To illustrate this, consider the following heap with 13 elements:

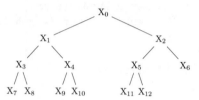

The subscripts indicate the numbering of the elements. The root is numbered 0. At level 1, from left to right, the elements are numbered 1 and 2. All the elements in the heap may be numbered in this manner level by level. The numbering is the index that an element occupies in the vector. There are 13 elements in the heap and, therefore, a vector of length 13 is needed. The vector elements are placed in the vector as follows:

X_0	X_1	X_2	X_3	X_4	X_5	X_6	X_7	X_8	X_9	X_{10}	X_{11}	X_{12}

Observe that from a parent index, i, the index for the root of its subheaps is easily computed. The index for the root of the left subheap is 2i + 1, and the index for the root of the right subheap is 2i + 2. For example, the left and right subheap roots for X_0 are indexed, respectively, by 2*0 + 1 = 1 and 2* 0 + 2 = 2, and the left and right subheap roots for X_4 are indexed, respectively, by 2*4 + 1 = 9 and 2*4 + 2 = 10. The following functions compute the indices for subheap roots:

```
;; natnum → natnum
;; Purpose: Return the index for the left subheap's root
(define (left-heap-root parent-index)
  (add1 (* 2 parent-index)))
```

```
;; natnum → natnum
;; Purpose: Return the index for the right subheap's root
(define (right-heap-root parent-index)
   (+ (* 2 parent-index) 2))
```

Further observe that given the index, i, for a subheap's root, the parent index may be computed. If i is even, the parent's index is the quotient of i-1 and 2. If i is odd, the parent's index is the quotient of i and 2. For example, the parent index for 12 is 5, and the parent index for 9 is 4. It is important to note that for a given vector, V, the valid subheap indices are in [1..(sub1 (vector-length V))]. In particular, observe that this vector interval does not contain, 0, the heap's root index because the root does not have a parent. A function for the index of a parent is written as follows:

```
;; natnum → natnum
;; Purpose: Return the parent index in the heap
;; Assumption: the given index is in
;;                    [1..(sub1 (vector-length V))]
(define (parent i)
   (if (even? i)
       (quotient (sub1 i) 2)
       (quotient i 2)))
```

The reference to V in the assumption is fine because this function is intended to be locally defined in the function that in-place sorts V.

93.4 The `heap-sort-in-place!` Mutator

93.4.1 Problem Analysis

In-place vector sorting using a heap requires two steps. The first mutates the given vector into a heap. The second sorts the vector that represents a heap. Observe that these are two different subproblems and, therefore, two different auxiliary functions are needed.

To sort a vector that represents heap, think about the vector as being divided into two parts. The first part contains the elements that must still be sorted. The second part contains the elements that are already sorted. That is, it contains the larger elements that are already in the correct place. This suggests that the function that sorts the elements needs the vector interval for the indices of the elements that still need to be sorted. Initially, this vector interval must include all the elements in the given vector.

To mutate a vector to represent a heap, elements must be rearranged such that a parent value is always larger than its children's value. This means that all children values must be processed. Ask yourself what vector interval contains the indices of all children values that must still be processed. The only value that does not have a parent and, therefore, is not a child is the heap's root. All other values have a parent. This informs us that initial vector interval for unprocessed children is from 1 to the length of the given vector minus 1.

93.4.2 Signature, Statements, and Function Header

The input is a vector of numbers to sort and the output is (void). The output is (void) because this function is only called to mutate the given vector. The effect is that the given vector's elements are rearranged in nondecreasing order. The result of the next steps of the design recipe is:

```
;; (vectorof number) → (void)
;; Purpose: Sort the given vector in nondecreasing order
;; Effect: The given vector's elements are rearranged in
;;              nondecreasing order
(define (heap-sort-in-place! V)
```

93.4.3 Tests

The tests must illustrate that the effect is achieved. The same vectors used to test qs-in-place! (from Sect. 92) are used to test in-place heap sorting given that both functions have the same purpose.[25] The tests are written as follows:

```
(check-expect (begin
               (heap-sort-in-place! V0)
               V0)
              (vector))

(check-expect (begin
               (heap-sort-in-place! V1)
               V1)
              (vector 3 7 10 11 17))

(check-expect (begin
               (heap-sort-in-place! V2)
               V2)
              (vector 12 20 22 22 23 27 31 37 44 46
                      60 60 62 67 74 75 77 80 85 86))
```

---

[25] Be advised that V0, V1, V2, V3, and V4 must be defined in the heap sorting program.

```
(check-expect (begin
                (heap-sort-in-place! V3)
                V3)
              (vector 0 1 2 3 4 5 6 7 8 9))

(check-expect (begin
                (heap-sort-in-place! V4)
                V4)
              (vector 0 1 2 3 4 5 6 7 8 9))
```

93.4.4 Function Body

Problem analysis and the mapping of a heap onto a vector revealed that
several auxiliary functions are needed. Therefore, the body of this mutator is
a local-expression. The local definitions needed include right-heap-root,
left-heap-root, and parent. In addition, it is clear that swap! is needed to
rearrange vector elements. Finally, problem analysis revealed the need for a
mutator, call it heapify!, to convert a vector into a heap and a mutator, call
it sorter!, to sort a vector representing a heap. The body of the mutator
may be written as follows:

```
(local [;; natnum natnum → (void)
        ;; Purpose: Swap the elements at the given
        ;;                  indices
        ;; Effect: V is mutated by swapping elements at
        ;;                  given indices
        (define (swap! i j)
          (local [(define temp (vector-ref V i))]
            (begin
              (vector-set! V i (vector-ref V j))
              (vector-set! V j temp))))

        ;; natnum → natnum
        ;; Purpose: Return the index for the right
        ;;                  subheap's root
        (define (right-heap-root parent-index)
          (+ (* 2 parent-index) 2))

        ;; natnum → natnum
        ;; Purpose: Return the index for the left
        ;;                  subhead's root
        (define (left-heap-root parent-index)
          (add1 (* 2 parent-index)))
```

```
;; natnum → natnum
;; Purpose: Return the parent index in the heap
;; Assumption: the given index is in
;;                    [1..(sub1 (vector-length V))]
(define (parent i)
  (if (even? i)
      (quotient (sub1 i) 2)
      (quotient i 2)))

;; ...
;; Purpose:
(define (sorter! low high) ...)

;; ...
;; Purpose:
(define (heapify! low high) ...)
        ⋮
    ]
  (begin
    (heapify! 1 (sub1 (vector-length V)))
    (sorter!  0 (sub1 (vector-length V)))))))
```

Observe that `sorter!` and `heapify!` still need to be designed and implemented as well as any auxiliary functions they may require.

93.5 The sorter! Mutator

93.5.1 Problem Analysis

To sort a vector representing a heap, we may think of the vector as divided into two parts: the unsorted part and the sorted part. Consider, for example, the following vector:

low				high		
100	31	87	4	543	750	757

The two parts of the vector are described as follows:

V[low..high] is a heap of unsorted elements

V[high+1..(sub1 (vector-length V))] contains V's largest numbers in nondecreasing order

The part of the vector that must be processed is the part containing the heap of unsorted elements. Its vector interval is given as input and may be processed from right to left. In this manner, at each step, high is added to the vector interval indexing the sorted elements in the rightmost positions of the vector.

If the given vector interval is empty, then there are no elements to sort, and (void) is returned. If the vector interval for the unsorted elements, [low..high], is not empty, then there is at least one element that must be moved from the unsorted part to the sorted part. What element should be moved from the unsorted part to the sorted part? The sorted part must contain the largest elements of the vector in nondecreasing order. This means that all the elements in the sorted part are larger or equal to any element in the unsorted part and that the largest element of the unsorted part should be moved to the sorted part. Where can the unsorted part's largest element be found? Observe that for our data definition of a heap, the largest element is always at the root of the heap. This means that if V[low] is swapped with V[high], then the element V[high..(sub1 (vector-length V))] contains V's largest elements in nondecreasing order. That is, one more number is added to the sorted part of the vector. After the swap, however, V[low..(sub1 high)] may no longer be a heap. The new root value must be trickled down to restore the heap before the sorting process may continue. Once V[low..(sub1 high)] is a heap, sorting may resume with the rest of the vector interval.

93.5.2 Signature, Statements, and Function Header

The input is a vector interval containing the unsorted elements, and the output is (void) because this function is solely called for its effect. The effect is that V's elements are rearranged in nondecreasing order. The assumption is that V[low..high] is a heap. The next steps of the design recipe yield:

```
;; [int int] → (void)
;; Purpose: For the given VINTV, sort the vector elements
;; Effect: V's elements in the given VINTV are rearranged
;;          in nondecreasing order
;; Assumption: V[low..high] is a heap
(define (sorter! low high)
```

93.5.3 Function Body

The function body must determine if the given vector interval is empty or not. If the given vector interval is empty, then (void) is returned as suggested by problem analysis. Otherwise, a begin-expression is used to properly sequence the needed mutations. First, the low and high elements are swapped. Second, the heap is restored for the elements in [low..high-1]. Third, the sorting process continues with the rest of the vector interval. The body of the function is:

```
(cond [(> low high) (void)]
      [else (begin
              (swap! low high)
              (trickle-down! low (sub1 high))
              (sorter! low (sub1 high)))]))
```

There are two observations to make. First, the design is based on structural recursion on a vector interval and, therefore, a termination argument is not required. Second, a new auxiliary function, trickle-down!, must be designed and implemented.

93.6 The trickle-down! Mutator

93.6.1 Problem Analysis

This mutator restores a heap in V[low..high] after a new value has been swapped into low. Given that only the root element has been changed, we may assume that all the elements in [low+1..high] are heap roots. The purpose, therefore, is to restore a heap rooted at low. Recall that the root element must be larger or equal to both subheap roots under it. Therefore, the root element must be swapped with the largest, if any, subheap root. Once swapped, under the root, we have a heap and either a binary tree or a heap. The subheap does not need to change. The trickling down process must continue with the other substructure. The trickling down process stops when V[low] is the root of a heap.

To accomplish this, the potential indices for the two children of the root are computed. We say potential because the root may have zero, one, or two children. The indices for the left child, lc-index, and for the right child, rc-index, are locally defined. Once these are defined, the mutator must determine how many children the root, V[low], has. If the left-child index is greater than high, then the root has no children in V[low..high]. This means V[low] is the root of a heap (with a single element) and (void) is returned because no more trickling down is needed. If only the right-child index is greater than high, then the root only has a left child. The mutator must determine if V[lc-index] and V[low] are out of order. If they are not out of order, then V[low] is the root of a heap, and (void) is returned because no more trickling down is needed. Otherwise, V[low] and V[lc-index] are swapped, and the trickling down process continues with [lc-index..high]. If the root has two children, then the index, mc-index, for the maximum

subheap root is determined, V[low] and V[mc-index] are swapped, and the
trickling down process continues with [mc-index..high].

93.6.2 Signature, Statements, and Function Header

The input is the vector interval, [low..high], that contains the elements that
must be restored to form a heap. This mutator is only called for its effect and,
therefore, (void) is returned. The purpose is to reestablish a heap rooted at
low. In order to restore a heap structure, all the vector elements, except low,
for the given vector elements must be (sub)heap roots. Therefore, we assume
that V[low+1..high] are heap roots. This is a safe assumption to make given
that this mutator is called after replacing the a heap's root with a new value.
The next steps of the design recipe yield:

```
;; trickle-down!: [int int] → (void)
;; Purpose: For the given VINTV, reestablish a heap
;;              rooted at low
;; Effect: Vector elements are rearranged to have
;;              a heap rooted at low
;; Assumption: V[low+1..high] are all heap roots
(define (trickle-down! low high)
```

93.6.3 Function Body

The body of the mutator is a local expression that defines the index, respectively, lc-index and rc-index, for the root of the left and right subheaps.
As outlined in the problem analysis, the mutator must determine if V[low]
has zero, one, or two children in the given vector interval. Therefore, the
local-expression's body is a cond-expression with three stanzas. Observe
that V[low] has zero children if the left child's index is greater than high,
it has one child if only the right child index is greater than high, and, otherwise, it has two children. If V[low] has no children, then it is the root
of one-element heap, and (void) is returned. If V[low] only has one child,
then it must be determined if V[lc-index] is less than V[low]. If it is, then
(void) is returned because V[low] is a heap root given that V[lc-index]
is a heap root. If it is not, then V[low] and V[lc-index] are swapped, and
the trickling down process recursively continues with [lc-index..high]. If
V[low] has two children, then the maximum child, V[mc-index], is compared with V[low]. If V[low] is greater than or equal to the maximum child,
then it is a heap root and (void) is returned. Otherwise, V[low] is swapped
with V[mc-index], and the trickling down process recursively continues with
[mc-index..high]. The body of the mutator is:

```
(local
  [(define rc-index (right-heap-root low))
   (define lc-index (left-heap-root low))]
  (cond [(> lc-index high) (void)];; root has no children
        [(> rc-index high)          ;; root only has a left child
         (if (<= (vector-ref V lc-index)
                 (vector-ref V low))
             (void)
             (begin
               (swap! low lc-index)
               (trickle-down! lc-index high)))]
        [else ;; root has two children
         (local
           [(define mc-index (if (>= (vector-ref V lc-index)
                                     (vector-ref V rc-index))
                                 lc-index
                                 rc-index))]
           (cond [(>= (vector-ref V low)
                      (vector-ref V mc-index))
                  (void)]
                 [else (begin
                         (swap! low mc-index)
                         (trickle-down! mc-index high))]))])))
```

Observe that every recursive call is made with a vector interval in which only
the root element of a heap has been swapped. This means that any children
of the root's index are heaps and the mutator's assumption is satisfied.

93.6.4 Termination Argument

A recursive call is only made when V[low] has one or two children. That is,
the index of any child must be less than or equal to high. Every recursive
call is made with an interval formed by a child index and high. Eventually,
the given vector interval becomes empty or V[low] is a heap root and the
mutator terminates.

93.7 The heapify! Mutator

93.7.1 Problem Analysis

This mutator receives as input, [low..high], a vector interval. The goal of
this mutator is to rearrange V's elements into a heap rooted at low. How can
this be done? We know from the heap data definition that the root must be

greater or equal than the root of any existing child. This suggest that if a parent element is less than a child element, then the parent and the child elements must be swapped. Otherwise, they do not have to be swapped. The question now is how is this swapping process done. In other words, should the given vector interval be processed from `low` to `high` or vice versa? If the given vector interval is traversed from `low` to `high`, every time a child is swapped with its parent, the child must be propagated up the heap until the top of the heap is reached or the child is less than or equal to the parent. To illustrate this process, consider transforming the following binary tree into a heap:

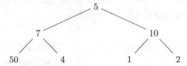

The 5 has two children that are larger than it and it is swapped to the largest of the two to obtain:

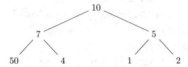

The 10 does not have to be further propagated up the tree because it is at root. The process continues with the 7 which is swapped with 50 to obtain:

The propagation up the tree must continue because 50 is larger than, 10, its parent to obtain:

The next element to process is 5. It is bigger than both of its children and no swapping is needed. The process proceeds with all the elements at the bottom level. None have children and no swapping is required. Observe that the elements now form a heap. This approach requires an auxiliary function to propagate a value up the tree.

Alternatively, the given vector interval may be processed from `high` to `low`. If a child is less than its parent, then they are swapped. Let us explore this approach using the following binary tree:

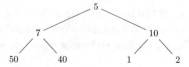

The first elements processed are 2 and 1. Neither of these are greater than their parent and, therefore, no swapping takes place. Observe that we now know that 2 and 1 are heap roots. The next element to process is 40. It is bigger than, 7, its parent and they are swapped to obtain:

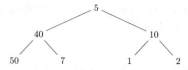

The new right binary tree rooted at 7 is a heap and nothing more needs to change. The next element to process is 50. This is larger than, 40, the parent value and a swap is needed to obtain:

The new binary tree rooted at 40 is a heap and nothing more needs to be swapped. Observe that 40 through 2 are heap roots. The next element to process is 10. It is bigger than its parent and they are swapped yielding:

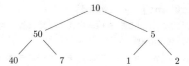

Observe that 5 through 2 are now heap roots. The next element to process is 50, and it must be swapped with its parent to obtain:

Observe that 10 is not a heap root because one of its children, 40, is larger. This means that 10 must be trickled down to restore the heap. This yields:

There is no need to process the root because it does not have a parent and the process may stop. Observe that the binary tree is now a heap. This approach suggests that an auxiliary function to trickle down an element to restore the heap is needed.

What conclusion can we reach? Should the vector interval be processed from low to high or vice versa? Clearly, it may be done either way. Recall, however, that a function to trickle down an element to restore the heap has already been designed and implemented. Therefore, processing the interval from high to low means that there is no need to design a new auxiliary function. For this reason, the design presented revolves around processing the interval from high to low.

93.7.2 Signature, Statements, and Function Header

The input is a vector interval and the output is (void). The purpose is to transform the elements in the given vector interval into a heap. The effect is that vector elements are rearranged to form a heap rooted at the low end of the given vector interval. We assume that the given vector interval only contains valid indices into the heap and that low is greater than 0. These assumptions are necessary to guarantee that indexing errors into V cannot occur. We also assume that V's elements indexed by any i in [high+1..(sub1 (vector-length V))] are heap roots. This assumption must hold in order for trickle-down! to restore the heap. The next steps of the design recipe yield:

```
;; heapify!: [int int] → (void)
;; Purpose: Transform the elements in the given VINTV
;;          into a heap
;; Effect: Rearrange the vector elements to form a heap
;;          rooted at low
;; Assumptions:
;;  low > 0 Given VINTV is valid for V
;;
;;  Given VINTV is valid for V
;;
;;  Elements indexed in [high+1..(sub1 (vector-length V))]
;;  are heap roots
(define (heapify! low high)
```

93.7.3 Function Body

If the given vector interval, [low..high], is empty, there are no elements to make into a heap, and (void) is returned. If the given vector interval is not empty, a local variable is defined for high's parent index. If the parent element is greater than or equal to the high element, the parent and the high elements form a heap, and the process continues with the rest of the heap. Otherwise, a begin-expression is used to sequence the needed mutations: the parent and high elements are swapped, the heap rooted at high is restored, and the process continues with the rest of the vector interval. The body of the function is:

```
(cond [(> low high) (void)]
      [else
       (local [(define parent-index (parent high))]
         (cond [(>= (vector-ref V parent-index)
                    (vector-ref V high))
                (heapify! low (sub1 high))]
               [else
                (begin
                 (swap! parent-index high)
                 (trickle-down! high
                               (sub1 (vector-length V)))
                 (heapify! low (sub1 high)))])])]))
```

This completes the in-place heap sorting's design and implementation. Run the program and make sure all the tests pass.

93.7.4 Complexity and Performance

The mutator, heap-sort-in-place!, performs two actions: rearranges V's elements to form a heap and then sorts the elements. Assume that the given vector is of length n. The complexity of the heap-sort-in-place! is heapify!'s complexity plus sorter's complexity.

The mutator sorter! is called with a vector interval of size n containing the valid indices into the given vector. This mutator processes the given interval by making n recursive calls. In the worst case, for each recursive call, two elements are swapped, and a call to trickle-down! is made. This means that the complexity of sorter! is given by the product of n and the complexity of trickle-down!. Before the swap is performed by sorter!, V[low] is the root of a heap. This means that approximately half of the elements are in the left subheap and half of the elements are in the right subheap. The difference in height between the two subheaps is at most 1. After the swap is performed, V[low] is the root of a binary tree whose left and right subtrees are heaps whose heights differ by at most 1. In the worst case, trickle-down! always performs a recursive, after swapping the root element, with one of the subheap roots until the given vector interval is empty. How many recursive calls are made? Given that the two subheaps are roughly of the same size, each recursive call reduces the size of the heap to process by a half. This makes trickle-down!'s complexity $O(\lg(n))$. Thus, sorter!'s complexity is $O(n * \lg(n))$.

The mutator `heapify!` makes n recursive calls to process the given vector. In the worst case, every recursive call requires a call to `trickle-down!`. This means that its complexity is $O(n * lg(n))$.

The above analysis informs us that `heap-sort-in-place!`'s complexity is $O(n * lg(n)) + O(n * lg(n))$ or simply $O(n * lg(n))$.

Does this make a difference in performance? Recall that quick sorting's potential weakness is receiving as input a vector that is sorted or that is in reversed order because its complexity becomes $O(n^2)$. In such a case, heap sorting is expected to be faster. To test this hypothesis, the following test vector and state variables are defined:

```
(define N 10000)
(define TV (build-vector N (λ (i) i)))

;; (vectorof number)
;; Purpose: Vector to test quick sorting
(define TV1 (void))

;; (vectorof number)
;; Purpose: Vector to test heap sorting
(define TV2 (void))
```

The following experiment is executed five times:

```
(begin
  (set! TV1 (build-vector N (λ (i) (vector-ref TV i))))
  (set! TV2 (build-vector N (λ (i) (vector-ref TV i))))
  (time (qs-in-place! TV1))
  (time (heap-sort-in-place! TV2)))
```

The CPU times, after subtracting any garbage collection time, for each experiment are displayed in the following table:

	Run 1	Run 2	Run 3	Run 4	Run 5	Average
Quick sorting	2828	2984	3031	3187	3094	3024.8
Heap sorting	47	31	46	31	31	37.2

The empirical data clearly suggests that when given a sorted vector, heap sorting is faster than quick sorting. In every experiment, heap sorting is about two orders of magnitude faster, and the average for each experiment reflects this observation.

6 Redesign `heapify!` to process the given vector interval from left to right.

Fig. 76 Mutator for empirical in-place sorting algorithm experiments

```
;; natnum (listof ((vectorof number) → (void))) → (void)
;; Purpose: Run empirical study with vectors that have lengths
;;            that are multiples of 1000 in [1000..natnum*1000]
(define (empirical-study factor lst-of-sorters)
  (local
    [(define NUM-RUNS 5)


     (define V (build-vector (* factor 1000) (λ (i) (random 10000000))))


     ;; (vectorof number) natnum (listof ((vectorof number) → (void)))
     ;; → (void)
     ;; Purpose: Time the given in-place sorters using the  given vector
     ;;            the given number of times
     (define (run-experiments V runs sorters)
       (local [;; (listof ((vectorof number)→(void)))→(void)
               ;; Purpose: Run n experiments
               (define (run sorters)
                 (if (empty? sorters)
                     (void)
                     (local [;; (vectorof number)
                             ;; Purpose: Copy of V to sort
                             (define V1 (build-vector
                                         (vector-length V)
                                         (λ (i) (vector-ref V i))))]
                       (begin
                         (display (format "Sorter ~s: "
                                          (add1 (- (length lst-of-sorters)
                                                   (length sorters)))))
                         (time ((first sorters) V1))
                         (run (rest sorters))))))]
         (if (= runs 0)
             (void)
             (begin
               (display (format "    RUN ~s\n" (add1 (- NUM-RUNS runs))))
               (run sorters)
               (run-experiments V (sub1 runs) sorters)))))]
    (if (= factor 0)
        (void)
        (begin
          (display (format "Experiments for length ~s \n" (* factor 1000)))
          (run-experiments V NUM-RUNS lst-of-sorters)
          (newline)
          (newline)
          (empirical-study (sub1 factor) lst-of-sorters)))))
```

94 Empirical Project

A natural question that arises is whether in practice in-place quick sorting or
in-place heap sorting is better especially considering that it is unlikely that a

given vector that is sorted or in reversed order is given as input. This means that the number of steps performed by both algorithms is proportional to n * lg(n) and we need to determine which performs better. Answering this question, therefore, requires experimentation and the collection of empirical data.

Figure 76 displays a mutator to time different vector-sorting algorithms on random vectors of varying lengths that are a multiple of 1000. It takes as input a natural number and a list of sorting mutators. The given natural number is the maximum factor of 1000 for the length of a vector. The mutator returns (void) because it is only needed for its effect: output timing data to the screen. The main mutator, empirical-study, locally defines the number of runs that are performed by each sorter and a random number-vector of length 1000 * factor. The given factor is processed using structural recursion. If the given factor is 0, then all the experiments have been executed, and (void) is returned. Otherwise, a message displays the vector length for the next experiments, and a mutator, run-experiments, to execute the experiments is called. After the experiments are executed, two blank lines are printed to the screen, and the experiments for the remaining vector lengths are executed.

The mutator run-experiments takes as input a (vectorof number) to sort, a natural number for the number of experiments to run, and a list of the in-place sorting mutators. It returns (void) as it is only called for its effect to print empirical data for each experiment. The number of experiments is processed using structural recursion. If the number of experiments to run is 0, then (void) is returned. Otherwise, a message with the run number is displayed on the screen, a mutator (run) is called to time all the sorters, and the rest of the runs are recursively performed.

The mutator run takes as input a list of in-place sorters and returns (void). Its purpose is to time all the given sorters using the vector, V, defined by empirical-study. The given list of sorters is processed using structural recursion. If there are no more sorters to time, (void) is returned. Otherwise, a local copy of V to sort is defined, a message for the sorter used is displayed, the first sorter is timed, and the rest of the sorters are timed recursively.

Empirical data to determine if in-place quick sorting or in-place heap sorting is better in practice may be gathered as follows:

```
(empirical-study 15 (list qs-in-place! heap-sort-in-place!))
```

When the above expression is evaluated, qs-in-place! and heap-in-place! are timed using random vectors of numbers whose lengths are a multiple of 1000 in [1000..15000]. For each vector length and each sorter, after subtracting any garbage collection time, the average CPU time may be computed. You will, of course, need to gather the numbers manually by scrolling through DrRacket's interactions window. For each vector length, the average CPU time may be plotted as displayed in Fig. 77. The figure reveals that neither algorithm is always superior. We can divide the x-axis into three vector-length intervals: [1000..3000], [4000..7000], and [8000..15000].

Fig. 77 Empirical results for in-place quick and heap sorting

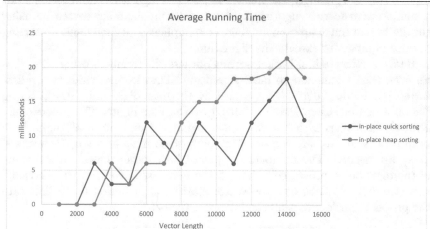

In the first interval, on average, there is no difference in performance between the two sorters. This informs us that in terms of execution time, it does not matter which sorter is used. In the second interval, sometimes quick sorting is faster, and other times, heap sorting is faster. Observe that the difference in performance is relatively small. Therefore, we may conclude that in terms of execution time, it does not matter which sorter is used. In the third interval, after the plotted line for each sorter intersects, we see a change in performance. Quick sorting is consistently faster than heap sorting. This suggests that for large vectors (i.e., vectors of length greater than or equal to 8000), quick sorting performs better and ought to be used.

94.1 Radix Sorting

The sorting algorithms studied so far are *comparative sorting algorithms.* That is, they are based on comparing elements to each other. If sorting `n` numbers requires comparing each number to the other `n-1` numbers, then the number of comparisons needed is `O(n²)`. This, for example, may occur with insertion sorting. Quick and heap sorting reduce the number of comparisons needed to `O(n * lg(n))` by not comparing every number to every other number.

Is it possible to do better? Observe that if the input vector is of size `n`, then at least `n` steps are needed to sort the vector because each element must be placed in the right place. Can a vector be sorted in `O(n)` steps? This would be optimal because the number of steps is proportional to the input's size. Surprisingly, the answer is yes. The algorithm, however, is a not a comparative sorting algorithm. Instead, the numbers are sorted by using the digits that make up each number. For simplicity, we shall focus on sorting natural numbers to explain the algorithm.

Radix sorting (a.k.a. bucket sorting) orders the numbers using their digits from least significant to most significant. That is, the numbers are first sorted by the ones digit. Once sorted by the ones digit and without losing the obtained ordering, they are sorted by the tens digits. The process successively continues with the next most significant digit until all digits have been processed. To sort the numbers by a given digit position, 10 buckets, [0..9], are needed. The numbers are placed in a bucket based on the value of the digit being processed. After all the numbers have been "bucketized," they are dumped back into the vector starting with bucket 0. To illustrate the process, consider sorting the following vector:

918	82	87	31	780	103	4

The numbers are bucketized based on the ones digit. This yields the following buckets:

B0	780
B1	31
B2	82
B3	103
B4	4
B5	
B6	
B7	87
B8	918
B9	

The contents of each bucket is dumped back into the vector starting with the 0 bucket to obtain:

780	31	82	103	4	87	918

Observe that the numbers are no longer randomly placed in the vector. The numbers are sorted by the ones digit. The numbers are now bucketized by the tens digit to obtain:

```
B0 103 4
B1 918
B2
B3 31
B4
B5
B6
B7
B8 780 82 87
B9
```

The numbers are once again dumped into the vector starting with bucket 0 to obtain:

103	4	918	31	780	82	87

Observe that the numbers are not randomly placed in the vector. They are sorted by the tens and ones digit. The sorting process continues by bucketing the numbers by the hundreds digit to obtain:

```
B0 4   31 82 87
B1 103
B2
B3
B4
B5
B6
B7 780
B8
B9 918
```

The numbers are dumped into vector starting with bucket 0 to obtain:

4	31	82	87	103	780	918

There are no more digits to process and the sorting process stops. Observe that the vector is sorted.

94.2 The Project

7 Design and implement a function to find the number of digits in the longest integer in a (vectorof integer).

8 Design and implement an interface for a bucket of integers. A bucket of integers offers the following services:

```
add!:   mutates a bucket to add a given integer
dump!:  dumps the bucket elements into the given vector
   starting at the given index and mutates the bucket to
   become empty
size:   returns the number of elements in the bucket
elems:  returns a vector containing the bucket elements
```

9 Design and implement a mutator to sort a vector in place using radix sorting. Be mindful that an integer may be negative. First design and implement your mutator assuming that all vector elements are nonnegative. Afterward, decide how to refine your program to sort a vector that includes negative integers.

10 Determine the complexity of in-place radix sorting assuming there are n digits among all the integers in the given vector.

11 Design and implement a mutator to sort a vector in place using insertion sorting.

12 Perform an empirical study comparing in-place radix, quick, heap, and insertion sorting. Use vectors with lengths of multiples of 500 up to a maximum length of 20,000.

95 What Have We Learned in This Chapter?

The important lessons of this chapter are summarized as follows:

- An alternative to allocating auxiliary data structures is to perform operations in place.
- In-place operations mutate data as a computation progresses.
- Referential transparency is lost when using in-place operations.
- Vectors may be used to represent data for in-place operations.
- In-place operations may make programs faster, but this is not always the case.
- Quick sorting may be implemented as an in-place operation.

- A max-heap is a data type that is either empty or has a root element and two subheaps such that the root element is greater than or equal to the root values of its subheaps if these are not empty.
- Heap sorting in place divides a vector into two pieces: a heap of unsorted elements and the sorted elements.
- At each step, heap sorting in place moves the root value to the set of sorted elements, places the deepest rightmost value at the root, and trickles this value down to restore the heap. This process is repeated until the set of unsorted elements becomes empty.
- A heap is mapped onto a vector, V, by placing the heap's root value in V[0] and placing position i element's subheap roots at 2i+1 and 2i+2.
- Heap sorting's complexity is O(n * lg(n)).
- Empirical data suggests that in-place heap sorting is significantly faster than quick sorting when the data is in sorted or in reversed sorted order.
- Empirical data suggests that in-place quick sorting is faster than heap sorting for large data sets.
- The collection of empirical data may be automated.
- Radix sorting is a non-comparative algorithm.
- Radix sorting sorts a set of numbers by progressively sorting them from least significant to most significant digit.

Chapter 18
The Chicken and the Egg Paradox

An ancient philosophical paradox is concerned with the origins of interrelated elements. It is popularly known as the *chicken and the egg paradox*. Philosophers have asked themselves whether the chicken or the egg came first. Answering this question has been problematic because it has been believed that every chicken is born from an egg and every egg is laid by a chicken. If the chicken came first, how did the egg it was born from come into existence? If the egg came first, what chicken laid that first egg? In essence, the circular relationship between chickens and eggs makes it a problem to determine how chickens and eggs got started.

In the world around us, many things are related in a circular manner beyond the chicken and the egg paradox. For example, bank clients and bank accounts are related in a circular manner. Every bank client has one or more accounts, and every account is owned by a bank client. Employees and employers are also related in a circular fashion. An employer has one or more employees, and every employee works for an employer. Books and authors are related in a circular manner. Every author has penned one or more books, and every book has one or more authors.

How can circular data be represented in a program? This is the problem that we explore next. To make the discussion concrete, the representation of a bank is used. A bank has multiple clients. That is, the number of clients is arbitrary. A natural representation for a bank, therefore, uses a list. A bank is defined as follows:

    A bank is a (listof client)

The next task is develop a data definition for clients and for accounts.

© The Author(s), under exclusive license to Springer Nature Switzerland AG 2022   499
M. T. Morazán, *Animated Program Design*, Texts in Computer Science,
https://doi.org/10.1007/978-3-031-04317-8_18

96 The Paradox in Programming

The representation of clients in real-world programming at a bank is complex
and large. We shall adopt, however, a simple definition in order to focus on
the issue of circularity in programming. At a minimum, every client has a
name and at least one account. This is a finite number of characteristics,
and, therefore, a client is represented as a structure. The client's name may
be represented as a string. Given that the number of accounts a client has
is arbitrary, a list is used for their representation. The data and structure
definitions for a client are:

```
#|
   A bank client is a structure:
        (make-client string (listof account))
   with a name and a nonempty list of accounts.
   |#
```

```
(define-struct client (name accounts))
```

Observe that the `client` data definition is meaningless without the `account`
data definition. Our next task is to develop the data definition for `account`.
An account in real-world programming at a bank is also complex and large.
Once again, in order to focus on circularity issues, we adopt a simple definition. Every account has a balance and an owner. It is appropriate to use a
structure to represent an account. The balance may be represented by a nonnegative number, and the owner is a client. The data and structure definition
for an account are:

```
#|
   A bank account is a structure:
        (make-account number client)
   with a nonnegative balance and an owner.

   |#
```

```
(define-struct account (balance owner))
```

The next step of the design recipe asks for sample clients and accounts
to be defined. Let us define a client named "Ada Lovelace" that has a single
account with a balance of 1000. The desired definition is:

```
(define CLIENT1 (make-client
                "Ada Lovelace"
                (list (make-account
                      1000
                      CLIENT1))))
```

In order to create Lovelace's `account`, we need a `client` representing Lovelace. Alas, the needed `client` cannot be constructed because it requires the client being defined. Let us try building an account for Lovelace first. The desired definition is:

```
(define ACCT1 (make-account
              1000
              (make-client "Ada Lovelace"
                           (list ACCT1))))
```

Alas, the `account` for Lovelace cannot be defined because it requires the `account` being defined. We have the chicken and the egg paradox in programming. We are unable to determine which to construct first.

97 Solving the Paradox

Given that neither a client nor an account can be created first using the constructors for the respective structures, a new type of constructor is needed. A *generalized constructor* builds incorrect structure instances. Mutation is used to correct the values in the instances. As problem-solvers, we need to decide which structure type is returned by a general constructor.

A generalized constructor may be written for any structure in a circular dependency, and later fields are mutated to correct the structure instances. For example, to build a `client`, the client's name and the initial balance of the first account may be used to build a `client` with no accounts. Observe that this violates the data definition for a `client`. Later the client's list of accounts is mutated to add the first account. We now proceed to design and implement a generalized constructor for `clients`.

97.1 Problem Analysis

To build a new client, an incorrect client is constructed with an empty list of accounts. The incorrect client is used to build a new account. Upon building the account, the incorrect client's accounts field is mutated to be a list containing the constructed account. In this manner, the build client is corrected, and it is returned as the value of the constructor.

97.2 Sample Expressions and Differences

To construct a `client`, an incorrect instance is locally defined with an empty
list of accounts. In the body of the `local`-expression a `begin`-expression is
used to perform two actions. The first constructs an incorrect account using
the given initial balance and the locally defined client and then mutates
the client's accounts to be a list containing only the constructed account.
Observe that this mutation corrects both the incorrect client and the incorrect
account. The second is to return the now correct locally defined `client`.
Sample expressions for the generalized constructor are:

```
;; Sample expressions for build-new-client
(define HOPPER (local [(define new-client (make-client
                                            "Grace Hopper"
                                            '()))]
                  (begin
                    (set-client-accounts! new-client
                                           (list (make-account
                                                  847
                                                  new-client)))
                    new-client)))

(define RHODES  (local [(define new-client (make-client
                                            "Ida Rhodes"
                                            '()))]
                  (begin
                    (set-client-accounts! new-client
                                           (list (make-account
                                                  1301
                                                  new-client)))
                    new-client)))
```

Observe that there are two differences among the sample expressions: the
name of the client and the initial balance for the first account. This informs us
that the generalized constructor for clients needs two parameters. We name
these differences `name` and `init-balance`.

97.3 Signature, Statements, and Function Header

The inputs are a string for the name and a positive number for the initial
balance of the first account. The purpose is to create a new client with the
given name and a single account with the given initial balance. It is assumed
that the given initial balance is positive. The next steps of the design recipe
yield:

```
;; string number → client
;; Purpose: To build a new client with given name
;;           and a single new account that has the
;;           given balance
;; Assumption: The given initial balance is positive
(define (build-new-client name init-balance)
```

97.4 Tests

The tests using sample computations illustrate that the constructor returns the defined values for the sample expressions when the differences are given as input. These tests are:

```
;; Tests using sample computations for build-new-client
(check-expect (build-new-client "Grace Hopper" 847)  HOPPER)
(check-expect (build-new-client "Ida Rhodes"   1301) RHODES)
```

To write tests using sample values, we need to understand a little about how ASL internally represents circular data. To do so, let us examine the value obtained by constructing a new client for Ada Lovelace with 1000 as the initial balance for her first account:

```
> (build-new-client "Ada Lovelace" 1000)
(shared ((-0- (make-client "Ada Lovelace"
                           (list (make-account 1000 -0-)))))
   -0-)
```

Circular data in ASL is represented as a shared value. A shared value names all the structures that are shared (in circular data) as a number between dashes. In the example above, the client for "Ada Lovelace" is named -0-. Observe that this client is shared with the account it contains. The value appears after the shared declarations. In this case, the value is -0- or equivalently the client for "Ada Lovelace". We can write tests using sample values as follows:

```
;;  Tests using sample values for build-new-client
(check-expect
  (build-new-client "Ada Lovelace" 1000)
  (shared ((-0- (make-client
                  "Ada Lovelace"
                  (list (make-account 1000 -0-)))))
     -0-))

(check-expect
  (build-new-client "Mary Kenneth Keller" 431)
```

```
(shared ((-0- (make-client
                 "Mary Kenneth Keller"
                 (list (make-account 431 -0-)))))
  -0-))
```

97.5 Function Body

The function body is obtained by abstracting over the sample expressions. Wherever a difference is used, it is substituted with the corresponding parameter. The function body is:

```
(local [(define new-client (make-client name '()))]
  (begin
    (set-client-accounts!
      new-client
      (list (make-account init-balance new-client)))
    new-client))
```

This completes `build-new-client`'s design and implementation. Run the tests and make sure they all pass.

1 Design and implement a generalized constructor for a new account.

98 Adding Clients to a Bank

Armed with the power to create new clients, we can design and implement a mutator to add accounts to a bank. This means that the bank must be a state variable. To simplify our task, we assume that every client in a bank has a unique name. We shall follow the steps of the design recipe for mutators displayed in Fig. 57.

98.1 Problem and Data Analysis

A bank is represented as a state variable whose value is a list of clients. Every time an account is constructed for a new client, the bank is mutated to add the client.

98.2 State Variable Definition

A bank is a list whose purpose is to store all the clients of the bank. We assume that every client in the bank has a unique name to simplify searching for a client. The bank state variable is defined as follows:

```
;; (listof client)
;; Purpose: Store the clients of a bank
;; Assumption: Every client has a unique name
(define bank (void))
```

98.3 Bank Initializer

The initializer is a mutator used to make **bank** an initial value. In this case, the initializer takes no input and sets **bank** to the empty list. The initializer is:

```
;;  → (void)
;; Purpose: Initialize bank
(define (initialize-bank!) (set! bank '()))
```

98.4 The add-account! Mutator

98.4.1 Problem Analysis

To add an account, the client's name and the new account's initial balance are needed. The mutator must determine if the given client already exists. If it does exist, then a new account is constructed using the given initial balance and the existing client. The new account is added to the front of the existing client's account list. Otherwise, a new client is constructed using the given initial balance and the given name. The new client is then added to the front of **bank**.

98.4.2 Signature, Statements, and Function Header

The inputs are a string and a number for, respectively, the client's name and the new account's initial balance. The purpose is to add a new account for the given client's name with the given initial balance. The effect depends on whether or not **bank** has a client with the given name. If so, a new account with the given initial value is added to the front of the existing client's account list. Otherwise, a new client is added to the front of **bank** that has a single

account with the given initial balance. The mutator assumes that the given
initial balance is positive. The results for the next steps of the design recipe
are:

```
;; string number → (void)
;; Purpose: Add an account for the given client's name
;;           with the given initial balance
;; Effect: A new client, if necessary, is added to the
;;         front of bank and a new account is added to
;;         the front of the client's accounts
;; Assumption: The given balance is positive
(define (add-account! name balance)
```

98.4.3 Tests

The tests must illustrate that a new account is correctly added to bank. Writing bank's value after several accounts are added, however, is cumbersome
and error-prone. To simplify writing tests, a function to transform bank into
a list may be designed and implemented. Such a function uses map to transform each client into a list. Transforming a client creates a list that starts
with the client's name and contains the balance for each account the client
owns. To create the list of balances for a given client, map is used to extract
the balance from every account. The function to transform bank into a list
is:

```
;;   → (listof (cons string (listof number)))
;; Purpose: Transform bank information into a list
(define (bank->list)
  (map (λ (client)
         (cons (client-name client)
               (map (λ (acct) (account-balance acct))
                    (client-accounts client))))
       bank))

;; Tests for bank->list
(check-expect (begin
                (initialize-bank!)
                (bank->list))
              '())

(check-expect
 (begin
   (set! bank (shared ((-1- (make-client
                             "Frances Allen"
                             (list (make-account 500 -1-)))))
                 (list -1-)))
```

```
  (bank->list))
(list (list "Frances Allen" 500)))
```

Armed with a function to transform bank into a list, writing tests for add-account! is not cumbersome. The tests initialize bank, add 0 or more accounts, and transform bank into a list. Tests are written as follows:

```
(check-expect (begin
               (initialize-bank!)
               (bank->list))
              '())

(check-expect (begin
               (initialize-bank!)
               (add-account! "Joan Clarke" 1000)
               (bank->list))
              (list (list "Joan Clarke" 1000)))

(check-expect (begin
               (initialize-bank!)
               (add-account! "Joan Clarke" 1000)
               (add-account! "Katherine Johnson" 100)
               (add-account! "Joan Clarke" 6500)
               (add-account! "Jean E. Sammet " 830)
               (bank->list))
              (list (list "Jean E. Sammet " 830)
                    (list "Katherine Johnson" 100)
                    (list "Joan Clarke" 6500 1000)))
```

98.4.4 Function Body

The mutator's body locally defines the result of searching bank, using filter, for a client with the given name and encapsulates the generalized constructor for a client. The local-expression's body determines if the search found a client. If so, a mutation to add a new account to the front of the found client's account list is performed. Otherwise, a new client is constructed, and bank is mutated to add the new client to its front. The local-expression's body is:

```
(local [(define client-search (filter
                               (λ (c)
                                 (string=? name
                                           (client-name c)))
                               bank))
```

```
;;   → client
;; Purpose: To build a new client with name and a
;;            single new account that has init-balance
(define (build-new-client)
  (local [(define new-client (make-client name '()))]
    (begin
      (set-client-accounts! new-client
                            (list (make-account
                                   balance
                                   new-client)))
      new-client)))]
  (if (not (empty? client-search))
      (local [(define the-client (first client-search))
              (define new-acct (make-account
                                balance
                                the-client))]
        (set-client-accounts!
         the-client
         (cons new-acct (client-accounts the-client))))
      (set! bank (cons (build-new-client) bank))))
```

The encapsulated generalized constructor has no parameters because the
needed name and balance are in scope and may be removed from the signature and the function header. Observe that in the local-expression's body,
the call to the generalized constructor has no arguments.

This completes add-account!'s design and implementation. Run the tests
and make sure they all pass.

---

2 A bank may have several branches. Each branch is a bank that may
be represented as a list of clients. Design and implement an interface for
banks that offers one service: adding an account. Define several branches
and add several accounts to each. Make sure that client names are repeated among the branches, and make sure that your tests illustrate that
changes to one branch do not affect a different branch.

---

3 A mutable list, mlist, is either:
  1. empty
  2. A structure (make-pair X pair)
Design and implement a mutator, (make-circular-mlist! mlist),
for circular mlists. It takes as input a nonempty mlist. It returns the
given mlist if it is circular. Otherwise, it mutates the end of the given
mlist to be the given mlist.

4 Design and implement a program that represents a library as a list of authors. Every author has a name and a list of penned books. Every book has a title, an ISBN number, and a list of authors. Include in your program a function to find a book using an ISBN number and a function to find the authors of a book given a title.

5 Design and implement a program that represents a population as a list of nonempty children. A child is either `empty` or a structure, `(make-child string child child)`, with a name and 0–2 parents. A nonempty parent must be a member of the population. Include a mutator to add a child to the population.

99 What Have We Learned in This Chapter?

The important lessons of this chapter are summarized as follows:

- In the world around us, many things are related in a circular manner.
- A circular dependency prevents the direct construction of any structure in it.
- A data definition that has a circular dependency with other data definitions is meaningless on its own.
- A generalized constructor builds incorrect instances of all the structures in a circular dependency and then uses mutations to correct them before returning its value.
- A generalized constructor requires the concrete values needed to build all instances of the structures in the circular dependency.

Part V
Epilogue

Chapter 19
Where to Go from Here

Congratulations! You have taken your next step into the exciting and wonderful world of problem-solving and programming. Hopefully, you have felt your mind expand and your problem-solving skills grow as you progressed through the pages of this book. You are well-prepared to continue your journey honing problem-solving skills in the realm of programming and beyond. There is still much to learn, and the next steps ought to be as or more exciting. Remember that all good things must...continue!

Where should you go from here? There are many paths you may follow but make sure that you always design the solutions to problems even if future textbooks (or for that matter professors or supervisors) do not. Go ahead and design your programs to be recursive, and, if necessary, refactor them to use state variables and mutation. Always remember that mutation is like a hammer that clobbers everything it touches. Sometimes, problem-solving requires more finesse and a screwdriver, not a hammer, ought to be used. That said, mutation does have its role in problem-solving, and you ought to use it when necessary. In more advanced courses, when you study an algorithm presented this book, like quick sorting or heap sorting, count the number of mutations used, and compare it with the number of times `set!` or `vector-set!` is used here. This should explain how easy or hard it is to understand the algorithm.

For the more immediate future, here are some suggestions for you:

- Pursue excellence. Strive to become the best problem-solver you can.
- Learn or teach yourself a new programming language every semester and summer. Learn in this context refers to mastering the abstractions (not the syntax) offered. Some suggestions:

  - Learn about lazy evaluation by writing programs using `Haskell` or `Clean`.
  - Learn about object-oriented programming by writing programs using `Java` or `Scala`.
  - Learn about macros by writing programs using `Racket`.

© The Author(s), under exclusive license to Springer Nature Switzerland AG 2022   513
M. T. Morazán, *Animated Program Design*, Texts in Computer Science,
https://doi.org/10.1007/978-3-031-04317-8_19

  – Learn about logic programming by writing programs using `Prolog`.

- Learn about the implementation of programming languages. This is fundamental to understand the technology that you are just beginning to use. Unfortunately, many Computer Science programs have moved away from requiring a course in programming languages. This means that it is very likely that learning about the implementation of programming languages must be born from your own initiative.
- Do not shy away from Math! Pursue courses in calculus, discrete mathematics, numerical analysis, numerical methods, linear algebra, discrete probability, and automata theory. Math can be the source of many insights in problem-solving.
- Attend talks by invited speakers in your department. It is very likely that your department has a weekly seminar where faculty members and outside speakers are invited to give talks. Attend these and learn about the research that is done in Computer Science.

My dear young reader, would you be surprised that I am jealous of you? Indeed, I am. You are only at the beginning of the adventure! Enjoy it! I know I did and I hope you will too!

P.S. Just like this textbook has helped you remember to help others as you progress, your experience is valuable to those that are not so far along on this wonderful adventure.

Printed in the United States
by Baker & Taylor Publisher Services